CANADA

A PEOPLE'S HISTORY

DON GILLMOR & PIERRE TURGEON

CANADA

A PEOPLE'S HISTORY

VOLUME ONE

WITH A FOREWORD BY MARK STAROWICZ AND GENE ALLEN

M&S

Cloth editions published 2000, 2001
Trade paperback editions published 2002

National Library of Canada Cataloguing in Publication

Gillmor, Don
    Canada : a people's history. – Trade pbk. ed.

Published in conjuction with series, Canada, a people's history on CBC Television.

V.1 by Don Gillmor & Pierre Turgeon; with a foreword by Mark Starowicz and
Gene Allen – V.2 by Don Gillmor, Achille Michaud & Pierre Turgeon; with
and afterword by Mark Starowicz and Gene Allen.

Includes bibliographical references and index.
ISBN 0-7710-3324-9 (v.1). – ISBN 0-7710-3336-2 (v.2)

1. Canada – History.   I. Michaud, Achille   II. Turgeon, Pierre, 1947-
III. Canadian Broadcasting Corporation   IV. Title.

FC164.G54 2002   971   C2002-903221-0
F1026.G46 2002

We acknowledge the financial support of the Government of Canada through the Book
Publishing Industry Development Program for our publishing activities. We further
acknowledge the support of the Canada Council for the Arts and the Ontario Arts
Council for our publishing program.

Typeset in Janson by M&S, Toronto
Book design by Kong Njo

Printed and bound in Canada

McClelland & Stewart Ltd.
The Canadian Publishers
481 University Avenue
Toronto, Ontario
M5G 2E9
www.mcclelland.com

1 2 3 4 5   06 05 04 03 02

CBC/Société Radio-Canada

Executive Producer	Mark Starowicz
Senior Producer and Editor	Gene Allen
Senior Editor	Mario Cardinal
Visual Research	Ron Krant and Hélène Bourgault
Maps	Stephen Dutcheshen and Paul Ryu

McClelland & Stewart Ltd.

Chairman	Avie Bennett
President and Publisher	Douglas Gibson
Senior Editor	Dinah Forbes
Managing Editor	Jonathan Webb
Copy Editor	Catherine Marjoribanks
Art Director	Kong Njo

Historical Advisers

Ramsay Cook, General Editor, *Dictionary of Canadian Biography*

Jean-Claude Robert, Chair of the History Department, Université du
   Québec à Montréal

Olive Dickason, Adjunct Professor, University of Ottawa, and author
   of *Canada's First Nations*

CONTENTS

Foreword by Mark Starowicz / ix

Foreword by Gene Allen / xiii

1   THE CENTRE OF THE WORLD / 1

2   THEY THAT GO DOWN TO THE SEA IN SHIPS / 43

3   THE GOLDEN AGE OF NEW FRANCE / 75

4   BATTLE FOR A CONTINENT / 107

5   A QUESTION OF LOYALTIES / 143

6   JOURNEY TO THE SEA / 179

7   REBELLION AND REFORM / 217

8   CONFEDERATION / 255

Bibliography / 293

Index / 297

FOREWORD BY MARK STAROWICZ

I'd like to begin by thanking Dulcie Way of Savage Cove, Newfoundland, who saved our lives.

On July 27, 1998, the first history of Canada for the television age started photography on a rented twelve-metre boat in the Strait of Belle Isle between Newfoundland and Labrador, where Jacques Cartier and John Cabot sailed centuries earlier. A violent storm rose, night closed in, and we started to take on water.

The heaving sea boiled into the engine room, rose quickly through the bunks and up to the wheelhouse. The captain radioed "Mayday! Mayday!" as all electrical systems shorted and our cabin filled with smoke. Then darkness. We struggled through the rising water to the deck. At this point, the Canadian History Project, on its maiden shoot, comprised five sodden people standing on a smoking boat in frigid waters, far from land.

On the listing deck, senior producer Gene Allen stood calling for help into the blackness. My thirteen-year-old daughter, Caitlin, was strapping a lifejacket on my Radio-Canada colleague Louis Martin. I was at the bow, signalling S-O-S with the flashlight.

Two hours later, we spotted the lights of a commercial fishing vessel. Our lives had been saved by an elderly woman in Savage Cove who had heard the mayday on her marine radio. She had recognized our location and kept ringing phone numbers in Anchor Point, sixteen kilometres away, until she woke up Captain Bruce Genge, who mustered a rescue party. The whole community of Anchor Point was waiting for us with blankets and food.

The next day we drove to Savage Cove to thank our lady of the airwaves, Dulcie Way, and her husband, Llewellyn, a retired fisherman. The walls of their bungalow were filled with pictures of their grandchildren. She spotted Caitlin, rushed up, and hugged her: "My dear, if I'd known you were out there I'd have swum out for you myself!"

The Ways gave us tea and asked if we were covering some big news story. No, we said, we were filming the history of Canada.

"Well," said Dulcie Way, "it's about time."

The next three years were among the most extraordinary in my life. My memory is a collage of war canoes churning through the water and sails billowing against the sky, freezing pre-dawn mornings on the battlements of Louisbourg, midnights spent reading through detailed e-mails from historians, turbulent management meetings with head office over the cost of cameras and editing equipment.

What can I tell you as you hold this book?

First, I had the privilege of working with the most painstakingly honest and caring people I have ever met in my life. This extraordinary mix of journalists from French and English Canada worked achingly hard and faced insane deadlines. One military doctor told me a significant number of them exhibited every symptom of combat fatigue. What united us all, however, was the knowledge that, whatever we had done before, this was the work of our lives.

Second, no television series, no book, no library of books, could ever encompass the history of Canada. This a narrative work, not an academic work. I was reminded of the importance of this when a high school teacher stood up in the huge plenary session of the conference Giving the Past a Future in Montreal in January 1999 and said, "There has been a narrative cleansing of Canadian history." He is right. We have bleached the dramatic narrative out of Canadian history and reduced it to social studies units in our schools. If you want a sociological history, or a military or diplomatic history, seek elsewhere. If you want to get a sense of what it felt like to be an eleven-year-old girl in the Loyalist exodus, a nineteen-year-old Hudson's Bay Company clerk seeing the Rocky Mountains for the first time, or a terrified eighteen-year-old Acadian refugee at the Plains of Abraham, then this is the right book. Not only does it describe the great and the famous, apparently in control of their destinies, it gives voice to the people who bobbed like corks in the great seas of history, in control of very little.

Everyone in this project has had his or her own points of reference. The most important for me were my children. My eldest daughter, Caitlin, almost drowned on the first day of shooting. Later, Madeleine, my youngest, accompanied me on many shoots. One day, at Louisbourg, she was costumed as an extra in a scene re-enacting the bombardment. An explosive charge went off, and I watched as Madeleine was engulfed in black smoke. My heart stopped. Everything was fine, because our special effects people are brilliant.

But I did say, as we drove back to the motel in Sydney, "Don't tell your mother." I thank their mother, Anne Wright Howard, for her patience as I dragged our daughters through marine disasters, cannonades, and invasions.

Some day, twenty years from now, someone of Caitlin and Madeleine's generation will look at this body of work – I hope with respect for what we did – and determine that this series and this book must be redone; that what is needed is a new vision of our past, one that is informed by their needs, their context, and the historical research of their time. Then they will fight the interminable battles to assemble the capital, the cameras, the historians, and the writers to refresh this history. And they will find the heirs of Claude St. Laurent and Hubert Gendron at Radio-Canada, Gene Allen and Gordon Henderson at the CBC, Avie Bennett at McClelland & Stewart, and Antoine del Busso at Editions Fides. And they will do the next People's History. And that is as it should be. This is the first history of Canada for the television and Internet age. It must not be the last.

History must be constantly renewed. But let's not bequeath our children a gap of another generation. We have left so many extraordinary stories out; there are such rich paths still to be followed. With whatever residual authority I may possess, I pray that this series leads to the creation of a permanent History Department at the CBC and Radio-Canada, and that the new media platforms we have launched remain a vibrant portal to our heritage.

The credit for this body of work belongs to the Canadian Broadcasting Corporation and la Société Radio-Canada. No other institution in this country would ever have undertaken such a perilous enterprise. But, as Graham Spry, the founder of Canadian radio, said, "Every generation will have to refight the battle for national broadcasting." Unless we protect and nurture this extraordinary institution today, the Canada of twenty years from now will be a poorer place.

I came to this country, to Montreal, when I was eight years old, speaking neither French nor English. My genetic provenance has no link with the early stories of Canada, except through the transcendent humanity of people seeking refuge and hope for their children. That is the single, uniting theme of Canadian history, from 15,000 years ago till the last jetliner that landed yesterday: Hope. I descend from neither the *filles du roi*, nor the Loyalists, nor the aboriginal nations. Yet their stories are also my own; since I am Canadian, they are my ancestors. They are also the ancestors of the Haitian, the Sudanese, the Vietnamese, and Chinese Canadians among us. But remember also that the stories of those who came here, from the famines of Africa, from the gas chambers of central Europe, from rafts tossed on the South China Sea, from the refugee camps of the world, these now belong to Canada, to the native peoples, to the French and to the English. Their history has become our history, and ours belongs to them. All of our children are in the same schoolyards.

Finally, I'd like to honour the memory of my parents, who helped shape history. My late father, Captain Stanislaw Starowicz of the Royal Air Force, flew fifty-five missions over France and Germany when everything looked dark, and received the Cross of Valour four times. My late mother, Lieutenant Barbara Kielb of the Polish Resistance, full of love of literature and music, carried bombs through German lines and finally received the Cross of the Warsaw Uprising from President Lech Walesa. The two of them were perfectly ordinary working people, one a mechanic at Air Canada, the other a clerk at General Electric. No one looking at my parents as they travelled on the Montreal Metro would have guessed their stories.

My daughters, in turn, take the subway home from school each afternoon. I've always told Caitlin and Madeleine, paraphrasing Leonard Cohen: Watch the faces. There are heroes on the buses, and legends on the subway.

We are all the grandchildren of history. We just have to lift the silence politely, and ask gentle questions.

Then listen. Just listen.

FOREWORD BY GENE ALLEN

This book diverges in many ways from the television series on which it is based – which is as it should be. A book, after all, is not a television program; it has its own life. But having watched closely as both the series and the book took shape, I can also see the deep connection between them – a connection based on the power of the first-person narratives and testimony that form the backbone of both.

We are not the first to have discovered the treasure trove of autobiographies, diaries, letters, and other first-person accounts that give a face and a voice to Canada's past. For decades, the Champlain Society has been making the most famous of these widely available; many more have been published under other imprints. But all of us involved in the making of the series and the book were astonished by how many first-person accounts are now available – there are literally hundreds of them, covering virtually every region of the territory that became Canada, and from every era of its history.

Together they paint a remarkably vivid portrait of the people who shaped Canada's past. I don't believe there is a modern travel writer as engaging as Gabriel Sagard, the inquisitive, sympathetic, and witty Récollet friar who was one of the first Europeans to spend time with the Huron in the early seventeenth century. Despite years of studying Canadian history, I had never read David Thompson's *Narrative* until now. It is a wonderful tale, full of keen-eyed observations about the land and its inhabitants. We hope that after having seen the series and read this book, our audience will hear the voice of Hannah Ingraham whenever the Loyalists are mentioned, or Marie-Claude Chamois when someone speaks of the *filles du roi*. It will be a worthy tribute to the work of Don Gillmor and Pierre Turgeon if it inspires their readers to explore this rich storehouse themselves.

This book was written and edited while we were in the throes of producing a large and complex television series, and it could not have been done without the skill and hard work of many people. I would like to acknowledge in particular the invaluable contribution of my colleague Mario Cardinal in coordinating the production of the French-language material and editing the text. Richard Fortin and Frédéric Vanasse went beyond the call of duty to write the captions and sidebars for Chapters 3, 7, and part of Chapter 2. Hubert Gendron's first-rate script for Episode 3 of the television series became Chapter 3 of the book with only slight changes. In Toronto, Rachel Brown capably and cheerfully handled a dozen different duties, including tracking down the sources of innumerable quotations. All our producers, directors, and researchers co-operated wholeheartedly with Don and Pierre despite their own deadline pressures. Among our academic advisers, Ramsay Cook, Jean-Claude Robert, Olive Dickason, and Jean-Paul Bernard found time to provide detailed commentary on draft chapters that saved us from many errors of fact and interpretation; any that remain are, of course, our responsibility, not theirs. Doug Gibson and Dinah Forbes at McClelland & Stewart have been enthusiastic backers of this project from the beginning and provided ample encouragement and support whenever it was needed. Finally, I cannot say enough about the talent, professionalism, and good humour of Don Gillmor; he actually appears to thrive on chaos to such an extent that he must have been a TV producer in another life.

THE CENTRE OF THE WORLD

"In the beginning of the world, all was water." So begins the creation myth of the Yakima, as related in the nineteenth century by Coteeakun, the son of a native chief. "Whee-me-me-ah, the Great Chief Above, lived in the sky, above the water, all alone. When he decided to make the world, he went down to the shallow places and began to throw up great handfuls of mud. Thus he made the land. We do not know this by ourselves, we were told it by our fathers and grandfathers, who learned it from their fathers and grandfathers. We were told the Great Chief Above made many mountains. . . . Some day the Great Chief Above will overturn those mountains and rocks. Then the spirits that once lived in the bones buried there will go back into them. Now, those spirits live in the tops of the mountains, watching their children on the earth and waiting for the great change which is to come . . ."

The story of life in North America before the arrival of Europeans can be found in the sporadic archaeological evidence that survives. But it is also passed on to us through the oral tradition of the continent's first inhabitants. While the archaeological record is the more factually reliable, the oral legacy is often more compelling and speaks to a larger, metaphorical truth. These stories teach, record history, and offer entertainment. Unconfined by a conventional western narrative structure, with circular themes and wild,

Manellia and Adelik
(*John Ross, National Archives of Canada, C-133832*)

surreal tangents, they often resemble dreams: the collective wisdom and nightmares of a people. Knowing the extreme climactic and geographic realities of the country, the natives allied themselves with nature, both physically and spiritually, and their stories speak of these alliances, as well as the inevitable betrayals.

The first Amerindians came from Asia, most likely crossing the land bridge that occasionally spanned the Bering Strait during the ice ages, or skirting its shore in small boats. Called Beringia, the land bridge was 2,000 kilometres wide, and it would emerge and be submerged again several times during the Pleistocene age. Its most recent surfacing came 14,000 years ago, during the last great Ice Age, but the first migration might have been as early as 40,000 years ago.

The most widely accepted theory holds that early *Homo sapiens* followed herds of bison, antelope, and mammoth as they moved south, along a corridor paralleling the west coast to the southern tip of South America. When the ice retreated north, it scraped across the land, melting into lakes and forming moraines, and small groups of hunters followed in its wake. The continent was settled in a looping pattern that almost closes to a circle with the prairie settlement of the natives of the northwestern plains, who arrived from the south and the east.

Independent cultures developed at different times, shaped by their immediate environments. On the west coast, about 7000 BC, a culture formed around salmon fishing and whaling. Whales were important to a village, supplying food, oil, sinew, and bone, and the whale hunt incorporated a spiritual element. The hunter fasted before the hunt, abstained from sex, and bathed several times daily with increasing intensity, scouring himself with shells until his skin bled. The hunt was a seduction; the whale chose its killer and would submit only to a worthy suitor.

The Nuu'chah'nulth of Vancouver Island had a whaling prayer that reads like a cross between a Christian litany and an erotic courtship. "May I cause the whale to emerge from the head area, may it come up my canal. May

Interior of a Clallum winter lodge, Vancouver Island (*Paul Kane, National Gallery of Canada, 6923*)

it listen to my words. . . . May I cause embarrassment to my fellow whalers, may it surface right where I am on the water, that it may wait for me. May I cause it to become lame when I start paddling after it. May I bend its mind to my advantage. That the females would want me, that the female whales would want to marry me. That it may look away from my fellow whalers. That all females would favour me, that they would catch my spear. That it would put my harpoon point under its bosom, that I may cause it to roll on the sea as I would spear it fatally. Only me they would love, me most of all."

It was not just the whaler who had to endure the rituals. His wife also had to scrub herself raw. "Between her thighs is where she has to rub, the whale hunter's wife, rubbing until it breaks open at her crotch with the sharp vines of the wild blackberry." As she rubs, she recites her own prayer: "May you not look at my husband when he is paddling towards you, that you may stop there on the water when he comes near you." The village's prosperity was dependent on the whale hunt, but the hunt had a moral element, too; it provided a moral structure. The whale judged the hunters and their wives, divined their fidelity and their worth.

The Nuu'chah'nulth were hunting grey whales, which can grow to more than twelve metres in length. Their boats were the same length, dugouts made from a single tree, planed and burned to a smooth finish then elaborately painted with ochre. They used three-metre harpoons tied to a bark rope. Attached to the rope were twenty or thirty inflated sealskins that impeded the whale's diving once he was harpooned, a technology shared with the Inuit and Aleut to the north.

The chief had to strike the first whale. When one was taken, there was a prolonged feast to celebrate the fact, at which the whale's various parts were apportioned according to rank. The whale was always honoured in death, to ensure that more would return the following year.

A thousand years after the west coast culture took shape, a Plains culture formed around the buffalo. The buffalo supplied the Plains natives – Blood, Sarcee, Peigan, and Blackfoot, among others – with almost everything they needed. The hides were dressed and made into clothing and stretched onto poles to construct teepees. The sinews were used for bowstrings, and the stomachs were made into kettles. In a Blackfoot hunting story, the Old Man creates humans out of clay and then blows life into them. "They asked him, 'What are we to eat?' He made many images of clay in the form of buffalo. Then he blew breath on these, and they stood up: and when he

Ninoch-Kiaiu, a Blackfoot Chief
(*Kari Bodmer, Jocelyn Art Museum*)

Top left: Medicine Masks of the Northwest Coast tribes
(*Paul Kane, Stark Museum of Art*)

made signs to them, they started to run. Then he said to the people, 'Those are your food.' They said to him, 'Well, now, we have those animals; how are we to kill them?' 'I will show you,' he said. He took them to a cliff, and made them build rock piles; and he made the people hide behind these piles of rock, and said, 'When I lead the buffalo this way, as I bring them opposite to you, rise up.'"

The buffalo hunt involved most of the village, including women and some children. It was a dangerous and delicate process that yielded the meat and skins the village would need for the season. The buffalo had to be successfully herded by drovers or fire into a corral. In the foothills they were usually herded over a cliff to their deaths in a wild, bloody ritual.

Certain especially advantageous sites were coveted by more than one tribe, and their use prompted political alliances. Several bands might co-operate on a particular hunt, or agree to what was tantamount to a time-sharing agreement. At Head-Smashed-In, near present-day Lethbridge, Alberta, the traffic was so heavy that an independent native police force was established to ensure that everyone followed the rules. The site was in use for five thousand years, and thirty separate routes to the cliff have been uncovered by archaeologists. Because the migratory patterns of the buffalo tended to follow the same route, the same jumps could be used annually. At some sites the buffalo bones are more than ten metres deep.

The Plains natives were spread thinly over a huge territory with a population density of less than one person per twenty-five square kilometres. Their world was defined by the sky and a distant horizon. A spiritual people, they worshipped the sun in an intense ritual that could last for several days.

In the far north, for the Inuit and Aleut, simply surviving was paramount, and their legends are particularly bloody, filled with tales of accidents and starvation. One Inuit myth tells of a woman who had lost her husband.

The buffalo was one of the few mammals to survive the Ice Age, feeding on the prairie grasses in the lee of the Rocky Mountains. The estimated 50 million buffalo were the most valuable resource for the Plains natives. Their meat provided food, and their hides were used for clothing, shelter, blankets, and shoes. The bones were made into tools, the horns, bladder, and paunch used as containers, and the dried dung was burned as fuel. (*National Archives of Canada*, C-403)

MEDICINE PIPE STEM DANCE ◆ Jacques Cartier was one of the first Europeans to encounter tobacco, an experience he described in his journal: "They have a plant, of which a large supply is collected in summer for the winter's consumption. They hold it in high esteem, though the men alone make use of it in the following manner. After drying it in the sun, they carry it about their necks in a small skin pouch in lieu of a bag, together with a hollow bit of stone or wood. Then at frequent intervals they crumble this plant into powder, which they place in one of the openings of the hollow instrument, and, laying a live coal on top, suck at the other end to such an extent that they fill their bodies so full of smoke that it streams out of their mouths and nostrils as from a chimney. They say it keeps them warm and in good health, and never go about without these things. We made a trial of this smoke. When it is in one's mouth, one would think one had taken powdered pepper, it is so hot." From *The Voyages of Jacques Cartier* (*Paul Kane, Stark Museum of Art*)

"The woman, who was depending on charity, had become a burden of which they wished to rid themselves. So they put all her belongings into the sealskin boat, and when they were on their way they seized the woman and cast her overboard. She struggled to regain the side of the boat, and when she seized it they cut off her fingers.

"The woman, in her despair, screamed her determination to have revenge. . . . The thumb became a walrus, the first finger a seal, and the middle finger a white bear. When the former two animals see a man they try and escape, lest they be served as the woman was. The white bear lives both on the land and on the sea, and when he perceives a man, revengeful feelings fill him and he determines to destroy the person, who he thinks mutilated the woman from whose fingers he sprang."

Huron natives (*National Archives of Canada, C-9892*)

This story, like many, has several versions. In another telling, it is a father killing a daughter who is clinging to the side of the boat. He cuts off her fingers, but she manages to hang on. He cuts off her hands, but she still clings. He finally cuts off her arms and she drifts away, offering a curse, and her severed limbs form various animals.

The Inuit adapted to one of the most extreme ecosystems on earth: an almost barren land and a plentiful sea. They wore caribou skins for warmth and were able to create everything they needed from bone, ivory, antler, or the limitless expanse of snow, from which they constructed houses. They were the last of the aboriginal peoples to arrive in North America, coming from Siberia around 2000 BC, and they moved with the seasons to hunt seals, polar bears, walruses, and beluga whales on the coast, caribou and musk-ox on the tundra. They lived in small societies built around a few families. In summer, the men danced under the pale night sky, banging a tambourine-like drum, singing a song of their triumphs.

In Huron mythology, a woman conceives twins who quarrel in her womb. One is born and the other refuses to follow. Instead, he bursts through his mother's side, killing her. She is buried in the earth, and from her head grows squash, her breasts sprout corn, and her limbs produce beans.

The Huron, who occupied the area between Lake Simcoe and Georgian Bay in present-day Ontario, were successful farmers. They arrived in central Canada during the Paleo-Indian period, about 9000–8000 BC, at a time when a glacier bisected Ontario and the Champlain Sea covered the St. Lawrence Valley. A small group, they initially lived off the caribou. However, as the climate warmed and the glacier retreated, the spruce forest became boreal, and the Huron adapted to the changing landscape. They began farming around AD 800, and as a stable agricultural society, their numbers quickly grew. They eventually formed a confederacy of approximately thirty thousand people called Huronia. Living in longhouses within fortified villages, they had three thousand hectares under cultivation, controlled trade in the area, and bartered their produce for fur and meat.

Corn was the Huron's most significant agricultural development (though their planting of tobacco is arguably more famous). Corn does not grow in the wild; it needs to be cultivated. By the time the Europeans arrived, 150 varieties of corn were being grown, from southern Chile to Ontario, a botanical coup that had evolved through the ministrations of centuries of Amerindian farmers. It was an efficient, ubiquitous crop, and some cultures believed it possessed human qualities, that it wept when it failed to grow.

The numerous native cosmologies have common themes but differ in the details. Some of the stories share themes with Judeo-Christian mythology. The creation myths of the Mi'kmaq, Cree, Iroquois, and Squamish all echo the story of Noah and the Flood. In the Cree version, the Creator made the animals and the people, and they fought until the earth was red with blood. To wash it clean he delivered a rain that lasted for weeks, covering the earth and drowning every living thing except an otter, a beaver, and a muskrat. The muskrat dove and retrieved a piece of the old earth, and from that an island grew, and life began anew with a fresh moral foundation. The Mi'kmaq believed that Kji-Kinap made the world and blew life into a stone that was shaped like a man; the Huron believed that Aataentsic, the Creator, fell through a hole in the sky onto the back of a great turtle with the earth on its back; the Haida were released from a giant clamshell by a raven; the Athapaskan Beaver believed humans crawled through a hollow log to reach earth.

Harmony and reciprocity are central ideas in most native religions. The importance of dreams is recognized. Trees and animals are invested with spirits; occasionally inanimate objects such as stones are as well. Man is part of nature, and nature is an interdependent rather than a hierarchical system.

This close relationship with nature was ritualized for males. In 1954, an ancient Sarcee named Pat Grasshopper described the vision quest, a puberty ritual undergone by Sarcee boys. "To get some of the spirit power from nature, and to find a spirit that would be his protector through life, a boy would go out alone, on his guardian spirit quest. He would first bathe until he was very clean, and then he would live for three or four or five days without food. After he had fasted, he would have a vision, and a spirit would speak to him. It would give him a special song and special power." To ignore these spirits was to court disaster. In times of crisis they could be summoned for guidance. It was part of the complex pact with nature.

Native women with children (*National Archives of Canada, C-99228*)

"In ancient times, warfare and feuding were endemic in the land of the Mohawks," wrote one of the chiefs of the Six Nations at the beginning of the twentieth century. "Here warriors roamed the countryside, killing and scalping the inhabitants of settlements that lay scattered across the forest." Male prisoners were tortured to death in lengthy ceremonies: the prisoner's skin was stripped in pieces, his fingers cut off, fire applied to his genitals, his scalp taken and the ghastly wound cauterized with pitch. Though it was extraordinarily violent, there were elements of compassion. The victim was given water, and his wounds were tended to before the ritual continued – a grisly pas-de-deux between torturer and prisoner. It ended finally with his beheading on a scaffold. It was to everyone's advantage if the prisoner died well. The villagers ate parts or all of his body and absorbed his courage. Warriors prepared for this ordeal their whole lives with a death song that they sang to themselves.

In a myth resembling the story of Christ, a saviour named Dekanah-widah emerged to end the hostilities. The "Heavenly Messenger" was sent by the Great Spirit and born to a virgin mother in a Huron village near the Bay of Quinte. He became the founder of the Five Nations Confederacy (later to become the Six Nations).

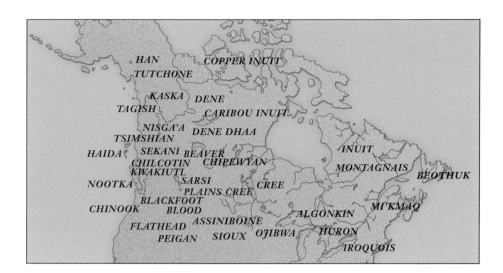

Native North America
circa 1500 AD

Dekanahwidah first crossed Lake Ontario in a stone canoe and went to the Onondaga (near present-day Syracuse, New York) to deliver his message of conciliation. Using diplomacy, threats, and displays of his supernatural powers, he negotiated for peace. The Seneca were convinced of his authority after Dekanahwidah produced a solar eclipse. The Five Nations – the Mohawk, Oneida, Cayuga, Onondaga, and Seneca (the Tuscarora became the sixth nation, joining in the eighteenth century) – formed a political alliance that allowed for peace among the Iroquois. "The land shall be beautiful," they declared, "the river shall have no more waves, one may go everywhere without fear." The Tree of Peace was planted, a white pine with roots that would reach to the four corners of the earth. Beneath it was a cavern in which the weapons were buried.

Was Dekanahwidah a prophet's dream, a man to whom the powers of a god were ascribed, or pure myth? Different versions of the story abound. But the birth of the Five Nations Confederacy is an established fact; it was probably created sometime in the fifteenth century. In 1654 the Jesuit missionary François-Joseph Le Mercier described the Confederacy as an alliance already long established. And a century later, Benjamin Franklin wrote that it "appears indissoluble."

Like the morality tales of western literature, the oral history of North America's native people included cautionary stories. One Kwakiutl legend describes the familiar, ruinous allure of materialism. The chief of the First-Ones obtained a huge amount of copper, which was called Causing-Destitution. The copper was sold for profit, and various people were killed for it, so Causing-Destitution was hidden in the ground to prevent any more deaths. But it was later discovered by a new generation.

"Then they dug, and behold, it was Causing-Destitution. A fathom and a half was the size of the copper. It was called Causing-Destitution because there was nothing that was not paid for it. It made the houses empty. Twenty canoes was its price; and twenty slaves was its price; and also ten coppers tied to the end was its price; and twenty sewed blankets was its price; and twenty mink blankets was its price; and one hundred boards was its price; and forty wide planks was its price and twenty boxes of dried berries added to it and twenty boxes of clover and also ten boxes of hemlock-bark was its price; and forty boxes of grease was its price; and one hundred painted boxes was its price; and two hundred mats was its price; and two hundred cedar blankets was its price; and two hundred dishes was its price."

Materialism was the root of evil; it led to jealousy, death, and familial rivalries. One way to exorcize it was through the potlatch, a ceremony in which one gave away one's possessions. The potlatch was an elegant way of dealing with economic inequality within the village and keeping the peace with neighbouring bands. It was also a way of establishing influence: the more you gave away, the more powerful you were.

There are several tantalizing theories of early European contact: the Phoenicians, the Carthaginians, and St. Brendan the Navigator, a sixth-century Irish monk, have all been proposed as the first to land in North America. But the first documented contact was with the Norse in AD 1000, who met with either Dorset or Beothuk natives in Labrador, and whose brief and gloomy stay is recorded in Norse myth. The Vikings built sod houses on the coast and repaired their ships using local iron deposits. When the natives brought furs to trade for metal implements, the Vikings were hesitant to give them weapons, and the relationship soured. The Norse called the natives "Skraelings," from *skraelingjar*, meaning small and withered. They reminded the Norse of trolls and were described as "ill-favoured men with ugly hair on their heads." The skirmishes between the two groups did not abate, and the Vikings finally left.

The next visit was not for five centuries, when Giovanni Caboto, or John Cabot, came to Newfoundland. Then followed a steady stream of Basque, Spanish, English, and Portuguese fishermen, French explorers, and English colonists.

Kluskap, a Mi'kmaq spirit, warned of this assault: "There will be white people who come and take this forest away from you. But I am going north, to make a place for you where no white person can ever come. No white person shall ever enter there. And this place will be a place where you may not come while you are alive. You will only travel there after you die on the Earth World."

In Huron mythology, the direction to escape the whites was west, the direction of death. The world was ruled by twins, Good Brother and Evil Brother, and in an epic battle Good killed Evil, who returned in a dream, saying, "I am going to the far west. Hereafter all men will go to the west after death." The Nuu'chah'nulth thought the whites were fish who had been transformed into men and had the faces of dog salmon.

The Squamish thought the whites were simply dead. When they saw a Spanish ship for the first time, a Squamish observer noted: "The people

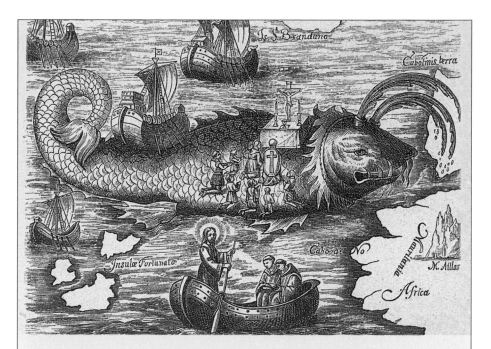

SAINT BRENDAN ◆ Saint Brendan was an Irish cleric who died around AD 577. He sailed around Ireland and Scotland and possibly much farther, according to a stubborn legend that has him visiting the shores of North America.

"They came within view of an island, which was very rugged and rocky, covered over with slag, without trees or herbage, but full of smiths' forges. St. Brendan said to the brethren; 'I am much distressed about this island; I have no wish to enter it or even to approach it – yet the wind is driving us directly towards it as if it were the aim of our course. . . . The brethren cried aloud to the Lord 'Hear us, O Lord, the God of our salvation.' But St. Brendan encouraged them: 'Why are you alarmed? Fear not, for no evil shall befall us, as we have here only a helper on our journey. . . .'

"One of the inhabitants came forth to do some work; he was all hairy and hideous, begrimed with fire and smoke. When he saw the servants of Christ near the island, he withdrew . . . crying aloud 'Woe! Woe, Woe!'

"'Soldiers of Christ, be strong in faith unfeigned and in the armour of the Spirit, for we are now on the confines of hell.'" From Saint Brendan's *Navigation* (*Illustration to Navigatio Brendani, Mary Evans Picture Library*)

did not know what it was. At first they believed that the ship was a floating island with sticks growing on it, and cobwebs were hanging from the sticks. . . . As they approached this monstrous thing they could see that it was a canoe of tremendous size. . . . Then as they rested their paddles and looked at this great canoe, they saw a man on board. He was walking on the deck. They thought he was dead – walking; that he was from the spirit world, and that he was carrying his coffin on his back. . . . You must understand that this man had a big beard, which was something new to the people, and above this great mass of black beard his face was white. Now, the only pale faces the people had ever seen were on dead men."

MARCO POLO ABOUT TO DEPART FROM VENICE ON HIS TRAVELS TO ASIA ◆
Marco Polo left Venice for the Orient in 1275 and spent time in the court of Kublai Khan, the grandson of Genghis
Khan. Polo established the first sustained link between Europe and the east, initiating lucrative trade.
(*Bodleian Library, Oxford*)

The Europeans were not dead, but they brought death with them.
Smallpox, measles, influenza, diphtheria, typhus, and mumps all raged
through the native populations. Their immune systems were vulnerable
to the alien viruses, and as much as 90 per cent of the North American
native population was killed by imported diseases, the silent gift that
crept westward.

Giovanni Caboto was an Italian navigator authorized by King Henry VII
of England to "seek out, discover and find whatsoever isles, countries,
regions or provinces of the heathen and infidels." On June 24, 1497, five

THE CAPTURE OF CONSTANTINOPLE ◆ All of Europe's trade with the east was funnelled through Constantinople. When it fell into the hands of Muslims, that door was effectively closed. This fuelled the impetus to search for a route to the Orient by sea in the other direction. (*The Taking of Constantinople, Jacopo Negretti Palma, Bridgeman Art Library, British Museum*)

years after Christopher Columbus had sailed to the West Indies, Caboto, who had adopted the anglicized name John Cabot, landed somewhere in Labrador or Newfoundland; historians have been unable to determine the precise location. There he raised a cross and the banner of England, claiming the territory for Christianity and his royal patron.

Following a trail inland, Cabot and a few of his men came to a clearing with a dead campfire and a short stick that had been carved and painted. The abandoned site might have belonged to the Beothuk, and it was a fitting introduction to a tribe that would prove so elusive. Cabot collected fresh water, then got nervous and returned to his ship.

MAP OF THE NEW WORLD DISCOVERED BY JOHN CABOT IN 1497 ◆ "That Venetian of ours who went with a small ship from Bristol to find new islands has come back and says he has discovered mainland 700 leagues away, which is the country of the Grand Khan, and that he coasted it for 300 leagues and landed and did not see any person; but he has brought here to the king certain snares which were spread to take game and a needle for making nets and he found certain notched trees so that by this he judges that there are inhabitants. Being in doubt he returned to his ship; and he has been three months on the voyage; and this is certain. And on the way back he saw two  islands, but was unwilling to land, in order not to lose time, as he was in want of provisions. The king here is much pleased at this; and he [Cabot] says that the tides are slack and do not run as they do here. The king has promised him for the spring ten armed ships as he [Cabot] desires and has given him all the prisoners to be sent away, that they may go with him, as he has requested; and has given him money that he may have a good time until then. And he is with his Venetian wife and his sons at Bristol. His name is [John Cabot] and he is called the Great Admiral and vast honour is paid to him and he goes dressed in silk, and these English run after him like mad, and indeed he can enlist as many of them as he pleases, and a number of rogues as well. The discoverer of these things planted on the land which he has found a large cross with a banner of England and one of St. Mark, as he is a Venetian, so that our flag has been hoisted very far afield." August 23, 1497, Lorenzo Pasqualigo, writing to his brothers Alvise and Francesco in Venice (*Bridgeman Art Library, British Museum*)

Four years later a Venetian diplomat named Pietro Pasqualigo wrote of native captives – possibly Beothuk – that he had seen in Lisbon, kidnapped by a subsequent explorer. "They are of like colours, figure, stature, and respect, and bear the greatest resemblance to the Gypsies," Pasqualigo wrote. Clad in the skins of animals, "they may appear mere savages, yet they are gentle, and have a strong sense of shame, and are better made in the legs, arms and shoulders than it is possible to describe . . . admirably fitted to endure labour, and will probably turn out the best slaves that have been discovered up to this time." This did not turn out to be the case; virtually all of them died, most on the voyage and the rest soon after landing.

The Beothuk were among the first natives to be paraded in Europe as the exotic face of the New World. Keen to avoid contact with the early European fishermen, they retreated from the coast. Their campfires were sometimes stumbled upon but the natives themselves were rarely glimpsed. Their insistent absence bred fear; they became mythic. In the course of their limited contact with Europeans, they contracted various diseases and were hunted by fearful colonists. By the beginning of the nineteenth century their numbers had dwindled from several hundred to just a handful. The last survivor was a woman named Shawnadithit, and her history became the history of her people.

In 1823, English trappers found a Beothuk woman and her two daughters in a state of starvation near Exploits Bay. The woman's husband was hiding nearby and attempted to come to their rescue but fell through the

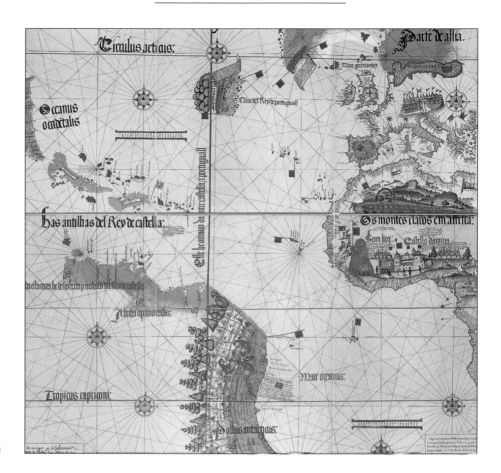

Map of the world by Alberto Cantino, 1502 (*Library of Congress*.)

ice while crossing a creek and drowned. The women were taken to St. John's and fed and clothed, then returned to Exploits Bay with gifts that were intended as peace offerings for the Beothuk. It was hoped that this would start a new chapter in the bleak relations between the two cultures. Within days the mother and one of the daughters died, probably of tuberculosis. The survivor, twenty-two-year-old Shawnadithit, walked alongside the River Exploits until she reached the English settlement. There she spent almost five years working as a maid known as Nancy, for a man named John Peyton, Jr.

William Cormack, an explorer and agriculturalist, became alarmed at the disappearance of an entire culture, and on October 2, 1827, he formed the "'Beothuk Institution,' for the purpose of opening a communication with, and promoting the civilization of the Red Indians of Newfoundland." His efforts came too late. At this point, Shawnadithit was already one of the only Beothuk left to communicate with. When Cormack learned of her existence, he had her brought to his institution, despite the protests of Peyton, who valued her as a nanny. She, in effect, became the Beothuk Institution, supplying Cormack with his only first-hand information on the tribe. "We have traces enough left to cause our sorrow that so peculiar and so superior a people should have disappeared from the earth like a shadow," Cormack wrote.

By then Shawnadithit was twenty-six, with a placid face and scars from gunshot wounds on her hand, arms, and leg. She was already dying of

tuberculosis and sometimes talked to the spirits of her mother and sister. Cormack tried desperately to improve her English to the point where she could tell the story of her people. She had a gift for drawing and outlined the tribe's dismal history in a series of detailed pictures. Her version of events accurately matched what was then known about the Beothuk.

In 1810, Governor Sir John Thomas Duckworth had sent a small party headed by Captain David Buchan into the interior to make friendly contact with the "Red Indians," so called for their custom of painting their bodies with ochre. Hostages were exchanged as a gesture of trust: two of Buchan's men were left at the Beothuk camp, while two natives went with him, intending to return with gifts. The Beothuk were worried that Buchan was going for reinforcements and killed the two English hostages with arrows. Shawnadithit, who was nine at the time of the incident, described how her mother had beheaded the two men.

Nine years later, Governor Sir Charles Hamilton offered a reward of one hundred pounds to anyone who could bring a "Red Indian" back to St. John's. Soon afterwards, a group of Englishmen surprised three Beothuk: Shawnadithit's aunt and two uncles. One of the native men was killed in the ensuing battle and his corpse was measured, to document his considerable size. The woman, Demasduit, was captured and given the name Mary March, in part after the month in which she'd been caught. By the summer she was dying, and Captain Buchan was given the task of taking her back to her people. She died en route, and Buchan left her body at the site where she had been captured. When Cormack went on a discouraging search for the Beothuk

DEMASDUIT (MARY MARCH) ◆ In 1819, Demasduit was captured by John Peyton, Jr., who had been paid by the governor of Newfoundland to bring back a Beothuk native. Her husband was killed trying to defend her and his killers measured his corpse to determine the size of someone who could fight half a dozen men. Demasduit was taken to St. John's where she demonstrated an uncanny ability to mimic those around her. She quickly picked up some English and was given the name Mary March. Once she could communicate, she told her captors that she had an infant child. This news precipitated a wave of protest among local citizens, who wrote to Governor Charles Hamilton, demanding that she be returned to her people and her child. Hamilton hoped that Mary March could become a link between the Beothuk and white settlers in Newfoundland, a way of establishing a diplomatic relationship. Unknown to Mary March or her captors was the death of her baby from starvation, two days after her capture.

The citizens of St. John's proposed to engage thirty men from Twillingate, who were familiar with the woods, to escort her home. "Upon meeting with the Natives," the citizens' committee advised, "they will deliver up the woman to her friends, as the offering of peace, and the best pledge of sincerity, together with such presents as may be deemed suitable, should they be able to induce two or three of the Chiefs to accompany them to Twillingate, they will return immediately, but should the Indians want confidence the party will secure themselves from attack, and remain some days in the country with the view of dissipating their doubts by daily acts of confidence and kindness."

Governor Hamilton acquiesced to the citizens' wishes, but by the time an expedition was mobilized, Mary March was dying of tuberculosis. Captain David Buchan headed the expedition, taking March, along with goodwill gifts for her people: 27 looking glasses, 24 knives, 9 strings of beads, 36 tin pots, dishes, and kettles, 36 awl blades. But Buchan could not find her tribe. Mary March said she only wanted to find her child, and then she would return to St. John's. She did not manage either, and died on January 8, 1820.

Buchan thought that returning her body to the site where she had been kidnapped would still constitute a gesture of goodwill. He had a coffin built and trimmed with red cloth. Two wooden dolls that Mary March had liked were placed in the coffin and a copper plate engraved with her name was fixed on it. Sixty men went inland with the coffin on a sled, covering eight kilometres a day. After fifteen days they found snowshoe tracks which led to a recently abandoned storehouse and wigwams. Five days later they reached the campsite where Mary March had been taken. Buchan built a platform and placed the coffin on it, with the presents surrounding it. He spent two weeks searching for the Beothuk, without luck. The natives were never far, though. They had been following Buchan, observing his progress. When they were sure that he and his party were gone, they took Demasduit's body out of the coffin and placed her in the burial hut that held her husband and child. (*Lady Henrietta Hamilton, National Archives of Canada, C-092599*)

JACQUES CARTIER ◆ "To declare unto you the state of the Savages, they are people of a goodly stature, and well made, they are very white, but they are all naked: and if they were apparelled as the French are, they would bee as white and as fayre: but they paynt themselves for feare of heat and sunne burning.

"In stead of apparell, they weare skinnes upon them like mantle; and they have a small payre of breeches, wherewith they cover their privities, as well men as women. They have hosen and shooes of lether excellently made . . . They eate good meate, but all unsalted, but they drye it, and afterward they broyle it, aswell fish as flesh. They have no certaine dwelling place, and they goe from place to place, as they thinke they may best finde foode, as Aloses in one place, and other fish, Salmons, Sturgions, Mullets, Surmullets, Barz, Carpes, Eeles, Pinperneaux, and other fresh water fish, and store of Porposes. They feede also of Stagges, wilde Bores, Bugles, Porkespynes, and store of other wilde beastes. And there is as great store of Fowle as they can desire.

"Touching their bread, they make very good: and it is of great myll: and they live very well; for they take care for nothing else." From *The Voyages of Jacques Cartier (Théophile Hamel, National Archives of Canada, C-11226)*

François I, 1494-1547 (*Superstock*)

five years later, he came upon a burial hut containing the corpse of Mary March, still wearing the muslin dress that had been given to her.

At the time of her aunt's death, Shawnadithit estimated that there were thirty-one Beothuk left. Two English traders killed another of her uncles, then shot his daughter as an afterthought. By 1823, the year Shawnadithit was taken to Peyton's house, they were down to thirteen. Cormack reported: "The surviving remnant, she says, went by a circuitous route northerly, westerly and southerly from the Badger Bay waters to the Great Lake. Here ends all positive knowledge of her tribe, which she never recounted without tears."

In June 1829, nine months after moving to St. John's to become the living emblem of a vanished culture, Shawnadithit died of tuberculosis. Cormack was in England at the time and wrote her obituary for the London *Times*, describing her as the last of the Red Indians. Dr. William Carson put her skull and scalp in a tin box and sent it to the Royal College of Physicians in London with a description: "She was tall, and majestic, mild and tractable, but characteristically proud and cautious."

After Cabot's expedition, the British were too preoccupied at home with religious travails, war, and domestic politics to finance any more. Exploration was a distant priority. But in 1534, Jacques Cartier, backed by the French government, launched a major expedition to the New World.

Cartier was born in St. Malo, in Brittany, on the French coast, and it is possible that he went to Newfoundland as a sailor before his voyages of discovery. In one portrait, he is shown in profile, dressed as a nobleman, hawk-nosed, almost scowling. In 1534 he was commissioned by King François I of France to sail to the New World with the hope of finding a passage to the Orient, or at least finding gold (as the Spanish had in Latin America). Cartier left St. Malo on April 20 and arrived at Newfoundland on May 10. He then sailed on to Labrador, where he offered his first, famous impression of the country: "I am rather inclined to believe that this is the land God gave to Cain." He could not see a cartload of soil; it was a barren, unwelcoming landscape.

Cartier encountered natives in canoes who made signs that they wanted to trade. "We likewise made signs to them that we wished them no harm," Cartier wrote in the ship's log, "and sent two men ashore, to offer them some knives and other iron goods, and a red cap to give to their chief. . . . They bartered all they had to such an extent that all went back naked without anything on them; and they made signs to us that they would return on the morrow with more skins."

Trade was of marginal interest to Cartier, though, and he moved west, probing for a promising passage to the Orient. He explored the Strait of Belle Isle as a possible route, but was defeated by fog off Anticosti Island. As he moved westward, Cartier was encouraged at least by the land, which was more fertile than Labrador's, and by the abundance and exoticism of the

THE MI'KMAQ ◆ In the seventeenth century, Henri Membertu, chief of a small Mi'kmaq band, noted that its population began to diminish after the arrival of Europeans. Once, he said, his people had been as plentiful as the hairs upon his head. The Mi'kmaq lost as much as 85 per cent of their population through diseases contracted from Europeans.

Disease was the single greatest agent of destruction to natives in the New World. Though the Spanish conquistadors slew thousands, many more were killed by diseases the Spanish brought with them, which wiped out 95 per cent of the pre-Columbian native population. Smallpox alone killed almost half the Aztec population. The epidemic moved north, spreading to native populations in the Mississippi Valley.

Natives had never been exposed to European germs and so had no immunologic or genetic resistance to them. Smallpox, measles, influenza, typhus, and tuberculosis all took their toll. It was a one-way exchange; no New World microbes returned to Europe, causing devastation. The reason for this was that the diseases originated with domesticated animals, which were in abundance in Europe but relatively rare in the New World. Dogs were common among the northern natives, and llamas used in South America, but neither species was herded in the large groups – such as cattle – necessary for the successful spread of microbes. The conquest of two continents was largely accomplished through inadvertent, but at times deliberate, germ warfare. (*National Archives of Canada, C-810*)

wildlife. He stopped at Iles-aux-Oiseaux where his crew killed more than a thousand birds, many of them great auks, which by the mid-nineteenth century were hunted to extinction.

A flotilla of more than forty canoes brought Cartier his next encounter with the natives. Several of them approached and surrounded a lone longboat that was exploring the coast. "All came toward our longboat, dancing and showing many signs of joy, and of their desire to be friends," Cartier noted. Despite their intent, he was nervous of their numbers and motioned them to turn back. "And seeing that no matter how much we signed to them, they would not go back, we shot off over their heads two small cannon." The Mi'kmaq turned and paddled toward shore.

It is not surprising that Cartier was apprehensive about making contact. Fear, writes French historian Robert Mandrou, was the dominant emotion in sixteenth-century France. "Everything combined to produce fear: the material conditions of life, the precarious nature of the food supply, the inadequacies of the environment, and above all the intellectual climate." As well as their pragmatic worries, there was fear of the supernatural. "Adding to the fear of wolves was the fear of werewolves, or men changed into wolves by the hand of the Devil." Cartier brought these fears with him, and they infected his relations with the natives.

At the Baie de Gaspé, Cartier met the St. Lawrence Iroquoians, the group with whom he would have his most lasting relationship in the New World, one that would prove both beneficial and destructive to all involved. He presented them with gifts and was introduced to their leader, Donnacona. An alliance was soon formed and sealed with dancing and celebration.

The festive mood quickly vanished after Cartier had a ten-metre cross made and set up at Gaspé harbour. On it a wooden board was engraved "Long Live the King of France." The Frenchmen knelt before it and worshipped, looking to heaven. This caused some unease among the natives, who rightly felt that Cartier and his men had designs on their territories.

"When we had returned to our ships," Cartier wrote, "the captain [Donnacona], dressed in an old black bear-skin, arrived in a canoe with three of his sons and his brother; but they did not come so close to the ships as they had usually done. And pointing to the cross he made us a long harangue, making the sign of the cross with two of his fingers; and then he pointed to the land all around about, as if he wished to say that all this region belonged to him, and that we ought not to have set up this cross without his permission. And when he finished his harangue, we held up an axe to him, pretending we would barter it for his skin. To this he nodded assent and little by little drew near the side of our vessel, thinking that he would have the axe. But one of our men, who was in our dinghy, caught hold of his canoe, and at once two or three more stepped down into it and made them come aboard our vessel, at which they were greatly astonished."

Cartier told Donnacona that he would go to France and return with more iron goods to trade. He wanted to take two of the chief's adult sons, Domagaya and Taignoagny, as a gesture of faith between the men. "We dressed up his two sons in shirts and ribbons and in red caps, and put a little brass chain around the neck of each, at which they were greatly pleased." Donnacona bade his sons farewell and Cartier left. He made a cursory search for a passage to the west, then returned to France, arriving on September 5 with his two captives, an exotic anticlimax to his first voyage of discovery.

Cartier had failed to find the passage to the Orient, nor had he found gold, but he remained optimistic.

The following year, Cartier returned to Gaspé harbour with three ships instead of two, and 110 men rather than the 61 of his first voyage. Donnacona's sons, who accompanied Cartier, had told him of a great river,

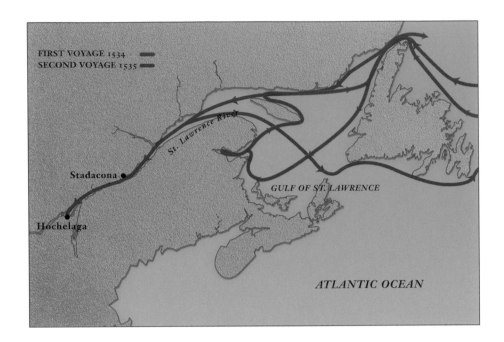

FIRST VOYAGE 1534
SECOND VOYAGE 1535

St. Lawrence River

Stadacona

Hochelaga

GULF OF ST. LAWRENCE

ATLANTIC OCEAN

The Voyages of Jacques
Cartier, 1534-1535

a lengthy route into the interior that no one had explored to the end.
Cartier was buoyed by this description; it sounded like the passage he was
seeking. But he did not entirely trust the two men, and so he first explored
the north shore of the Gulf of St. Lawrence, looking for a more promising
route. With no other leads to follow, Cartier finally accepted the guidance
of the chief's sons, which led him to the St. Lawrence River, his most significant geographical discovery.

Cartier reached the archipelago at Orleans, near the Iroquoian village
of Stadacona (the present site of Quebec City), where Donnacona was waiting. As Cartier's ship anchored, the chief came out and embraced his sons,
and they spoke of France. Gifts were exchanged and the mood was festive,
but a guarded suspicion lingered on both sides. "And all came over toward
our ships," Cartier noted, "showing many signs of joy, except the two
men we had brought with us, to wit, Taignoagny and Domagaya, who were
altogether changed in their attitude and goodwill, and refused to come
on board our ships, although many times begged to do so. At this time we
began somewhat to distrust them." The two sons also had reason to distrust
Cartier, having been kidnapped by him, but the mood of mutual suspicion
was tempered by a mutual desire for gain.

In the negotiations that followed, the chief's sons, who had learned
French, acted as interpreters, but Cartier suspected that Taignoagny was not
in fact presenting Donnacona's views but his own. Perhaps there was some
treachery in the translation? In his mind, Cartier cast Taignoagny as a
Shakespearean villain, an Iago, spreading suspicion and doubt among
all parties. Taignoagny told Cartier that his father was vexed because the
French were so heavily armed, while the natives were not. "The Captain
replied that for all Donnacona's grief, he would not cease to carry weapons
since this was the custom in France as Taignoagny well knew."

Jacques Cartier sailing up the St. Lawrence in 1535 (*Gudin Théodore, Versailles et Trianon*)

After promising to accompany Cartier up the St. Lawrence to the Iroquoian settlement of Hochelaga (at the present site of Montreal), Taignoagny then changed his mind, saying the river was not worth exploring. The French became convinced that Taignoagny "was a worthless fellow, who was intent on nothing but treason and malice."

As Cartier became more intent on going up the river to Hochelaga, Donnacona and his sons became more resistant to the idea. Donnacona might have wanted to control trade with the Europeans, and wanted a binding trade agreement with Cartier before he dealt with other bands. Perhaps he simply resented Cartier's intrusion into the interior in so bold a manner. The two sons had spent a year in France, and they might have glimpsed the imperial aims of Cartier's backer.

Having seen the power the Church held for the French, Donnacona and his people staged a religious pantomime to discourage the explorers. "On the next day," Cartier reported, "they devised a great ruse to prevent us still from going to Hochelaga. They dressed up three men as devils, arraying them in black and white dog-skins, with horns as long as one's arm and their faces coloured black as coal." They passed by the ship in a canoe, then returned to shore, where Donnacona and his men grabbed them and carried them into the wood. Taignoagny and Domagaya emerged from the trees, feigning astonishment. Taignoagny cried, "Jesus, Jesus, Jesus," and stared toward heaven. Dom Agaya joined in, calling out, "Jesus, Maria, Jacques Cartier," and he, too, looked upward.

A religious face-off ensued, with Donnacona's sons saying that their god, Cudouagny, had warned them that there would be enough snow and ice at Hochelaga to kill everyone. Since it was late September, with no sign yet of winter weather, this prediction did not carry much weight with the French. Cartier responded that Cudouagny was a fool; Jesus would keep

Jacques Cartier meets the Hochelagans. "We marched on, and about half a league thence found the land began to be cultivated. It was fine land with large fields covered with the corn of the country . . . and in the middle of these fields is situated and stands the village of Hochelaga, near and adjacent to a mountain, the slopes of which are fertile and are cultivated, and from the top of which one can see for a long distance. We named this mountain 'Mount Royal.'" (*Napoleon Sarony after Andrew Morris, National Archives of Canada, C-42247*)

them safe. Cudouagny would prove to be the more prescient in this theological tug-of-war, but for the moment it was agreed that the sons would accompany Cartier up the river.

For Cartier and his crews, the journey up the St. Lawrence offered the breathless wonders of the New World. They saw beluga whales and walruses for the first time, and there were new varieties of birds in huge numbers. They were well received by natives along the way, the meetings brokered by Donnacona's sons. They encountered five Iroquoian hunters who, Cartier wrote, "came to meet our boats without fear or alarm, and in as familiar a manner as if they had seen us all their lives. And when our longboats grounded, one of those men took me in his arms and carried me on shore as easily as if I had been a six-year-old child, so strong and big was that man."

At Hochelaga they were met by more than a thousand people. Gifts were exchanged, and the Hochelagans gave them fish and food in such quantity that "it seemed to rain bread." The men danced and the women wept with joy.

The Hochelagan leader, Agouhanna, who was partially paralysed, was carried in on a large deerskin and presented to Cartier. "He showed his arms and legs to me motioning to him to be good enough to touch them, as if he thereby expected to be cured and healed. On this I set about rubbing his arms and legs with my hands." Others came to Cartier: the lame, the blind, the elderly and ailing, "in order that I might lay my hands upon them, so that one would have thought Christ had come down to earth to heal them." Cartier addressed his impromptu assembly, reading from the Gospel of St. John: "In the beginning was the Word, and the Word was with God, and the Word was God . . ."

By the time Cartier had left Hochelaga and returned to his ships, the river had indeed begun to freeze, and they were forced to winter downriver at Stadacona. They quickly built a fort, with artillery pointing outward – an affront to Donnacona. The relationship between Cartier and the chief quickly deteriorated. The Stadaconans ceased to bring fish to the fort, and contact withered.

An outbreak of disease soon put an end to any hopes of friendly relations. By December, fifty natives were dead, and Cartier forbade any contact, lest it spread to his own men. But the French quickly began to exhibit symptoms, and they assumed that they had caught whatever the natives had. It is likely, though, that they were suffering from different maladies. The Stadaconans might have been infected by a virus borne by the French, while it seems clear that Cartier's men had scurvy. By the middle of February, fewer than 10 of Cartier's party of 110 men remained in good health. By the end of March 25 men were dead, and almost all the survivors were afflicted. Cartier, remarkably, was spared.

Cartier gave orders for the men to pray and had a statue of the Virgin Mary placed against a tree outside the fort. On Sunday, those who could move trudged across the snow for mass. They sang the seven psalms of David and prayed to the Virgin that her Son would have pity on them.

With his men enfeebled by scurvy, Cartier became even more nervous of Donnacona and his people, worried that the Stadaconans would attack if they knew how vulnerable the French really were. Since relations were so strained, each camp was unaware of how fragile the other was. The French were too weak to bury their dead in the frozen ground and simply covered them with snow. When natives came near the fort, Cartier would put on an elaborate charade in an attempt to demonstrate vigorous health. He would take two or three men outside the enclosure, one of his men observed, and "would pretend to beat them, and vociferating and throwing sticks at them, would drive them back on board the ships, indicating to the savages by signs that he was making all his men work below the decks, some at calking, others at baking bread and at other tasks; and that it would not do to have them come and loaf outside." Inside the boat the sick men weakly hammered the hull with sticks, trying to approximate the sounds of busy, healthy sailors.

When Domagaya approached one day, Cartier saw that, though he had been ill, he was now in good health, and asked what had cured him. Domagaya said that he had been healed by the foliage of the white cedar tree. In a fleeting fraternal mood, he had an infusion of the drink prepared for Cartier's men. Initially, they declined to take it, but a few of the more desperate finally drank it. "As soon as they had drunk it they felt better," Cartier wrote, "which surely must be ascribed to miraculous causes; for after drinking it two or three times they recovered health and strength and were cured of all the diseases they had ever had. . . . When this became known, there was such a press for the medicine that they almost killed each other to have it first; so that in less than eight days a whole tree as large and as tall as any I ever saw was used up, and produced such a result that had all the doctors of Louvain and Montpellier been there, with all the drugs of Alexandria, they could not have done so much in a year as did this tree in eight days." Credit for this miraculous cure was given to God, of course, rather than the Stadaconans.

By April, the ships were free of ice and Cartier planned to return home, with the dread that his second voyage, like the first, had ended in failure. But Donnacona suggested that there were riches to be discovered. "He assured us that he had been to the land of the Saguenay where there are immense quantities of gold, rubies, and other rich things, and that the men there are white as in France and go clothed in woollens," Cartier wrote. "He also told us that he had visited another region where the people, possessing no anus, never eat or digest, but simply make water through the penis. He told us furthermore that he had been in the land of the Picquenyans, and to another country whose inhabitants have only one leg and other marvels too long to relate."

Whether Cartier believed these marvels himself is not clear. His relationship with Donnacona was based on mutual distrust, and the tales of people who never ate must have strained his credulity. Nevertheless, Donnacona was a king and he told a good story. (French satirist François Rabelais later incorporated these tales, and Donnacona himself, into his book *Pantagruel*.) Cartier decided on a more ambitious kidnapping: "I had quite made up my mind to take Donnacona to France, that he might relate and tell to the king all he had seen in the west of the wonders of the world."

Donnacona and his sons were wary of going too near the ships; they knew that Cartier was preparing to leave, and they had been duped before. So, after assuring the chief that the king of France did not want any native hostages, Cartier took Donnacona and his sons by force, transporting them to the ship and holding them there. The villagers spent the night on shore, "howling and crying like wolves all night long, calling out incessantly, Agouhanna, Agouhanna, in the hope of being able to speak to him." But Cartier kept Donnacona below decks. The next day, Cartier told the chief that an interview had been arranged with the French king, and that Donnacona would receive gifts in France and would return to his people in ten to twelve months. Donnacona related this to his people from the deck and said goodbye. They sailed on May 6.

When Cartier arrived he had ten natives with him: besides Donnacona and his two sons, there were three men who had been captured with their chief and four children who had been given to Cartier as gifts. In France they were baptized and, according to an observer, "instructed in the love and fear of God and of His holy law."

Donnacona met with King François and described the great city of Sagana, where, he said, white men lived, and nutmeg, cloves, and pepper grew. A man named Lagarto was present for this speech and described it in a letter to John III, the king of Portugal. Lagarto said that Donnacona was

ANDRÉ THEVET ◆ "It is impossible for any living man," André Thevet wrote, "never having left a place, however good a rhetorician he may be, to describe foreign countries unless he wishes impudently to lie." There is no evidence that Thevet visited the New World, though he wrote about it extensively. But his interviews with explorers and captured natives did yield a vivid, if unreliable travel literature.

"On the Country of Canada. . . . Since this country in the north was discovered in our time by a certain Jacques Cartier . . . one of my best friends, from whom I have obtained bits of information, since he has explored the country from one end to the other . . . I decided to write briefly in this place what seems to me worthy of being written. What motivated me even more to do this was that I have not seen that anyone else has treated it, although the matter in my opinion is not without merit." (*Library of Congress*)

like the Devil tempting Christ, saying "'*haec omnia tibi dabo* [all of this I give to you],' so as to return to his own land, and it seems to me that this is what will happen. The King laughed and said that the Indian King was an honest man, and would not act other than he had said."

It is unlikely that Donnacona had been to a land where spices grew and Europeans lived. And it is just as unlikely that Cartier, who had spent a winter on the St. Lawrence, and knew Sagana, or Saguenay, to be north of this frozen expanse, believed the city to exist, at least in the way Donnacona described it. At any rate, Cartier and Donnacona were allied in this fiction; both wanted to return to Canada, and each needed the other to do so.

Donnacona never returned. André Thevet, a Franciscan and a friend of Cartier's, met with Donnacona on several occasions and provides one of the few glimpses into his last years in France. He was "chief over all others, who was called [Donnacona], who died in France in the time of the Great King François, who spoke our language very well and having lived there four or five years died a good Christian. I saw and spoke with him to be more certain of the singularities of his country, and he told me that his seniors had told him that when a man . . . came to earth the sky formed a new star . . . which appeared in the sky to be the guide of this man. Whereas on the contrary when a man . . . came to pass away and leave Canada, then a star was lost in the sky never to be seen again."

The British were lagging far behind in the race to wealth and empire. The Spanish and Portuguese were dividing up the hemisphere south of Florida and the French had Cartier, who was charting the St. Lawrence. After Cabot, the British waited thirty-nine years before launching a second expedition, and it turned out to be an eccentric blip in the annals of exploration.

Two years after Cartier sailed up the St. Lawrence, Richard Hore, an English gentleman, organized an expedition to the New World of two ships, a crew of ninety, and thirty gentlemen who were interested in exotic

MI'KMAQ VILLAGERS ◆ Jacques Cartier had predicted that the natives would be easy to convert to Christianity, but this didn't turn out to be the case. "There is scarcely any change in them after their baptism," wrote Father Pierre Biard, who came to Acadia in 1611 and stayed for three frustrating years. "The same savagery and the same manners, or but little different, the same customs, ceremonies, usages, fashions, and vices remain, at least as far as can be learned; no attention being paid to any distinction of time, days, offices, exercises, prayers, duties, virtues, or spiritual beliefs."

Biard had trouble convincing the Mi'kmaq that Christianity was a superior belief system. "[The natives] are exceedingly vainglorious," he wrote. "They think they are better, more valiant and more ingenious than the French; and what is difficult to believe, richer than we are. . . . It is self-love that blinds them, and the evil one who leads them on, no more nor less than in our France, we see those who have deviated from the faith holding themselves higher and boasting of being better than the Catholics."

Father Biard's first documented success came with Membertu, the Mi'kmaq chief who claimed to be more than one hundred years old and to have met Cartier. Christened Henri, after the late French king, he became the first native baptized in New France and something of a propaganda vehicle. Biard described him as "the greatest, most renowned and most formidable savage within the memory of man: of Splendid physique. . . . Grave and reserved; feeling a proper sense of dignity for his position as commander." He was introduced into the church with a singing of the Te Deum and a cannon salute into Port Royal.

Membertu was a critical exception, the mission's great hope. He was given a few days' training, gave up all but one of his wives, and resolved to live as a Christian. But on September 16, 1611, lying on his deathbed, Membertu had a change of heart. After confessing his sins, he said he wanted to be buried with his pagan ancestors; the bond with his people was stronger than this new relationship. Biard was angry and left the tent where Membertu lay. Two days later he returned, and claimed that Membertu had finally agreed to a Catholic burial, though the chief was too weak to make the sign of the cross on his own and had to be helped. (*National Gallery of Canada*)

adventure. They might have been trying to follow Cartier's route into the Gulf of St. Lawrence. After a ceremony of religious blessing in which they received the sacrament, they left England from Gravesend in the spring of 1536.

The crossing was long, more than two months, and their adventure was initially limited to spotting some Beothuk on Newfoundland. The natives fled, leaving a campfire with bear meat on a spit. But a more genuine, dismal adventure took shape after one of the ships became unseaworthy and the crew ran out of food. They had little luck hunting or fishing and scoured the inhospitable land for edible roots and herbs. An account of the voyage was given by one of the survivors, Sir William Buts: "But the famine increasing and the reliefe of herbes being to little purpose to satisfie their insatiable hunger, in the fields and deserts here and there, the fellowe killed his mate while he stouped to take up a roote for his reliefe, and cutting out pieces of his body whome he had murthered, broyled the same on the coles and greedily devoured them. By this meane the company decreased . . ."

The cannibals among the crew accounted for their shipmates by saying they had been killed by savages or wild animals. When one of the crew confessed to broiling and eating a shipmate's buttock, the captain invoked God, declaring "that it had bene better to have perished in body, and to have lived everlastingly, then to have relieved for a poore time their mortal bodies, and to bee condemned everlastingly, both body and soule to the unquenchable fire of hel. And thus having ended to that effect, he began to exhort to repentence, and besought all the company to pray, that it might please God to looke upon their miserable present state, and for his owne mercie to relieve the same. And such was the mercie of God, that the same night there arrived a French shippe in that port, well furnished with vittaile, and such was the policie of the English, that they became masters of the same."

They pirated the ship and left the French crew with the unreliable English one and no food, then returned home. Several months later, against great odds, the French sailors arrived in England in the rotting vessel, demanding compensation, which was granted by a sympathetic Henry VIII. British ambitions for the New World were not revived for several years.

It was not until October 1540 that Cartier was commissioned to undertake a third voyage. His mandate was to go to "Canada and Hochelaga and as far as the land of Saguenay" with people of diverse skills, including fifty prisoners to be used as indentured labour. But this commission was annulled by the king, and a new commission was issued to a Protestant, Jean-François de la Rocque de Roberval, who was to lead the voyage of colonization. Cartier would accompany him in a subordinate position.

In May 1541, Cartier left for Canada with five ships, 1,500 men, and the explicit blessing of the Vatican. In 1537, Pope Paul III issued the *Sublimus Dei*, stating that the natives of the New World could be considered human beings and were therefore capable of being converted to the Roman Catholic faith.

"To all faithful Christians to whom this writing may come, health in Christ our Lord and the apostolic benediction. The enemy of the human race inspired his satellites who, to please him, have not hesitated to publish abroad that the Indians of the West and South and other people of whom we have recent knowledge should be treated as dumb brutes created for our service, pretending that they are incapable of receiving the Catholic faith.

"We, who though unworthy, exercise on earth the power of the Lord and seek with all our might to bring those sheep of his flock who are outside into the fold committed to our charge, consider, however, that the Indians are truly men and that they are not only capable of understanding the Catholic Faith but, according to our information, they desire exceedingly to receive it."

This was not entirely true. While natives had shown some desire to receive the faith, it was not clear that they understood what it was they were receiving.

None of the natives Cartier had brought to France were on board when he returned. They had all died of disease, with the exception of a young girl whom they'd left in France.

Roberval was waiting for artillery and stayed behind in France. Cartier arrived at Stadacona and was greeted by the new chief, Agona. "And after the said Agona had inquired of me where Donnacona and the rest were," Cartier wrote, "I answered him, That Donnacona was dead in France, and that his body rested in the earth, and that the rest stayed there as great Lords, and they were married, and would not return back into their Country: the said Agona made no show of anger at all these speeches: and I think he took it so well because he remained Lord and Governor of the country by the death of the said Donnacona."

Agona might have seen the advantage of going along with Cartier's story, but it is unlikely that he believed it, and hostility quickly developed between the two camps. Cartier established a new settlement at the mouth of the Rivière du Cap-Rouge, and during the winter the natives kept the fort under siege and said they killed thirty-five of Cartier's men. In June, Cartier returned to France, but not before running into Roberval at St. John's harbour. Roberval ordered Cartier to return to Canada. Cartier agreed, but in the middle of the night, he sailed for France.

He believed that he was carrying riches that would impress his king, but the diamonds he had found turned out to be quartz, and the "certain leaves of fine gold" were iron pyrites. Cartier was never given another commission and seems to have retired to his estate in St. Malo. He died on September 1, 1557, at the age of sixty-six.

If not the first to reach what would eventually become Canadian shores, Cartier was the first to survey the coasts of the Gulf of St. Lawrence, and the first European to sail the St. Lawrence River, the country's most vital artery. He was a fundamental link between the Old World and the New.

Canada from the Voyage of Jacques Cartier (1491-1557) and his Followers (*Pierre Descaliers, Bridgeman Art Library, British Museum*)

For the next three hundred years, Europeans and the natives of the east coast continued their uneven relationship. But on the northwest coast, there was relatively little contact. Spanish ships came up to trade, but the first prolonged visit was from the renowned English navigator James Cook, who anchored at Ship Cove (now Resolution Cove on Vancouver Island) for a month in 1778. One of the most fascinating descriptions of native life here comes from Englishman John R. Jewitt, who lived among the Nuu'chah'nulth (Nootka) on Vancouver Island for more than two years (1803–1805) and kept a journal of his experience.

Maquinna was the chief of the Moachat band of the Nuu'chah'nulth, and Jewitt describes him in his journal as "a man of dignified aspect, about six feet tall in height and extremely straight and well proportioned: his features were in general good, and his face was rendered remarkable by a large Roman nose, a very uncommon form of feature among these people; his complexion was of a dark copper hue, though his face, legs, and arms were, on this occasion, so covered with red paint, that their natural colour could scarcely be perceived; his eyebrows were painted black in two broad stripes like a new moon, and his long hair, which shone with oil, was fastened over with white down, which gave him a most curious and extraordinary appearance. He was dressed in a large mantle or cloak of the black sea-otter skin, which reached to his knees, and was fastened around his middle by a broad belt of the cloth of the country, wrought or painted with figures of several colours; this dress was by no means unbecoming, but, on the contrary, had an air of savage magnificence."

Maquinna initiated the sea-otter trade for his own village of 1,500 and acted as a wholesaler for other tribes, taking their pelts to the Europeans and making impressive profits. He was a shrewd bargainer and became adept

JAMES COOK ◆ The son of a Scottish farmer, James Cook became Britain's pre-eminent explorer, circumnavigating the world twice and making invaluable contributions to the knowledge of world geography. He was also the first to deal successfully with the problem of scurvy, which often killed up to half a ship's crew on a long voyage. Experimenting with citrus extracts, sauerkraut, and other foods, Cook did not lose a single man to scurvy on his Pacific voyages, an unprecedented feat. When he visited Nootka Sound in 1778, Cook's crew included George Vancouver and William Bligh, who would go on to command the mutinous crew of the *Bounty*. Cook described the Nootka natives in his journal.

"Sometimes they wear carved wooden masks, or vizors, applied on the face, or to the upper part of the head, or forehead. Some of these resemble human faces, furnished with hair, beards, and eyebrows; others the heads of birds, particularly of eagles . . . and many of the heads of land and sea animals. . . . Whether they use these extravagant masquerade ornaments on any particular religious occasion or diversion, or whether they be put on to intimidate their enemies when they go to battle, by their monstrous appearance, or as decoys when they go to hunt animals, is uncertain.

"The houses are disposed in three ranges or rows, rising gradually behind each other, the largest being that in front and the others less. . . . The heights of the sides and ends of these habitations is seven or eight feet: the back part is higher than the front, by which means the planks that compose the roof slant forward; they are laid on loose, and are moved to let out smoke and admit air or light. . . . Many are decorated with images. These are nothing more than the trunks of very large trees, four or five feet high, set up singly or by pairs, at the upper end of the apartment, with the front carved into a human face, the arms and hands cut out upon the sides, and variously painted, so that the whole is a truly monstrous figure.

"The women were always properly clothed, and behaved with the utmost propriety; justly deserving all commendation for a bashfulness and modesty becoming their sex."

Cook knew that his exploration would inevitably lead to European settlement, and he was concerned that it would have a negative effect on the natives. On February 14, 1779, he was clubbed to death on Kealakekua Beach in the Sandwich Islands (Hawaii) by the local natives. (*John Webber, National Portrait Gallery, London*)

CAPTAIN COOK IN NOOTKA SOUND ◆ The oral history of Cook's visit is recounted by Gillette Chipps, a west coast native. "I am going to tell you about when the first white man appeared in Nootka Sound. The Indians were dancing around the island – they called the schooner an island. They said there's an island because big trees on it. . . . They say Indian doctors go out there singing a song, find out, try to find out what it is. Rattling their rattles around the schooner, go around, all see a lot of white men. . . . Pale face white man, they said it was the dog salmon and oh that's a spring salmon. . . . Red-faced men, big nose, and so they said it was coho. That was when the first white man appeared in Nootka Sound in the schooner." (*John Webber, National Archives of Canada, C-11201*)

Callicum and Maquinna, Chiefs of Nootka Sound. When the Spanish claimed ownership of the territory surrounding the Sound, both the English traders and the Nootka largely ignored the claim. After a Spanish captain arrested an English trader in a show of strength, Callicum paddled out to the Spanish ship to condemn the action. He was shot and killed while still in his canoe. In fear of further violence, the Nootka moved their village and stayed away from the sound for two years. (*National Archives of Canada, 2807*)

at playing the Spanish against the English. His influence stemmed, in part, from the wealth he attained and redistributed in potlatches. Through trading, Maquinna built up his base of power, both within his own tribe and among others on the coast.

The Europeans viewed the natives through a monochromatic lens, seeing only a race of primitives, one that was by turns endearing (when they were guiding them, procuring furs, or offering herbal cures) and a barbarous, godless impediment to occupation. But the Amerindians in Canada were part of a complex network of separate nations, with twelve different language groups and a host of dialects. There were differing political structures, long-standing rivalries, and a variety of spiritual beliefs. By 4000 BC, there were already complex trading networks among the natives. Trade demanded a common language, which was sometimes a separate dialect that both groups understood. It required protocol and laws. Whoever controlled a territory controlled the trade that went through it.

Houses at Nootka Sound
(*British Library Picture Library*)

Trading brought the Europeans and natives to a head-on cultural clash. Chiefs sometimes prostituted female slaves captured in battle, taking them out to the ships and offering them to the crew in return for goods. From this, the Europeans gained the erroneous impression of a lax morality, a sexual licence that did not exist. As a result, they sometimes raped native women. Inevitably, disasters of this sort poisoned the relationship between natives and Europeans.

In 1803, the *Boston*, an American trading vessel, came to Nootka Sound. Based in Massachusetts and captained by John Salter, it was the most extravagantly laden trade vessel to sail out of America. As was customary, Maquinna came aboard to welcome the captain and assess the trading possibilities. He offered Salter fresh salmon as a welcoming gesture and later received a gift, a double-barrelled rifle. With it he shot eighteen ducks and made a gift of them to Salter.

In the course of the hunt one of the locks on the gun had broken, and Maquinna told Salter that it was *peshak*, that it was bad. Salter assumed that the chief had broken it with misuse and called him a liar, among other insults, and gave the gun to nineteen-year-old John Jewitt, the ship's armourer, to repair. Maquinna had acquired a rudimentary knowledge of English in his more than two decades of trade, and he understood the tenor of Salter's slurs. While Salter was speaking, Maquinna rubbed his chest repeatedly, to keep his heart from rising in his throat and choking him, he later said. He swallowed his rage and stood mute.

The next day, Maquinna returned with several of his chiefs, bringing their usual gift of salmon. This time, he was wearing a wooden mask that had been carved to resemble a fierce animal. The natives danced wildly for the *Boston*'s crew, then stayed for dinner.

Shortly after they'd finished, Jewitt, who was below decks cleaning muskets, heard a commotion above him and ran up the stairs. One of the chiefs grabbed Jewitt by the hair, but lost his hold as he swung his axe. Jewitt missed being decapitated but was hit in the forehead, a clean gash across his skull, and he collapsed unconscious into the hold.

When Jewitt came to, he crawled up to the deck, where six blood-streaked, naked natives pointed daggers at him. Maquinna addressed Jewitt by name, having observed him at his trade during visits to the *Boston*. "John – I speak – you no say no; You say no – daggers come!" he said. He asked Jewitt a series of questions. Would he be Maquinna's slave for life; would he fight for him in his battles; would he repair the muskets and make knives for him? Maquinna recognized Jewitt's practical worth, and that would save his life.

Jewitt carefully answered yes to each question, and Maquinna led him to the quarterdeck, where the twenty-five heads of the *Boston*'s captain and crew were arranged in a neat line on a sheet of blood. Each head was brought to the armourer for identification. One of Jewitt's eyes was swollen shut from his wound and he blinked through the other, offering the grim roll call.

A second man, John Thompson, the ship's sail-maker, was found alive and spared after Jewitt convinced Maquinna that Thompson, who was twenty years older than Jewitt, was in fact his father. Jewitt threatened suicide if the older man was killed and reminded Maquinna that he would lose his services. Maquinna reluctantly spared Thompson.

Twenty coastal tribes came to survey the rich haul from the *Boston*. They put on dresses from the ship's trunks, put stockings on their heads, slung cartridge belts across their shoulders, and danced on the shore. There was a feast of whale blubber, smoked herring spawn, and dried fish. Jewitt noted: "On this occasion Maquinna gave away no less than one hundred muskets, the same number of looking glasses, four hundred yards of cloth, and twenty casks of powder, besides other things." It was the largest potlatch ever seen in that area, and it helped cement Maquinna's position as the most powerful man on the island.

Thompson, an American born in Philadelphia, despised the natives and was a bitter, resentful, occasionally violent slave. But Jewitt learned the language and did his best to fit in. He made fish hooks and knives for the various chiefs and ornaments for their wives and children. Maquinna's wife liked Jewitt, and her eleven-year-old boy became devoted to him. Maquinna prized him both as an armourer and as a novelty that he sometimes put on display during trade missions to other tribes. "I became quite an object of curiosity to these people," Jewitt wrote in his diary, "very few of whom had ever seen a white man. They crowded around me in numbers, taking hold of my clothes, examining my face, hands and feet, and even opening my mouth to see if I had a tongue. . . . Having undergone this examination for some time, Maquinna at length made a sign to me to speak to them. On hearing me address them in their own language, they were greatly aston-ished and delighted . . ."

THE CHINESE CONNECTION ◆ Among the tantalizing stories of early contact is the case of Hwui Shan, a Buddhist monk whose journal describes a trip across the "Great Eastern Sea" in AD 458. Chinese naval technology and navigation were a thousand years ahead of Europe, and the Chinese were already trading on the eastern coast of Africa. In his journal, Hwui Shan identified the Aleutian Islands as being 2,333 miles north of Japan, which would place him in the middle of the island chain. "Its people have marks on their bodies like those of wild beasts. Upon the foreheads they have three marks. If the marks are large and straight, they indicate those of the higher classes; but if they are small and crooked they are of the lower classes." In his trip to the Aleuts 1,300 years later, James Cook described the same kind of markings.

Hwui Shan called the Pacific Northwest the "Great Land of Rushing Waters" and described the residents. "The rudeness of their customs is the same as the people of Marked Bodies. . . . The people of the land are of a merry nature and rejoice when they have an abundance, even of articles that are of little value. Travelling visitors do not prepare food for their journeys and they have the shelter of the dwellings. They have no fortifications or walled cities."

There is a reference in west coast native oral histories to foreign visitors who predated James Cook. They are referred to as "The Eaters of Maggots," a possible reference to rice. Another bit of evidence is the remarkable similarity between the hats of the Nootka, as sketched by Gallo Gallina in the eighteenth century, and traditional Chinese hats. (*Gallo Gallina, National Archives of Canada, C-033614*)

In his journal, Jewitt retained the condescension of the European, but gained considerable insight into the perspective of the Nuu'chah'nulth. "Though they are a thievish race, yet I have no doubt that many of the melancholy disasters have principally arisen from the impudent conduct of some of the captains and crews of the ships employed in this trade, in exasperating them by insulting, plundering, and even killing them on slight grounds." Jewitt was a gifted amateur ethnographer, noting every detail of Nootka life, measuring the lengths of dwellings and canoes, observing the complex social hierarchy, and recording odd parallels with his own culture. "In decorating their heads and faces they place their principal pride," he wrote, "and none of our most fashionable beaus, when preparing for a grand ball can be more particular: For I have known Maquinna after having been employed for more than an hour in painting his face, to rub the whole off and recommence the operation anew when it did not entirely please him."

Maquinna was vain and complex, both political and principled, a charismatic chief whose vanity was balanced by a strict asceticism. His relationship with Jewitt eventually took on a familial tone. Thompson, in contrast to Jewitt, remained sullen and combative. He punched Maquinna's son on one occasion, an offence that would have cost him his life had

Jewitt not argued strenuously on his behalf. To ensure survival, Thompson needed Jewitt, who in turn depended on the capricious Maquinna.

In his happier moments, Maquinna had promised Jewitt that, should a ship come, he could leave with it. But news of the massacre had reached the European traders, likely gathering horrific embellishments en route, and no one came to trade.

Maquinna's interest in Jewitt was not shared among the villagers. "As for the others," Jewitt wrote, "some of the chiefs excepted, they cared little what became of me, and probably would have been gratified with my death." Many felt that, despite their marquee value and practicality, the two white slaves were liabilities; they were witnesses to a massacre and could bring ruin on the village. On one occasion, Maquinna had to use his club to defend Jewitt against angry chiefs.

There was an odd opportunity for revenge against the chiefs and an interesting cultural clash when one of the chiefs, Tootoosch, went mad. The natives were unable to cure his madness, and Jewitt offered that in his country the insane were confined, restrained, and sometimes whipped to make them better. Maquinna said he would try anything and Thompson was employed for the whipping, something he was happy to do. After a severe lashing with a whip made out of spruce boughs, which only enraged and injured Tootoosch, Maquinna ordered a halt to it, saying he would rather have him mad than whipped.

When Jewitt had been almost two years in Nootka Sound, Maquinna held a council at which it was decided that Jewitt should marry one of their women; it was time he was fully integrated into the tribe. If Jewitt did not want one of the local women, Maquinna said, they would go to another tribe and buy a bride. If he decided not to marry, he would be killed.

"Reduced to this sad extremity," Jewitt wrote, "with death on the one side, and matrimony on the other, I thought proper to choose what appeared to me the least of two evils, and consent to be married." Jewitt did not want any of the local women, so he and Maquinna and fifty men loaded two canoes and set out for the A-i-tiz-zart tribe, bringing muskets, cloth, and sea-otter pelts to buy a bride for Jewitt. On their arrival, they were feted with herring spawn and whale oil, and Maquinna asked Jewitt if he saw a woman he liked. He chose a seventeen-year-old beauty, Eu-stoch-ee-exqua, the daughter of the chief, Upquesta.

"Maquinna rose," Jewitt recounted, "and in a speech of more than half an hour, said much in my praise to the A-i-tiz-zart chief, telling him that I was as good a man as themselves." Maquinna told the chief that despite the fact that Jewitt was white and looked like a seal, he would make a good husband.

Jewitt seems slightly bloodless in his journal – it is what makes his chronicles so believable – and he approaches marriage with the same aloof pragmatism. His new wife was beautiful, small and well formed, with soft black hair and teeth of a whiteness rarely seen in Europe. Yet he was not happy. "A compulsory marriage with the most beautiful and accomplished

person in the world, can never prove a source of real happiness," he wrote, "and in my situation, I could not but view this connection as a chain that was to bind me down to this savage land, and prevent me ever again seeing a civilized country . . ."

Marriage was a psychological burden to Jewitt, an incremental step to actually becoming native. Maquinna used it as a wedge, arguing that Jewitt should adopt native customs now that he was married. He had to paint himself in their customary red and black. His European clothes were abandoned and he wore a breechcloth, so that he suffered constantly from the cold. His European self was being slowly eroded. One of the last bulwarks was his faith; on Sundays he retreated to the forest and prayed to his God.

Jewitt's life among the Nuu'chah'nulth, which had begun as an adventure, was beginning to take on an unwelcome permanence, which left him feeling desolate. He told Maquinna that his wife would have to be sent back to her tribe as he could no longer care for her in his miserable state. Apparently he was able to conquer his melancholy long enough to father a child, however, a son who is mentioned only in passing in his published journal. His wife pleaded to stay, saying that she would nurse him back to health. "I told her she must go," Jewitt wrote, "for that I did not think I should ever recover, which in truth I but little expected, and that her father would take good care of her. . . . I was greatly affected with the simple expressions of her regard for me, and could not but feel strongly interested for this poor girl, who in all her conduct towards me, had discovered so much mildness and

The interior of a house at Nootka Sound (*John Webber, Glenbow Collection*)

attention to my wishes; and had it not been that I considered her as an almost impossible obstacle to my being permitted to leave the country, I should no doubt have felt the deprivation of her society a real loss."

Maquinna's strategy with Jewitt had evolved from coercion, through familial bonding, to forced assimilation. The chief knew that one day another ship would come to the harbour. Would Jewitt try to leave? The answer came on July 19, 1805, when the *Lydia*, a trading ship out of Boston, anchored in the sound and fired three cannons in greeting. Its captain, Samuel Hill, was aware that Jewitt and Thompson might be there. Jewitt had written letters describing his plight and left them with a few chiefs during trading visits, asking them to pass them along to any ship that came by. Hill had been given one of these letters by a native chief named Ulatilla. In it, Jewitt had outlined the fate of the *Boston* and pleaded for the rescue of the two survivors.

Jewitt feigned indifference at the ship's arrival. The villagers were alarmed, though, and argued for the deaths of him and Thompson. At the very least, they should be taken a great distance into the bush until the ship had left, they said. The chiefs adopted a surprisingly conciliatory tone, and said that the two should be released. Maquinna, who had so often been Jewitt's protector, was now reluctant to let him go. The captives sat in limbo, unsure whether they would be rescued or killed.

Maquinna decided to go aboard the *Lydia* and assess its trading poten- tial, a decision that was met with strong opposition from both villagers and chiefs. They said it was dangerous and unnecessary; he would be killed by the white men. Maquinna replied that he had no fear and asked Jewitt to write him a letter of recommendation, stating that he and Thompson had been well treated.

As Maquinna watched, Jewitt wrote, "Dear Sir, The bearer of this letter is the Indian king by the name of Maquinna. He was the instigator of the capture of the ship *Boston*, of Boston in North America, John Salter captain, and of the murder of twenty-five men of her crew, the two only survivors being now on shore – Wherefore I hope you will take care to confine him according to his merits, putting in your dead lights, and keep- ing so good a watch over him, that he cannot escape from you. By so doing we shall be able to obtain our release in the course of a few hours."

When Maquinna asked Jewitt to read what he had written, he went over each line, fabricating a new narrative, saying that he had instructed the captain to give Maquinna molasses, biscuits, and rum, and stating that he had always been well treated.

"John, you no lie?" Maquinna asked, closely observing his face.

"Why do you ask me such a question, Tyee [Chief]?" Jewitt responded. "Have you ever known me to lie?"

"No."

"Then how can you suppose I should tell you a lie now, since I have never done it?"

In his play, *The Armourer's Escape*, Jewitt played the part of himself and even sang a song he had composed, "The Poor Armourer's Boy."

No thrush that e'er pip'd its sweet note from the thorn
Was so gladsome and lively as me,
Till lur'd by false colours, in life's blooming morn
I tempted my fortune at sea.
My father he wept as his blessing he gave,
When I left him my time to employ
In climates remote on the rude ocean wave,
Being but a poor Armourer Boy. . . .

From slav'ry escap'd, I, joyful, once more
Hail'd a civiliz'd land, but alone
And a stranger was I on a far-distant shore
From that which my childhood had known.
If such be life's fate, with emotion I cried,
Of sorrow so great the alloy;
Heaven grant that sole blessing that ne'er is denied.
To the friendless Poor Armourer Boy!

Maquinna examined his face, which was implacable, in part because it was covered in red and black paint. He said he believed Jewitt, and left in a canoe.

On board the *Lydia*, Maquinna presented Jewitt's letter to Captain Hill along with a gift of sea-otter pelts. Hill invited him into his cabin, gave him biscuits and rum, and had him arrested. Maquinna was surprised but offered no resistance. The canoe returned to shore without the chief, the paddlers conveying the message that Jewitt had betrayed him.

The women in the village wept and sank to their knees, begging Jewitt to stop the white men from killing Maquinna. The men took another approach, threatening to cut him into pieces the size of his thumbnail or slowly roast him alive. A trade was finally arranged, and Jewitt and Thompson were taken out to the *Lydia*.

Jewitt was dressed almost exactly as Maquinna had been when he had first come aboard the *Boston*. His hair had not been cut in more than two years and was piled on his head and held with a spruce twig. His face and entire body were painted in red and black and he was wrapped in a bearskin. Hill said he had never seen any human in so wild a state.

Maquinna was in irons but welcomed Jewitt. They spent a sleepless night together in the cabin as Maquinna reviewed their relationship. "John," he said, "you know when you [were] alone, and more than five hundred men were your enemies, I was your friend and prevented them from putting you and Thompson to death, and now I am in the power of your friends, you ought to do the same by me."

Jewitt had in fact already convinced Hill to release Maquinna, and he assured the chief that Thompson, who probably wanted to kill him, would be restrained. Jewitt felt a duty to recover what remained of the *Boston*'s cargo and arranged for a final trade. In the morning, the cargo was brought on board in exchange for the great trader, Maquinna.

Before getting in his canoe, Maquinna presented the captain with his mantle of four sea-otter pelts, which was greatly appreciated. Hill said he would be back at Nootka Sound in November and suggested that Maquinna have more skins ready for trade; they could do business.

The chief grasped both of Jewitt's hands and said he would never again ask for a letter of recommendation from anyone. He wept openly and said goodbye.

Jewitt was unexpectedly moved as well. "Notwithstanding my joy at my deliverance," Jewitt wrote, ". . . I could not avoid experiencing a painful sensation on parting with this savage chief, who had preserved my life, and in general treated me with kindness, and considering their ideas and manners, much better than could have been expected."

The *Lydia* headed north along the coast to trade with other bands, among them the Haida, whom Jewitt calls the Wooden-lips. He notes that all their trading was done by the women.

In November, the ship returned to Nootka Sound and Maquinna was overjoyed to see Jewitt, who came ashore, once several chiefs had gone out to the *Lydia* as hostages to ensure his safety.

"Ah John," Maquinna said. "You are afraid to trust me, but if they had come with you, I should not have hurt you, though I should have taken care not to let you go on board of another vessel."

Jewitt's son by Eu-stoch-ee-exqua was now five months old, and Maquinna said that once the child was weaned he would take him from the mother and raise him as his own, the coda to their complex relationship.

The *Lydia* next went to China, and Jewitt did not get back to Boston until 1807, five years after he had left England. But civilization did not prove as welcoming as the former captives had hoped.

John Thompson died in 1815 in Havana, Cuba, or in 1816 in Philadelphia, according to differing historical accounts. Jewitt married a woman named Hester Jones, with whom he had five children. Settled, finally, in a "civilized" place, Jewitt was obsessed by his experience on the West Coast. He published his diary as *a Journal Kept at Nootka Sound*, and peddled the book around New England in a horse-drawn cart. It was later rewritten by Richard Alsop, an author of some note, and appeared in 1815 as *A Narrative of the Adventures and Sufferings of John R. Jewitt; Only Survivor of the Crew of the Ship* Boston, *During a Captivity of Nearly 3 Years Among the Savages of Nootka Sound, with an Account of the Manners, Mode of Living, and Religious Opinions of the Natives*. Despite the awkward title, it received critical praise and was a modest commercial success, selling nine thousand copies. Jewitt sold the book door-to-door in the towns along the eastern seaboard and sent what money he could back to his family in Connecticut.

Jewitt's literary work was parlayed into a dramatization. He collaborated with playwright James Nelson Barker and the result, *The Armourer's Escape; Or, three years at Nootka Sound*, was a two-act melodrama/musical that ran for three performances at the Philadelphia Theatre in March 1817. Jewitt played himself and sang two songs, one of them in the language of the Nuu'chah'nulth. After the play's brief run, he returned to his life as a travelling salesman, constantly on the road, peddling his retailed adventures, offering the dramatic scar on his skull as validation. In a letter to his wife he complained that he had been plagued for weeks by "a violent pain in the head, right in the place where I was wounded." The pain in his head worsened, and Jewitt died of unstated causes in January 1821 at the age of thirty-seven.

Maquinna was last seen in 1825 by a Hudson's Bay Company trader visiting Vancouver Island. The chief was nearing seventy and hobbled by rheumatism but he still greeted the ships, anxious to trade.

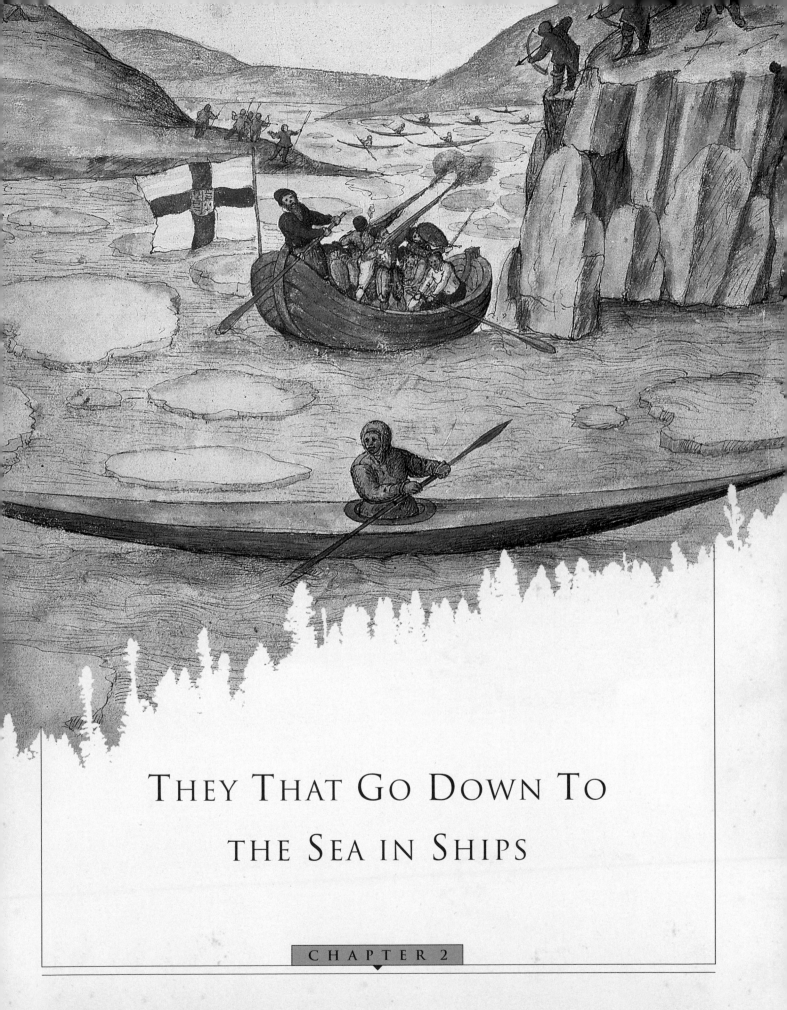

THEY THAT GO DOWN TO
the SEA in SHIPS

Elizabethan London was a loud, foul city of modest size, a city in which one of the main thoroughfares, London Bridge, was decorated with the severed heads of criminals, and a place where prostitutes were publicly whipped at well-attended floggings. In the mid sixteenth century, England was essentially poor and defiantly parochial. The royal court could not afford exploration, and the public did not have any real interest in the western hemisphere. At any rate, Spain had already claimed most of the New World's wealth. England was on the verge of grand imperial quests and an unrivalled prominence in literature (William Shakespeare arrived in London in 1587), but for the moment it was busy and squalid and concerned mostly with itself.

Spain was the dominant European power. It had the dreaded Armada – a navy of 125 armoured, formidable ships – and a treasury full of gold, mostly looted from the New World. The Spanish had led the way in exploring the western hemisphere and were now entrenched in America, throughout Mexico and the Caribbean and north as far as Florida. Catholic missionaries were claiming souls throughout the southern latitudes as fast as the conquistadors were sending them to their heavenly reward. Having destroyed the Aztec empire and taken its gold, Spain was now the richest and most powerful nation in Europe.

When Hernando Cortés landed on the shores of Mexico in early 1519, he had an army of four hundred foot soldiers and sixteen horsemen. That April, representatives of the Aztec ruler, Moctezuma II, attended the first Easter mass ever celebrated in Central America. Subsequently, Cortés ordered his own ships to be burned, eliminating any possibility of retreat.

At this time, there were more than 11 million Aztecs, but by November disease had begun to kill them. Cortés and his army massacred a great many others. (*The Taking of Tenochtitlan by Cortes, Bridgeman Art Library, British Embassy, Mexico City*)

England's only foothold in the New World was in the fishing waters off Newfoundland, which hosted dozens of English, French, Basque, and Spanish ships. Millions of tonnes of cod were taken off the Grand Banks, which had first been fished by Basques. Some of the fishermen had even begun to make contact with the people who lived on the Atlantic shores. The English would soon venture north, looking for a passage to China and its promised riches. But the exploration that would be in full bloom by the end of Elizabeth's reign was slow in starting.

England's spirit of adventure was given a tremendous boost by a little-known scholar named Richard Hakluyt. A Protestant clergyman and an Oxford scholar, Hakluyt's view of the world ranged well beyond the limited maps of the late sixteenth century. With missionary zeal, he took on the task of exciting the public imagination and overcoming the nation's political lethargy.

His interest had been sparked when he was an adolescent by an older cousin. "I found lying upon his board certain books of Cosmography with an universal Map . . . he pointed with his wand to all the known Seas, Gulfs, Bays, Straights, Capes, Rivers, Empires, Kingdoms, Dukedoms, and Territories of each part. . . . From the map he brought me to the bible and turning to the 107th psalm, directed me to the 23rd and 24th verses, where I read, that 'they which go down to the sea in ships, and occupying [their business in] great waters, these see the works of the Lord and his wonders in the deep.'"

In the largely unclaimed space of North America, Hakluyt saw an opportunity to gain new souls for Christianity, to convert the natives. "Now if they [the Catholic Spaniards and Portuguese] in their superstition, by means of planting in those parts, have done so great things in so short space," he wrote, "what may wee hope for in our true and syncere Religion, proposing unto ourselves in this action not filthy lucre nor vain ostentation as they indeed did, but principally the gayning of the soules of millions of those wretched people, the reducing of them from darkness to light, from falsehood to truth, from dumb Idols to the living god, from the deep pit of hell to the highest heavens."

Hakluyt's interest in America was also patriotic; he believed that England, like Spain, could become powerful through exploration and subjugation. He was convinced that the public was indifferent to exploration because they had not been properly informed of the romantic and daring exploits of their own explorers. "I both heard in speech," Hakluyt wrote, "and read in books other nations miraculous extolled for their discoveries and notable enterprises by sea. But the English of all others for their sluggish security and continual neglect exceedingly condemned. . . . We shall attempt to publish the maritime records of our own men, which are hitherto scattered and buried in dust."

Hakluyt decided to create a history of exploration, to trumpet the achievements of the English. This involved some juggling of the facts: Giovanni Caboto, the Italian explorer who was financed by the English court, would be claimed as native son John Cabot.

Opening page: Detail from John White's rendering of an Inuit attack on Frobisher and his men near Baffin Island. (*John White, British Museum*)

QUEEN ELIZABETH I ◆ To her subjects, Queen Elizabeth was a perennial virgin. Playwright Ben Jonson said of her, "She hath a membrana which rendereth her incapable of man." She was a shrewd and capable ruler who personified England. During the battle with the Spanish Armada, she gave a speech to her soldiers: "I know I have the body but of a weak and feeble woman, but I have the heart and stomach of a king, and of a king of England too, and think foul scorn that Parma or Spain, or any prince of Europe should dare to invade the borders of my realm." (*Robert Peake, Bridgeman Art Library, Private Collection*)

WILLIAM SHAKESPEARE ◆ When Shakespeare arrived in London in 1587, war with Spain was imminent. A year later, the English navy defeated the feared Spanish Armada and the victory was followed by a delirious outbreak of English patriotism, which the young Shakespeare used to great dramatic effect in his historical plays. His work closely reflected the times, using court intrigues and tapping into the sudden celebration of England's explorers. Michael Lok, one of Frobisher's backers (who was bankrupted by his protegé's explorations in the Arctic), was the model for Shylock in *The Merchant of Venice*. Richard Hakluyt merited a reference in *Twelfth Night*: "He does smile his face into more lines than is in the new map with the augmentation of the Indies." (*International Portrait Gallery*)

England's future lay across the ocean, Hakluyt felt, and he hoped to plant that idea in the popular imagination. His own future, however, lay in the dusty confines of libraries. He tried to accompany various voyages to the New World, but circumstances always prevented it, and he never saw the places he catalogued with such enthusiasm.

In 1582, Hakluyt produced a book, *Divers Voyages touching the discoverie of America*, which was a collection of first-person accounts. Among them was an account of Martin Frobisher's search for a Northwest Passage to China.

Frobisher was Hakluyt's opposite, a hot-tempered, muscular mariner and pirate who had turned to the search for a Northwest Passage as a way to make his reputation. "It is *still* the only thing left undone," Frobisher wrote, "whereby a notable mind might be made famous and remarkable." Frobisher's mind might not have been notable, but he was possessed of a natural courage and was an efficient navigator – both more useful qualities for an explorer. He was once taken hostage by an African chief and almost starved in Guinea. He plundered Spanish and French ships with Sir Francis Drake and was detained three times for piracy by English authorities, but he was released each time. He had the perfect temperament for an explorer.

In 1576, Frobisher was commissioned by Queen Elizabeth I to find the route to China, and he vowed to die rather than come home "without the discovery of Cathay." Elizabeth, the cleverest of Europe's monarchs, hoped for some financial payoff from Frobisher's voyage and was on hand to wave goodbye when he sailed in the spring of 1576 aboard the *Gabriell*.

He left in the company of a second ship, the *Michaell*. Intimidated by the ice near Greenland, the crew of the *Michaell* returned to England and reported that Frobisher and the *Gabriell* were lost. But Frobisher sailed on to Resolution Island, then continued north until he found an open waterway. He was sure that the strait, which he named after himself, separated two continents.

"The land on his right sailing westward he judged to be the continent of Asia," one of his officers, George Best, reported, "and there to be divided from the firm of America, which lyeth upon the left hand."

Frobisher's conviction was reinforced when he encountered what he believed were Asians. "[Frobisher] perceived a number of small things fleeting in the sea far off whych he supposed to be porposes or seals or some kind of strange fish," Best wrote. "But coming nearer he discovered them to be men in small boates made of leather."

When the Inuit paddled up to the *Gabriell*, they communicated through hand signals, which Frobisher optimistically interpreted as confirmation that he had found the Northwest Passage. He understood that one of the Inuit would pilot him farther and sent five crewmen to row the Inuk ashore and prepare for the trip. They landed out of sight of the ship. Two of his men reappeared on the horizon, then mysteriously turned back. None of them was ever seen again. Frobisher searched for them but could not find any trace.

Shaken by this event, and without the guide he had expected, Frobisher returned to England. Before setting sail, though, he captured an Inuk who had approached the ship in a kayak, hoping to trade. "Knowing well how they greatly delighted in our toys and specially in the bells," Best wrote, "he rang a pretty lowbel, making wise that they would give him that same that would come and fetch it. He let the bell fall and caught the man fast and plucked him with his main force – boat and all into the bark, out of the sea."

Frobisher now had an Asian, proof of his discovery of a Northwest Passage. But his prisoner did not adapt to confinement. "Once he founde himself to be captive," Best wrote, "he bit his tongue in twain within his mouth . . . he did not die thereof, but lived until he came to Englande." He demonstrated his skills with a bow and arrow by shooting swans on Queen Elizabeth's lawn at Hampton Court. "And then he died of colde."

In London, Frobisher had been given up for dead, so he was given a hero's welcome when he returned. Though Frobisher's Asian prisoner soon died, he lent the trip an exotic authenticity. There was even greater excitement when it was reported that some of the mineral samples Frobisher had brought back contained gold. England could have its own northern source to rival Spain's southern gold mines.

Another expedition was outfitted, this time to find gold rather than a route to China. Frobisher's supporters formed the Cathay Company, under royal charter, to finance this new voyage. Among the backers was Queen Elizabeth herself, who put up one thousand pounds and lent Frobisher a 200-tonne ship, the *Ayde*. But the pragmatic queen contained her enthusiasm for the venture; she named the new country *Meta Incognita*, "Of Boundaries Unknown."

Six weeks later, Frobisher was mining ore and claiming the Arctic territory for England. "[On] the top of a high hill," Best wrote, "our men [made] a columne or cross of stone heaped up to a good height . . . and solemnly sounded a trumpet and said certaine prayers and honoured the place by the name of Mount Warwick." They mined two hundred tonnes of ore and loaded it onto the ships.

Frobisher found a few scraps of European clothing at an abandoned village site and concluded that his men from the previous voyage had been murdered. According to Inuit oral history, though, they had spent the winter, then built a boat and sailed away. Frobisher attacked a group of Inuit, hoping to kidnap one and get information about his men. In the skirmish that followed he was struck in the buttock by an arrow, but he managed to capture a man, woman, and child to bring back to England.

Like their predecessor, all three Inuit died within a month of landing in England. More bad news arrived when the assayers expressed doubt about the value of the ore. But Frobisher was a hearty salesman, his backers were still eager, and the royal court was desperate enough to launch a third voyage.

On his last trip, in 1578, Frobisher intended to build a permanent settlement. His expedition was on an enormous scale: fifteen ships, four hundred

Eskimo man and Eskimo woman and baby (inside hood). Frobisher thought these Inuit were Asians, proof that he had found the Northwest Passage to China. All three died within weeks of arriving in England. (*John White, British Museum*)

Martin Frobisher (1539-94),
Frobisher's mines on eastern
Baffin Island were discovered
in 1861 by Charles Francis Hall,
who was led to the location by
Inuit. Frobisher's house, camp-
sites, a blacksmith's shop, and
stone quarries were all found,
the best-preserved remains
from the Age of Exploration.
(*Dono Gualteri Charlton,*
Bodleian Library, Oxford)

men, and lumber enough to build the colony. But his search for gold was
cursed with the bad luck that would plague English exploration for the next
thirty years. The crew of one ship deserted and sailed back to England,
and the ship carrying the lumber sank, ending any hopes of a settlement.
Frobisher persevered, mining 1,100 tonnes of ore and bringing it back to
England, but his cargo turned out to be iron pyrite, "fool's gold." The
Cathay Company was ruined, and Frobisher's reputation was in tatters.

After this disaster, Frobisher returned to the lucrative business of piracy, which was officially illegal though privately condoned by the shrewd
Elizabeth. With Francis Drake, Frobisher raided Spanish settlements in
the Caribbean and returned with sixty thousand pounds, some of which was
turned over to the Crown. In 1588, his reputation gained legitimacy when he
served as a commander in that year's epic victory over the Spanish Armada.
Frobisher was knighted, and returned to pirating with the title of Sir. In
1594, he was shot in a battle with the Spanish and died of his wounds.

While Frobisher's voyages were commercial failures, they inspired new
hope for the discovery of the Northwest Passage, pushed back the frontiers
of geographical knowledge, and kindled public interest in the New World.

Another man who fired the adventurous spirit of the English was
David Ingram, a sailor who wandered England in those days, stopping in
taverns and telling stories of America for the price of a drink. "The towne
[is] half a myle longe and hath many streates farre broader than any streate
in London," he said, describing a city he had been to in America. "There is
a great abounance of gold, sylver and pearle, and . . . dyvers peaces of gold
some as bigge as [my] finger, otheres as bigge as [my] fist."

Ingram had worked on a privateer's ship in the Gulf of Mexico and
claimed to have jumped ship and walked north to Cape Breton. En route, he
said, he saw the city of Norumbega (located in what is now New England).
"Genirallye all men weare about there armes dyvers hoopes of gold and
silver which are of good thickness," Ingram wrote. "The women of the
country gooe aparyled with plates of gold over there body much lyke unto an
armor." The possibility of gold was a potent lure, and Ingram's account was
publicly cheered, initially at least, by Hakluyt; in the second edition of his
book, he would question the veracity of Ingram's glittering tale.

The idea of Norumbega took root in Humphrey Gilbert's imagination.
He was the second son of a wealthy English gentleman who had been
educated at Eton and Oxford before joining the army and seeing action in
Ireland, France, and Holland. Gilbert took an early interest in America,
though originally from a military point of view. He wrote a letter to the
queen titled, "A discourse how hir Majestie may annoy the king of Spayne."
In it he suggested capturing Spanish fishing boats that were anchored off
the coast of Newfoundland while their crews were on shore drying fish. It
would be an easy task, he argued, but the queen dismissed the idea.

As a second son, Humphrey Gilbert was landless. According to the
system of primogeniture that existed in England, his father's estate would be

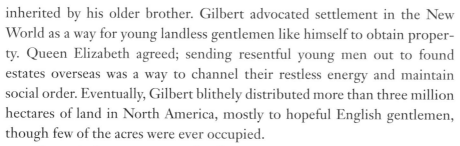

FRANCIS DRAKE ◆ In 1577 Drake left England on a voyage to circumnavigate the globe, a feat first accomplished by Ferdinand Magellan and his crew in 1519-22. He successfully plundered Spanish ships en route and in 1579 claimed San Francisco Bay for England, naming it New Albion. He returned to England in 1580, the first English captain to have sailed completely around the world. *(Jodocus Hondius, National Portrait Gallery)*

SIR HUMPHREY GILBERT ◆ When his ship, the *Squirrel*, was being tossed in the storm that eventually took his life, Gilbert allegedly called out to his sister ship, *The Golden Hind*, "We are as neare to Heaven by sea as by land." *(Van De Passe, National Portrait Gallery)*

inherited by his older brother. Gilbert advocated settlement in the New World as a way for young landless gentlemen like himself to obtain property. Queen Elizabeth agreed; sending resentful young men out to found estates overseas was a way to channel their restless energy and maintain social order. Eventually, Gilbert blithely distributed more than three million hectares of land in North America, mostly to hopeful English gentlemen, though few of the acres were ever occupied.

In 1578, the queen granted Gilbert a patent to find a suitable site for a colony, "to discover, searche, finde out and view such remote heathen and barbarous landes countries and territories not actually possessed of any Christian prince or people." This restricted him to North America north of Florida, beyond the territories occupied by Spain. He was given viceregal powers to claim and dispense titles to land and full power to defend it against other encroaching Europeans.

Gilbert set out in November with ten ships and 570 men, but his ambition to build a colony quickly collapsed. Spain had an organized system for teaching the principles of ocean travel, which was one of the reasons for its success abroad. But England had no system (though Hakluyt had argued for one), and inevitably, its explorers were reduced to employing pirates (some of them reprieved from execution), the most experienced sailors, for their voyages of discovery. As a result, four of Gilbert's ships deserted the convoy to pursue piracy. Two of the remaining vessels were leaky and had to return for repairs, while supplies were insufficient in the others. None of them made landfall in Newfoundland. The trip was a financial disaster and a blow to Gilbert's reputation.

On the evidence, Gilbert did not seem a likely candidate for a second attempt, but the zeal for exploration was growing. Richard Hakluyt's *Divers Voyages touching the discoverie of America* included the first publication of

Cartier's journals, Cabot's record of his 1497 voyage, Giovanni da Verrazzano's search for a Northwest Passage in 1524, Frobisher's more recent attempts, and dozens of lesser-known documents. Information on colonization, flora, fauna, soil, and natives was enlivened with the heroic accounts of explorers – a lengthy, wild, and contradictory compendium of everything that was known or imagined about North America.

Hakluyt supported Gilbert's second venture, which proposed to establish a settlement in North America at David Ingram's mythical Norumbega. Steven Parmenius, a Hungarian poet who had roomed with Hakluyt at Oxford, wrote an epic poem that prematurely celebrated Gilbert and glossed over recent disasters.

> . . . How many valiant sons and dauntless hearts
> This land has raised! A host of noble men
> And scores of leaders stand as witnesses:
> Among them, him to whom the muses rise
> In acclamation, him to whom the wise
> Minerva gladly listens, – England's pride,
> Great Humphrey Gilbert.

Both Hakluyt and Parmenius wanted to join Gilbert on his voyage, to experience the world they had talked about at Oxford. Parmenius was taken on as official poet, commissioned to write an epic poem to Gilbert's heroic accomplishments. Hakluyt was ready to go as well but was instead sent to Paris by the queen to act as chaplain to the English ambassador. He appealed to Sir Francis Walsingham, the secretary of state: "I am most willing to go now in the same this present setting forth, and in the service of God and my country to employ al my simple observations, readings and conference whatsoever. . . . Because the time is exceeding shorte, I wold desire your honour's present aunswere; upon sight whereof, with winges of Pegasus, I wold fly [to] England." But Walsingham declined to use Hakluyt's services in America.

Gilbert left in June 1583 with five ships, the *Delight*, the *Bark Raleigh*, the *Golden Hind*, the *Squirrel*, and the *Swallow*. Elizabeth, her enthusiasm by now somewhat dampened, remarked at the embarkation that Gilbert was a man "noted of not good happ [luck] by sea." She was right, and the second voyage began as a dismal repetition of the first. The crew of the *Bark Raleigh* deserted after two days, due to sickness and inadequate supplies. The *Swallow*'s crew, chiefly pirates, robbed a French ship despite orders not to. The weather was vile and it took them fifty days to make the crossing.

After arriving in Newfoundland (near present-day St. John's), Gilbert ordered an elaborate tent set up on shore; then, using trumpets and couriers, he summoned the thirty-six fishing boat captains who were in the harbour. He boldly announced to the collected English, Spanish, French, and Portuguese fishermen that he was Lord Paramount and claimed the land for

MERMAIDS ◆ Richard Whitbourne, who lived in Newfoundland from 1583 to 1620, described the mermaids he claimed to have seen in St. John's harbour. "Now I will not omit something of a strange creature which I first saw there in the year 1610 . . . which very swiftly came towards me, looking cheerfully on my face, as it had been a woman . . . it seemed to be so beautiful . . . having round about the head many blue streaks resembling hair. . . . This I suppose was a Mermaid." The mermaid mythology likely started from sailors' descriptions of the dugong, a cetacean that has a defined head and nurses its young by holding them to its breast with a flipper. (*Theil Dreyzehender, from Americæ, Memorial University of Newfoundland*)

England. A rod and a piece of turf were handed to him as part of the odd ceremony. English law would rule and the Church of England would be supreme. "If any person should utter words sounding to the dishonour of Her Majesty," he told his audience, "he should lose his ears and have his ship and goods confiscated."

Gilbert declared sovereignty over a principality that went five hundred kilometres inland and doled out land to his captains. Fishing licences were issued to the foreign fishermen. Many of them did not speak English, and they regarded Gilbert's impromptu coronation as an unlikely theatre piece. They had been fishing off the Grand Banks for decades and had formed a relatively peaceful international society.

Gilbert had intended only to stop for supplies before continuing on to Norumbega, but he grew to like the rocky, uninviting coast. "His mind was wholly fixed upon the Newfoundland," wrote Edward Haies, one of Gilbert's captains, who kept a record of the voyage. "Lying down his determination in the spring following for his disposing of his voyage then to be re-attempted, he . . . reserved unto himself the north, affirming that this voyage had won his heart from the south and that he was now become a northern man altogether."

Stephen Parmenius did not share Gilbert's enthusiasm for Newfoundland's possibilities. He was disappointed by its raw, barren space and was having trouble mustering an epic poem. His years of armchair adventuring had prepared him for something more exotic. "The manner of this Country . . . what shall I say, my good Hakluyt, when I see nothing but a very wildernesse?" he wrote to his old Oxford friend. "Whether there bee any people in this Country I know not, neither have I seene any to witnesse it . . . when we have served, and supplied our necessitie in this place, we purpose by the helpe of God to passe towards the south, with so much the more hope every day, by how much greater the thinges are, that are reported of those Countries, which we go to discover. . . . Adewe, my most friendly, most sweete, most vertuous Hakluyt: In Newfoundlande, at St. John's Port, the sixt of August, 1583. Steven Parmenius."

By the time Hakluyt received his friend's letter in Paris, Parmenius was dead. Gilbert's grandly claimed empire had unravelled almost immediately. Some of the pirates who had been recruited for the voyage had reverted to type and looted fish from the foreign vessels. Then there were deserters and a wave of sickness. Gilbert sent the malcontents and the ailing home in the *Swallow* and set sail down the Atlantic coast. But the *Delight*, carrying Parmenius, as well as all the maps, charts, and specimens, went aground, broke up, and was lost. The news that his closest friend had died at sea came to Hakluyt at about the same time as Parmenius's last letter.

Gilbert was down to two ships now, the *Squirrel* and the *Golden Hind*. Without maps or charts, he could not make the trip south; he had no choice but to return to England. Gilbert sailed home in a state of despair, savagely beating his cabin boy in frustration. Near the Azores, the *Squirrel*, carrying Gilbert, went down in a storm. He was last seen by Edward Haies, sitting on deck with a book in his hand, yelling into the wind. All hands were lost. The *Golden Hind* arrived home on September 22, bearing bad news and only a tentative claim to Newfoundland. Gilbert had not left a garrison on Newfoundland to enforce any of his declared notions of empire. As soon as he had weighed anchor, his government and laws had vanished.

Richard Hakluyt dutifully entered Edward Haies's journal of the voyage into his collection of exploration literature. It was a difficult time for Hakluyt. He had lost his best friend, and the last five voyages to the New World by Frobisher and Gilbert had been failures. In Paris, he received more discouraging news: the French were planning a colony of their own in North America. "The Duke Joyeuse, the Admiral of France, and the cardinal of Bourbon and their friendes, have had a meeting to send out certayne ships to inhabit some place for the north part of America and to carry thither many friars and other religious persons," Hakluyt wrote. "This was told to me by . . . André Thevet, the King's cosmographer."

Thevet was Hakluyt's French counterpart, a scholar whose energies went toward explaining the New World, and who, like Hakluyt, had never been there. Thevet had known Jacques Cartier and had met Donnacona. Where Hakluyt was long on research and short on imagination, Thevet was the opposite. His interpretation of North America was fanciful and his theories idiosyncratic. "It would seem that all these northern peoples are thus courageous," Thevet wrote. "In the tropics and around the equator are the contrary, because the excessive heat of the air draws their natural warmth out and dissipates it so they are only hot on the outside and cold on the inside. The [northerners] have their body heat closed and kept inside them by the external cold, which therefore renders them robust and valiant: for the strength and virtue of all parts of the body depend on this natural warmth."

Thevet was the first to put forth the idea of the "noble savage" that Jean Jacques Rousseau would later espouse. "They live in continual health and peace and have no occasion to be envious of one another because of their property or patrimony – for they are all almost equal in possession and are

SIR WALTER RALEIGH ◆ A poet and adventurer, Raleigh despaired at the power of Spain and its king, Philip II: "How many kingdoms he hath endangered, how many armies, garrisons, and navies he hath, and doth maintain, the great losses which he hath repaired, as in Eighty-eight above an hundred sail of great ships with their artillery, and that no year is less infortunate, but that many vessels, treasures, and people are devoured, and yet notwithstanding he beginneth again like a storm to threaten shipwreck to us all; we shall find that these abilities arise not from the trades of sacks and Seville oranges, nor from aught else that either Spain, Portugal, or any of his other provinces produce; it his Indian gold that endangereth and disturbeth all the nations of Europe."

In 1584, Raleigh sailed to North America and claimed over three thousand kilometres of its coastline for England, naming the territory Virginia, after the virgin queen, Elizabeth. It was disastrously settled by 225 colonists; in 1590 an English ship arrived to find no trace of them. Raleigh was Sir Humphrey Gilbert's half-brother and a favourite of Elizabeth I, who knighted him. He wasn't a favourite of her successor, King James I. The king accused Raleigh of plotting against the Crown and had him executed in 1618. (*Attributed to "H," National Portrait Gallery*)

all rich in mutual contentment and degree of poverty. They also have no place designated for administering justice because they do no wrong to each other. They have no laws . . . other than that of nature. . . . They have neither cities nor castles nor machines of war like us."

The natives also represented a huge reservoir of unclaimed souls, and Hakluyt, the Protestant clergyman, wanted them claimed for his God. But he also saw a more practical reason for colonizing North America, one the French had already exploited. "In Paris," Hakluyt wrote, "I have seen in one man's house the value of 5000 crowns wirth of furres, as sables, beavers, otters, and other sortes which he bought . . . from the men of St. Malo. . . . [These] are brought out of the most northerly parts of those countreys whereunto *our* voyage of inhabiting is intended."

Hakluyt hoped to spur the English to further exploration by writing a policy paper titled "Discourse of Western Planting." He gave it to Sir Walter Raleigh, who in turn passed it on to the queen, who effectively ignored it. (The paper was finally published three hundred years later in Maine, one of the places in which he advocated settlement.) Hakluyt emphasized the need for an English settlement on North American soil, arguing that the queen had lawful right to the land between Florida and the Arctic Circle. If they did not move quickly, either the Spanish would move north or the French would make claims. Hakluyt suggested that if they secured settlements, then a Northwest Passage to China would inevitably be found. A colony would occupy the unemployed, provide a military base, and bring more glory to the Protestant religion.

Another motive was to limit the expansion of the Spanish empire in America. Hakluyt advocated fomenting rebellions among the natives against their Spanish oppressors and humiliating the Spanish king, Philip II: "He will

King James I was short, oddly proportioned, and drooled, the result of a malformed tongue. He was vicious, often drunk and crude, but also multilingual, well educated in the classics, and an able writer. He wrote a prescient book condemning the use of tobacco, another on the divine right of kings, and he sponsored the writing of what we know as the King James version of the bible. (*Paul van Somer, Bridgeman Art Library, Prado, Madrid*)

in shorte space become a laughinge stocke for all the worlde. . . . His olde bandes of souldiers will soone be dissolved, his purposes defeated, his power and strengthe diminished, his pride abated, and his tyranie utterly suppressed."

King Philip, however, was planning his own attack on England, tired of high-seas piracy by the English, which largely went unpunished. By 1587, Elizabeth knew war was coming. She also knew she could not afford one. Much of England's meagre treasury was spent in keeping Protestantism alive, both within the country and on the continent. A considerable amount of money went to keeping up appearances; the royal court was an opulent wonder that dazzled visitors and locals alike, but it was a glittering façade. Elizabeth was borrowing money in Antwerp at high rates of interest, using goods from the merchants of London as collateral.

In 1588, Philip II's invincible Armada – all 125 oversized ships – entered the English Channel, intent on invasion. Sir Francis Drake, along with Sir Walter Raleigh and Martin Frobisher, commanded the much smaller English navy with its more manoeuvrable ships. The English harassed the Spanish northward, up the coast of England and Scotland, where the violent North Sea weather dashed the clumsy Spanish ships against the rocks. Half of the Armada was destroyed at sea against the inhospitable shores of Scotland and Ireland. The rest limped home, defeated.

Hakluyt saw this as Divine Providence. "I think that never was any nation blessed . . . with a more glorious and wonderful victory upon the Seas, than our vanquishing of the dreadful Spanish Armada," he wrote. "But why should I presume to call it our vanquishing; when as the greatest part of them escaped us, and were only by God's outstretched arm overwhelmed in the Seas, dashed in pieces against the Rocks, and made fearful spectacles and examples of his judgement unto all Christendom."

Spain's European dominance was over, and the race to the New World began with new fervour.

In 1605, the first French settlement in North America was established at Port-Royal, on the Bay of Fundy. Five years later the English set up their own colony. In 1610, a Bristol merchant named John Guy petitioned King James I to set up a colony on Newfoundland, hoping it would afford "furs, heath, pitch, turpentine, boards made of pine trees, masts, and yeards for small shipping, soapeashes, staggs, skins and hawks of all sorts, together with seal, skins and trane made of seals, and very like to afford either copper or iron mines, which in regard of the quantity of woods and fair rivers might easily raise great profit."

James I added to this list Hakluyt's aim of claiming souls, "thinking it a matter and action well beseeming a Christian King to make true use of that which God from the beginning created for mankind, and thereby intending not only to work and procure the benefit and good of many of our subjects but principally to increase the knowledge of the Omnipotent God and the propagation of our Christian faith."

There was a problem, though, in finding anyone in Newfoundland with whom to share their Christian faith. The Beothuk, who were indigenous to the territory, were nowhere to be found when Guy and thirty-nine colonists established what was intended to be the first permanent settlement in Newfoundland at Cuper's Cove (now Cupid's Cove) in 1610. In any case, that first winter they were too busy trying to survive to seek out natives to convert. Guy's colonists were plagued by pirates and beset with scurvy, which killed four of his people. Despite these problems, and little luck in either farming or finding minerals, Guy remained optimistic, writing to his partners that all was well.

In October 1612, Guy and eighteen colonists spent a month in search of the Beothuk, who had retreated from the coast as the fishery developed, avoiding contact with the whites – the only natives to do so. Guy was sailing along the coastline when he saw a campfire near the tip of Trinity Bay. He sent one man ashore with a white flag, and two Beothuk men approached him carrying a white wolf skin. What followed was the first, and probably last friendly meeting between the Beothuk and Europeans.

Guy described the scene in his journal: "The savages passed over a little water stream towards Mr. Whittington, dancing, leaping and singing, coming together, the foremost of them, presented unto him a chain of leather full of small periwinkle shells, a splitting knife and a feather that stuck in his hair. The other gave him an arrow without a head; and the former was requited with a linen cap and a hand towel, who put presently the linen cap upon his head: and to the other he gave a knife: and after hand in hand, they all three did sing and dance."

Guy came ashore with more of his men and they were joined by eight Beothuk, who had been lingering warily in canoes. A curious party ensued. The Beothuk "danced, laughing & making signs of joy & gladness, sometimes

John Guy was a Bristol merchant and city sheriff, part of a small group of businessmen who requested the charter to settle Newfoundland. After serving three years as the colony's first governor, Guy suddenly quit and returned to England. The Newfoundland Company went bankrupt in 1631; it wasn't until after 1650 that settlement in Newfoundland flourished. (*Provincial Archives of Newfoundland and Labrador*)

Robert Hayman is considered the first "Canadian" poet. Among the 100 poems he wrote praising Newfoundland was this paean, " A Skeltonicall Continued Ryme, In Praise Of My Newfoundland."

Although in cloaths, company, buildings faire,
With England, New-found-land cannot compare,
Did some know what contentment I found there,
Always enough, somewhat to spare,
With little paines, lesse toyle, and lesser care,
Exempt from taxings, ill newes, lawing, feare,
If cleane and warm no mater what you weare,
Healthy and wealthy, if men careful are
With much much more than I will now declare,
I say if some wise men knew what this were,
I'd believe they'd live no other where.

striking the breasts of our company & sometimes their own. . . . Signs were made unto them that . . . bread and drink should be brought ashore . . . bread, butter, and raisins of the sun to eat and beer and aquavitae to drink. And one of them blowing in the aquavitae bottle it made a sound, which they fell all into laughter at. . . . After they had all eaten and drunk, one of them went to their canoe & brought us deer flesh dried in the smoke or wind, and drawing his knife . . . he cut every man a piece and that savoured well."

Finally, one of the Beothuk signalled that it was time to leave. He gave Guy's men the white wolf skin and took the white flag of the English and put it in his canoe before departing. When Guy awoke the next morning, the weather had suddenly turned colder. He returned to the site of the party but the Beothuk were gone: ". . . we found all things remaining there, as it was when we parted. . . . It began to freeze and there was thin ice over the sound and because we heard nothing more of the savages, we began to return."

They had arranged, through signs, to meet again the following year. But the winter was punishing, and Guy, frustrated by the new colony, quit as governor of Newfoundland and returned to England. An English fishing boat passed by Trinity Bay several years later and saw the Beothuk assembled on the shore, perhaps expecting a reprise of their party with Guy. The ship's captain assumed that they were planning to attack his ship and fired a cannon at them. The Beothuk disappeared into the woods and stayed there for the next two hundred years, trying to avoid whites.

Richard Hakluyt died in 1616 at the age of sixty-four, never having seen the world he spent his life studying and promoting. He lived in relative poverty – most of his books were self-financed. His masterwork, *Principall Navigations, Voyages and Discoveries of the English Nation* (1589), was 825 pages long and the closest he came to a popular success. But his books remain the most valuable source of information on early exploration. Without Hakluyt's diligent harvesting of journals, many of the first-person accounts, including Jacques Cartier's, would have been lost. And yet, with the exception of his stint in Paris, Hakluyt never travelled far from his Oxford library.

His work was his reward. "I call the work a burden," he wrote, "in consideration that these voyages lay so dispersed, scattered, and hidden in several hucksters' hands, that I now wonder at myself, to see how I was able to endure the delays, curiosity, and backwardness of many from whom I was to receive my originals." His books were a journey, and he experienced some of the same hardships as his heroes, the explorers. "What restless nights, what painful days, what heat, what cold I have endured," he wrote. "How many long & changeable journeys I have travelled; how many famous libraries I have searched into; what variety of ancient and modern writers I have perused; what a number of old records, patents, privileges, letters, etc. I have redeemed from obscurity and perishing; into how manifold acquaintance I have entered; what expenses I have not spared . . . the honour and benefit of this common weale wherein I live and breathe hath made all difficulties seem easy, all pains and industry pleasant, and all expenses of light value and moment unto me."

Hakluyt's accomplishment was to make the English realize that they were no longer an island on the edge of the world, but a power at its centre – a view they would not give up for at least three centuries.

Though England was becoming a powerful player in the game of exploration, it was France that was first to establish a permanent colony in North America. New France – which owes its name to the Italian explorer Giovanni da Verrazzano, who called it *Nova Gallia* in 1523 – evolved through two phases of settlement. The first belonged to Jacques Cartier, the next to Samuel de Champlain.

The first phase failed because it was motivated by a pipe dream. François I of France was intent on challenging Spain's supremacy in Europe, which came from the immense wealth taken from the mines of Mexico and Peru. In 1534 he ordered Cartier to sail to Canada "to find passage to Cathay and . . . a great hoard of gold and other rich goods." But Cartier returned with worthless pyrite and mica. François I was never going to be able to defeat Charles V with a shipload of Canadian pebbles. He quickly lost interest in North America.

Jean-François de la Rocque de Roberval's voyage of colonization came to a bad end as well. On his trip across the Atlantic in 1542 to join Cartier, who had established a settlement at Charlesbourg-Royal, he found out that his wife, Marguerite, was sleeping with one of the crew. Roberval abandoned his wife, her lover, and a servant on a little island in the Gulf of St. Lawrence. His attempt to establish a colony was unsuccessful – the winter was disastrous and his people were wracked with illness – and he returned to France to hear the galling news that Marguerite had been rescued, surviving her lover, the servant, and the newborn child she had had to bury herself on the barren island. A Protestant, Roberval was among many killed by Catholics while leaving church in the early days of the French Wars of Religion.

By the end of the sixteenth century, the lure of wealth in North America had rekindled interest, though France was no longer the rich, powerful kingdom it had once been. When Henri IV made his royal entry into Paris on March 22, 1594, France lay in ruins. The court at Fontainebleau had rivalled the splendours of the palaces of the Medici family, but the kingdom had been exhausted by civil and religious wars. The cities had seen their populations shrink, some by as much as two-thirds. The state of finances was deplorable. Even the king was poor. "My shirts are all torn, my doublet has gone through at the elbow," wrote Henri IV, "and my soup-pot is often upside down." His conversion to Catholicism surely had less to do with his famous words – "Paris is certainly worth a mass!" – than with the impossible task he would have faced as a Protestant trying to rule a Catholic country. Henri IV received absolution from the Pope, then set about rebuilding his kingdom – and surrounding himself with upright and devout Protestants.

Henri IV. Henri de Navarre, born in 1553, was raised a Protestant, but he renounced his faith to become king of France. His reign was dedicated to the reconstruction of his kingdom, which had been ravaged by the Wars of Religion. He was enthusiastic about the commercial potential of North America and encouraged Samuel de Champlain's backers to form private companies on a model developed by the Dutch. He was murdered May 14, 1610, by a Catholic fanatic. (*Château de Versailles, Giraudon, Art Resource*)

The Beaver Hunt. "The beaver does everything well. He provides us with stoves, axes, swords, knives: in fact, the beaver does everything." A Montagnais quoted by Paul Le Jeune in *The Jesuit Relations*. Indians and Europeans both benefited from the beaver trade. (*Chiedal, Glenbow Collection*)

Henri IV encouraged the manufacture of luxury goods: gold and silver fabrics, tapestries, and crystal. But the economic reconstruction of the kingdom was largely the responsibility of the Surintendant Général of finance, the Duc de Sully. He made the countryside safe once again, drained marshes, and drafted a plan for a canal system. Sully told the king that ploughing and pasturage were the foundation of France. Exploration would be nothing but a huge expense, and would prove to be of little value.

But the king hoped that furs taken from the New World would do for France what the gold of Peru had done for Spain. Taking his minister's skepticism into account, Henri established his fur-trading expedition but would not risk public finances in the enterprise.

Natives smoking fish. The first Mi'kmaq Champlain encountered on the Acadian coast lived partly off fish that they caught in inshore waters. (*Le fumage du poisson, Théodore de Bry, Stewart Museum*)

In 1603, drawing inspiration from the English and Dutch systems, Henri founded a company for the colonization of New France, headed by one of his most loyal supporters: Aymar de Chaste, vice admiral of Normandy. The company was given the monopoly over the fur trade in the territory ranging from present-day Philadelphia all the way to Cape Breton. Its leading shareholders were mostly burghers from Dieppe and St. Malo who dreamed of dramatic profits. The investors were prepared to finance the colony that the Crown demanded in exchange for a commercial monopoly. The fact that 70 per cent of the members of some expeditions died during the first winter did not faze the investors. At the time, a human life was often worth less than a beaver skin.

Two months later, Chaste died. But one of his last acts was to send to the New World a man who would make a lasting mark there. His name was Samuel de Champlain. Born in Brouage in 1567, Champlain was the son of a sea captain, and he had learned early on about navigation and warfare. He wrote in his book *On Savages*: "After serving as a sergeant in the King's Army for several years, which was stationed in Brittany under Maréchal d'Aumont, de St. Luc and Maréchal de Brissac, and up to the time when His Majesty reduced Brittany to obedience in the year 1598, and then disbanded his Army, I found myself with neither responsibilities nor work, and thus determined to avoid idleness, by finding a way to travel to Spain." Aboard a Spanish vessel, he explored the eastern coast of South America. As a member of the expedition sent out by Chaste in 1603, he went up the St. Lawrence as far as Tadoussac, then all the way to the Lachine Rapids. When he returned to France, Champlain found that the Huguenot Pierre du Gua de Monts had taken over the monopoly, and the two men planned to return to North America the following spring.

The very Catholic territory of New France was, in the beginning, a mostly Protestant undertaking. Champlain himself might have been a

Protestant, as his biblical first name seems to suggest. In 1604, Champlain and de Monts set out for Acadia, the name given by the French to the region that roughly corresponds to today's Maritime provinces. They planned to establish a permanent trading post there. A Catholic priest accompanied them, but de Monts himself served as Huguenot pastor. Quarrels broke out on board between the two denominations, an unhappy legacy of the Wars of Religion at home that would continue to create bitterness and divisions among the French.

They decided to spend the winter on the island of Ste. Croix, but the fierce winds and an outbreak of scurvy prompted the colonists to seek a milder climate. They followed the Atlantic coast southwards, but were attacked by natives when they tried to disembark. The crew buried their dead in graves marked with wooden crosses, then got back on the ship. The natives dug up the dead and threw the crosses into the sea.

De Monts and Champlain returned to the Bay of Fundy, where they built the settlement of Port-Royal. De Monts then went back to France to reassure his partners, who blamed him for investing too heavily in settlements to the detriment of the fur trade. Champlain stayed to see the winter through, and to offset the effects of winter depression among his men he created the Order of Good Cheer. They organized festivities and staged a play called *The Theatre of Neptune in New France*, written by Marc Lescabot, who would become the first historian of Canada and eventually write *A History of New France* (1609).

In 1606, de Monts managed to send reinforcements, which he placed under the command of one of his old comrades-in-arms in the Huguenot army, Baron Jean de Biencourt de Poutrincourt. But de Monts lost his battle with the creditors, who put the company into receivership and struck down the monopoly. The colonists, including Champlain himself, returned to France, but Poutrincourt stayed on, acquiring the title of governor of Acadia. By assuring the continuous occupation of the colony, he made Port-Royal the first permanent French settlement in Canada.

Port-Royal. Founded in 1605 by Samuel de Champlain and Pierre du Gua de Monts, Port-Royal was the first permanent settlement in Canada and the oldest on the continent north of Florida (Saint Augustine, in Florida, was founded in 1565). Destroyed by the British in 1613, Port-Royal was rebuilt by Scottish colonists before being given back to France under terms of the 1632 Treaty of Saint-Germain-en-Laye. Port-Royal was retaken by the British in 1710, given up by France under the Treaty of Utrecht (1713), and renamed Annapolis Royal. (*Bibliothèque nationale de France*)

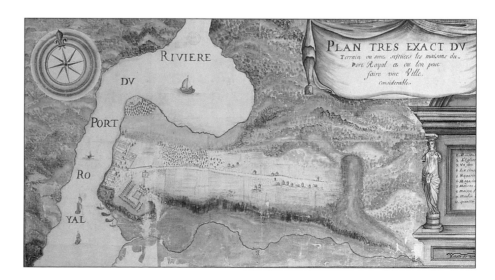

ABITATION. DE QVEBECQ

Abitation de Quebecq. In 1608, Champlain's twenty-eight men stayed in Canada over the winter and built the settlement of Quebec at the foot of Cap-Diamant. (*Samuel de Champlain, from Les voyages du Sieur de Champlain, 1613, Stewart Museum*)

Poutrincourt, in his fragile Acadian outpost, converted to Catholicism. Back in France, de Monts managed to find backers for a second expedition. This time he put Champlain in charge, delegating to him the title of lieutenant-general of New France. De Monts also gave Champlain the responsibility of picking the exact location of the future colony. He thought it should be in the interior of the country, at the heart of the native trading networks. The monopoly was worth nothing as long as he was trying to enforce it from the Atlantic coast; he would need a whole fleet to prevent European merchants from encroaching. But he could protect the St. Lawrence River. The new company's permanent colony would give it a huge advantage over European competitors.

In the spring of 1608, two vessels crossed the Atlantic, the *Lévrier*, under the command of François Dupont-Gravé, and the *Don de Dieu*, under the command of Champlain. On June 3, when Champlain arrived in Tadoussac, Dupont-Gravé's pilot came to greet him in a rowboat. The pilot informed him that Dupont-Gravé had tried to impose his monopoly on the Basque and Spanish captains who were already there, but they had answered him with their muskets and cannons. He took Champlain to the bedside of Dupont-Gravé, who was still alive but seriously wounded. Together, they negotiated a truce with Darache, the leader of the Spaniards, which allowed Dupont-Gravé's men to start trading with the Montagnais.

Champlain continued his journey in a light and manoeuvrable craft designed for river travel. He passed Ile aux Coudres, Rivière du Gouffre, and Cap Tourmente, which had all been named by Jacques Cartier. Champlain did not like what he saw, describing the coast as a "mountainous and very dreary land." But he was delighted with the Ile d'Orléans, which marked, in his words, "the beginning of the lovely and fine land of the great river."

From there, he looked for a site worthy of the settlement he wanted to create, and on July 8, he found it. Champlain, both a cartographer and a soldier, was struck by the incredible natural beauty of the site, but also its military advantages: the cliffs rose ninety-eight metres above sea level. He also noted that, at this point, the St. Lawrence was only one kilometre wide; a battery of cannons could cut off an invader's access to the hinterland and its riches. Champlain decided to call his colony by its Algonkin name, Quebec, which means "the place where the river narrows."

Workers started cutting trees to build the settlement. "The first thing we built," Champlain wrote, "was a magazine to safely store our supplies." A warehouse and three large buildings quickly sprang up in the forest, fortified by ditches and a picket palisade, with platforms from which cannons watched over the river. It was an imposing sight.

France's enemies immediately understood that Champlain was locking up control of the river, and they decided to intervene. Champlain was tending his garden when a sailor came up to him, asking to speak in private. The two men went into the woods. The sailor said that the locksmith Antoine Natel, along with four others, had been hired by the Basques and Spaniards to murder Champlain. The sailor added that the enemies would land as soon as they had heard that their conspiracy had been successful.

When Champlain summoned Natel, he shook with fear and immediately denounced his accomplices and their leader, Duval, the second locksmith of the settlement. "Go about your business," said Champlain. Then he invited the conspirators to come at sundown, to have some wine. When they arrived, they were quickly arrested and thrown into prison. Champlain promised to pardon them if they confessed, but after they signed statements, he had them clapped in irons. There was a perfunctory trial, in which Duval was condemned to death, and Champlain sent three of the others, whom he disdainfully referred to as his "gallant ones," back to France, saying that they deserved to hang. He ordered Duval strangled, then decapitated, and had his head exhibited on a stake in the most prominent part of the fort, "to set an example for those remaining, that they wisely fulfill their duty in the future, and that the Basques and Spaniards of whom there were many thereabouts could not repossess it." The foreign conspirators made a hasty return to Tadoussac.

Champlain also calculated the effect of the severed head on the natives who lived around the settlement. For the Huron and Montagnais who were already trading furs with the French in Tadoussac, the message was clear: Champlain was a dangerous enemy, as well as a valuable ally in their ongoing war against the formidable Iroquois. To entice the native trappers to bring their furs to Quebec, Champlain offered his military support to two chiefs: the Montagnais Anadabidjou and the Algonkin Yroquet.

He was not up against a united empire. Instead, there were many federations and alliances; no single group wielded centralized power. There were frequent wars, and Champlain had to choose which alliance would offer the greatest advantage. After courting the Montagnais, the Algonkin, and the Etchemin, he sought an alliance with the powerful Huron confederation, which had a population of thirty thousand living in small towns between Georgian Bay and Lake Simcoe. "I promised to help them in their wars, as much to force them to love us as to assist me in my undertakings and discoveries, which could not succeed without their help." Champlain needed the native trappers: without them, there was no fur trade.

But first he had to survive the killing cold. He had already endured three winters in Acadia, and he knew what to expect once the snow started falling: "All those who were with me were well-clothed, sleeping in good beds, well-heated and nourished." Despite his precautions, though, when winter set in, the residents of Quebec began to die. "Scurvy attacks those who take proper care of themselves as well as the most miserable people," Champlain noted. "Eighteen got it and ten died from it." But he did not know the cause of what he called "the distemper of the land." One theory was that the illness was caused by vapors that rose from the soil and infected the air outside. Champlain's own observations brought him to believe that the disease could be caused by "eating too much salty food and vegetables, which heat the blood and spoil the interior parts."

Cartier had not thought to pass on the remedy he had been given by the natives – an herbal tea made from the foliage of white cedar called *annedda*, without which all the French explorers would have died in 1535. And the native nations that knew of this remedy had disappeared, victims of epidemics, driven off by more warlike bands, or attracted to more fertile soil elsewhere. The small towns of Hochelaga and Stadacona, with their longhouses and corn crops, had vanished without a trace.

At the end of November, the locksmith Natel, the only surviving conspirator, died of scurvy. A month later, it was the turn of Bonnerme, the surgeon. Then Champlain himself began to show symptoms. But at last – after months of suffering, agony, and death – spring brought deliverance. "It is strange to contemplate that two to three yards' depth of snow and ice on the river can melt in less than 12 days," Champlain wrote. "On April 8, the air was still fairly cold. Some of those suffering [from scurvy] have recovered. On June 5, a boat arrived in our settlement bringing me much joy and comfort. Only eight of the original twenty-eight inhabitants remained alive, and even then, half of us were very weak." The survivors could finally get out into the sunlight, leaving behind the tomb-like building Champlain had constructed. They were scrawny and filthy, and looked more like the vanquished than rivals of the Spanish conquistadors.

In the spring of 1609, the chiefs Anadabidjou and Yroquet introduced Champlain to a Huron chief who also wanted to wage war on the Iroquois. Champlain headed out on the warpath with three hundred natives and nine Frenchmen. He welcomed the opportunity to explore new territories, to become the first European to thrust so far into the interior of the continent.

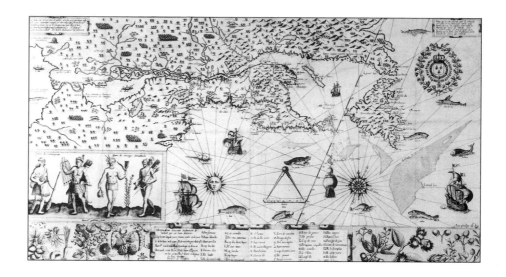

Map of New France, 1613. Champlain's talents as a cartographer and illustrator served him in good stead, helping to attract the interest of wealthy French backers. (*Samuel de Champlain, from* Les voyages du Sieur de Champlain, *1613, Stewart Museum*)

A Huron told him that to the south there was a lake, then another, and then a river that went all the way to Florida. But as the expedition continued southwards, fear of the Iroquois set in. After a few days, most of Champlain's party returned home. Only a handful agreed to penetrate deeper into enemy territory. Champlain would have to face the Iroquois with only sixty natives and two Frenchmen at his side.

They finally encountered the enemy at Ticonderoga Point, between the Green Mountains and the Adirondacks. The warriors in both camps spent the evening preparing for battle. "The whole night," Champlain wrote, "was spent in dancing and singing, in both camps, with many insults being proffered. Our men told the Iroquois they would see a kind of warfare they had never seen before."

At dawn, two hundred Iroquois attacked. Champlain stood behind his own warriors with his musket. His two French companions were in the woods, waiting for his signal. The strategy was simple: "Our men told me that the men with big head-dresses were the chiefs and there were only three of them. We recognized them by their feathers that were much larger than those of their companions. They told me to do what I could in order to kill them."

Encouraged by the yells of his allies, Champlain moved to the fore-front, his armour shining in the sunlight. "Our men called out to me with loud yells and opened into two bodies to let me through. I stood out in front of them, and I aimed straight at one of the three chiefs and with a single shot two of them dropped to the ground. I had put four bullets in my harquebus. The Iroquois were very astonished that two men could be slain even though they wore armour made of cotton thread and wood, able to withstand their own arrows. A great panic came over them. As I was reloading, one of my companions fired a shot that so startled them that seeing their chiefs dead before them, they lost courage and fled into the depths of the woods."

The victory added considerably to Champlain's prestige among the natives, who saw him as a great warrior and a man of his word. Their alliance was sealed in blood. "We parted, making fine declarations of friendship," Champlain wrote. "They asked me if I didn't wish to come to their country, to help them as their brother. I promised to do so."

The three gunshots fired by the French set off a chain of hostilities that were to prove almost fatal for New France. The Iroquois, now mortal enemies of the French, united to oppose them, bringing together five great nations: the Mohawk, the Oneida, the Onondaga, the Cayuga, and the Seneca. At the request of the Huron, Champlain took on the Iroquois in 1610, at the mouth of the Richelieu River, and then again in 1615. These incidents were the first violent skirmishes in a rivalry between two political and economic powers that would endure for a very long time.

Champlain's victory made the Iroquois understand that, without European weapons, they could not defeat the Huron, whom they were battling for control of the fur trade. The Iroquois got much-needed guns from Dutch merchants, who had begun to use the Hudson River as a means to penetrate the interior of the continent. The Dutch, who were in the area for fifteen years, settled in Fort Orange, very close to the Mohawk River, in the heart of the Iroquois empire. The new colonists sought neither to convert the natives nor to explore new countries: they only wanted to get rich quickly.

When the chiefs of the Five Nations understood that they could trade furs for guns, they decided to tolerate the presence of Fort Orange (later to be known as Albany), and New Holland became their arsenal. The pastor Johannes Megapolensis was one of the few religious leaders from the Netherlands who tried to bring Christianity to the Mohawk. Six years of effort produced pitiful results. "When I pray, they laugh at me," he wrote in his journal. The Iroquois did not care for the theology of their neighbours – but they had the greatest respect for their abilities as gunsmiths.

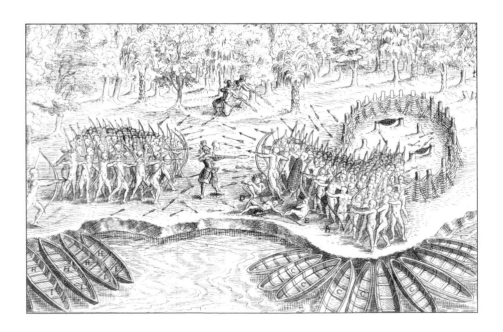

The Defeat of the Iroquois at Lake Champlain. The military alliance of the French with the Huron led to permanent commercial ties between them. Because of the traditional enmity of the Iroquois and the Huron, the Iroquois were consequently enemies of the French. (*National Archives of Canada*, C-5750)

IROQUOIS MAN AND IROQUOIS WOMAN ◆ The Iroquois Confederacy consisted of five nations: Mohawk, Seneca, Cayuga, Onondaga, and Oneida. The Mohawk nation, which inhabited the region around Lake Champlain, was often in conflict with the French colony on the St. Lawrence. Yet, after 1660, missionaries resettled the so-called sedentary Mohawk close to Montreal. The Canadiens lived in relative harmony with Mohawks until the end of the French regime.

For the French colony to spread its influence over the continent, Champlain had to learn how to travel along its only roads: the lakes and rivers. The natives knew this huge network by heart. Champlain realized that their knowledge was the key to power, and he sent some of his men to live among them. He called these ambassadors *truchements*, a combination of translator and ethnologist.

One of the first *truchements* was Etienne Brûlé, an eighteen-year-old who was one of the eight survivors of the winter of 1608. Champlain referred to him as "my boy" and sent him to live among the Huron, to learn everything he could about them.

After several weeks of travel by canoe, Brûlé arrived on the shores of Lake Huron, at one of the villages of Huronia. In the company of hunters, he explored neighbouring territories. From warriors, he learned the cunning stratagems of forest warfare. The women taught him the laws and language of their people, and the elders taught him the traditions. Brûlé came back to Quebec transformed by this immersion in native culture. "On the thirteenth day of June," wrote Champlain, "two hundred savages brought Etienne Brûlé back, who arrived dressed as a savage. He was pleased with the treatment he had received. He explained to me everything he had seen over the winter and what he had learned from them. He had learned their language well." Brûlé was soon joined by others: François Marguerie, Duvernay, Desmarets, Jean Nicollet, and Nicolas Marsolet.

Not content simply to listen to the tales told by his *truchements*, Champlain decided to go directly to the land of the Huron, where he found a far more complex society than he had imagined. "In this stretch of land there are eighteen villages," he wrote. "They have a total of 30,000 souls. Their cabins are covered with the bark of trees, and a space at one end where they keep their corn. In one cabin, there is place for twelve fires and twenty-four families. The men go out to other nations to trade and to barter what they have for what they lack."

Huron Village. When Champlain visited Huronia in 1615, he found thirty thousand people living in eighteen small towns. His previous encounters with nomadic natives had not prepared him for such a complex and well-organized civilization. (*National Archives of Canada*, C-001994)

Soon France insisted that Champlain send out another kind of ambassador, the missionary, whose task it was to propagate the Catholic faith in North America. Three missionaries were brought over in 1615, but they faced a difficult task. The Huron resisted conversion, since they had their own god. "It is the belief of the Hurons," wrote the Recollet friar Gabriel Sagard, "that the Creator is named Yoscaha, and has a grandmother named Ataensiq. That he sows wheat, works, drinks, eats, and sleeps like other men. That all the animals of the world belong to him. That he is of a very good nature and everything that he does is well done. They also believe that certain spirits dominate all rivers, voyages, trading, wars, celebrations and maladies. They believe that souls are immortal and, on departing the body, go to dance and rejoice."

The natives were not the only ones wary of conversion; the French merchants also objected. "The greatest hindrance," explained Sagard, "came to us from the French. . . . Most of them did not wish us to convert the Savages. They were fearful that the beaver trade would fall off; that was the only purpose of their voyage. O my God, my blood freezes in my veins, at the realization that for them, a beaver skin was more important than the salvation of a people."

Between 1608 and 1628, Samuel de Champlain risked his life by crossing the Atlantic twenty times. To replace de Monts, who had lost his monopoly, Champlain needed investors and colonists. In 1610, Champlain married Hélène Boullé, daughter of the king's lord chamberlain, who brought him an impressive dowry of 6,000 livres, which helped to fill the coffers of the Company of Merchants. Hélène was only twelve years old and the marriage could not be consummated for another three years. After the wedding, Champlain left her in the charge of her father, planning to reclaim her after she matured.

Armand-Jean Du Plessis, Cardinal and Duke of Richelieu, was nicknamed "The Red Eminence." His political career was devoted to restoring absolute monarchy in France and to weakening the power of the Hapsburg dynasty in Europe and America. Champlain gained Richelieu's support for his American enterprises and could not have found a more powerful protector. (*Giraudon/Art Resource, Musée Conde, Chantilly*)

Boullé's dowry was not enough, however, to secure his colony. Revenue from trading was unstable and depended on the military successes of the allies of the French in the New World. At the time of Henri IV's death in 1610, the Protestant companies of the north lacked the political clout to guarantee the survival of the French presence in North America, and with the appointment of Marie de Medici as regent, the Catholics controlled the political landscape. Champlain needed a powerful and Catholic protector, and from this time onward, the tone of his writings changed. Where he had written mostly of military exploits, Champlain now maintained that the salvation of one soul was worth more than the conquest of an entire empire. Was this some mystical conversion – or a practical one, like that of Henri IV? It is impossible to sound the depths of this man, who described everything about the countries he explored without saying a word about himself.

In an effort to find new investors, in 1618 Champlain presented the Paris chamber of commerce with an inventory of the natural riches of Canada. "The immense forests are full of wood as far as the eye can see," he wrote. "There must be 900,000 livres' worth of wood. The soil contains minerals of every sort. More than 1,000,000 livres. The rivers, lakes and oceans are brimming with fabulous quantities of fish. 2,000,000 livres. Without counting what has already produced the wealth of the merchants of France. The traffic and trade of hides is not to be underestimated, sable, beaver, fox, lynx, the hides of deer, moose, buffalo are things from which, at present, it is possible to derive 400,000 livres."

Champlain argued that his colony would bring France some 6 million livres of revenue per year, and in 1627, he managed to convince the most powerful man in France, Cardinal Richelieu, of the same thing. Richelieu established the Company of the One Hundred Associates and made Champlain in effect the governor of the new colony.

Champlain's first priority was to send more colonists. The One Hundred Associates raised funds and sent ships with four hundred passengers, but they never reached their destination. France and England were engaged in hostilities, and the convoy was intercepted near Tadoussac by the Kirke brothers. The Kirkes had been born in Dieppe, France, to a French mother and English father, and as Protestants they had sought refuge in England from the Cardinal's persecution. The eminent prelate had decided that heretics would no longer have the right to emigrate to New France, and the fleet that he had sent out to Quebec was full of missionaries of the true faith. The Kirkes belonged to the Calvinist bourgeoisie that had underwritten the development of Quebec. They were well informed about what was going on in the little colony, and had no intention of letting Richelieu have his way.

The Kirke operation seemed to put an end to the dream Richelieu had of creating a totally Catholic New France. The Kirkes demanded the surrender of Quebec. Champlain refused, but, lacking any fresh supplies, he was forced to surrender the following spring: "Louis Kirke landed about 150 armed men and took possession of the settlement. He came to the fort to drive me out. He planted the English flag on one of the bastions, sounded the drum, assembled his soldiers and fired the cannon to signal his joy."

Champlain was granted all the honours of war, and was escorted by one of the Kirkes to England, where he learned that the war between France and England had been over for three months by the time Quebec had surrendered. Champlain immediately launched a campaign to annul the conquest of New France, and Charles I of England agreed to return Canada to France, on condition that Louis XIII pay him the dowry of one million livres that he still owed.

At the request of Richelieu, Champlain returned to New France. Quebec had been devastated by the Kirkes, and now he faced the daunting task of rebuilding it. His next priority was to convert the natives to the Catholic faith, though his motives were more commercial than religious. "There are enough people in these places who hope to have a number of Frenchmen and Religious to instruct them in our faith. This will increase the practice of religion and ensure an incredible trade in furs." Catholic Huron would go to heaven, but in the meantime, they would bring France as many beaver skins as possible.

By 1634, Champlain was old and tired. But his colony had taken root; it now had four hundred inhabitants and an active mission in Huronia. One dark note was the fate of his protegé Etienne Brûlé, who made a fatal mistake by trading with the Iroquois. The Huron were furious, and allegedly tortured, killed, and ate him. Terrified by Champlain's possible reaction to the death of a man he considered his son, the Huron decided not to come down to Quebec to trade. Champlain sent them a message: they had nothing to worry about. Perhaps Champlain's response was simply pragmatic, or possibly he resented the fact that Brûlé had traded with the English during the occupation of Quebec. Champlain bore grudges and did not forget easily.

In 1635, after winter had set in, Champlain died peacefully in the city he had founded. Quebec owed its existence to his tenacity and perseverance. Through his many alliances, wars, court intrigues, and manoeuvres in matters of religion, Champlain stubbornly clung to the dream of creating a profitable colony for France. In the thousands of pages he wrote, he always remained discreet about himself, but not about his love for the colony he'd founded.

The task of bringing Christianity to the natives of New France fell to the missionaries of the Society of Jesus, known as the "soldiers of Christ" because of their success in converting "pagans" in Asia, Africa, and South America. The Jesuits now faced a fresh challenge: converting thirty thousand souls in Huronia. Paul Le Jeune and his fellow missionaries, Charles Lalemant and Jean de Brébeuf, were not welcomed by the Huron. "The Hurons would have preferred well-armed Frenchmen to these men in long robes who had no harquebuses," Le Jeune wrote. The missionaries promised that they would paddle and offered presents, but the Huron were not interested in salvation. Still, Le Jeune declared that he would rather go among

PAUL LE JEUNE ◆ Superior of the Jesuits of Quebec 1632–39, Paul Le Jeune was the first editor of *The Jesuit Relations*. Through his writings, Father Le Jeune had a huge influence in Roman Catholic circles and helped inspire a group of devout believers to found Montreal as a Christian community for the conversion of natives. *(René Lochon, National Archives of Canada, C-021404)*

ISAAC JOGUES ◆ The life of the Jesuit Isaac Jogues testifies to the strength of missionary faith during the Roman Catholic Counter-Reformation. In August 1642, he was captured and tortured by the Iroquois, before being released. Nevertheless, he insisted on returning among them in 1645 as an ambassador of peace. On October 18, 1646, he was slain by a single axe stroke. He was thirty-nine years old. *(National Archives of Canada, C-034204)*

them than reach earthly paradise. "It would never do," he wrote, "for everyone to know how fine life is in the horrors of these forests, in the compelling darkness of such barbarity. Otherwise, we would simply have too many people trying to come here."

Life among the Huron was not easy for the missionaries. They lacked tables and household utensils, ate on the ground, and drank out of tree-bark cups. They had neither salt nor fruit nor bread nor wine, except the wine that was kept for mass. Their bed was a long piece of tree bark on which they laid out a cover. "We won't even talk about the sheets," one Jesuit wrote. "These people have neither towers, nor cities, nor temples, nor masters of any science or art. They know neither reading nor writing."

The Jesuits had little success. One native priest, a shaman, engaged them in theological argument, claiming that the Christian God did not live in Canada, and that was why he did not believe in Him. He maintained that native souls might not have been made the same as European ones, that they did not go to the same place after death. Besides, he concluded, who had ever returned from that land beyond death to describe it?

The missionaries persisted. In Quebec, the superior of the Jesuits kept a diary of what life was like in Huronia. In it each soul was duly accounted for. The diary was finally published as *Relations of the most remarkable events that have occurred during the mission of the Fathers of the Company of Jesus in New France*. Translated into Latin, Italian, and German, the *Relations* were devoured by a passionately devout readership in Europe. In France, they sparked an apostolic zeal for the "savages" of Canada.

Among the zealous was a group of Catholic militants who wanted to return to the original idealism of the Gospels. In 1641 they landed in New France and the next year founded a Christian village – Ville-Marie – on the island of Montreal. This colony was the product of the visions of a provincial financier, Jérôme le Royer de la Dauversière, to whom God had spoken of this mission in a dream. Le Royer and his wife invested their fortune in this undertaking. They recruited volunteers, among whom were Jeanne Mance, age thirty-four, and Paul de Chomedey de Maisonneuve, a soldier in his thirties who commanded the expedition.

In Quebec, the Jesuits and the governor tried to dissuade them from their undertaking. "On account of the war with the Iroquois," wrote Governor Montmagny, "this plan cannot hold out against their raids. The scheme of this new company is so absurd that it would be better to call it the foolhardy enterprise."

"Sir," replied de Maisonneuve, "what you say would be correct had I been sent to choose a site; but as it was determined by my company that I would go to Montreal, it is for me a question of honour, and you will find it good that I go up there to begin a colony, even though every tree of this island were to change into an Iroquois."

Ville-Marie was born of a dream: to bring pious natives and Frenchmen together to create a new people of God. But this dream was never fulfilled. After ten years, the devout colonists gave up. Jérôme le Royer was ruined by the muddle of his own business dealings. De Maisonneuve was recalled to France and died in Paris. Only Jeanne Mance stayed on.

Huronia, meanwhile, was devastated by disease. Influenza, measles, and smallpox brought by the Jesuits and *coureurs des bois* swept through the nation. An old Huron woman confided in Mother Marie de l'Incarnation, who had founded the Ursuline convent in Quebec in 1641: "The black robes are casting spells on us and making us die. They came into a village where everyone was doing just fine: as soon as they arrived, everyone died. They went to visit some cabins in other settlements, and it is only the places where they never set foot that have been spared death and illness. Unless they are quickly put to death, they will end up devastating the country, so that neither young nor old will live there any longer."

Between 1610 and 1640, half the Huron population of Georgian Bay died in different epidemics. The shamans sought to preserve ancestral customs and accused the missionaries of poisoning them. "I will never allow my wife to be baptized," a Huron told one of the Fathers. "I hate the Faith, and I hold the God of the believers in contempt: get out of here and don't speak of it again." An Algonkin chief told Father Le Jeune that his dreams and prophecies did not contain one ounce of truth. The Huron were demoralized, and they sometimes drove away the "black robes," as the missionaries were called, by flinging stones at them.

The Iroquois, who had undertaken to invade and destroy Huronia, made the Jesuits into the sort of martyrs they apparently wanted to be. "We

Marie de l'Incarnation. Born Marie Guyart in Tours in 1599, Marie de l'Incarnation was the first superior of the Ursulines of New France. At the age of thirty-two, this widowed mother of a thirteen-year-old boy decided to become a nun. Answering God's calling, she left in 1639 for New France to convert young native women. Her abundant correspondence is a mixture of spiritual writings and revealing accounts of life in the early years of New France. She died in Quebec in 1672, without ever seeing her native country again. (*Attributed to Hugues Pommier, Archives des Ursulines de Québec*)

THE MARTYRDOM OF FATHERS BRÉBEUF AND LALEMENT ◆ By the seventeenth century, the Roman Catholic Society of Jesus already had considerable missionary experience. It had established missions around the world to convert "heathens." But the Jesuits' presence in Huronia proved costly; seven of them were slaughtered. The Canadian martyrs were canonized in 1930. (*Joseph Légaré, National Archives of Canada, 18795*)

THE MASSACRE OF THE HURON ◆
"Since the faith entered into their hearts and they began to adore the Cross of Jesus Christ, He shared with them a part of this Cross, exposing them to miseries, torments and cruel deaths. In a word, this people has been wiped off the face of the Earth," wrote Paul Ragueneau in *The Jesuits Relations*, 1650. In 1649, the Iroquois annihilated the Huron, and put an end to the French-Huron alliance. A tragedy for the Huron, this was a major setback for the missionaries and merchants. (*Le Massacre des Hurons par les Iroquois Vers, Musée de Québec*)

may be on the point of shedding our blood," wrote Le Jeune, "and to sacrifice our lives in the service of our good Master Jesus Christ. It seems that his goodness wants to accept this sacrifice from me for the remission of my great and manifold sins. If He should want us to die at this very hour, then what a glorious hour it is for us! If God bestowed on me the grace of going to Heaven, then I would pray to God for the poor Hurons."

In 1648 and 1649, the Iroquois attacked and massacred the Huron, who were by now weakened by illness. The Huron had no European weapons – the French had refused to sell to them – and were divided by the presence of so many Christian converts among them. They could no longer resist. The Jesuits Daniel, Jogues, Lalemant, and Brébeuf were taken prisoner, tortured, and executed.

"About twelve hundred Iroquois came," a Huron remembered. "They took their anger out on the Fathers: they stripped them naked; they tore their fingernails off. They rained blows on their shoulders with sticks, on their kidneys and stomach and legs and face, and no part of their body was spared this torment."

The Iroquois then laid waste to Huronia. Of the thirty thousand Huron, a few thousand survived: some were adopted by the Iroquois, some resettled in the west, and some decided to live on the Ile d'Orléans under the protection of the cannons of Quebec. "Since the faith entered into their hearts," wrote Father Le Jeune, "and they began to adore the Cross of Jesus Christ, He shared with them a part of this Cross, exposing them to miseries, torments and cruel deaths. In a word, this people has been wiped off the face of the Earth."

It was the end of a prosperous and vibrant culture. Forty years after meeting Champlain, the powerful Huron nation had disappeared, killed by the fur trade, the crucifix, and the Iroquois.

"My brother," a Huron chief said to a Frenchman, "your eyes cheat you when you look at us: you think you are seeing living beings, whereas we are only the spectres and souls of the departed."

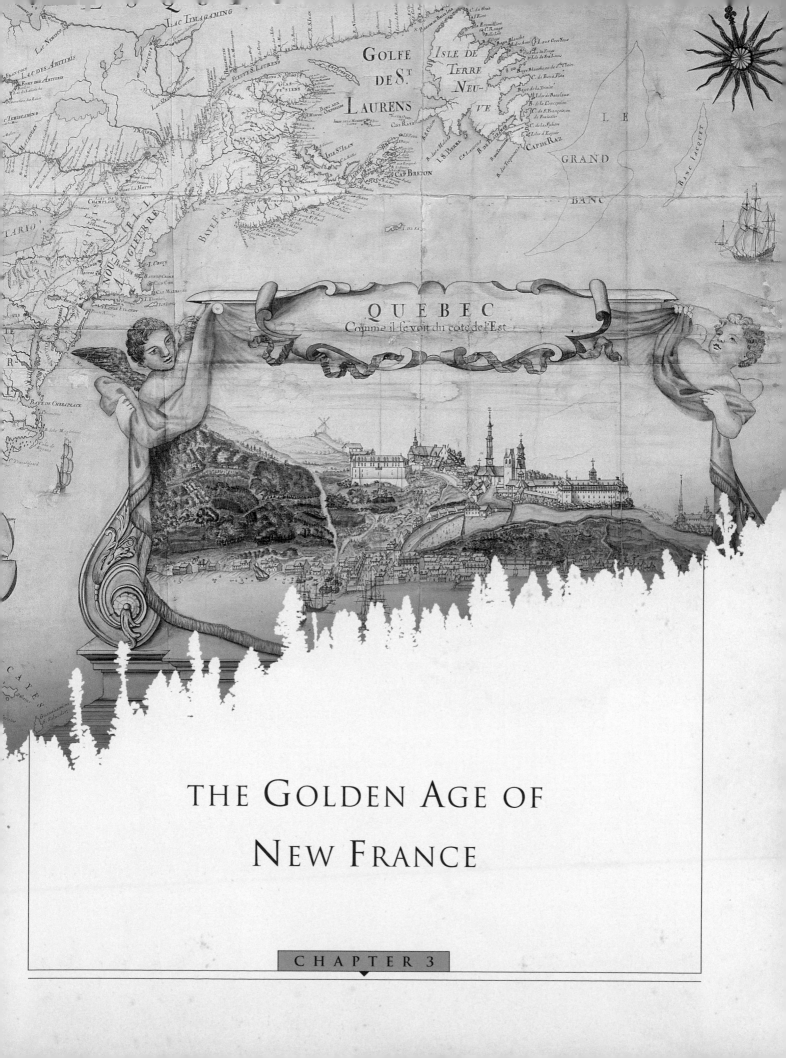

THE GOLDEN AGE OF
NEW FRANCE

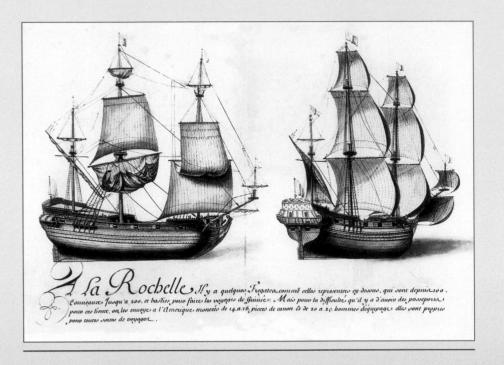

A la Rochelle Il y a quelques Fregates comme celles representées cy-dessus, qui sont depuis 100. tonneaux. Iusqu'à 200. et bastries pour faire les voyages de Guinée: Mais pour la difficulté qu'il y a d'auoir des passeports pour ces lieux, on les enuoye à l'Amerique, montées de 14.a.16. pieces de canon et de 20 a 25. hommes d'équipage: elles sont propres pour toutes sortes de voyages.

T hroughout the seventeenth century, the Iroquois were a military power to be reckoned with. Battles in 1626 brought them victory over the Mohican and gave them control over the Hudson Valley. They invaded the territory of the Huron in the 1640s, then intensified their campaign against the settlers of New France. *The Jesuit Relations* described the Iroquois fearfully: "They come like foxes in the woods. They attack like lions. They flee like birds. They could pass before Quebec in broad daylight and nobody would be able to pursue them or recover the captives they had seized." The Iroquois were masters at guerrilla warfare, striking with quick, devastating raids that kept their casualties to a minimum.

The 12,000 members of the Five Nations – this number grew considerably through the practice of adopting prisoners – could summon 2,200 disciplined warriors. The little French colony on the St. Lawrence River had only 350 inhabitants. This tiny foothold was left to defend itself when the French Crown refused to help.

Beginning in 1643, the Iroquois attacked the outposts of Montreal (Ville-Marie) and Trois-Rivières, disrupting trading and agriculture. "The store in Ville Marie has not bought a single beaver skin from the Savages over the last year," one Jesuit wrote. "In Trois Rivières, the few stragglers to be found thereabouts have been put to work fortifying the place. The store

The frigates of La Rochelle. Most ancestors of French Canadians came to America on board ships built at La Rochelle. For 150 years, the harbour of La Rochelle, on the west coast of France, was the main point of departure for North America. Nearly all of Canada's trade with France passed through this town. (*Musée de la Marine, Paris*)

in Quebec reeks of poverty. The Iroquois have shut down the entire trade in beavers, which has always been one of the great resources of the country." The Iroquois effectively seized control of the fur trade, blocking French access to the interior and preventing other native nations from trading with New France.

"Our enemies the Iroquois are preventing us from enjoying the commodities of the country," wrote merchant Pierre Boucher. Boucher had arrived in Quebec at the age of thirteen and would go on to become the governor of Trois-Rivières. "We cannot go hunting, or fishing, for fear of being killed, or of being taken by these villains; and we cannot even plough our fields, or make hay, without continually putting ourselves at risk: for they throw up ambushes on every side and it only takes a single bush to shelter or rather conceal six or seven of these barbarians, who rush out at you any which way. So you can imagine that we are always on our guard and that a poor man is never safe for long if he wanders off from the others. A woman always worries that her husband, who departed in the morning to work, will be killed or captured, and that she will never see him again."

From 1645 to 1665, the colony was in a state of siege. Settlers no longer cleared the land. There was not a single horse in all of New France. "It would cost a lot to bring horses from France," Boucher wrote. "There are few people willing to undertake the expense; and it is feared that once the horses arrived, the Iroquois would kill them, as they have done with our other livestock, which would be a serious setback for the people who had paid to bring them over."

Ten per cent of the population had been killed in Iroquois raids, and the colony was demoralized. In 1643, three colonists were killed at the very foot of the palisade of Montreal. The next year, de Maisonneuve, founder and governor of the city, barely escaped death during an abortive sortie against two hundred enemy warriors surrounding his fort. Throughout the following night, he could hear the screams of his comrades being tortured.

This bad news stemmed the already waning tide of immigration. In Quebec, Mother Marie de l'Incarnation, the founder of the Ursuline convent, feared for the survival of the French presence in North America. "There are not enough forces in all the land to resist them," she wrote. "If France does not come through for us, we will, in short, either have to leave or die."

The guerrilla campaign continued sporadically for the next fifteen years. But in the first days of May 1660, a young Montreal officer by the name of Adam Dollard des Ormeaux abandoned the colonists' strictly defensive strategy. He left the fort to protect the passage down the Ottawa River of a large convoy of furs piloted by Pierre Radisson. But des Ormeaux and his sixteen men were captured by the Iroquois. All were massacred, with the exception of five prisoners, whose flesh, according to *The Jesuit Relations*, was distributed to the allies of the Iroquois, "so that they all could taste of the flesh of Frenchmen." In the colony as a whole, the Mohawk killed fifty inhabitants and captured a hundred more. The situation was desperate.

King Louis XIV of France.
(*Hyacinthe Rigaud, Superstock*)

France was not interested in helping its North American colony. It was engaged in a war with Spain, and bitterly divided by the Fronde, a series of civil wars in which the nobility rose in rebellion against the absolute monarchy. In 1661 Prime Minister Jules Mazarin, who had always seemed indifferent to the fate of New France, died. The colonists seized on this opportunity and sent Pierre Boucher to France to plead their case before the king.

Louis XIV was only twenty-two years old and newly crowned, but he already dreamed of creating a great empire, and he did not want to inaugurate his reign by losing his colony in the New World. He realized that New France would never prosper as long as it was treated as a purely commercial operation, so he abolished the One Hundred Associates, and Canada ceased to be the property of a private company. It now reported directly to the royal administration, through a governor and an intendant, just as the French provinces did.

The king also understood that a military presence would be necessary to deter the Iroquois. "The Iroquois, who are all perpetual and irreconcilable

Jean Talon, intendant of New France from 1665 to 1668 and from 1670 to 1672, was responsible for its renewal. Canada was placed under the direct authority of King Louis XIV and was expected to become a viable colony, competing with British, Dutch, and Spanish colonies in the New World. Talon presided over the only big wave of immigration in the colony's history, reorganized the administration, and supported the growth of agriculture and industry. But the king's interest in New France proved short-lived and there was little follow-up to Talon's work. (*Frère Luc, Musée des augustines de l'Hôtel-Dieu de Québec*)

enemies of the Colony," read a royal memorandum, "have, through the massacre of a great number of Frenchmen and by the inhumanities they commit against those who fall in their clutches, prevented the country from being more populated than it is at present. The King, in order to provide an appropriate remedy, has resolved to wage war unto their very households, so that they may be entirely exterminated."

Louis sent experienced troops who had just returned from a victorious campaign against the Ottoman Turks. "On the 17th and 19th of June 1665, two vessels arrived in Quebec," the Jesuit superior François-Joseph Le Mercier wrote in *The Jesuit Relations*, "with four companies of the Carignan-Salières Regiment. On the 30th of the same month, two sails were spotted in the distance, which filled us with great joy. There is no way to express the delight of the entire people."

Along with the soldiers came the first representatives of the Crown: Governor Daniel de Rémy de Courcelle; the commander of the troops, Alexandre de Prouville, the Marquis de Tracy; and the intendant, Jean Talon, who had already served as intendant in the French province of Hainault. During this extraordinary summer, Quebec, a town of seventy houses, saw its population double. Marie de l'Incarnation believed that the colony, and her convent, were saved. "All the vessels have arrived, and have brought us the rest of the army with the most distinguished persons that the King has sent to save the country," she wrote. "They had all believed they would perish in storms during the crossing. They were made to understand that this is a holy war, in which the glory of God and the salvation of souls is at stake."

The 1,200 men of the Carignan-Salières Regiment were undoubtedly motivated more by their pay than by concern for the Catholic faith. They were freely enlisted men who had signed on for three years. Some of the most experienced officers had refused to come to America, for fear that their careers would suffer if they were too far from the eyes of the court. But newer recruits, like Captain François Tapie de Monteil, hoped to use the posting as a route to promotion.

A third of the troops were set to work building forts along the Richelieu River, the main invasion route of the Iroquois. "I was ordered to camp on the river with seven companies in order to build a fort at the mouth of Lake Champlain," the Marquis de Salières wrote in his *Memoirs*, "without so much as a carpenter, or any other workman to help and very few tools besides. I arrived with 350 men, many of whom were suffering from stomach problems because of heavy rains and the cold. They were badly dressed, barefoot and had no pots in which to cook their lard and make a bit of soup."

By early winter, the soldiers had built three rudimentary forts. But the new governor, de Courcelle, did not plan to let them sit idle. The thirty-nine-year-old aristocrat – impulsive and foolhardy – was experiencing his first winter in Canada, and he chose January to attack the Iroquois in their territory. The Marquis de Salières tried to dissuade him, without success.

A SOLDIER'S PUNISHMENT ◆ Corporal punishment was part of daily life for soldiers and militiamen. Canadiens had a reputation for being undisciplined if they did not respect their officers. "It is true," wrote Father Charlevoix, "that when they are well led, there is nothing too great for them to undertake, whether on land or at sea. But for that, they need to have huge respect for their commander. The late Mr. D'Iberville, who had all the good qualities of the nation, without any of its shortcomings, could have brought them to the ends of the Earth." (*Anne S. K. Brown Military Collection, Brown University*)

"When I wanted to find out what condition our soldiers were in for this enterprise, I saw that everything was badly arranged," wrote de Salières, "the soldiers have no snowshoes, very few axes, one cover, no hooks, having only one pair of moccasins and one pair of socks. Seeing everything that was lacking, I told the captain that it would be a miracle if they did anything worthwhile."

On January 29, 1666, de Courcelle left Fort St. Louis with five hundred soldiers and two hundred Canadien volunteers, too impatient to wait for his native guides. They wandered lost for four weeks in the forest. "During this expedition which we undertook in the month of January," wrote Captain de Monteil, "we lost four hundred men, who literally froze to death while marching, and then dropped to the ground. We had expected to make a surprise attack on an enemy village, but we did not succeed because our guides froze to death along the way."

The survivors made it to the little post of Schenectady, where the English had just replaced the Dutch. The English saved de Courcelle's men from certain death. The Iroquois they had been intent on fighting had not even noticed them. The governor's punitive expedition had punished only its own members.

In the summer of 1665, the commander of French troops in America, the Marquis de Tracy, arrived from the Antilles and in the fall of the following year he launched a second, and far more ambitious, incursion. Six hundred soldiers joined an equal number of Canadian militiamen, Pierre Boucher among them, and a hundred native allies. The column made its way south of Montreal to the Lake Champlain area, where it planned to attack.

The soldiers came across five large villages, but they were deserted. The weather was getting colder, and de Tracy realized that it would be a mistake to pursue the enemy. He gave orders to set fire to the villages and stocks of grain. On November 5, the army arrived back in Quebec. The regiment still had not engaged in battle, but the colony felt triumphant.

"There is something wonderful at work in this whole business," wrote Marie de l'Incarnation, "because if the Iroquois had stood their ground, they would have created a lot of trouble. But this defeat has inflicted on them the worst possible humiliation. Their country has been laid waste: it is too late in the season to rebuild; what little grain survived the burning of the harvest will not be enough to feed them."

The Iroquois, who were suffering an epidemic of smallpox, did not starve. But they had their first glimpse of the new military strength of the French. The chiefs of the Five Nations decided to sign a peace treaty rather than fight them. The Iroquois Confederacy continued to hinder the thrust of Europeans into the west, but it was not about to destroy New France the way it had destroyed Huronia.

"Ever since the King had the goodness to extend his care to this country by sending the Carignan-Salières Regiment," wrote Father François-Joseph Le Mercier, "we have seen noteworthy changes in Canada, and we can say that it is no longer the country of horrors and hoar-frost that has been described so unfavourably, but a real New France."

The soldiers were getting ready to return to France, but Louis XIV decided otherwise. "The expedition against the Iroquois having been completed, the King desires that the soldiers of the Carignan Regiment

France bringing the faith to the Indians of New France was one of the first large pictures painted in New France (around 1670). It shows the beginnings of the conversion of the Huron by Jesuit missionaries. France was embodied in Anne of Austria, who was regent during the minority of her son Louis XIV and was one of the most ardent propagandists of the Roman Catholic Counter-Reformation. (*Attributed to Claude François, also known as Frère Luc, Archives des Ursulines de Québec*)

remain in the country, offering each of them the means to set himself up and even to help him procure some cleared land."

Seigneuries were offered to the officers. Under the feudal regime, the seigneur received income from the tenant farmers inhabiting his lands, ground their grain at his mill, and subjected them to various duties. The soldiers were offered both land and money. Three hundred and fifty soldiers declined the royal offer and returned to France – among them the Marquis de Salières and Captain de Monteil – but four hundred members of the expedition decided to remain in the colony.

Captains Pierre de Sorel and Antoine Pécaudy de Contrecœur and Lieutenant François de Verchères received seigneuries along the Richelieu River, and so became both colonists and the first line of defence against future Iroquois attacks. Lieutenant René Gaultier de Varennes married the elder daughter of Pierre Boucher and went into business with his father-in-law. The soldiers who were supposed to have exterminated the Iroquois to the last man, but had actually not killed anyone, became the forefathers of an entire nation. Some of them became good settlers, as the king had hoped. But others, after their initial taste of adventure, headed back into the forest to pursue the fur trade.

In the summer of 1665, a vessel had arrived in Quebec bearing a much greater surprise for the inhabitants than mere soldiers. "On July 16, a ship arrived from Le Havre bringing horses, which the King planned to establish in the country," wrote Father Le Mercier. "Our savages have never seen horses before, and stood admiring them, wondering that the French moose, for that is how they call them, should be so gentle and so easy for men to handle."

Louis XIV had now been on the throne for ten years, and he had one grand ambition: to eclipse the other powers of Europe and become master of the world. His first weapon would be economic rather than military, and to wield it he enlisted the help of Jean-Baptiste Colbert, his intendant for finance and minister of marine.

The king, wrote Colbert, "has undertaken a war of money against all the States of Europe. He has created companies, which like armies attack them everywhere, and since the greater part of trade is conducted in foreign colonies, we deemed it necessary to consider maintaining, protecting and building up the colonies already established."

In New France, the biggest obstacle to building a prosperous colony was an acute lack of women. The arrival of so many soldiers meant that the population was two-thirds male. A royal program to supply women was initiated, and the *filles du roi* arrived by the hundreds.

"The 100 girls whom the King sent this year have just arrived," wrote Marie de l'Incarnation on October 29, 1665. "And almost all of them are already provided for. He will send another 200 next year, and corresponding numbers in future years. He is also sending men to be married, to say nothing of those who make up the army. It is astonishing to see how the

Jean-Baptiste Colbert, Louis XIV's minister of marine, was the chief architect of royal policy during the early reign of the Sun King. His ambition was to make France the greatest European power and the centre of a world empire. He ordered Jean Talon to turn New France into a colony strong enough to put a stop to British ambitions in America. (*Chateau de Versailles, Giraudon /Art Resource*)

country grows and multiplies." Over seven years, the royal government sent more than a thousand young women to New France, mostly from the Paris region and the diocese of Rouen. Many were paupers, with no future in France. The king provided them with a dowry ranging from 50 to 300 livres.

One of these women was Marie-Claude Chamois. "I was baptized at St. Gervais de Paris and raised by my mother till the age of 13 in the Faubourg St. Antoine," she recalled. "I had no choice but to leave, if I was to escape the rages of my own brother, who did not respect in my person the holy laws of Nature, Religion and Law."

Marie-Claude Chamois was the youngest of four children from a comfortable family living in Paris. In 1669, she ran away from home. A priest took charge of her and sent her to an institution where abandoned women, poor children, and the mentally ill were housed. "I was sent first to the Hôpital de la Pitié in 1669, from where I was transferred to the Hôpital de la Salpêtrière."

The following year, she sailed for New France. "I was chosen to join the women heading for America, and rather than beg for the support of my mother, I preferred to give up my homeland, make a perilous voyage and arrive in a new world. I remained there in silence, far from my country, without friends, or support of any kind, or parents, condemned to perpetual exile." She arrived in Quebec in October 1670 and married François Frigon, a resident of Batiscan. She was fourteen years old.

"There are all kinds of girls," Marie de l'Incarnation wrote. "Some of them very coarse and hard to manage. Some others, being of good birth, are more honest and will prove more satisfying to the King."

In France, it was said that the women who were sent to the colony were prostitutes. Pierre Boucher, who had come to New France as an indentured servant, defended their honour. He wrote, "It is not true that this type of girl comes here, and those who say so are being contemptuous. If, by any chance, amongst the girls who come, some have a bad reputation or a bad attitude during the passage, they are returned to France." What the women had in common was their poverty and their ability to have children.

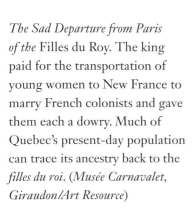

The Sad Departure from Paris of the Filles du Roy. The king paid for the transportation of young women to New France to marry French colonists and gave them each a dowry. Much of Quebec's present-day population can trace its ancestry back to the *filles du roi.* (*Musée Carnavalet, Giraudon/Art Resource*)

"The girls sent over last year are married and almost all are pregnant or have had children, which is proof of the fertility of this land," Jean Talon wrote to the king in 1670. There was an economic incentive to produce a large family as well. Talon ordered that all inhabitants who had ten living children, born in wedlock, "neither priests . . . nor nuns, will be paid a pension of 300 livres per year; and those who have 12, will receive 400 livres more; that all boys who marry at 20 or less and all girls at 16 or less, will receive 20 livres on the day of their wedding."

This policy produced the desired result. Catherine Ducharme and Pierre Roy had eighteen children. Marie Hatanville, a widow with eleven children under fifteen years of age, married a fourth time; her new husband was a widower with seven children. Marie-Claude Chamois and François Frigon had seven children, the ancestors of everyone in North America bearing the surname Frigon. Seven was an average number of children for the *filles du roi*; fewer than the average number born to Canadien women.

"If things continue the way they have for the last two years," Father Le Mercier wrote, "Canada will be unrecognizable, and we will see our forests turning into cities and provinces that one day may resemble those of France."

Pierre Boucher was now a merchant and a seigneur looking for servants in France. "All the poor would be much better off here than in France," he argued, "as long as they weren't lazy; there is no lack of work here, and people couldn't say what they say in France, that they have to fend for themselves because nobody is willing to offer them any work."

Importing indentured labourers was a profitable business. Boucher brought over a hundred, whom he rented to colonists. For the duration of the contract, which usually lasted three years, the indentured labourer belonged to his master. He did not have the status of habitant. He could not take part in the fur trade and could not get married. Some indentured labourers worked as house servants, but most did heavy work, such as clearing the land. The indentured labourer earned the very low wage of 75 livres per year, from which food, lodging, and clothing were deducted. After three years of labour, sometimes under harsh conditions, he often ended up owning only his clothes, his gun, and his liberty. In 1665, one-quarter of the males under fifteen years of age were indentured labourers. Fugitives ran the risk of hanging, the whip, the stock, and hot irons. But these punishments were very rarely applied, and most indentured workers lived as members of the family.

Between 1664 and 1671, roughly one thousand indentured labourers came to the colony. About half of them stayed. The rest jumped onto the first ship they could after getting their *congé*, a passport-like document allowing them to return to France. In a letter to Colbert, Talon complained that such departures threatened the collective survival of the colony: "This colony will hardly be strengthened by the way people are heading back to France, because as much as you may promote the arrival of fresh people, several people headed back this year, and many more are waiting to head back next year, owing to the ease with which they can acquire a *congé*." Of the 15,000 French who came to North America between 1608 and the end of the century, only 3,400 stayed in Canada.

In 1667 the minister of marine took action: "His Majesty considers it a serious problem which he must try to resolve, and for that purpose he forbids any Frenchmen from returning to this kingdom, unless those making the request have a wife and children and a considerable establishment in this country, although His Majesty recognizes that it is important no Frenchman should believe he is kept in the new country by force."

What the new country offered was hope of advancement, though it took time. Marie de l'Incarnation wrote, on October 29, 1665: "There are many poor people here and the reason is that when a family creates a household, it takes two or three years before they have enough to eat, not to mention enough clothing, furniture and a whole range of little things needed for the upkeep of a household; but once these hardships are behind them, they start to feel more comfortable, and if they conduct themselves well, then they become rich over time, as much as a new country like this will allow."

On April 30, 1672, at the age of seventy-two years, after a long illness, Marie de l'Incarnation died in Quebec. Before dying, she had one last message for the son she had abandoned in France more than thirty years earlier. To her great satisfaction, Claude Martin had become a Benedictine monk, and he regularly corresponded with her. "Tell him that I always kept him with me, in my heart." Upon her death, she was revered as a saint, and today she is considered one of the Church's greatest mystics.

François-Joseph Le Mercier left the colony in 1672. The Jesuits needed his services in Martinique.

Another bloody war had broken out in Europe, and France was no longer able to send men to the colony. That November, Talon was called home, leaving most of his projects unfinished. But the French colony did not fall apart. There were only four thousand inhabitants but their roots were strong. Men like Pierre Boucher and the veterans of the Carignan-Salières Regiment had found a home.

Between 1667 and 1680, merchants set out into the interior of the continent, where they created new alliances with native peoples. Hundreds of Frenchmen left the colony for the *Pays d'en Haut* (the area around the Great Lakes) and a new breed of traders, the *coureurs des bois*, emerged. An anonymous chronicler described their lives to the Comte de Pontchartrain in a document bearing the picturesque title *Historical brief on the ill effects of bringing the beaver together under one hand*. "The life of the *coureurs des bois* is one of continual idleness, which leads to all sorts of excesses," the unknown writer claimed. "They sleep, smoke, drink spirits and often ravish the wives and daughters of the savages. They live in a state of complete independence: they account for their actions to nobody: they recognize no superior, no judge, no laws, no police, no subordination."

New France began as a very small colony, but over the course of twenty years French explorers claimed territories from Hudson Bay to the Gulf of Mexico in the name of their king. They discovered the great Mississippi River. They created new alliances with native nations, and they established a threat to New England. This was accomplished in a climate of anarchy, often against the express will of Louis XIV, the Sun King.

It was Intendant Jean Talon who initiated this expansion. From the time of his arrival in 1665, he dreamed of a great French empire in America. The minister of marine, Jean-Baptiste Colbert, warned him to be careful. "It would be better to keep to a well-defined region which the colony will be in a position to maintain," he wrote on April 6, 1666, "than to cover too big a stretch of land, a part of which it might one day be necessary to abandon, to the detriment of His Majesty's and the Crown's reputation."

Colbert was right to be worried. In 1670, New France still had fewer than 10,000 inhabitants, while the English colonies had more than 100,000. In Albany, the English offered better prices to the natives for their furs, and they also provided alcohol. François de Laval, bishop of Quebec, in histrionic language, described the effects of this policy in his *Pastoral Letter, February 24, 1662*: "The village or the cabin where savages drink spirits is an image of hell: fire is flickering about on all sides: they hack away with axes and knives, spilling blood everywhere; everywhere are heard dreadful yells and howling. They are at each others' throats, they rip each others' ears off. The father and mother throw their little children onto hot coals or into boiling caldrons."

As problems increased, native leaders demanded that the traffic in spirits be stopped, and Monseigneur de Laval issued a threat: "Since we are obliged by the duties of our position to oppose with all our power this flood of disorder, we hereby proclaim the excommunication of all those who give, in whatever manner, intoxicating drinks to the savages, unless it be one or two cups per day of the ordinary little measure that is given to French labourers, in other words, two small shots of spirits per day." Not surprisingly, commercial competition won out over religious fears.

The new governor, Louis Buade, Comte de Frontenac, became the main promoter of expansion. The fifty-year-old aristocrat, heavily burdened with debts, saw his position in Canada as an opportunity to rebuild his personal fortune. He formed a partnership with René-Robert Cavelier de La Salle, who was from a rich family in Rouen, and who had abandoned the priesthood because of "moral weakness." La Salle endorsed the use of alcohol in trading with the natives. "It is up to laymen alone to decide what is good or bad for trade," he said, "and not up to ecclesiastics."

Frontenac entrusted La Salle with his fort, Cataracoui (now Kingston), which immediately led to conflict with the merchants of Montreal, who accused Frontenac of abusing his position for private gain. The conflict

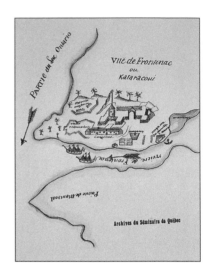

Fort Cataracoui, later named Fort Frontenac. In ordering the construction of Fort Cataracoui (at the present site of Kingston, Ontario), Le Comte de Frontenac, governor of New France, launched a policy of unbridled expansion that displeased Louis XIV. Frontenac also antagonized Canadien merchants who considered that the governor's personal interest in the fur trade amounted to unfair competition. (Vue de Frontenac ou Kataracoui, *Musée d'Amerique française*)

VIEW OF THE QUAI DE LA RÂPÉE (LA SALPÊTRIÈRE) 1716 ◆ La Salpêtrière was operated by the General Hospital of Paris. Originally a gunpowder factory, it was a shelter for beggars, prostitutes, the homeless, and orphans. Many of the women who came to New France as *filles du roi* had spent time here. (*Pierre-Denis Martin, Photothèque des Musées de la ville de Paris 98*)

became so bitter that the clergy got involved. On Easter Day, 1674, Abbé Fénélon denounced Frontenac from the pulpit. "A good governor," he said, "is satisfied with the emoluments paid by the prince without disturbing commerce and without offending those persons unwilling to share their profits with him. He does not oppress the people in pursuit of his own interests, while claiming to act in the name of the monarch."

It was the beginning of a turbulent time. The Intendant Jacques Duchesneau complained to the court: "Everyone contravenes the King's orders. People don't hide it any longer and even head off with astonishing insolence to trade in the villages of the savages. I ruled against the *coureurs des bois*, against the merchants who provide them with goods. All that has been useless because several powerful families of the country are deeply involved and the governor lets them do it and even shares in the profits with them."

Some people, such as the explorer Louis Jolliet, looked for a compromise and proposed "that the habitants be allowed to give them alcohol in their homes and in those places where it is traded in moderation, and that any disorders meet with punishment."

"Frenchmen unworthy of the name derive huge profits from this disgraceful commerce," an anonymous observer wrote, "because once they have intoxicated the savages, they strip off their clothes, their weapons and anything else they may have sold them beforehand. Some Frenchmen have admitted to getting 15,000 livres worth of beaver skins out of a single barrel of spirits worth no more than 200 livres."

Expansion into the interior of the continent continued. Louis Jolliet and Father Jacques Marquette explored the Mississippi River to the mouth of the Arkansas. Nicholas Perrot, an interpreter, was also part of the expedition and took possession of the huge territory around the Baie des Puants (present-day Green Bay, Wisconsin). The king finally ordered Frontenac to stop encouraging this expansion, but Frontenac appealed to his allies at the court and received permission to explore the Mississippi region. With Frontenac's backing, La Salle used this royal authority to expand the fur trade and create a monopoly.

In the autumn of 1679, La Salle undertook a series of expeditions along the Mississippi that would last more than four years. La Salle dreamed of becoming the Great Discoverer, so as "not to leave to anyone else the honour of finding the South Sea route, and thereby the way to China." He was obsessed by a desire for glory. He got lost in the forest, incited native wars, and lost some of his men, but he finally achieved his goal.

"In the name of His Majesty, I take possession of this land Louisiana," he announced on April 9, 1682, "with its adjacent harbours, ports, bays and straits and all its nations, peoples, provinces, cities, towns, villages, mines, fisheries, and rivers contained in Louisiana, from the mouth of the great river called the Ohio and also along the Mississippi and the rivers flowing into it." La Salle was dressed for this momentous occasion in a scarlet coat trimmed with gold braid.

The king, however, was not interested in La Salle's new territory. "The discovery of Sieur de La Salle is quite useless," declared Louis XIV, "and such enterprises should be prevented in the future."

La Salle did not give up easily. On his maps, he tampered with the location of the mouth of the Mississippi, putting it 250 leagues (1,200 kilometres) farther to the west. He then persuaded the king that it would be the ideal place to put a colony that would serve as a base to attack the Spaniards to the south. The fraud paid off. La Salle was named commander of the entire territory and was sent one hundred soldiers and a thirty-six-gun warship.

With his new authority, La Salle sailed from France to the Gulf of Mexico but soon got lost. For two years he wandered, without maps, in the marshes of the Mississippi delta. Some of his troops died; others revolted. He was a merciless, unloved leader who pushed his men to their limits. Five of them finally decided to kill him. On the morning of March 19, 1687, Pierre Duhaut shot La Salle in the head. They stripped him bare and took his possessions, including the scarlet coat.

In the ten years between 1672 and 1682, the French took possession of much of the continent. But they paid a high price. Frontenac's policy had

The murder of La Salle. "A steadfast personality, courage and tireless work helped him overcome everything, and would have brought him glorious success, had all of these fine qualities not been offset by a haughty manner, which often made him unbear-able, and by harshness towards the men under his command, which caused their hatred and finally was the cause of his death," said La Salle's companion Henri Joutel. Robert Cavelier de La Salle was murdered in Texas by members of his expedition on March 19, 1687. (*From* Nouveau voyage d'un Pais plus grande que l'europe, *National Archives of Canada*, C-099233)

Quebec *circa* 1683
(*De L'Amerique, Musée du Québec*)

scattered the colony's resources, wreaked havoc with its native alliances, and upset the merchants, administrators, and clergy. Louis XIV, exasperated, recalled Governor Frontenac to France.

In Europe, France and England were at peace, but in North America, there were tensions. "It is intolerable to consider," noted Thomas Dongan, governor of New York from 1682 to 1688, "that wherever a Frenchman goes forth in America, it becomes part of Canada." Dongan worked to set the Iroquois against the French: "The King my master has forbidden me to supply arms and munitions against the French; but you should not be alarmed by this interdiction: you will lack nothing you need to mete out justice; I would supply you at my own expense."

The Iroquois sought to control the fur trade, to take furs to the English in Albany rather than the French in Montreal. The French were now trading directly with the tribes of the west: the Illinois, the Miami, and above all the Ottawa, all traditional enemies of the Iroquois. "Everyone agrees," wrote Intendant Jacques Duschesneau, on November 23, 1681, "that if the Iroquois continue their conquests without opposition, they will become masters of all the Ottawa, and will take the fur trade over from the English. It is absolutely necessary for us either to make friends with them, or to annihilate them."

Frontenac had convinced the king that the Iroquois were not a threat, so he had not fortified the colony or trained the militia, and on his departure, the French were not strong enough to defend their native allies. The Iroquois were triumphant in the west. Governor Joseph-Antoine Le Febvre de La Barre, Frontenac's successor, had little inclination for military adventures and did not react. New France's native allies felt abandoned.

Nicolas Perrot arrived from France at the age of sixteen to work as a servant. He became a *coureur des bois*, then an interpreter, and finally a merchant. The most skilful French diplomat among the natives of the west, he was given the job of winning them over to support the French in their war against the Iroquois.

"When they sought reasons to make war on each other," Perrot wrote in *Brief on the Morals, Customs, and Religion of the Savages of North America*, "I made them understand that this would disturb the peace of their families, and that they would be better off supporting each other against the Iroquois, who were their common enemy." He was so determined and convincing that seven nations made him their honorary chief. He was given the name Metaminens, "the Man with Iron Legs."

Perrot allied the natives with the French by turning them against the English: "When the English wanted to entice them with presents, I made them understand that they were going to ally themselves with traitors who had poisoned some of the nations that lived among them. And that after intoxicating the men, they had sacrificed and kidnapped their women and children to send them to islands far away, from which they never returned."

In order to defend the colony from the renewed Iroquois threat, Louis XIV named a new governor: Jacques-René de Brisay, Marquis de Denonville. But the French troops Denonville inherited were unfit for combat, and the Canadien militiamen were undisciplined. It took two years of preparation before Denonville was ready to face the Iroquois. In 1687, he launched an expedition against the Tsonnontouan, one of the Iroquois nations.

"It was time, Your Majesty," Denonville wrote to the king, "that we did to the Iroquois what we came to do, to re-establish France's reputation, which had been lost among all the savage nations. It is common knowledge that if we had not marched on Tsonnontouan, and if he had not been humiliated, then all the Ottawas and Hurons would have yielded to the Iroquois and settled under the protection of the English."

The French learned how to tame winter from their native allies. Here, members of the Oneida nation of the Iroquois Confederacy are arriving on snowshoes. By the time this ink drawing was completed (1686), Canadiens had completely adopted native techniques of travel. (*Claude Chaucetière, Les six premiers sauvages de la prairie viennent d'Onneiout sur les neiges, Archives départementales de la Gironde, Bordeaux*)

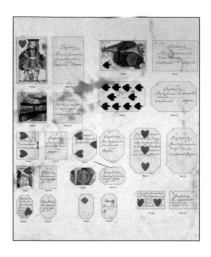

Playing-card money. The first Canadian cash consisted of playing cards. Playing-card money was invented by Intendant Jacques De Meulles in 1685. When he could not pay his soldiers because the ship bringing their wages was late, he distributed playing cards that could later be exchanged for coins. Playing cards were used as money until the end of the French regime. (*Henri Beau, National Archives of Canada, C-17059*)

The allied nations wanted the French to annihilate the Iroquois. Instead Denonville entered into secret peace negotiations with them. Kondiaronk, the powerful Huron chief of Michilimackinac, felt betrayed when he found out. He was afraid that once the Iroquois made peace with the French, they would then be free to attack him.

In the summer of 1688, at l'Anse à la Famine on the shores of Lake Ontario, Kondiaronk laid a trap. He ambushed an Iroquois delegation on its way to Montreal, killed a few of them, then let the others go. "Go my brothers, I am freeing you, and sending you back among your people, even though we are at war with you," Kondiaronk told them. "The Governor of the French himself forced me to commit such a black deed, and I will only be consoled when your five nations have rightly taken vengeance."

Kondiaronk, who was nicknamed "the Rat," was well known to the French and well respected. He ate at the table of Frontenac, who admired his intelligence. "The Rat came back alone after his expedition," wrote Father Pierre-François-Xavier de Charlevoix, "and someone asking him where he came from, he replied he had just destroyed the peace and he added: 'Let's see how Ononthio (the Governor) gets out of this one.'"

In the spring of 1689, the French and Iroquois took up peace negotiations again. But in Europe, war had broken out between France and England. The new governor of New York, Sir Edmond Andros, was the first to learn the news, which he shared with his allies, the Iroquois.

The news, however, had not yet reached New France, where, despite Denonville's efforts, the majority of Canadiens lived in unfortified villages. On August 5, 1689, at dawn, 1,500 Iroquois warriors attacked the village of Lachine: 24 colonists were killed, more than 70 were taken prisoner, and 56 of the 77 houses were razed.

François Vachon de Belmont, superior of the Sulpicians and seigneur of Montreal, gave one account of the horrors of the attack in his *History of Canada*: "After this total victory, the unhappy band of prisoners was subjected to all the rage which the cruellest vengeance could inspire in these savages. They were taken to the far side of Lake St. Louis by the victorious army, which shouted ninety times while crossing to indicate the number of prisoners or scalps they had taken, saying, we have been tricked, Ononthio, we will trick you as well. Once they had landed, they lit fires, planted stakes in the ground, burned five Frenchmen, roasted six children, and grilled some others on the coals and ate them." Later, a few prisoners managed to escape, and some were released in prisoner exchanges. Others were adopted by the Iroquois, among them Marguerite Barbary, born that year, and her sister Françoise. In all, forty-two inhabitants of Lachine were never heard from again.

News of the war between France and England finally reached the colony in October, and with it came a new governor: the Comte de Frontenac, now sixty-seven years old, was back. He immediately ordered an attack on New York, but it was too late in the season. That winter the colony was in desperate straits. The Iroquois harassed its outposts repeatedly, then disappeared into the forest like shadows. Frontenac decided to act: he sent Canadian militiamen to attack the English.

Nicolas D'Ailleboust de Manthet, the brothers Jacques Le Moyne de Sainte-Hélène and Pierre Le Moyne d'Iberville, and 114 other Canadiens all joined the fight. With them came Christian Iroquois from the Sault-Saint-Louis mission. Their target was the fortified village of Schenectady. The Canadiens attacked shortly after midnight, on February 14, 1690.

In a letter to Governor Andros, the mayor of Albany, Pieter Schuyler, wrote: "We deeply regret to inform you of our deplorable situation, which is the result of a horrible and murderous massacre, simply without precedent in this part of America. Two hundred Frenchmen and Indians swooped on the village and assassinated sixty men, women and children in the most barbarous fashion. The cruelties committed in this place cannot be described, neither by spoken word nor in writing. Pregnant women were disembowelled, their children thrown live into the flames, and their heads smashed against doors and windows."

The attack on Schenectady and two similar expeditions launched almost at the same time had the desired effect: the English colonists were terrified. But their response was swift and devastating. On October 16, a fleet of thirty-four ships, among them four great warships, appeared in the St. Lawrence at Quebec. The fleet was from Boston and was commanded by Admiral William Phips, who had already seized Port-Royal the previous May. For the second time in its brief history, Quebec was under siege.

The next day Phips sent Major Thomas Savage to demand the surrender of Quebec and the entire colony. Phips insisted on receiving an answer within the hour. "The only reply I have to make to your general," Frontenac retorted, "is from the mouth of my cannons and the firing of my guns. May he learn that this is no way to summon a man like me."

Frontenac had had time to assemble three thousand militiamen and marines. Phips tried to land his men at the mouth of the St. Charles River, but Jacques Le Moyne de Sainte-Hélène, who was mortally wounded in the encounter, rebuffed them. The artillery up on the ramparts caused great damage to Phips's fleet, and his men were already suffering from smallpox. On October 24, after eight days of siege, he left, worried that ice would imprison his ships.

The war between France and England continued another seven years, though this proved to be the only major English attack on Canada.

Near the end of the seventeenth century, the French colony was still very fragile. The economy was suffering as Europe's taste for beaver skins declined, and with the fur trade no longer profitable, Louis XIV ordered all western outposts to be closed in 1696. Two years later, Frontenac died in Quebec at the age of seventy-six.

A Canadien on snowshoes going to war. "In wartime, the only people we can arm for the defence of the colony and send out to manhandle and harass the English are the habitants, because they alone can go forth in canoes in summertime, and on snowshoes in wintertime, eating only a little flour, fat and tallow; they alone can make forced marches through the woods for three or six months at a time, stand up to the rigours of cold weather, and live out of the barrel of their gun, hunting and fishing as they go," wrote Louis Franquet, the king's engineer. Throughout the French regime, Canadien militiamen had the reputation of being invincible. (*National Archives of Canada, C-113193*)

Phips before Quebec. On October 16, 1690, an armada, transporting 2,000 Massachusetts militiamen, 1,000 English soldiers, and 1,500 natives, appeared before Quebec. On October 21, the French pushed the invaders back to Beauport, where they set sail. Before suffering this defeat at Quebec, Phips's fleet had laid waste to the Acadian coast and had seized Port-Royal. (*Rouargue frères, National Archives of Canada, c-006022*)

There was peace with the Iroquois, though. Smallpox epidemics had winnowed their numbers, and they called for a stop to hostilities with New France, and other native nations followed their example. In the summer of 1701, 1,300 native delegates, representing more than forty peoples, met in Montreal, despite a violent outbreak of influenza, to sign a peace treaty putting an end to nearly one hundred years of fighting. Most of the chiefs had seen their nations exhausted and laid waste by war, and they wanted a peace that would be guaranteed by the French.

The meeting was held according to Iroquois ritual, with a ceremony honouring the dead, an exchange of presents, and long speeches. The new governor, Hector de Callières, welcomed the delegates, and Nicholas Perrot acted as interpreter for all the nations of the west. First, the prisoners

The Great Peace. The peace treaty of 1701 consolidated French-native alliances, and this allowed France to occupy and explore the northern half of America during the first part of the eighteenth century. This extraordinary document illustrates the encounter of two completely different civilizations. (*National Archives of Canada, c-018474 and c-018475*)

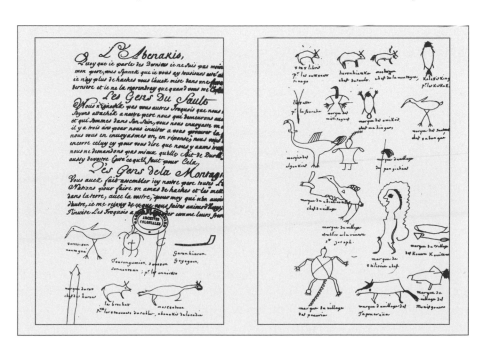

The Port-Royal Hospital. Under the *ancien régime*, social services – in particular the care of the sick – were provided by women's religious communities. (*Louise Madeleine Cachin, Giraudon/Art Resource, Château de Versailles*)

captured in the incessant wars of the last few years were exchanged. Then several tribes replaced their fallen warriors with enemies taken in battle, whom they adopted.

Kondiaronk, the formidable Huron chief of Michilimackinac, represented his people. "If he had been born a Frenchman," wrote the chief administrator of the marine, Le Roy Bacqueville de la Potherie, "he was of a character to manage the thorniest matters of a powerful State. His words were like oracles, and when the Iroquois knew that he was getting ready to strike at them, they did everything to avoid confronting him. He had the deep sentiments of a worthy soul, and nothing of the savage about him."

Kondiaronk was the most important speaker at the assembly. "The waterfalls, the rapids, and a thousand other obstacles," he declared, "hardly seemed difficult for us to overcome, compared to the desire we had to see you and to meet together with you here. We found many of our brothers lying dead along the river. Rumour had it that a great illness raged at Montreal. The many bodies that we found all along the way, bodies eaten away by the birds, were convincing proof of this. However, we made a bridge of all those bodies so that we could walk firmly forward." Kondiaronk died the next night, at fifty-two years of age, and a grand funeral was held in the streets of Montreal.

The treaty was signed on August 4, 1701, but a devastating winter followed, putting an end to celebration. Another influenza epidemic broke out, and more than 10 per cent of the population died. Jeanne-Françoise Juchereau was the superior of the Hôtel-Dieu, and her hospital was overwhelmed. "There were so many deaths," she wrote, "that the priests were unable to bury the dead and minister to the dying, and bodies were brought every day to the church and in the evening they were buried together, sometimes fifteen, sixteen or eighteen at a time. That lasted several months, and

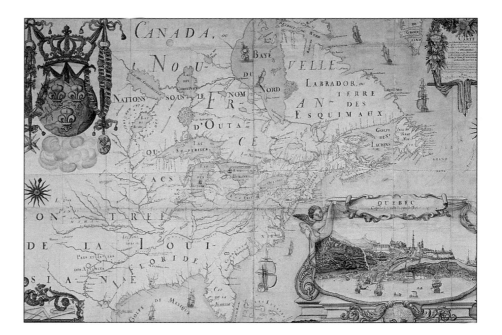

Map of North America, 1688. At the end of the seventeenth century, New France stretched from Hudson Bay to the Gulf of Mexico, from Newfoundland to the Prairies. (*Jean-Baptiste-Louis Franquelin, Service historique de la Marine, France*)

more than 2,000 deaths were registered on the death rolls in Quebec alone, without speaking of the surrounding region."

There were economic consequences as well. "All these deaths are upsetting trade in this country, because of the many debts left behind by the dead merchants, almost all unredeemable," François de Beauharnois wrote to his minister on April 27, 1703. The gloomy toll of the bells was heard so often that ringing them was finally forbidden.

At the beginning of the eighteenth century, France and England were at war once again, and in North America, the French were winning, despite the enormous numerical superiority of their enemies. New France had only 17,500 inhabitants, where the English colonies had 251,000. But this time the Iroquois remained neutral, an advantage for the French, who now controlled even more of the continent. Canadien soldiers – Frenchmen born in the colony – struck fear in the hearts of Englishmen. The most famous was Pierre Le Moyne d'Iberville.

D'Iberville was the first Canadien to be dubbed a Chevalier of the Order of Saint Louis, the highest military distinction in the kingdom. He belonged to one of the most remarkable families in Canada. His father, Charles, had come to Canada at the age of fifteen as a servant working for the Jesuits. When he died, forty-four years later, he was a seigneur and one of the richest merchants in Montreal. All the Le Moyne sons were fearless warriors. For Canadiens, successful trade and military feats provided the most direct route to achieving their ambition: glory and a noble title.

D'Iberville won victories all over the continent. With only a handful of militiamen and natives under his direct command, he threw the English out of Hudson Bay, then attacked Newfoundland. "It is well known how important for England is the fishery of Newfoundland," he wrote, "and the wealth

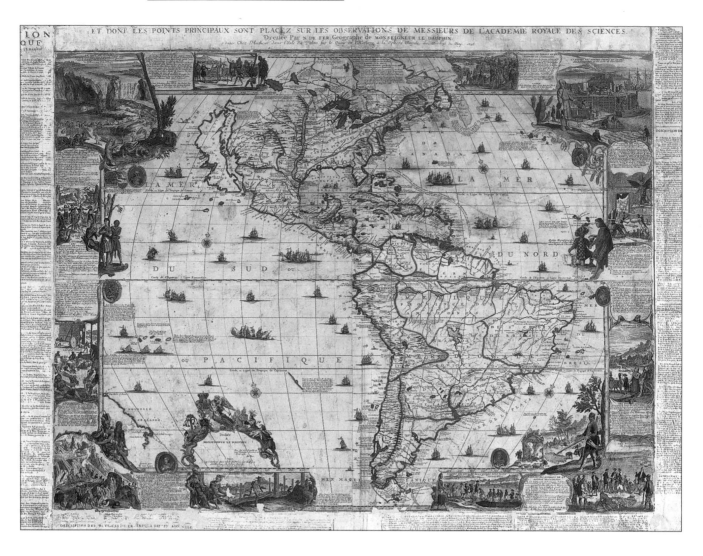

she draws from the trade she undertakes in dried cod for Portugal, Spain and Italy, the damage she would suffer from the ruin of her establishments, and the advantages the French would thereby gain."

In November 1696, d'Iberville attacked the Newfoundland outports, leading 120 militia and Mi'kmaq warriors. He met with resistance when he went on to besiege St. John's, but after he burned the houses and had a prisoner publicly scalped, the defenders quickly surrendered.

In 1701, Louis XIV commanded d'Iberville to found a post at the mouth of the Mississippi River to block the expansion of the English colonies toward the interior of the continent: "If France does not take this part of America in order to possess a colony strong enough to resist England, then the English colony which is becoming very powerful will grow at such a rate that in less than a hundred years, it will be strong enough to take all of America and drive out all other nations." D'Iberville's brother, Jean-Baptiste Le Moyne de Bienville, became governor of the territory, and in 1718 he founded New Orleans.

In North America, the French were victorious and expansionist, but back in Europe the colony was being dismantled, treaty by treaty. On

America divided into its main parts, 1698. Around 1700, the Spanish empire was still more developed than either the French or British colonies of North America. (*Nicolas de Fer, National Archives of Canada,* NMC-26825)

Renard, the slave. In all, there were 2,087 slaves in Canada during the French regime. Most of them (1,685) were natives from the west. They were used as domestic servants and were often treated like members of the family. Compared with the 250,000 black slaves in France's sugar-producing islands in the Caribbean in 1745, and as many again in the British colonies of North America, slavery was marginal in New France. (Esclave Renard, *c. 1732, Bibliothèque nationale de France*)

April 11, 1713, in Utrecht, Holland, France signed a treaty putting an end to the War of Spanish Succession. Louis XIV secured the throne of Spain for his Pretender, Philippe d'Anjou, who would soon reign as Philip V, but in exchange, he had to give up a large part of his colonial empire. He had no choice: war had bled his kingdom dry. De Pontchartrain, the colonial minister, explained the concessions the Sun King had to make: "His Majesty ceded to the Kingdom and to the Queen of Great Britain the Bay and Strait of Hudson, all of Acadia, as well as the island of Newfoundland. His Majesty is only keeping the island of Ile Royale and all the others located in the mouth of the Gulf of St. Lawrence."

In Acadia, there were 1,800 farmers settled and working the land. De Pontchartrain invited them to move to Ile Royale (Cape Breton). "I am persuaded," he wrote, "that the inhabitants of Acadia will not have to pledge allegiance to the Queen of England, and will be able to withdraw without the English interfering in any way."

The treaty gave them one year to move.

In 1717, one of the first pioneers of New France died: Pierre Boucher, seigneur of Boucherville. He had arrived as a mere servant employed by the Jesuits in 1641, but had become, by the time of his death at the age of ninety-five, the most highly regarded man of the colony. He left more than 150 descendants. Nicolas Perrot also died in 1717, but in poverty, on a plot of land at Bécancour.

Compared to New England, with its 446,000 inhabitants, New France seemed a small colony, comprising just 28,000 souls. Population growth came from births alone; there was little immigration. The lack of manpower was acute. In a letter dated October 26, 1720, addressed to the council of the marine, Intendant Michel Bégon proposed a solution tried in other American colonies: "The French colonies of the islands of America were only established and only became prosperous by means of negroes. The English colonies of Boston and New York right down to Carolina only started flourishing when negroes were brought there. These examples leave no doubts as to the advantage the colony would derive from the service of negroes."

At their peak, there would be only 402 black slaves in the colony, almost all of them domestic servants. More often, native slaves, Pawnee, were bought from tribes in the west.

In February 1716, Governor Philippe de Rigaud de Vaudreuil noted the large number of smugglers sent to the royal prison ships, and he proposed that the king send 150 of them to Canada each year. They would be distributed among the inhabitants as indentured labourers for a three-year period, after which they would be free, although they would not be allowed to return to France. New France would not become a penal colony, however. The royal tribunals exiled only a few thousand convicts. The future of Canada lay neither in the cargoes of slave ships nor in penal servitude. It lay in the cradle.

EX-VOTO OF MONSIEUR ROGER, 1717 ◆ An ex-voto is a picture placed in a church to give thanks for the grace of God or for the intercession of a saint. During the French regime, crossing the Atlantic was so dangerous that the wretched passengers needed the protection of all the saints (here, Saint Anne and Saint Mary) if they hoped to arrive safe and sound in Quebec. (*Musée de Sainte-Anne-de-Beaupré*)

France's chief interest in North America had always been the fishery. Continuing access to the Grand Banks of Newfoundland was essential to its survival. After ceding Newfoundland and Acadia to England, France decided to consolidate its sole possession on the Atlantic coast, Ile Royale, and, in 1720, the most imposing military fortress anywhere in North America was built there. Counsel to the boy king Louis XV, who came to the throne in 1715, declared that he was determined to start building up the fortifications in Ile Royale by focusing on Louisbourg, "the most important part, both for its advantages over other ports in the fishery, and for its location."

Four years later, Etienne Verrier, the engineer managing construction, proudly told the king: "The fortification of this city seems so vast in all its parts that the King may count it as the greatest stronghold in all of America." Troops of the marine made up the greater part of its population and workforce, but the soldiers did not like it there. They were isolated; the climate was dreadful; the fog rarely lifted. There were frequent mutinies.

Initially, the strategic location of Louisbourg annoyed the English colonies. Later, it threatened them, and the Bostonians were determined to destroy it.

By 1750, New France had fifty thousand inhabitants. Agriculture, particularly wheat, was one of the main industries. A typical habitant family had a few cows, one or two pigs, a dozen chickens, a horse or two, a pair of oxen for ploughing, and a flock of sheep for wool. The family farmed an area between 25 and 50 hectares, made up of a large wheat field, pasture, and a stand of trees that would provide a constant supply of firewood for winter. The family was self-sufficient, more so than a family in France at the same time, because whatever the land did not produce could be supplemented with fur trading, hunting, and fishing.

Farms were established along both shores of the St. Lawrence and Richelieu rivers, facing the waterway and stretching upland in parallel strips toward the forest. They belonged to the seigneurs, who granted them to tenant farmers, known as *censitaires*, in exchange for rent and services. Seigneurs and *censitaires* were under an obligation to clear the land, though a number of them failed to do so in the time period set out, often because trading in the forest seemed more attractive and offered the potential of nearly instant wealth.

HABITANTS ◆ Louis Franquet, the king's engineer, wrote about the habitants: "They don't work hard enough at farming, they prefer to go hunting, fishing, or to become sailors or go into trade, thereby leaving the countryside to settle in the cities, which by becoming overpopulated will drain the country of its inhabitants. . . . The cities are becoming overpopulated and the countryside is being emptied out; which is leading to a drop in land cultivation and the production of foodstuffs needed to keep the country going. The fact of there being so many people in the cities is leading to greater consumption and as a result to greater scarcity." Several European observers noted a big difference between the European peasantry and Canadian habitants, including Intendant Gilles Hocquart, who wrote: "They are naturally rebellious. They are fond of honours. They like to consider themselves brave, and are extremely sensitive to any sign of contempt or the slightest punishment." (*Henri Beau, National Archives of Canada, c-001247*)

The intendant took action on the king's behalf: "I hereby order that one year from the date of publication of this ruling . . . the inhabitants of New France to whom His Majesty has accorded lands in Seigneuries, who have not cleared their domain, and who do not have habitants required to cultivate and settle these lands, failing this and the period of time having expired, it is His Majesty's desire that said lands be returned to the Crown."

These proclamations often had no effect whatsoever, because the deadlines could be impossible to meet. "The habitant must start by cutting down the dense trees around his house," wrote Ruette d'Auteuil, the king's general prosecutor, on January 20, 1706, "cutting them to agreed lengths, which can be handled by men as well as by women, by hoeing the land for several years with his bare hands and among the fallen trees, by pulling up what remains of the tree trunks which are cut five to six feet above the snows, by digging ditches required in humid places, and by providing for upkeep and the needs of his family, which are excessively costly on account of the length and rigour of the winters."

It would take the habitants several generations to tame the winter and use it to their advantage. They learned to use the cold to conserve food. They built houses that withstood frost and thaws. They made very warm clothes and learned from the natives to travel on snowshoes. They took advantage of winter to make necessary repairs to buildings and tools and to cut and split wood for the following year.

It was a century in North America before winter became something other than an enemy. In 1716, Quebec authorities issued a decree: "Sledding is forbidden in the streets of this city, whether on sleds, or skates, or otherwise, and adult offenders will face a penalty of ten livres. As for children, they will be kept in prison until their fathers and mothers have paid the penalty."

In 1730, Justice Pierre Raimbault denounced another favourite winter sport of the habitants: "In the city of Montreal, all those who drive sleighs or other carriages, officers as well as others, take delight in going through the streets at a full gallop. There have been several accidents this winter: most of these swaggering habitants bring their horses into the city without breaking them in, in order to race them better and smash into anyone they encounter in the streets."

In 1753, a ruling banned people from gathering "for the purpose of making snowballs and throwing them at passers-by or even at each other. The penalty for infractions is a 50 livres fine."

Marie-Elisabeth Bégon, widow of the governor of Trois-Rivières, hated the cold, even though she had been born in Montreal. This fifty-three-year-old Canadian belonged to the new local aristocracy. "The news is that everyone here is learning how to dance," she wrote in 1749. "People are endeavouring to stand out at the ball they hope Monsieur Bigot will give here."

The little Versailles that Quebec had become was condemned by the clergy. "The curate preached a sermon this morning about balls," Madame

Habitants. In New France, the term "peasant" was considered an insult. Canadiens were "habitants," that is, they were familiar with the country, and they had gained that familiarity through a long struggle against the harsh elements and living conditions of New France. (Habitants de Canada, *Laval University*)

Marie-Élisabeth Bégon, the wife of Michel Bégon, governor of Trois-Rivières, kept up an extensive correspondence with her son-in-law Honoré-Michel de la Rouvillière de Villebois, a man almost her age, with whom she seems to have been very much in love. Her letters show that high Canadien society knew how to enjoy life without worrying too much about the strictures of the Church. (*Henri Beau, National Archives of Canada, C-010599*)

Bégon wrote to her son-in-law in Louisiana. "You know him and you will not be surprised at the way he spoke, saying that all gatherings, balls and parties were disgusting, that the women who brought their daughters along were adulterous. He said: 'What has been the result of all these abominations? Quarrels and shameful illnesses.'"

In another letter to him, Madame Bégon wrote, "I have to tell you about a jest from Mme La Ronde when she married. You know that the priest, before giving the sacrament, must know if the spouses are well informed. He asked her if she knew what the sacrament of marriage is. She answered that she did not know, but if he was curious to find out, she would give him news in four days. The poor priest looked down and did not say a word."

Some French aristocrats, such as the Intendant Gilles Hocquart, had a poor opinion of Canadiens and looked down on them. "They are naturally unruly," he observed. "They are fond of honours and like to consider themselves brave. They are extremely sensitive to any sign of contempt or the slightest punishment. They are vindictive, drink spirits heavily, and are not very truthful."

CANADIEN WOMAN AND MAN ♦ "I do not know whether we should count as one of the shortcomings of our Canadiens the good opinion that they have of themselves. It is at least certain that this opinion gives them the confidence to undertake and accomplish things that would not seem possible to other peoples. It has to be admitted that they have excellent qualities. We have nowhere in the Kingdom a Province where the blood is generally finer, the height more advantageous and the body better proportioned. Their skill and address are unequalled: the cleverest Savages don't paddle their canoes any better in the most dangerous rapids and don't shoot more accurately." From the *History and General Description of New France* by Father Pierre-François-Xavier de Charlevoix. (*Bibliothèque de Montréal*)

But Father Pierre-François-Xavier de Charlevoix saw a society becoming ever more refined: "Nowhere else is our language spoken with greater purity. No trace of an accent can be heard; a lively spirit, gentle and polite manners are shared by all; and boorishness, whether in language or in behaviour, is unknown even in the most remote countryside."

The Jesuits had a college in Quebec as early as 1635, the first in North America, where they taught the same curriculum offered in France. But the young Canadiens preferred practical instruction. Father Charlevoix wrote that "many people are convinced they are not suited to the branches of knowledge which require a good deal of application and serious study. But nobody can challenge their rare talent for mechanical arts; they have practically no need of masters to excel and one sees people every day who succeed in all crafts without doing any apprenticeship at all."

Towards the middle of the eighteenth century, a fifth generation was born in the colony. Canadien society had become much more urban and gradually very distinct from French society. In 1749, Marie-Elisabeth Bégon went to France. She detested the long winters and was looking forward to the trip, since she had been told that everything was better there than in Canada. But she was bitterly disappointed.

"I find every day, reasons to reproach all those people I have heard saying that in France everything is done marvellously well," she wrote on October 29, 1750. "In France, everything comes easily; in France, people are obliging, and finally in this country, I thought that with money you could acquire anything you needed. But in truth, if I had been fool enough to believe it, I would have been very much mistaken, because I find nothing here is better than in Canada, except in December, January and February;

all the rest is worse." In France, she was known as "the Iroquois lady" at the court at Versailles. She never returned to Canada, and she died in 1755.

It is most likely that Acadia got its name from Arcadia, the garden of the gods in Greek mythology. The region boasted some of the richest soil in America and seemed immune to disease; no epidemics of typhus, cholera, or scurvy occurred there. The French lived in harmony with the Mi'kmaq, who became allies and often their in-laws, as marriages between the two peoples were frequent. But Acadians lived along the border between two great powers that held each other in mortal contempt. Acadia was handed back and forth between France and England at least six times in less than a hundred years.

In 1713, when Acadia was finally ceded to England, it was home to 1,800 peaceful farmers, most of whom decided to stay on their land. They were French Catholics, and their new sovereign was an English Protestant, who was demanding an oath of allegiance. The Acadians stalled, then refused. A delegation from the settlement of Beaubassin explained to the governor of Port-Royal (which the English called Annapolis Royal), "When our ancestors lived under English domination, they were never required to take such an oath."

There were not enough Englishmen to force the Acadians, and above all Lieutenant-Governor Thomas Caulfield wanted them to stay in the country. "If the French leave," he wrote, "we will never be able to support English families here, and protect them from harassment by the Indians, who are the worst enemies imaginable."

In 1718, five years after the transfer of Acadia, the English again demanded an oath of allegiance to the king. This time the Acadians of Grand-Pré, Beaubassin, and Port-Royal requested the assistance of their former sovereign, and sent this petition to the governor of Louisbourg: "Today it appears that we are being forced either to take the oath of allegiance or to leave the country. We are unable to do either. We are determined never to take the oath because we are the good and true subjects of the Very Christian King [of France], and we cannot give this up, without appropriate conditions, which were promised by the Court of France and were always refused by the Court of England. As our current position is very difficult, we beg you to honour us with your generous counsel."

Governor Richard Philipps informed London in 1720 that the Acadians "will never take an oath of allegiance, nor will they ever leave the country."

The Board of Trade agreed: "As to the French inhabitants of Nova Scotia who appear so wavering in their inclinations we are apprehensive they will never become good subjects to His Majesty . . . for which reason we are of opinion they ought to be removed as soon as the Forces which we have proposed to be sent to your protection shall arrive in Nova Scotia . . . but you are not to attempt their arrival His majesty's positive order."

Nothing happened for ten years, and by 1730, the Acadian population had doubled. Philipps wrote that "they constitute a powerful group, which like Noah's offspring are spreading across the face of the province." Philipps and his assistant, Lawrence Armstrong, managed to get the Acadians to take the oath, on the condition that they were exempted from the duty of bearing arms. This clause appeared in the documents that the habitants had to sign. Philipps recommended that it be "written in the margin, next to the French translation, in the hopes of overcoming their repulsion, little by little." However, it was not included in the oath itself, which read, "I promise and swear by my Faith as a Christian that I will be entirely faithful and will truly obey His Majesty King George II, whom I acknowledge as the sovereign lord of Acadia or Nova Scotia, so help me God." Philipps could reassure London that four thousand Acadians had taken the oath.

There is no doubt that the promise not to bear arms was made. Father Charles de Goudalie de Grand-Pré and the notary Alexandre Bourg Belle-Humeur were witnesses: "We certify that His Excellence Lord Richard Philipps has promised to the habitants of Mines and other rivers tributary, that he exempts them from taking arms and from waging war against the French and the savages and that the said French have committed themselves and have promised never to take arms against the kingdom of England."

The Acadians thought they had found a way to safeguard their way of life. Starting in 1730, the English called their new citizens "neutrals" or "French neutrals."

The winds of hatred were blowing across America, and Acadia was at the centre of the storm. Louisbourg was such a threat to the commercial leadership of Boston that in 1745 the governor of Massachusetts, William Shirley, led an expedition against the fortress and captured it. Three years later, England returned Louisbourg to France, which provoked consternation and rage in Boston.

In 1749, the English built Halifax, their own fortress on Chebucto Bay. France and England had never agreed about the exact limits of Acadia. France believed that it had ceded only a strip of land along the coast, while England understood that it had obtained all territory south of the St. Lawrence. Conflict was inevitable.

Officially, France and England were at peace. But the French encouraged the Mi'kmaq to harass the English. The governor of Canada, the Marquis de la Jonquière, had to act secretly: "It is desirable that the Savages succeed in destroying the plans of the English as well as their establishment in Halifax. It is up to the missionaries to negotiate with the Savages and to direct their actions. Reverend Father German and Abbé Le Loutre will have no difficulty making the best use of them."

Acadia was a powder keg. It was no longer possible to be neutral, but the Acadians did not know that. On August 9, 1755, a correspondent for *The New York Gazette* wrote: "We are now upon a great and noble Scheme of sending the neutral French out of this Province, who have always been secret

John Winslow. In 1755,
Lieutenant Colonel John Winslow
of Massachusetts was in charge
of deporting Acadians from the
towns of Beaubassin and Grand-
Pré. Just before issuing the first
deportation order, he announced:
"The part of duty I am now upon
is what tho[h] necessary is Very
Disagreeable to my natural make
& Temper, as I Know it Must be
Grievous to you who are of the
Same specia." It was one of
the rare expressions of sympathy
the ten thousand Acadian depor-
tees received. In the British
colonies and in England there
was widespread satisfaction that
the problem of the French
neutrals of Nova Scotia had been
definitively resolved. (*The Pilgrim
Society, Plymouth*, MA)

enemies, and have encouraged our Savages to cut our Throats. If we effect their Expulsion, it will be one of the greatest Things that ever the English did in America; for by all the Accounts, that Part of the Country they possess, is as good Land as any in the World: In Case therefore we could get some good English Farmers in their Room, this Province would abound with all Kind of Provisions."

In the month of July, the new governor, Charles Lawrence, demanded that the Acadians take a new oath, this time without conditions. The Acadians refused: "We and our forefathers having taken . . . an oath of allegiance which was approved several times, in the name of the King, we will never be so inconstant as to take an oath which changes even one word of the conditions and privileges which our sovereigns and forefathers have obtained for us in the past."

This proved the last straw for Lawrence, who decided to expel the recalcitrant Acadians. On August 11, 1755, he announced to Lieutenant Colonel John Winslow, of Massachusetts, who was in Grand-Pré, "You must collect the inhabitants together in order to their being Transported in the Best Manner in your Power by Stratagem or Force as Circumstances may require, but above all I desire you would Not pay the Least attention to any remonstrance or Memorial from any of the inhabitants."

Winslow declared, "I therefore order and strictly enjoin by these presents to all the inhabitants as well of the above named districts as all the other districts, both old men and young men as well as all the lads of ten years of age, to attend at the church at Grand Pré on Friday the 5th Instant at Three of the clock in the afternoon." Once they were brought together, Winslow addressed the population. "Your lands and tenements, cattle of all kinds and live stock of all sorts are forfeited to the Crown with all other your effects, saving your money and household goods, and you yourselves to be removed from this province."

By now, Acadia had been British for forty-two years. Almost all its people had been born British subjects. In the summer of 1755, there were in Acadia 12,000 inhabitants of French origin. That year, 7,000 were expelled. The *dérangement*, or deportation, lasted five years. A total of 10,000 Acadians went into exile.

John Thomas, a doctor under Winslow's command, kept a meticulously detailed journal during the autumn of 1755: "September 2nd. Pleasant day. Major Frye sent Lieutenant John Indocott's detachment to the shore, with orders to burn the village at a place called Peteojack. September 18. Very strong gusts of wind, with rain and snow. Major Prible returned from an expedition with his men, who had burned 200 houses and barns. November 19th. Cold. We rounded up 230 head of cattle, 40 sows, 20 sheep and 20 horses and we came back. We have started moving the inhabitants out. The women were very distressed, carrying their newborns in their arms; others brought along in carts their infirm parents and their personal effects. In short, it was a scene in which confusion was mixed with despair and desolation."

The majority of Acadians were deported to the American colonies, where they were not welcome. "The French neutrals arouse the general discontentment of the population, because they are papist zealots, lazy and of a quarrelsome mind," declared the governor of Virginia, Robert Dinwiddie. "We have very few Catholics here, which makes the population very anxious for its religious principles and makes it fear that the French shall corrupt our Negroes."

Jean Labordore and the seven members of his family reached Salem, Massachusetts. In a petition, he complained of his treatment by the local authorities: "Having at length refused him oxen to fetch home his wood which he always cut himself, and left them now . . . without victuals or firing, and in a kind of house without doors or roof for when it rains they are obliged to shift their bed from part of the wett to leeward . . . having told one of the selectman that we were afloat in the house he said I must build a boat and sail it."

One-third of the deported Acadians died of typhoid, smallpox, and yellow fever. Another third settled in Louisiana. The rest were scattered throughout France, England, and the Antilles. Once the deportation was over, only 165 French families remained in Acadia, fewer than 1,000 people.

In 1756, the winds of war blowing across North America became a hurricane.

BATTLE FOR A CONTINENT

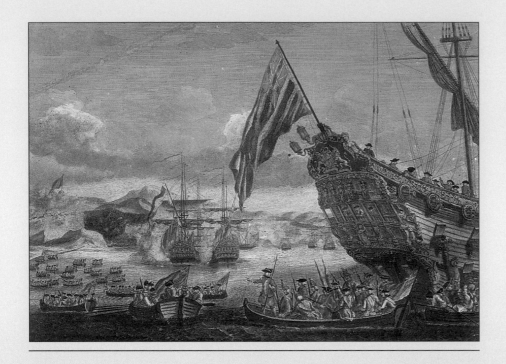

"I left Paris on the 15th of March 1751," an eighteen-year-old Frenchman known only by his initials, J.C.B., wrote in his journal. "I was tormented with a desire for travel. I sought information about the best country to live in; about Louisiana and Canada, the only place to which recruits were then taken. . . . The sailors told me that Canada was more healthy, although its climate was colder."

Like Jonathan Swift's Gulliver travelling in Brobdingnag, J.C.B. experienced in Canada a fantastic, oversized world. After joining the army as a gunner he canoed on the blue immensity of Lake Erie and stood under Niagara Falls, soaked and awed. He saw passenger pigeons flying south in their millions, "so numerous that they seem to be a heavy cloud, and they often fly so low that it is easy to kill them with guns or even clubs." In a single day he and his fellow soldiers killed 130 rattlesnakes, and he was briefly pinned to the ground by a bear before it was frightened away. The first deaths he saw came at a celebration for the Duke of Burgundy's birthday when a lighted wick fell into a box of fireworks, setting them off. Five soldiers standing beside J.C.B. were pierced with rockets and killed, and four others were seriously wounded. But J.C.B. emerged unscathed, and received fifty francs from the intendant for his luck.

The Expedition against Cape
Breton in Nova Scotia, 1745
(*H. Stevens, National Archives
of Canada, C-001090*)

He spent most of his time in wilderness army posts, preyed upon by scurvy and nervous of France's allies, the natives. In his diary he outlined their scalping technique in clinical detail. "The French and the English were accustomed to pay for the scalps," he noted, "to the amount of thirty francs' worth of trade goods. Their purpose was then to encourage the savages to take as many scalps as they could." The natives, adept traders, began to man-ufacture scalps from horsehide, selling them to whoever was buying.

In the mid eighteenth century, the French laid claim to the largest part of the continent. A Catholic, French-speaking society of sixty thousand was centred in the cities of Quebec and Montreal, in the fortress of Louisbourg, and spread thinly through villages along the St. Lawrence and in small forts that advanced French territory into the interior. The French cemented alliances with the natives, enabling them to control the west, a frail empire that ran from Fort Detroit to Louisiana at the mouth of the Mississippi River. The much more populous English colonies, from Halifax to Savannah, were hemmed in east of the Allegheny Mountains – a source of great frustration and bitterness. The natives, comprising approximately two hundred nations, lived uneasily between the two groups. Many natives sided with the French, though it was a fragile alliance, and they resented the English presence. The natives were also divided among themselves by traditional rivalries.

For the French and English, North America represented an empire of incalculable size and wealth. To the natives, it was a homeland. "We have great reason to believe you intend to drive us away and settle the country or else why do you come and fight in the Land God has given us," a native chief lamented. "In a little while, if we find a bear in a tree there will immediately appear an owner of the land to challenge the property, and hinder us from killing it, which is our livelihood."

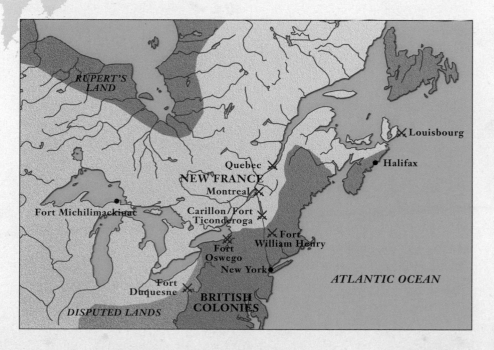

The Seven Years' War, 1756-1763

In the years after 1750, North America frequently became a bloody battleground, in a prelude to what would become Europe's most monumental confrontation, the Seven Years' War (1756-63). Even before war was formally declared, the British tried to take the French fort at Niagara and failed. In 1755, they forcibly expelled ten thousand Acadians who refused to take an oath of allegiance to the king. A third of the deported Acadians died of disease or misadventure; the rest became refugees. In the west, the natives, supported by the French, drove out the English colonists who were pushing into the Ohio Valley. Three thousand settlers were killed or captured, thousands more driven away.

In May 1755, J.C.B. was at Fort Duquesne (near present-day Pittsburgh, Pennsylvania) when a group of Ottawa natives returned from Virginia with twenty-five prisoners. Ten of them were offered to the commander of the fort as a gift, but not before being subjected to the native practice of running the gauntlet. "One of the ten prisoners handed over was a young girl named Rachile. . . . This girl, like the others, received the bastonnade [gauntlet] when she reached the fort, and almost lost an eye from the blows she suffered." She was nursed back to health by the fort's surgeon and married a Canadien, who had fallen in love with the pretty, tragic survivor. When the natives heard that an ally had married one of the enemy, they demanded her return. "The commander saw no better way to save the young couple from their enemies than to send them in disguise at night by boat with provisions and two guides who would take them to Louisiana. Three months later, news came of their safe arrival and settlement at New Orleans." The happy story of Rachile illustrates the complex politics of the continent, with the English, French, Canadiens, the many native nations, and the Thirteen Colonies all engaged in a shifting, complex dance.

The illusion of a formal peace between the English and French was maintained despite frequent, venomous skirmishes. But on July 8, 1755, Britain finally severed its diplomatic ties with France, and the following year it declared war. It was a world war, the first, and North America would be the site of its most famous battle and one of its greatest prizes.

Quebec was the centre of France's operations in North America, and in 1756, it became a wartime city, filled with soldiers and refugees. New France's governor general was Pierre de Rigaud, the Marquis de Vaudreuil, a sixty-year-old colonial aristocrat born in Quebec, a big man who favoured directness. He was commander-in-chief of the army.

Louis-Joseph, the Marquis de Montcalm, had been sent from France to command the *troupes de terre*. Montcalm was forty-seven, a career soldier from a distinguished French family who had begun his military training at the age of nine. He was short, impatient, determined, and vain, Vaudreuil's physical and temperamental opposite. The two men despised one another; both wrote regularly to France, informing their superiors of the other's perceived shortcomings.

The Marquis de Montcalm. "I shall always say, happy he who is free from the proud yoke to which I am bound. When shall I see my château of Candiac, my plantations, my chestnut grove, my oil-mill, my mulberry trees? O good God! Goodbye; burn my letter." Montcalm writing to the Chevalier de Bourlamaque, March 23, 1759 (*National Archives of Canada*, C-27665)

PIERRE DE RIGAUD DE VAUDREUIL DE CAVAGNIAL ◆ In an age of arranged marriages, the Marquis de Vaudreuil's marriage was an anomaly. He married Jeanne-Charlotte de Fleury Deschambault in 1746 in Louisiana. She was a sixty-three-year-old widow with no property, Vaudreuil an ambitious forty-eight-year-old moving upward through the world of colonial politics. They remained devoted to one another until her death seventeen years later.

Vaudreuil became governor general of New France in January 1755, shortly after George Washington attacked the French Fort Duquesne (Pittsburgh), signalling the start of eight years of fighting. He had been desparate to get the appointment, but his entire tenure in New France was consumed by war.

Through guerrilla tactics and shrewd deployment of his limited military resources, Vaudreuil was able to thwart the larger British forces and American militia. But the differing styles of warfare between the French regulars and the Canadien militia created internal tensions. These weren't helped by the personality clash between Vaudreuil and the Marquis de Montcalm, who had been sent from France to bolster the military effort. By 1756, Vaudreuil was in poor health and wanted to leave for France. He praised the Canadiens and natives and was critical of the French soldiers, writing to a friend, "Canada at the moment is in chaos. If I were not to return to France I should go out of my mind. I have not received one word about my return that I strongly requested at the turn of the year. Since I could expect nothing were I to be crippled in this country, and I can expect no great thanks for the vital services that I render here, I shall return to Franc, without permission, if the state of my health requires it. At present the war is waged in Canada as in France, with the usual panoply and baggage train. It is only the poor Canadians who are not in the like case, always being off on forays with the Indians and bearing the brunt of the enemy's fire."

Vaudreuil opposed Montcalm's decision to engage Wolfe on the Plains of Abraham, advising that he wait for the rest of the French force to arrive. The battle was lost, but the French still held Quebec. If the English were unable to take the city, they would have to leave before the St. Lawrence River froze. Vaudreuil sent an order to the commander of the Quebec garrison, Jean-Baptiste-Nicholas Roch de Ramezay, telling him not to capitulate, that supplies and reinforcements would arrive soon. But Ramezay did not receive the order in time and surrendered the city on September 18. (*National Archives of Canada, C-10612*)

"Monsieur Montcalm has got so quick a temper," Vaudreuil wrote to the minister of the marine, "that he goes as far as to strike the Canadians. I had urgently recommended him to see that the land officers treat them well; but how could he keep them in order, if he cannot restrain his own vivacity? Could a worse example be given . . . ?"

Vaudreuil, in turn, was described as "a timid man and one who neither knows how to make a resolution or to keep one once made." Vaudreuil held to the belief that Quebec was secure; Montcalm saw only its vulnerabilities.

There was also a glaring difference between Montcalm's European views of warfare and the guerrilla tactics of the New World, which Vaudreuil subscribed to. The European strategy was to bring large forces directly to bear on each other, then deliver a single, well-timed volley that would devastate the enemy. Battles tended to be brief and casualties were high. Though governed by a strict code of manners, "civilized" warfare could be more destructive than the natives' tactics, which inflicted specific cruelties on a smaller number of the enemy.

In the first battles of the war, Montcalm took Fort Oswego on the south shore of Lake Ontario, then, on August 9, 1757, Fort William Henry at the southern tip of Lake Champlain. He used traditional tactics, employing siege guns and French soldiers. With an army of 3,600 men he defeated Major-General James Abercromby's force of 15,000, a stunning tactical rout.

By contrast, Vaudreuil assigned the Canadiens and natives to conduct raids that were designed to destroy the enemy's morale. A settlement of Germans in the Mohawk Valley was attacked: sixty dwellings and granaries were burned, fifty people killed, and thirty-two scalps taken. One hundred and fifty people, mostly women and children, were taken prisoner.

Montcalm hated these tactics. "It is no longer the time," he said, "when a few scalps, or the burning of a few houses is any advantage or even an object. Petty means, petty ideas, petty councils about details are now dangerous, and a waste of time."

There was another objection to the Canadian style of war: the worry that the Europeans would abandon the gentleman's pretense that marked warfare, that they would embrace the savagery of the new landscape. Louis Antoine de Bougainville, aide-de-camp to Montcalm, kept a journal of his experience in Canada that is one of the most perceptive records of the war. He was diminutive, overweight, asthmatic, but he possessed a good military mind. He had already written two books on mathematics and was a keen observer. Bougainville immersed himself in the native culture, though he held on to his European sensibilities. "Their souls are as black as pitch," he wrote of the natives. "It is an abominable way to make war; the retaliation is frightening, and the air one breathes here is contagious of making one accustomed to callousness."

Bougainville admired the courage of the natives, however, and he was a pragmatist. He knew that the French needed their skills, especially as trackers. "They see in the tracks the number that have passed, whether they are Indians or Europeans, if the tracks are fresh or old, if they are of healthy or of sick people, dragging feet or hurrying ones, marks of sticks used as supports. It is rarely that they are deceived or mistaken. They follow their prey for one hundred, two hundred, six hundred leagues with a constancy and a sureness which never loses courage or leads them astray."

Bougainville attended a council with the Nipissing, Algonkin, and Iroquois, at which each chief stood up and sang a war song. When Bougainville was implored to do the same, he adopted the listing cadence of the natives' music and repeated the phrase "Trample the English underfoot" until he was exhausted. The next night he was adopted by the Iroquois in a tribal ceremony and given the name Garionatsigoa, meaning "Great Angry Sky." "Behold me then," he wrote in his journal, "an Iroquois war chief!"

Bougainville saw the alliance with the natives as a necessary evil. There were dozens of native nations, and they were frustratingly decentralized.

LOUIS ANTOINE DE BOUGAINVILLE ◆ "The entire English army advanced to attack me. I retreated before them and posted myself so as to cover the retreat of our army, to join with it, or to march again against the enemy if it was judged proper.

"The Marquis de Montcalm died the next day of his wounds. He had conducted a campaign worthy of M. de Turenne, and his death caused our misfortunes. It was believed necessary to abandon the Beauport camp all standing and to withdraw behind Jacques Cartier River, eleven leagues from Quebec, which the enemy at once besieged.

"I took it upon myself (and the Marquis de Vaudreuil approved) to remain with my corps at Cap Rouge and Lorette. There I reassembled the remnants of our army and got provisions into Quebec.

"On the eighteenth I marched with six hundred men to throw myself into [Quebec], and the Chevalier de Lévis, arrived the evening before from Montreal, advanced the army to get within range of attacking the English. I was only three-quarters of a league from Quebec when I learned that the city had surrendered. It had been bombarded for sixty-eight days. I was forced to retrace my steps, for the English army moved to march against me.

"Such was the end of what up to this moment was the finest campaign in the world. We spent three months in bivouac. Just the same, the English hold only the walls and the King holds the colony." The last entry from *The American Journals of Louis Antoine de Bougainville, 1756-1760 (Granger Collection)*

Decisions to wage war involved lengthy and, to the French mind, unnecessary meetings and consultations. To include the natives among their forces also presented logistical problems. Crops had failed and food was scarce; feeding several thousand more men was a burden, and Bougainville marvelled at the natives' extraordinary appetites. Occasionally, the natives killed French settlers as well. Bougainville feared that the Europeans would lose something of themselves in their association with the natives' "savagery." "This country is dangerous for discipline," he wrote. "Pray God that it alone suffers from it."

A shared European sensibility occasionally united the British and French against the natives. When the British surrendered Fort William Henry in 1757 to Montcalm, the natives felt they deserved the spoils of war. When they stripped the English soldiers and began to massacre them, the French leapt to their defence. "The Marquis de Montcalm rushed up at the noise," Bougainville wrote, ". . . several French officers risked their lives in tearing the English from the hands of the Indians. . . . Finally the disorder quieted down and the Marquis de Montcalm at once took away from the Indians four hundred of these unfortunate men and had them clothed. The French officers divided with the English officers the few spare clothes they had." Vaudreuil managed to ransom some of the prisoners the natives had taken away, though some had been killed and one eaten.

The British felt that this debacle violated the rules of war and held the French responsible. They refused to honour the terms of surrender that they had agreed to. The European style of war and its quaint protocol was beginning to unravel.

LOUISBOURG IN 1764 ◆ After the British took Louisbourg, they destroyed it with particular zeal. "The King is come to a Resolution that the said Fortress, together with all the works, and Defences of the Harbour, be most effectually and most entirely demolished; And I am in consequence thereof, to signify to you His Majesty's Pleasure, that you do as expeditiously as the Season will permit, take the most timely and effectual Care, that all the Fortifications of the town of Louisbourg, together with all the Works, and Defences whatever, belonging either to the said Place, or to the Port, and Harbour, thereof, be forthwith totally demolished, and razed, and all the Materials so thoroughly destroyed, as that no use may, hereafter, be ever made of the same." Letter from William Pitt to Major General Jeffery Amherst (*National Archives of Canada*, C-5907)

The decisive military victories were welcome news in France, but the colony was suffering. It was a time of famine, horsemeat, recurring smallpox, savage battle, and uneasy alliances. At Quebec, the citizens saw their meagre rations reduced to two ounces of bread per day in April 1757. A month later there was no bread at all. "The distress is so great that some of the inhabitants are reduced to living on grass," Bougainville wrote. There was a feeling of abject despair in the colony. The next year, the French writer Voltaire gave voice to that sentiment in his novel *Candide*, wondering if it was worth fighting over a few acres of snow.

The British and their allies were proving to be no match for the French in the war in Europe, and Prime Minister William Pitt supported the radical proposal of concentrating Britain's resources in North America. If they could not beat the French in Europe, perhaps a decisive blow could be struck in Canada.

The first step was to capture Louisbourg, the French fortress that guarded the entrance to the St. Lawrence River. It sat on Ile Royale, in a fortified town that had become a detested symbol for the British. It was the centre of the French fishing industry, a key military site, and a training base for the French navy. French privateers used Louisbourg as a base for

Sir Jeffery Amherst was given the
novel rank of major general in
America, in command of the force
sent out to take Louisbourg.
Though Amherst was forty at the
time, he was only a junior officer
and had never commanded troops
in action. King George II wasn't
convinced he was the man for
the job. The Duke of Newcastle,
who was prime minister, appealed
to the king's mistress, Lady
Yarmouth, to lobby on Amherst's
behalf. The king agreed, and
Amherst left in March, 1758.
(*National Gallery of Canada, 8004*)

their plunder of New England's ships, and in 1744 they captured a New England fishing outpost at Canso, Nova Scotia. A year later, fed up with these attacks, a New England force attacked Louisbourg. It was a motley collection of ships and citizens aided by a British naval force from the West Indies. After a seven-week siege, the fortress was surrendered and its people deported to France. But in the peace treaty of 1748, Louisbourg was restored to the French.

A potent symbol of the French empire, it was now defended by a garrison of 2,400 men, 400 militia, and 10 warships. In 1758, the British sent a massive force – 39 ships, more than 12,000 troops, and almost 2,000 mounted guns – to attack the fortress.

The siege began with European decorum, as the British commander, General Jeffery Amherst, sent two pineapples to Marie-Anne Drucour, wife of the French governor, Augustin de Drucour. In return, the governor sent Amherst several bottles of champagne. After this gesture of politesse, the bombardment began, and the British gunboats rained hundreds of shells into the town. "All the women and a great number of little children came out, running to and fro, not knowing where to go in the midst of bombs and balls falling on every side," Drucour reported. "It seems the British intention is not just to breach the walls but rather to kill everyone and burn the town." The hospital was destroyed and food supplies were low. Marie-Anne Drucour fired three cannons each day herself as an inspiration to the gunners and earned the name "La Bombardière."

Governor Drucour knew Louisbourg could not hold against the British attack. His plan was simply to delay the British ships. If he kept them engaged until midsummer they would not have time to continue up the St. Lawrence and attack Quebec before winter set in. By late July, the siege had lasted for almost two months. The town was strewn with rubble, the batteries almost ruined. Only five cannons were still able to fire, and the walls had crumbled to such an extent that the enemy, if they managed to land on the rocky coast, would be able to walk right in. The dead piled up like cordwood.

Near the end of July, Drucour felt that he had held out long enough to delay the British, and on July 26 he wrote to General Amherst, offering to discuss terms of surrender. Amherst's chilly reply arrived quickly: "We give your excellency an hour to determine on the only capitulation we are willing to grant, which is, you surrender yourselves prisoners of war." Drucour accepted the terms and surrendered. He was despised by the people for holding out for so long, and scorned by the soldiers for giving up. The evening before, priests had spent the entire night performing hurried marriage ceremonies for every girl in Louisbourg, worried that they might otherwise fall into the heretical, Protestant arms of the conquering British. It was the first substantial British victory in three years of fighting.

The people of Louisbourg were deported, and in France, Drucour was disgraced for relinquishing the fortress. He died four years later in poverty. Marie-Anne, "La Bombardière," died two months afterwards.

On William Pitt's orders, Louisbourg was to be "totally demolished, and razed, and all the materials so thoroughly destroyed, as that no use may, hereafter, be ever made of the same."

Among the British invaders was a thirty-one-year-old brigadier-general named James Wolfe. He had distinguished himself by gaining the first landing on Ile Royale, at Anse de la Cormorandière, a place so dangerous and rocky that the French had not seen any need to defend it. A British soldier described the landing: "One boat in which were twenty grenadiers and an officer was stove and every one drowned. The difficulty of landing at this place was such that they thought the devil himself would not have attempted it." Wolfe got his first taste of glory and the beginning of a reputation for recklessness.

He had already been in the military for seventeen years, the veteran of battles in Scotland and Belgium. His father was a lieutenant-general; his mother was controlling, melancholy, and self-absorbed. Wolfe was an unlikely warrior, a thin, homely, humourless, and excitable man who suffered from rheumatism and bladder infections. Socially, he was awkward, and so he had spent time in France trying to refine his manners, learning the language, conversing stiffly with local coquettes. Amid the opulent sweep of Versailles he had been presented to the king and queen. Wolfe lacked the skills for seduction but shunned prostitutes – a reluctant celibate who was convinced he would die young.

Wolfe believed that there was still time to sail up the St. Lawrence River and take Quebec that year, but Amherst and the rest of the command did not agree. The day after the surrender of Louisbourg, Wolfe wrote his mother, "I hope to be with you by Christmas; though I protest to you that I had much rather besiege a place than pass four weeks at sea." Among his other ailments, Wolfe suffered horribly from seasickness, and ocean voyages always left him thinner and paler.

Upon hearing of Wolfe's feat at Louisbourg, William Pitt decided that he was the man to lead the assault on Quebec. He sent word for Wolfe to remain in Canada, but it arrived too late; he had already started back, and he spent the winter in London.

Wolfe was both ambitious and insecure, and he fretted over the immensity of his new task. "I am to act a greater part in this business than I wished or desired," he wrote to his uncle, Major Walter Wolfe. "The backwardness of some of the older officers has in some measure forced the Government to come down so low. I shall do my best, and leave the rest to fortune, as perforce we must when there are not the most commanding abilities."

Others shared Wolfe's doubts. Even William Pitt, who had appointed him, was worried. During dinner at Pitt's home one evening, Wolfe left the table, retrieved his sword, and pantomimed the slashing of imaginary enemies. Pitt observed this unhinged theatre and, after Wolfe had left, commented, "To think that I have committed the fate of my country and of my ministry into such hands." Wolfe had not had much wine that evening; he was not drunk, and several people suggested that he might be mad. When King George II heard of the dinner party incident, he was buoyed. "Mad is he?" said the king. "Then I hope he will bite some of my generals."

Despite his physical frailty and self-doubt, Wolfe had a zeal for war. His inherent fatalism was fuelled by the various afflictions that already tormented him at thirty-one. He was a dying man seeking a noble death, and he led his troops accordingly.

Wolfe knew something of the military situation in Canada, and the knowledge did not cheer him. "[General James] Abercromby is a heavy man & Brig Provost the most detestable Dog on earth, by everybody's account," he wrote. "These two Principal Officers hate one another; now to serve in an army so circumstanced is no very pleasing business."

The unpleasantness of the military situation was matched by the climate. In a letter to his mother he wrote, "The Early Season in this Country, I mean the months of April & May, are intolerably cold & disagreeable – June & July are foggy, August rainy – September has always a Tempest – October is generally a dry and fair month and the winter sets in early November." Barely one good month out of twelve.

He felt the people were no better: "These colonies are deeply tinged with the Vices & bad Qualities of their mother Country & indeed many parts of it are Peopled with those that the Law or necessity has forced upon it . . ."

What the country had, in Wolfe's opinion, was enormous potential. "They have all the materials ready, Nature has refused em nothing & there will grow a People out of our little spot (England) that will fill this vast space, & divide this great Portion of the globe with the Spaniards, who are possessed of the other half." Wolfe showed prescience in his prediction, though the pie would not be divided quite the way he envisioned.

Wolfe left London with of a quarter of the British navy, which was in the command of Admiral Charles Saunders. It was an extraordinary fleet: 29 ships of the line, each carrying up to 800 people; 22 frigates; 80 transport ships; and about 55 smaller craft. They were carrying 15,000 soldiers, 2,000 cannon, and 40,000 cannonballs, as well as surgeons, ministers, prostitutes, children, and livestock. The fleet stretched for 150 kilometres up the St. Lawrence River, a floating city with a population larger than Quebec's.

As they cruised up the river, the small villages and farms on the banks nervously made preparations. "We have settlements now on each side of us," wrote John Knox, an Irish lieutenant on board HMS *Success*. Knox kept a journal that became the most accurate British account of the war. "The land uncommonly high above the level of the river; and we see large signal fires every where before us. . . . The country-people, on the south shore, are removing their effects in carts, and conducting them, under escorts of armed men, to a greater distance."

Wolfe had come to fight the French, not the Canadiens. Hoping to discourage the habitants from joining the fighting, he wrote a manifesto in French and had it nailed to the door of a church in Beaumont. "The formidable sea and land armament which the people of Canada now behold in the heart of their country," he wrote, "is intended by the King, my master, to check the insolence of France, to revenge the insults offered to the British colonies, and totally to deprive the French of their most valuable settlement in North America." Wolfe said the king of England had no quarrel with the "industrious peasant" and expected he would take no part in what was essentially a European war. If the Canadiens joined the battle, Wolfe warned, they would be mercilessly crushed, their houses and crops destroyed. Wolfe's heavy-handed tactic only reinforced the Canadiens' resolve, and his men were continually plagued by farmboys and old men firing at them from the woods.

On June 27, 1759, Wolfe's fleet landed at Ile d'Orléans, downriver from Quebec. It was Wolfe's first opportunity to see the fortress – a discouraging sight. The cliffs were steep, the walls imposing, and the north shore was defended for at least ten kilometres downriver by several thousand troops. The plan that he had come with – to land at the flats at Beauport, below the city – would have to be abandoned. He would have to find another way of taking Quebec.

The shore was fortified in part because of intercepted intelligence. Bougainville, who had gone to France for the winter, had got hold of a letter written by General Amherst that outlined in detail Pitt's plan to take Quebec. They had hoped to land troops downriver and approach Quebec from the east. Now, Montcalm was one step ahead in what would become a tense chess match between two generals.

At midnight on June 28, while Wolfe was trying to come up with a new plan, Montcalm launched his own attack. Boats and rafts carrying gunpowder were chained together and sent with the current toward the anchored English fleet. Aboard each craft, a man awaited the signal to ignite his cargo before plunging into the river. But one of the boats exploded too soon and the others took it as the signal to ignite theirs. The element of surprise was lost.

"Nothing could be more formidable than these infernal engines on their first appearance," John Knox wrote. "They were certainly the grandest fireworks (if I may be allowed to call them that) that can possibly be conceived, every circumstance having contributed to their awful, yet beautiful appearance; the night was serene and calm, there was no light but what the stars produced, and this was eclipsed by the blaze of the floating fires . . . the profuse clouds of smoke with the firing of the cannon, the bursting of the grenades, and the crackling of the other combustibles; all of which reverberated thro' the air, and the adjacent woods . . . afforded a scene, I think, infinitely superior to any adequate description." The boats missed their mark and burned, gloriously but uselessly, until morning.

A second attempt at fireboats was tried and thwarted. Wolfe was angry at the tactic and wrote Montcalm a letter. "If you send any more fire-rafts,"

French Fireships Attacking the English Fleet at Quebec, 1759 (*Dominic Serres, Samuel Scott, National Archives of Canada, C-004291*)

he warned, "they shall be made fast to the two transports in which the Canadian prisoners are confined in order that they may perish by your own base invention."

Montcalm had an army of 15,000, but he knew he would need more troops. Before winter closed the St. Lawrence, he had sent a message to France, asking for 4,000 men. The answer arrived just before Wolfe and his fleet, on the ship that carried Bougainville. There were fresh provisions but a mere 400 troops. The French minister of the marine, concerned with the war on the home front, had said, "We can't worry about the stables when the house is on fire." Worse, many of the new troops were sick or dying from fever. The Quebec hospital could not hold all the ailing soldiers, and some were sent to the General Hospital outside the walls. Ten nuns died after contracting the fever. Instead of the reinforcements he needed, Montcalm got a medical crisis that strained the city's thin resources.

He also got desolate news from home: one of his daughters had died, though he would never find out which one. In his last letter to his wife, he wrote, "I would renounce every honour to join you again; but the King must be obeyed. The moment when I see you once more will be the brightest of my life. Adieu, my heart! I believe that I love you more than ever."

Wolfe, too, was forlorn. Against his mother's strenuous protests, he had become engaged to a woman named Katherine Lowther just before sailing to Canada. They had spent only a few weeks together. On parting, she had given him a locket containing her portrait in miniature, which he wore around his neck, and a copy of Thomas Gray's "Elegy Written in a Country Churchyard." He read regularly from it: "The boast of heraldry, the

MADAME DE POMPADOUR ◆ Louis XV's mistress was described as a woman "whom every man would have liked to have as his mistress and who was very tall for a woman, but not too tall. A round face, all the features regular, a superb complexion, very well made, a superb hand and arm, her eyes were rather pretty than large, but with a fire, a wit, a vicacity that I have never seen in any other woman. She was rounded in all her forms as in all her movements."

She was also an influential and effective adviser to the king, helping to broker deals with other European powers. She ruled his court and took an active interest in the Seven Years' War, having the paintings in her boudoir replaced with large maps. She kept track of French victories and defeats by marking their location with beauty spots from her vanity table. (*Boucher de Pompadour, Alte Pinokthek, Munich, Bridgeman Art Library,* BAL *8545*)

pomp of power, / And all that beauty, all that wealth e'er gave, / Awaits alike the inevitable hour: / The paths of glory lead but to the grave." It was a passage perfectly suited to Wolfe's ongoing presentiment that he would die young.

Montcalm hoped to survive, but he had been predicting military defeat for the French in Canada for months, writing to the minister of war that it was inevitable.

As they approached one of the great battles in history, neither general was fuelled by optimism.

The battle began with a lengthy siege of Quebec, a town that was already more than one hundred and fifty years old. It was a sophisticated urban centre, with grand architecture and a society that mirrored that of France – a colonial Versailles. The local aristocracy included Angélique-Geneviève Péan, the wife of Michel-Jean-Hugues Péan, adjutant at Quebec. "All the elegant people meet at his house," an observer noted, "and here life is carried on after the fashion of Paris."

The fashion of Paris was further mimicked when the twenty-five-year-old Angélique became the mistress of the forty-five-year-old intendant, François Bigot. With a pragmatic shrug, her husband simply accepted the situation and profited from her contacts. In France, King Louis XV's mistress, Madame de Pompadour, ruled through a combination of beauty, charm, and shrewdness. Angélique followed her example, proving to be an adept mediator and power-broker. She presided over grand dinners, clever entertainments, and nights of excessive gambling; it was a corrupt, profligate society that included Vaudreuil and, reluctantly, Montcalm, who was critical of it. Vaudreuil even set up a faro table at his house to accommodate the gamblers.

François Bigot's tenure in New France was corrupt, competent, and reluctant. He repeatedly and unsuccessfully applied for postings back in France. While he was stuck in Quebec, however, he made the best of it, amassing a personal fortune. He was paternalistic to the point of tyranny and stood accused of systematically starving the people of New France. But he brought order: the streets were paved and public shootings were curtailed. Bigot operated as the governors of most colonies acted, which was to their own advantage, on a governmental model borrowed from Paris. Beneath his wayward example there was a descending hierarchy of mistresses, relatives, friends, and toadies who benefited hugely from their lonely postings.

The excess of the administrators was at odds with the near starvation of the people. The citizens of New France were already fifth-generation Canadiens, and the divide between the Canadiens and the French was palpable and widening. Montcalm was acutely aware of these divisions within New France but was resigned to his role as protector. "I shall do everything to save this unhappy colony or die," he said. Bougainville wrote to his family of the resentment between the French and the Canadiens. "What a country, my dear brother, and what patience is needed to bear slights that

people go out of their way to lay on us here. It seems as though we belonged to a different nation, even a hostile one."

While the aristocracy gambled and the townspeople endured, the nuns struggled to establish a suitable moral climate. They battled the risqué fashions of France, which arrived every spring and occasionally undermined decency, and they served as nurses, educators, and social workers. They developed business skills and trades and brought the disparate citizens together under the authority of the Church. They would prove to be the city's most valuable resource during the long, destructive siege of Quebec.

It started at nine o'clock on the night of July 12, with a rocket briefly lighting the pale sky to signal the assault. Batteries of cannon and mortars kept up a steady barrage until morning, sending cannonballs into the streets and smashing walls. Firebombs made of iron baskets filled with pitch, tar, and powder were lobbed over the walls, spreading destruction. Mother Marie de la Visitation was head of the order of nuns that ran the General Hospital, and she described the desperate scene in a letter. "Let us now, dear Mothers, endeavor to give you some of the details of a war and captivity, which our sins have drawn upon us. . . . During one night, upwards of fifty of the best houses in the Lower Town were destroyed. The vaults containing merchandise and many precious articles, did not escape the effects of the artillery. During this dreadful conflagration, we could offer nothing but our tears and prayers at the foot of the altar at such moments as could be snatched from the necessary attention to the wounded."

A View of the Cathedral, Jesuits College, and Récollet Friars Church, taken from the Gate of the Governor's House, 1761 (*National Archives of Canada, C-361*)

A view of the inside of the
Jesuits' church, Quebec, 1761
(*Richard Short, National Archives
of Canada, C-351*)

On August 10, a shell ignited barrels of brandy in a wine cellar and the flames spread, burning down the church of Nôtre Dame des Victoires. The elegant sanctuary collapsed into a half-walled ruin. The roof of the Récollet Friars' church was pierced by cannonballs and its pews smashed into useless piles of lumber. The Jesuits' church and the nunnery suffered the same fate. More than half the town was in ruins.

"In addition to these misfortunes," Marie de la Visitation noted, "we had to contend with more than one enemy; famine, at all times inseparable from war, threatened to reduce us to the last extremity; upwards of six hundred persons in our building and vicinity, partaking of our small means of subsistence, supplied from the government stores, which were likely soon to be short of what was required for the troops. In the midst of this desolation, the Almighty, disposed to humble us, and to deprive us of our substance, which we had probably amassed contrary to his will, and with too great avidity, still mercifully preserved our lives, which were daily periled, from the present state of the country. Our enemy, informed of our destitute condition, was satisfied with battering our walls, despairing of vanquishing us, except by starvation."

Wolfe was not satisfied with just battering the town walls. He wrote to his mother of his frustration: "My antagonist has wisely shut himself up, in inaccessible entrenchments, so that I can't get at him, without spilling a torrent of blood, and that perhaps to little purpose. The Marquis de Montcalm is at the head of great number of bad soldiers & I am at the head of a small number of good ones, that wish for nothing so much as to fight him – but the wary old fellow avoids an action; doubtful of the behavior of his army."

Wolfe had to get his troops back to England before the ice made the St. Lawrence impassable. While waiting for starvation to draw his enemy out, he endured constant skirmishes with natives and Canadiens, which resulted in regular casualties. The French were being bombed into numbness and the British slowly bled. If Montcalm could simply endure, he would win this war of attrition.

Wolfe faced opposition even within his own camp. His three brigadiers were members of the aristocracy. James Murray, Robert Monckton, and George Townshend viewed their leader as a career officer of the middle class, and they questioned whether he had the will or imagination for the job. Townshend drew caricatures of Wolfe, whose misshapen form lent itself to the task. One of the unflattering sketches was passed around the mess tent, and was finally intercepted by Wolfe himself. He glanced at his twisted likeness and crumpled the paper. "If I live," he said, "this shall be inquired into; but we must beat the enemy first."

Townshend was not found out, but his discontent was obvious. "I never served so disagreeable a Campaign as this," he wrote. "Our unequal Force has reduced our Operations to a scene of Skirmishing, Cruelty & Devastation. It is War of the Worst Shape. A Scene I ought not to be in. . . . Genl Wolfe's health is but very bad. His generalship, in my poor opinion – is not a bit better, this only between us. He never consulted any of us till the latter end of August, so that we have nothing to answer for . . ."

Wolfe was infuriated by Montcalm's inaction, while at the same time the doubts of his officers and the unrelenting rebellions of his body were steadily wearing him down. He could not decide how to attack, and most of the summer was already gone. The brigadiers thought Wolfe should land upriver and initiate an attack at Pointe-aux-Trembles or Deschambault. Wolfe waffled. At one point he ordered three different actions in the course of five hours, cancelling each as soon as he had ordered it.

Without consulting his officers, he ordered an invasion downriver at Beauport, where Montcalm's army was entrenched. Four thousand men landed onshore and moved up the heavily fortified hill. They were picked off at will, unable even to return fire. Four hundred and forty English were killed or wounded compared to seventy French. The injured British were taken to the General Hospital, under the care of Marie de la Visitation. The Marquis de Vaudreuil observed the French victory from the heights and announced that Quebec was safe.

"When the French are in a scrape," Wolfe wrote, "they are ready to cry out in behalf of the human species; when fortune favours them, none more bloody, more inhuman. Montcalm has changed the very nature of war, and forced us, in some measure, to a deterring and dreadful vengeance."

General George Townshend
(*after Gilbert Stuart,
Royal Ontario Museum*)

James Wolfe. "The weather has been extremely unfavourable for a day or two, so that we have been inactive. I am so far recovered as to do business, but my constitution is entirely ruined, without the consolation of having done any considerable service to the State, or without any prospect of it." September 9, 1759, Wolfe's last letter to England, addressed to Lord Holdernesse (*J.S.C. Schaak, National Portrait Gallery*)

Wolfe, who had fought in Scotland at Culloden, a bloody and barbarous battle in which the wounded were slaughtered as they lay, was being disingenuous. He had come to Quebec prepared to destroy civilians if necessary. In a March 6 letter to Jeffery Amherst, written on the voyage over, Wolfe had written, "If, by accident in the River, by the Enemy's resistance, by sickness, or slaughter in the Army, or, from any other cause, we find that Quebec is not likely to fall into our hands, I propose to set the Town on fire with shells, to destroy the harvest, houses, cattle . . . to leave famine and desolation behind me."

After his stunning defeat at Beauport, Wolfe gave the order to burn the Canadian countryside from Kamouraska to Point Levy. Twenty-three villages and 1,400 farmhouses were torched. It was a task that sickened some of his men. Lieutenant Malcolm Fraser of the 78th Highlanders described one scene: "There were several of the enemy killed and wounded, and a few prisoners taken, all of whom the barbarous Captain Montgomery, who commanded us, ordered to be butchered in a most inhuman and cruel manner; particularly two I sent prisoner by a sergeant after giving them quarter."

The butchery was interspersed with odd moments of European decorum. When prisoners were taken from Pointe-aux-Trembles, Wolfe invited some of the nobler women to dine with him in his tent. They chatted happily in French, reminiscing about Paris and joking about Montcalm's reluctance to venture outside the walls.

By August 19, Wolfe was feverish, bedridden, and paralyzed with indecision. He had just learned of his father's death, and in his last letter to his mother he wrote that he planned to quit the service at the first opportunity. There were four weeks left before he would be forced to take the world's most potent naval force home to winter in England, to become a national symbol of impotence. His reputation would then be irredeemable.

Montcalm was also weary and disheartened. Earlier, he had written the minister of war requesting that he be recalled to France. His health and finances had been destroyed by this violent landscape, he said. His pay was overdrawn by 30,000 livres. He missed his wife and despaired at the contradictions and unpalatable alliances that his job required. In a letter to the Chevalier de Lévis, his second-in-command, he asked, "When the devil will this play in Canada and our part in it be over?"

As hints of autumn appeared, Wolfe was fading. "I found myself so ill, and am still so weak," he wrote, "that I begged the general officers to consult together for the general utility. *They are all of the opinion* . . . to draw the enemy from their present situation, and bring them to an action. *I have acquiesced in* their proposal, and we are preparing to put it into execution."

Wolfe's three brigadiers planned an invasion fifty kilometres upriver, between Pointe-aux-Trembles and St. Augustin. On September 9, five thousand men were in landing boats ready to attack. But they were delayed by rain.

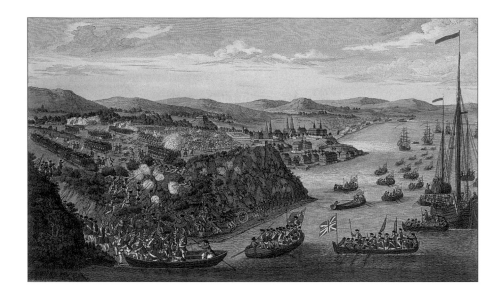

The View of the Taking of Quebec (*National Archives of Canada*, C-001078)

The next day, Wolfe wandered upriver, surveying the imposing north shore, wondering how to seduce it. An idea came to him, one that had the suicidal earmarks of his landing at Anse de la Cormorandière, or the order to charge the hill at Beauport. To the dismay of his officers, he cancelled the existing plan and, shortly before midnight on September 12, he landed between four and five hundred men upriver at Anse au Foulon, a site that offered no plausible route to the fortress. They spent six hours climbing a narrow goat path up the fifty-metre cliff, then overpowered the French sentries at the top.

At 5:00 a.m. Wolfe stood on the Plains of Abraham, an abandoned farmer's cornfield, overgrown and dotted with clutches of bushes. Though Quebec was only a few kilometres distant, a small hill, Buttes-à-Neveu, obscured the view from the city. The top of the hill was within cannon range of Quebec, so Wolfe reluctantly placed his men at the bottom. There were not enough troops for the customary triple line, allowing for the delicate choreography of shooting, kneeling, and loading that the British favoured. Instead he set up two lines and had each man load two musketballs, to maximize their firepower. A light rain misted the fields.

Montcalm was at Beauport with the bulk of his troops, anticipating another mule-headed British assault on the hill. He knew as well as Wolfe that time was running out; a desperate assault would have to be risked or the British fleet would limp home in ignominy. Montcalm's men had been up all night guarding Beauport, and as Wolfe's men were assembling on the Plains, the French soldiers were going to sleep.

The British were soon spotted and word reached a disbelieving Montcalm, who ordered his army awake and quick-marched them to Quebec, an hour away. Bougainville was a three-hour march away, with his three thousand troops stationed to defend against a landing farther upriver. When he got the message of the English landing, he marshalled his army and marched east.

On the Plains, Wolfe's men assembled into an incongruous regimental mosaic. The 78th Regiment, known as the Fraser Highlanders, had the plaids, broadswords, and pipers that had been at Culloden, where some of them had fought for Charles Edward Stuart, known as Bonnie Prince Charlie. Now they were being commanded by a man who had fought against them with the forces of England's Hanoverian monarchy in that historic disaster. Wolfe had suggested recruiting the Highlanders as mercenaries, noting their ferocity and fearlessness – they had the reputation of being one of the toughest units in the British army. And, he commented, it would be "no great mischief" if they were killed. Sergeant James Thompson, Simon Fraser, Alexander Fraser – these were the names of men from Highland Catholic families whose homes had been destroyed by the English. Now they were in their employ, doing what they knew best – fighting – this time against other Catholics.

Closest to the cliffs was the 35th Regiment, made up mostly of displaced Irish farmers and unemployed labourers, including Michael Clinton, John Darby, Abel Skittle. Beside them was the 43rd, commanded by John Knox and made up of unemployed English boys from the Midlands – James Rutherford, Robert Acton, Edward Stone.

Advancing toward this awkward alliance were French soldiers who had been on half rations for months and awake for thirty-six hours. For the most part landless and unemployed, they threw themselves into battle sporting romantic *noms de guerre*: François Mouet, twenty-four, *Sansquartier* ("Gives no Quarter"); Antoine Mouret, twenty-one, *LaDouceur* ("Sweetness"); Barthélemy Girave, twenty-seven, *Prestaboire* ("Likes a Drink"). Like the army they were facing, few of them had heard of Quebec until they had been shipped there.

The French army was joined by Canadien militia – the Bouchers, Repentignys, Courtemanches, d'Argenteuils – defending one hundred and fifty years of history, land, and family.

The French also had their native allies, Iroquoian and Algonkin warriors who were ferocious in battle but flexible as to the outcome between these two warring European tribes. The Algonkin had changed sides before, scornful of the vanquished.

Montcalm marched his men to the crest of Buttes-à-Neveu where they formed a line. The rain had stopped and it was pleasantly warm. Montcalm was worried that the British army facing him was part of a two-pronged attack, that there was another, larger invasion planned for Beauport. He felt he had to deal quickly with this threat, then return to Beauport.

The battle began with random sniper fire coming from the cornfields and the woods. At 8:00 a.m., the British artillery began firing. "We had two pieces of short brass six pounders playing on the enemy," John Knox wrote, "which threw them into some confusion, and obliged them to alter their disposition, and Montcalm formed them into three large columns; about nine the two armies moved a little nearer each other."

Montcalm rode the length of his line, shouting the question, "Are you tired?" The game, untruthful response was a resounding "No!" At 10:00 the French shouted "*Vive le Roy!*" and the battle formally began.

"The enemy began to advance in three columns," Knox wrote, "with loud shouts – two of them inclined to the left of our army, and the third to our right, firing obliquely at the two extremities of our line."

The French line, made up Canadiens and French troops who had not trained together, was moving in a disordered fashion. Maurès de Malartic, a French officer, observed the problem: "We had not got twenty paces when the left was too far in the rear and the centre too far in front. . . . The Canadiens who formed the second rank and the soldiers of the third fired without orders and, according to custom, then threw themselves on the ground to reload. This false movement broke all the battalions." They had fired too soon, and their volleys were ineffectual and disruptive.

The ragged French line stopped forty metres away from the British and fired again. Redcoats slumped as the crude balls ploughed through flesh and shattered bone. Before he gave the order to fire, Wolfe was spotted in his new uniform by a sniper and shot through the wrist. The wound was dressed with a borrowed handkerchief and at 10:15 Wolfe raised his cane, giving the order to fire: the last military order of his life.

Sections of the French line collapsed as the massive volley ripped through them. The Highland yell was taken up, the piper played "Lovat's March," and the Fraser Highlanders charged with their broadswords, hacking through the retreating French army. A full British bayonet advance followed in their awful wake.

Wolfe was shot in the groin and had to be helped forward. A third shot, into his chest, was fatal and he slumped to the ground, happily receiving the whispered news that the enemy was in retreat.

On the other side of the line, Montcalm received a mortal wound below his ribs just as he was about to enter the Saint-Louis gate. He was carried by his men to the General Hospital.

The Scottish Highlanders pursued the retreating army to the woods. "I can remember the Scotch Highlanders flying wildly after us," Joseph Trahan, an Acadian soldier, later wrote in his journal, "with streaming plaids, bonnets and large swords – like so many infuriated demons – over the brow of the hill. In their course, was a wood, in which we had some Indians and sharpshooters, who bowled over the *Sauvages d'Ecosse* in fine style. Their partly naked bodies fell on their face, and their kilts in disorder left a large portion of their thighs, at which our fugitives on passing by, would make lunges with their swords, cutting large slices out of the fleshiest portion of their persons."

The bloodied Highlanders waited until the British troops caught up and resumed pursuit, but they were fired on from sharpshooters stationed on the ramparts of Quebec and cannon barges on the St. Charles River. "It was at this time," wrote Malcolm Fraser of the Highlanders, "and while in

THE DEATH OF WOLFE ◆ Benjamin West was an American artist from Pennsylvania and his famous painting was done in 1770, eleven years after Wolfe's death. "Wolfe must not die like a common soldier under a bush," West wrote. "To move the mind there should be a spectacle presented to raise and warm the mind and all should be proportion'd to the highest idea conceiv'd of the Hero. A mere matter of fact will never produce the effect." West ignored the facts and framed his subject with a dramatic sky, fabulous light, and a large supporting cast. The most jarring fiction is the native man sitting in the contemplative pose to the left of Wolfe. For one thing, the natives fought alongside the French, not the English. But the Mohawk embodies the popular European idea of the noble savage, an idea that wasn't embraced by Wolfe himself.

The Death of General Wolfe was a huge hit and gave the public the exalted death they craved. When it was unveiled at the Royal Academy, there was a long line-up. The elite jumped the queue, among them William Pitt, Horace Walpole, Lord Grosvenor, and King George III. West quickly produced five copies for various well-paying patrons, including the king. While this was among the least accurate of the many renditions of Wolfe's death, it was the most dramatic, and the most popular, and it emerged as the definitive version. (*Benjamin West, National Gallery of Canada*)

the bushes that our Regiment suffered most. . . . Captain Thomas Ross was mortally wounded in the body by a cannonball from the hulks, in the mouth of the River, of which he died in great torment. . . . I received a contusion in the right shoulder, or rather breast . . . which pained me a good deal. . . . We suffered in men and officers more than any three regiments in the field."

Joseph Trahan ran toward the city walls. "I was amongst the fugitives and received in the calf of the leg a spent bullet, which stretched me on the ground. I thought it was all over for me; but presently I rose up and continued to run towards the general hospital, in order to gain the Beauport Camp over the bridge of boats."

The Death of Montcalm. Montcalm, like Wolfe, inspired a number of heroic paintings. The most bizarre version shows Montcalm dying on the battlefield, flanked by a palm tree and South American-looking natives. In the background, Wolfe can be seen, dying less heroically. (*National Archives of Canada*)

He was able to make Quebec, one of the lucky ones, but it was a woeful place. "On my way to the Beauport camp, I came to a bake-house, in which the baker that day had baked an ovenful of bread. Some of the exhausted fugitives asked him for food, which he refused, when in a fit of rage at such heartlessness, one of them lopped off his head with his sword. The bloody head was then deposited on top of the pile of bread. Hunger getting the better of me, I helped myself to a loaf all spread with gore, and with my pocket knife removing the crust, I greedily devoured the crumb."

The wounded were hauled to the hospital. "We witnessed the carnage from our windows," Marie de la Visitation wrote. "It was in such a scene that charity triumphed, and caused us to forget self-preservation and the danger we were exposed to, in the immediate presence of our enemy. We were in the midst of the dead and dying, who were brought to us by the hundreds, many of them our close connexions; it was necessary to smother our grief and exert ourselves to relieve them . . ."

The French retreat was covered by the Canadien snipers in the woods. They put up a fierce resistance before many of them were driven off the cliff.

Shortly after 11:00, Bougainville arrived with his troops, but the battle was over. On the field were sixty-seven British dead, almost six hundred wounded. Two hundred and twenty French were dead and more than four hundred wounded. Had Montcalm waited for Bougainville, the French could have won the battle. Had he simply declined to engage Wolfe at all, he could have won the day.

Both the English and French dead were stripped of their equipment and uniforms and their naked bodies pushed into common, unmarked graves on the Plains.

Wolfe achieved his noble death. The cannon of the fleet fired a salute to him, and his body was put in a barrel of rum to preserve it on the voyage back to England. In London, his coffin was carried through streets filled with silent mourners, and he was buried beside his father at Greenwich.

Montcalm died of his wounds at the General Hospital, glad, he said, not to have seen the fall of Quebec. There were no coffins left, so his body was put into a makeshift box and buried in a crater made by a British cannonball that had landed in the Ursuline nuns' chapel.

On September 18, 1759, the British flag was raised near the top of Mountain Street in Quebec. They had taken the city, but it was a desolate prize. Benoît-François Bernier, the former commissioner of war in Quebec, now a prisoner, observed, "Quebec is nothing but a shapeless mass of ruins. Confusion, disorder, pillage reign even among the inhabitants. . . . Each searches for his possessions, and not finding his own, seizes those of other people. English and French, all is chaos alike."

The British fleet returned to England, leaving a small garrison to hold the city. General James Murray had taken over from Wolfe. Those who remained were faced with a familiar problem: the failure of the crops and encroaching famine. As winter threatened, British soldiers worked uncomfortably alongside the Canadiens, collecting a desperate harvest of rotting crops and roots.

The British military looked more like medieval peasants than a triumphant force, their European uniforms inadequate to the December cold. "Our guards, on the grande parade, make a most grotesque appearance in their different dresses," John Knox wrote, "and our inventions to guard us against the extreme vigour of this climate are various beyond imagination: the uniformity, as well as the nicety, of the clean, methodical soldier, is buried in the rough fur-wrought garb of the frozen Laplander."

With famine came the familiar blight of scurvy, which killed far more British than the French army had. "The scurvy, occasioned by salt provisions and cold," noted Malcolm Fraser, "has begun to make fierce havock in the garrison, and it becomes every day more general. In short, I believe there is scarce a man of the army entirely free from it. . . . Numbers of sick and dead since September 18th, 1759: Sick: Two thousand, three hundred and twelve. Dead: Six hundred eighty-two." The skin of the dead turned black and their bodies bloated into obscene balloons. The ground was frozen and they were buried in snowbanks, waiting for spring.

Outside the walls of Quebec, there was another problem for the British. In Montreal, General François-Gaston de Lévis, the officer who had replaced Montcalm, planned to recapture Quebec. He still had an army of seven thousand and sent word to France to send four thousand more. Unlike Montcalm, Lévis embraced the guerrilla warfare tactics of the Canadiens. He trained them to fight in harmony with the French troops, to avoid the disastrous clashing of the two on the Plains. They began to attack in a series of sorties around Quebec.

"The English were not safe beyond the gates of Quebec," Marie de la Visitation wrote. "General Murray the commander of the place, on several occasions was near being made a prisoner; and would not have escaped if our

Quebec in ruins, 1759. The French thought that the British cannonballs would not be able to reach the Upper Town, but they were wrong. The bombardment left much of the Upper Town in flames. (*Richard Short, National Archives of Canada, C-350*)

people had been faithful. Prisoners were frequently made, which so irritated the Commander, that he sent out detachments to pillage and burn the habitations of the country people. . . . We heard of nothing but combats throughout the winter; the severity of the season had not the effect of making them lay down their arms."

Throughout the long winter, both sides were cut off from Europe. Lévis hoped that the four thousand reinforcements he had asked for would come. He marched to Quebec with his army of seven thousand, which included three thousand Canadiens, three hundred natives, and eighty-three black soldiers.

On the morning of April 28, 1760, he stood on the Plains of Abraham, where Wolfe had stood seven months earlier. James Murray took his troops to Buttes-à-Neveu, where Montcalm had been. They were about to replay the battle of the Plains of Abraham, changing positions. "About eight-o'clock in the morning the whole garrison, exclusive of the guards, was drawn up on the parade," Malcolm Fraser wrote, "and about nine o'clock we marched out of Town with twenty pieces of Field Artillery. When we had marched a little way out of Town, we saw the advanced parties of the enemy nigh the woods about half a league distant from us. When we were about three quarters of a mile out of Town, the General ordered the whole to draw up in line of Battle, two deep, and take up as much room as possible."

Murray saw that the French lines had not fully formed, and he attacked, hoping to catch them in disarray. In doing so, and abandoning the high ground, he made the same mistake that Montcalm had made. The cannon sank in the spongy spring earth and the soldiers laboured in the muck. The two armies fired volleys into one another's lines for two hours until the British finally retreated. The French flag flew on the Plains of Abraham, though the Union Jack still flew over Quebec.

A View of the Orphans' or Urseline Nunnery, taken from the Ramparts, Quebec, Sept. 1, 1761 (*Richard Short, National Archives of Canada, C-000358*)

After the Battle of Sainte-Foy, as it was called, the armies waited to see whose navy would come up the St. Lawrence, to see who would be vindicated. After eleven days of suspense, a ship appeared. It did not have a flag, and it did not reveal its colours until it was in front of the ramparts; the British had won the transatlantic race. Pitt had sent twenty-two ships with reinforcements. France, after suffering defeats in Europe, had sent only five ships and four hundred men. "The gladness of the troops is not to be expressed," wrote John Knox. "Both Officers and soldiers mounted the parapets in the face of the enemy, and huzzaed, with their hats in the air, for almost an hour."

Lévis retreated to Montreal, and by May 9, three British armies commanded by General Amherst had converged on the city. Amherst denied Lévis the military honours of war, a fact that angered King Louis XV more than the capitulation itself when news finally arrived in France. In protest, Lévis and the French battalions burned their own colours. The traditional European style of war had given way to something else.

Vaudreuil, the maligned governor, managed to negotiate one adroit and critical concession in the Articles of Capitulation, a clause ensuring religious freedom: "The free exercise of the Catholic, Apostolic, and Roman Religion, shall subsist entire, in such manner that all the states and the people of the Towns and countries, places and distant posts, shall continue to assemble in the churches, and to frequent the sacraments as heretofore, without being molested in any manner, directly or indirectly." This was a dramatic concession, given that in Protestant England Catholics had no religious and severely restricted civil rights.

On September 8, 1760, half of the continent changed hands. George II now had sixty-five thousand new French-speaking Catholic subjects.

The Canadien militia returned to their villages and farms. Five hundred French soldiers who had married Canadien women were allowed to stay. A garrison of three thousand British troops remained in Quebec. The rest left, posted to the West Indies or Nova Scotia or the Ohio Valley. The colourful cast that had animated Quebec society quietly disintegrated. Angélique Péan sailed to France on the *Fanny*, in September 1760, accompanied by her husband, Michel-Jean-Hugues, and her lover, François Bigot.

In France, Michel was arrested and put in solitary confinement in the Bastille for his role in the mismanagement and loss of the colony, which was being called *l'affaire du Canada*. His sentence was reduced to a large fine, and he and Angélique moved to Orzain, where he died in 1782. Angélique dedicated the last twenty years of her life to helping the poor.

Bigot was also put in the Bastille, accused of corruption and mismanagement of the king's affairs. Though he was unquestionably corrupt, he was being judged by a corrupt judicial process: the government needed a scapegoat, and he was the best candidate. Bigot was found guilty and sentenced to death. But he, too, was given a reprieve; he was ordered to pay a fine, forfeit all his property, and live in exile. Bigot moved to Switzerland. Citing poor health, he asked for and received permission to return briefly to France, to take the waters. Instead he visited his old lover Angélique and his cuckolded friend. He died in exile in 1778.

Vaudreuil also left for France in 1760, and he too was arrested for his role in *l'affaire du Canada*. He was exonerated, but his wife died during the trial. Vaudreuil died in Paris in 1778.

Louis-Antoine de Bougainville fared the best of the French survivors. He was made a colonel and transferred to the navy. In 1766 he led a scientific voyage of exploration that landed in Tahiti. His descriptions of the natives there launched a debate in Europe about the superiority of "savages" over "civilized" people. A tropical flower was named in his honour. He distinguished himself militarily, scientifically, and as a judge, dying in Paris in 1811, where he was buried in the Pantheon.

The anonymous J.C.B. returned to France in 1761 and wrote his journal twenty years later. He intended it to be a travel book of sorts, though he was worried that it might be dated. So much had changed, he observed. The population had grown, there were new "places of settlement, the new routes of communication, the clearing of the ground, the felling of trees, and finally a soil which is more productive since the English took possession." Civilization was transforming the land.

John Knox returned to England, where his life became a series of mild misfortunes and bad timing that led to his retirement at half pay. He published his journal, the most complete and ambitious account of the battle for Quebec, but it sold only a handful of copies. The truth, unvarnished and presented at length, was unwelcome, and Knox died in obscurity in 1778.

Wolfe, on the other hand, became a virtual industry in death. Biographies, ballads, and epic poems piled up like newspapers. Paintings abounded,

Jean-Olivier Briand, Bishop of Quebec. Although Britain granted Quebec the right to practise the Catholic religion in the articles of capitulation in September 1760, it did not give permission for a new bishop to be anointed. Without a bishop, no new priests could be consecrated. The church was a legal entity, but destined to wither and die. Jean-Olivier Briand was the de facto bishop of Quebec and a shrewd politician. He worked for several years with British governor James Murray to persuade the king to allow Briand to be anointed by Rome. (*Archives nationales du Québec*)

William Pitt, First Earl of
Chatham. At the outbreak of
the Seven Years' War, William
Pitt boldly stated, "I am sure
I can save this country and
nobody else can." This turned
out to be the case. Under his
statesmanship, Britain further
expanded its empire. Pitt died
at the age of seventy, while his
son was reading Homer's *The
Iliad* to him. (*William Hoare,
The Carnegie Museum of Art*)

among them Benjamin West's lovely, incongruous portrait of Wolfe's death, attended by a kneeling, thoughtful native. There were more than a dozen versions of his dying words, from "Thank God, I die contented" to "Lay me down, I am suffocating." In death, his lofty ambitions were finally achieved.

In Europe, peace talks between England and France began in the spring of 1761. William Pitt was negotiating for the English. Plagued by gout for twenty-five years, he was imperious, sharp-tongued, and hated the French. The French negotiator was Etienne-François de Choiseul, a court gentleman who was offended by English arrogance in general and Pitt's arrogance in particular. Negotiations proceeded slowly.

Many British businessmen and politicians wanted to keep Guadeloupe, which British forces had also captured from France, and give Canada back to the French. Guadeloupe's sugar exports produced twice the revenue of Canada's fur exports, without the ongoing grief of governing sixty-five thousand Catholics.

Frustrated by the glacial pace of the negotiations, Choiseul finally jotted down a dozen lines on a piece of scrap paper. His suggested terms were: France would return Minorca and England would return Guadeloupe; the English would keep Canada but the French would retain fishing rights off the coast – the most valuable aspect of Canada, in his view. Pitt refused these terms and negotiations broke off. England then engaged in a weary war with Spain, though it had neither the money nor the appetite for more death.

Peace talks resumed in the summer of 1762 with both Pitt and Choiseul removed from the negotiating table. An agreement was reached on November 3, 1762, one that closely resembled Choiseul's hasty proposal. The French would give Canada to the English. In return they would receive fishing rights in the Gulf of St. Lawrence and deed to two islands – St. Pierre and Miquelon – on which to dry their fish.

The following year, the peace treaty was formally ratified in Paris and passed in the British parliament. Pitt's gout was inflamed and he crawled melodramatically to his seat in parliament to protest the terms. Choiseul, a pragmatist, felt that the Treaty of Paris was neither glorious nor profitable for the French, but the best they could hope for under the circumstances. He took limited joy in predicting to King Louis XV that the English would eventually be crippled by a revolution in the American colonies.

The territorial battles between the English and French had been resolved, but the natives had been excluded from the process. At Fort Michilimackinac, the Ojibwa Chief Minweweh spoke to English traders.

"Englishman, although you have conquered the French you have not yet conquered us! We are not your slaves. These lakes, these woods, and mountains were left us by our ancestors. They are our inheritance; and we will part with them to none. . . . Englishman, our Father, the king of France, employed our young men to make war upon your nation. In his warfare,

many of them have been killed; and it is our custom to retaliate, until such time as the spirits of the slain are satisfied. But, the spirits of the slain are to be satisfied in either of two ways; the first is the spilling of the blood of the nation by which they fell; the other, by covering the bodies of the dead, and thus allaying the resentment of their relations. This is done by making presents. Englishman, your king has not sent us any presents, nor entered into any treaty with us, therefore he and we are still at war."

The French defeat had disturbed a hundred and fifty years of alliances, and a new instability now loomed. For years the natives had tried to keep British and American settlers out of their traditional territories. But now the British occupied all the French forts in the interior, and new settlers were arriving in greater numbers. Part of the success of the French-native alliance lay in the fact that the French were traders and soldiers; they inhabited the land the way the natives did, lightly and seasonally. The English, on the other hand, were settlers, who marked the land into grids, clearing and cultivating it, moving west, disturbing the native hunting patterns.

Pontiac, the war chief of the Ottawa, was distressed by the changing face of the frontier, and he travelled among the native nations recounting a vision from the Master of Life: "This land where ye dwell I have made for you and not for others. Whence comes it that ye permit the Whites upon your lands. Can ye not live without them? . . . Drive them out, make war upon them. I do not love them at all; they know me not, and are my enemies,

Fireworks in Green Park to celebrate the signing of the Treaty of Paris in 1763 (*The Bridgeman Art Library, Private Collection*)

An East View of Montreal, Quebec, November 11, 1762 (*National Archives of Canada, C-2433*)

and the enemies of your brothers. Send them back to the lands I have created for them and let them stay there."

Pontiac made plans to capture the forts in the interior, which the British now held. Described as "proud, vindictive, warlike, and easily offended," Pontiac was a leader respected by all sides. On May 5, 1763, he addressed hundreds of Ottawa, Huron, and Potawatomi in the Grand Council.

"It is important for us, my brothers, that we exterminate from our lands this nation which seeks only to destroy us. You see as well as I that we can no longer supply our needs, as we have done, from our brothers, the French. The English sell us goods twice as dear as the French do and their goods do not last. When I go to the English commander and say to him that some of our comrades are dead, instead of bewailing their death, as our French brothers do, he laughs at me and at you. If I ask anything for our sick, he refuses with the reply that he has no use for us. From all this you can well see that they are seeking our ruin. Therefore, my brothers, we must all swear their destruction and wait no longer. Nothing prevents us; they are few in numbers, and we can accomplish it. All the nations who are our brothers attack them, – why should we not attack? Are we not men like them?"

A war plan was drawn up. Native forces captured Fort Pitt, Venango, and Fort de la Rivière au Boeuf. Pontiac's warriors arrived in sixty-five canoes at Fort Detroit, killed the settlers outside its walls, and laid siege to the fort. Ninety soldiers from Point Pelée were attacked outside its walls;

several were killed and forty-six were captured. Robert Navarre, a notary inside Fort Detroit, observed the gruesome scene.

"The savages disembarked their prisoners, one company after another, upon the strand and made them strip naked, and other Indians then discharged their arrows into all parts of their bodies. . . . The poor victims had to keep standing till they fell dead in their tracks and then those who had not engaged in the killing fell upon the dead bodies and hacked them to pieces, cooked them, and feasted upon them. Some they treated with different cruelty, slashing them alive with gun-flints, stabbing them with spears, cutting off their hands and feet and letting them bathe in their own blood and die in agony; others were bound to stakes and burned by children in a slow fire."

Pontiac was not able to bring the Canadiens to his side in a war with the English. He occasionally had to plunder their farms for food, which angered them. There was a problem in uniting the native nations, too. Some were being appeased by the English. As the siege of Detroit dragged on, members of Pontiac's own band drifted home for the hunting season. The native uprising appeared to be waning.

In October, Pontiac received word finally that the French had made peace with the English in Europe. He sent the commander of Fort Detroit a message. "My brother, the word that my father [the king of France] has sent to make peace I accept; all of my young men have buried their hatchets. I think that you will forget the bad things that have happened this past while. For my part I shall forget."

Pontiac did not forget, though. He continued to preach his message of war. It was the only hedge against assimilation, he argued. He astutely gauged the impact of the British settlers and felt it was better to take a stand while the natives still had the advantage in numbers. He seized on a divine message that had been delivered to the Abenaki: "I warn you that if you allow the English among you, you are dead, maladies, smallpox and their poison will destroy you totally . . ."

This turned out to be sadly prophetic. General Jeffery Amherst was suggesting a chillingly modern plan: biological warfare. They would send smallpox rather than soldiers to fight the natives. "I will try to inoculate the Indians by means of Blankets that may fall in their hands," Colonel Henry Bouquet wrote to Amherst, "taking care however not to get the disease myself. It is a pity to oppose Good men against them. I wish we could make use of the Spaniard's methods and hunt them with English Dogs."

An infected blanket was cut into small pieces that were placed in small tin boxes. They were given to a delegation of Ottawa natives at Fort Pitt who were told the boxes contained medicine and they should not open them until they were home.

In 1765 Pontiac finally signed a preliminary peace agreement. Pontiac stipulated that peace did not imply English ownership of the land. They had merely defeated the French, who were tenants, not owners, he argued. A final treaty was signed in 1766.

Pontiac taking up the war hatchet in 1763 (*Granger Collection, 4E233.12*)

The native uprising was over, and the war parties returned to their tribal lands, some of them carrying tin boxes. Andrew Blackbird, the adopted son of an Ottawa chief, wrote down the oral account of what happened when they were opened.

"Accordingly, after they reached home they opened the box; but behold there was another tin box inside, smaller. They took it out and opened the second box, and behold, still there was another box inside the second box, smaller yet. So they kept on this way till they came to a very small box, which was not more than an inch long; and when they opened the last one they found nothing but mouldy particles in this last box. . . . Pretty soon burst out a terrible sickness among them. The great Indian doctors themselves were taken sick and died. The tradition says that it was indeed awful and terrible. Everyone taken with it was sure to die. Lodge after lodge was totally vacated – nothing but the dead bodies lying here and there in their lodges. The whole coast of Arbor Croche . . . which is said to have been a continuous village some fifteen or sixteen miles long . . . was entirely depopulated and laid waste."

On April 20, 1769, Pontiac was assassinated by a Peoria native who resented the chief's new message of peace. He was buried by the French near St. Louis, Missouri, a revolutionary and visionary whose understanding of cultural politics would prove accurate.

In order to stabilize their hard-won, ill-defined territory, to ease the pressure caused by settlers moving west, London issued a royal proclamation declaring the interior of the continent to be native land: "We do hereby strictly forbid, on Pain of our Displeasure, all our loving Subjects from making any Purchases or Settlements whatever, or taking any possession of any of the lands above reserved, without our especial leave and License . . ." The carefully worded proclamation led to a temporary peace.

General James Murray, a survivor of Louisbourg, the Plains of Abraham, and the Battle of Sainte-Foy, was appointed governor over the territory. It was his job to forge a society out of the fractious citizenry and years of bloodshed. He oversaw sixty-five thousand French-speaking Catholics, whom he liked, and a handful of recently arrived English-speaking Protestant merchants, whom he detested. "All have their fortunes to make and I hear few of them are solicitous about the means where the end can be obtained," he wrote to a friend, "in general, the most immoral collection of men I ever knew." In addition to the merchants and French Canadians there was a small garrison of British soldiers and a few hundred disbanded soldiers who had elected to stay.

They made for an uncomfortable society. The merchants, led by Thomas Walker, an Englishman who had come to Montreal from Boston, demanded an elected legislative assembly, which, like the English model, would not allow Catholics to vote. He also wanted French Catholics to be prohibited from sitting on juries. Murray disagreed. "As there are but 200

SIR GUY CARLETON ◆ Guy Carleton was an Irish officer who fell into disfavour with George II, insulting his Hanoverian background by disparaging the military qualities of German mercenaries. William Pitt championed Carleton, though, and he went with Wolfe to Quebec in 1759 as quartermaster general. On the Plains of Abraham, Carleton commanded the 2nd Battalion of the Royal Americans and was wounded in the head. In 1766, he became acting governor of Quebec, and advocated that the English government retain elements of the French legal system rather than impose its own entirely.

"This System of Laws established Subordination, from the first to the lowest, which preserved the internal harmony they enjoyed until our Arrival, and secured Obedience to the Supreme Seat of Government from a very distant Province. All this Arrangement, in one Hour, We overturned, by the Ordinance of the Seventeenth of September One Thousand seven hundred and sixty four, and Laws, ill adapted to the Genius of Canadians, to the Situation of the Province, and to the Interests of Great Britain, unknown, and unpublished were introduced in their Stead; A Sort of Severity, if I remember right, never before practiced by any Conqueror, even where the People, without Capitulation, submitted to His Will and Discretion." Carleton to Lord Shelburne, December 24, 1767 (*National Archives of Canada, C-002833*)

Protestant subjects in the Province," he argued, "the greatest part of which are disbanded soldiers of little Property and mean Capacity, it is thought unjust to exclude the new Roman Catholic subjects to sit upon Juries, as such exclusion would constitute the said 200 Protestants perpetual Judges of the Lives and Property of not only 80,000 of the new Subjects, but likewise the Military of the Province . . ."

The fight over religious and constitutional rights was ongoing, but the first battle, surprisingly, was between the English merchants and the English military. Soon after arriving in Montreal, the merchant Thomas Walker was sued by his clerk and appeared in military court, where the clerk won his case. Walker was loudly contemptuous of the process, a contempt that blossomed when he lost on appeal. He accused the military court of being arbitrary and malicious. On August 10, 1764, a civil government was established, and Walker became one of the first civilian magistrates. From the bench he pursued his argument with the military in an arbitrary and malicious way.

The bitter relationship between merchants and military quickly descended into violence. On December 6, six men, armed and disguised, broke into Walker's home, beat him until he was "black as a hat," and cut off his ear. The trial to identify and prosecute his assailants was protracted and ended finally in acquittal for the defendants (though it was thought by many that they were in fact guilty). Walker accused a second man, John Disney, who was clearly innocent, and the local British population began to tire of Walker's determined spite. Disney was acquitted as well.

Walker left for London to argue his larger case: that there should be an elected, English-only assembly, no French juries, and that Murray should be recalled as governor. London disagreed. A declaration was issued stating that

The Boston Massacre. On March 5, 1770, British soliders, after being taunted by civilians, fired into a crowd in front of the Custom House, killing five men. Several soldiers and their commander were tried for murder but acquitted, prompting outrage throughout the Thirteen Colonies. (*Granger Collection*)

all citizens of Quebec had the right to sit on juries. Instead of having an assembly dominated by the English minority, there would be no assembly at all. But Walker did succeed in casting enough doubt on Murray to have him recalled.

His replacement was Guy Carleton, a forty-two-year-old brigadier-general who had been wounded on the Plains of Abraham. Carleton shared Murray's sensibilities; in order to be viable, he said, Quebec had to be accepted as a French colony. Carleton argued that the imposition of English law on a French and Catholic colony was barbaric and benefited no one. He nominated twelve Canadian seigneurs to his council, nine of whom had been awarded the Croix de Saint Louis for fighting the British in the Seven Years' War.

In 1770, Carleton returned to London to lobby for his vision of Canada to be made law. It took four years for the Quebec Act to reach the House of Commons. The act, once passed, guaranteed Canadiens the right to their religion, allowed Canadiens to hold public office, and restored French civil law, which upheld the seigneurial system of land ownership. Catholics now had rights that they did not have in Britain. Instead of assimilation or deportation, the Canadiens got a colony that in several important ways differed little from the world they had known before 1759.

There were objectors in the House of Commons, among them Lord Cavendish, who warned, "I should think it material not to give them directly their own law again; it keeps up that perpetual dependence upon their ancient laws and customs, which will ever make [them] a distinct people." The act was approved by a margin of fifty-six in favour, twenty opposed. Publicly, it remained unpopular, though. When George III came to sign the bill into law, he drove through angry mobs shouting, "No Popery!"

The American colonies also saw the Quebec Act as a betrayal. The recognition of French and Catholic rights and the extension of the colony to the Ohio Valley were among the "Intolerable Acts" that sparked a revolutionary fervour. A wave of expansionism and anti-Catholic sentiment swept through the colonies. Ministers preached to their congregations about the Protestant triumph and the defeat of Satan.

The new borders of Quebec curtailed American expansion. To their resentment, more than a million New England colonists were hemmed in by eighty thousand French Catholics. Newspapers and budding statesmen railed: "The finger of God points out a mighty Empire to our sons; the Savages of the wilderness were never expelled to make room in this, the best part of the continent, for idolators and slaves." Benjamin Franklin met with George Washington, Alexander Hamilton, and the other leaders of the American colonies to protest this development and resolved "that the last act of Parliament to establish the Roman Catholic religion and French law in the vast country called Canada is an extremely grave danger for the Protestant religion and for the freedoms and civil law of America; consequently, for the citizens and Christian Protestants, we must take the necessary measures to insure our security."

The Americans were already in an agitated state over what they saw as grossly unfair taxation, resulting from Britain's need to pay off its war debts. There was rioting in Massachusetts, and British troops were sent to restore order. On March 5, 1770, a mob charged British soldiers at the Custom House, who fired on them. It became known as the "Boston Massacre," and a stirring version of it was engraved, printed, and sold by Paul Revere, reinventing the scene as patriotic kitsch. Five years later, the colonies were in open rebellion. "The shot heard round the world" at Lexington on April 19, 1775, signalled chaotic revolution and a new threat to Canada.

A QUESTION OF LOYALTIES

In 1774, North America was beginning to suffer a new upheaval. Quebec had been conquered and the continent was now British, but the Thirteen Colonies were going through their own tortured identity crisis: would they remain colonies or become a republic? That question was being answered with the first salvoes of revolution. It was not only a fight with England but also a civil war, as neighbours turned on one another with a new, violent patriotism. Americans who were suspected by republicans of being loyal to the Crown were beaten and imprisoned, their farms confiscated, homes burned, women and children exiled. As the struggle for independence grew increasingly bitter, the American rebels viewed Quebec as either a valuable source of support or a serious military threat.

The rebels tried to recruit Canadiens to their cause. In October 1774, the Continental Congress wrote a manifesto to the people of Canada and had copies posted in Montreal and Quebec. In it, they urged Canadiens to "take a noble chance for emerging from a humiliating subjection under Governors, Intendants, and Military Tyrants . . ." It might look as though the Canadiens were living as free men, the Americans argued, but this was simply a veneer; their true masters were in London. The letter contained a hint of menace: "You are a small people, compared to those who with open arms invite you into a fellowship. A moment's reflection should convince

Perry's Victory on Lake Erie
(*Anne S. K. Brown, Military Collection, Brown University*)

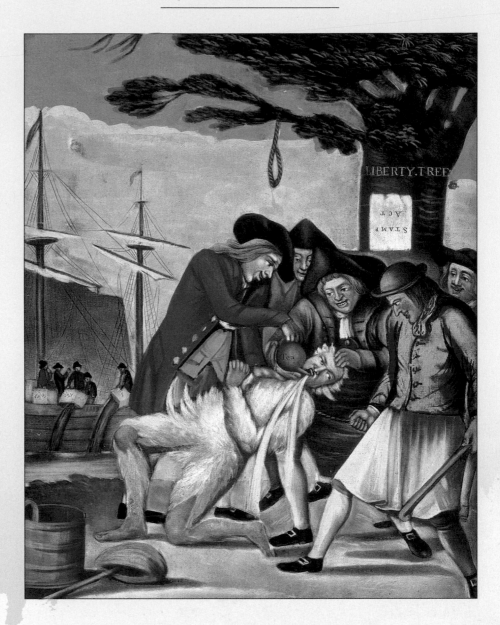

The Bostonians Paying
the Excise Man
(*John Carter Brown Library*)

you which will be most for your interest and happiness, to have all the rest of North-America your unalterable friends, or your inveterate enemies."

After reading the letter, with its threats, seductions, and flattery ("exerting the natural sagacity of Frenchmen, *examine* the specious device . . ."), most Canadiens chose to endorse neither side in the looming conflict between England and America. They saw the nascent American Revolution as nothing more than an argument between two brands of Englishmen. While the letter from Congress contained unfortunate truths about Quebec's colonial rule, it was also true that those who had written it had denounced Catholic Canadiens as satanic (though only in the English-language version). Most Canadiens realized that an alliance with the Americans would not necessarily produce the advertised happiness.

Some were won over, however, among them the perennially distempered Montreal merchant Thomas Walker. A large, one-eared man with a face the colour of brisket and a hatred of British military rule, he travelled the Quebec countryside spouting his enraged rhetoric, offering money and muskets to those who would join the Americans. Others took up the cause. Clément Gosselin, a carpenter from Ste. Famille, recruited volunteers along the south shore of the St. Lawrence River. Germain Dionne, a wealthy merchant from La Pocatière, guaranteed clothing and supplies for the new recruits.

On the other side was François Baby, a native Montrealer, veteran of the siege of Quebec, and a captain of the militia. All that fall and winter, Baby kept his eye on the pro-American propagandists. "They have helped and assisted with all their might the enemies of the government. They are preaching rebellion everywhere, urging the pillaging and arrest of the small number of zealous servants of the King; forcing the *officiers du Roi* to read the proclamations of the rebels from church doorsteps. They have raised holy hell."

On May 1, 1775, Quebec's controversial new constitution was inaugurated, and in Montreal a bust of King George III was defiled with coal and a rosary of potatoes placed around the neck. Attached was a wooden cross with the words "*Voilà le Pape du Canada ou le sot Anglois*" (Behold Canada's Pope, the English fool). No one claimed responsibility, and tensions escalated between English and French.

The dominant mood in Quebec was confusion. Walker told his American friends, "The bulk of the people, both English and Canadians . . . wish well to your cause. . . . Few in this colony dare vent their griefs but groan in silence and dream of lettres de cachet, confiscations and imprisonments, offering up their prayers to the throne of grace to prosper your righteous cause, which alone will free us from those jealous fears and apprehensions that rob us of our peace."

Thérèse Baby, a Montreal widow with five children, saw a different side. She wrote to her brother François: "You have certainly heard – the Bostonnais [Americans] are giving us quite a fright. . . . You cannot imagine the terror that has overtaken us all – women and men. Many people have sent off their documents and valuables to the country, many people are getting ready to leave altogether. I am saddened by all of this but then again it does make me laugh to see how some cowards can no longer hide their fear . . ."

When the militia was called up in Montreal to resist the Americans, few came forward, and the militia commander threatened to blow up the city himself if citizens did not enlist. In June, Governor Guy Carleton declared martial law as a desperate measure, but it had little effect. The seigneurs, Quebec's traditional landholding class, largely supported the British administration, which had confirmed their privileged position. But when they tried to get their tenants to take up arms to resist the anticipated American invasion, they were driven away with pitchforks. Carleton was faced with the alarming prospect of defending the province with a woefully inadequate force. "Not six hundred rank and file fit for duty upon the whole extent of this great river," he wrote to Lord Dartmouth, secretary for the colonies,

Before he was known as the mad king, due to periodic bouts of insanity, King George III was known as Farmer George, after his habit of walking the countryside and talking to the locals about crops and recipes. He thought that finding a wife was an inconvenience and entrusted a lord to do it for him; his marriage to Charlotte Sophia of Mecklenburg lasted for almost sixty years. During his reign the American colonies were lost but new ones were gained in India and Australia. George died in 1820 at the age of eighty-one, both mad and blind. (*William Beechey, Library of Congress*)

James Murray, the son of British aristocrats, did all he could as governor of Quebec to preserve the French-Canadian presence, for which he was criticized. "I glory in having been accused of warmth and firmness in protecting the King's Canadian Subjects and of doing the utmost in my power to gain to my royal master the affection of that brave, hardy people, whose emigration, if ever it should happen, will be an irreparable loss to this empire." Letter from James Murray to Lord Shelburne, August 20, 1766 (*National Portrait Gallery, London*)

"not an armed vessel, no place of strength; the ancient provincial force enervated and broke to pieces; all subordination overset and the minds of the people poisoned by the same hypocrisy and lies practiced with so much success in the other provinces, and which their emissaries and friends here have spread abroad with great art and diligence."

The strongest ally Carleton had was the Catholic Church. Years earlier, General James Murray had lobbied steadily to protect the Church's position in Quebec society and to get Jean-Olivier Briand anointed by Rome. Now Bishop Briand returned the favour. He announced that anyone who took up arms against the king would be denied the sacraments and the right to a Christian burial. But his threat of damnation had little effect; he was viewed as the king's man, on his payroll to the tune of two hundred pounds per year.

Among the Canadiens, the most forceful sentiment was in favour of a militant neutrality. They were rebuilding after the Conquest; they had been through one destructive war and were not anxious for another. Canadiens would not fight the Americans, but they would not join them either, at least not in sufficient numbers. This was a problem for George Washington, the commander of the American forces, who saw the province as a key military objective. "I need not mention . . . the great importance of this place [Quebec], and the consequent possession of all Canada, in the scale of American affairs. . . . To whomsoever it belongs, in their favour, probably, will the balance turn. If it is ours, success, I think, will most certainly crown our virtuous struggles; if it is theirs, the contest, at least, will be doubtful, hazardous and bloody."

On June 27, 1775, the Continental Congress instructed American troops to invade Quebec. One unformed country made the decision to attack another, and both would further define themselves during the course of the struggle.

The Americans attacked from two directions. Richard Montgomery, a former British army captain, now an American brigadier-general, led one force of a thousand men up Lake Champlain and along the Richelieu River toward the St. Lawrence. They planned to attack Fort St. Jean, then take Montreal.

The second army of 1,200 men was led by Benedict Arnold. Arnold's name would later enter the American lexicon as a synonym for treachery, but he began the revolution heroically. He planned a surprise attack on Quebec, moving north from the mouth of the Kennebec River in Maine, crossing into Canada on the Dead River, then travelling up the Chaudière River to emerge on the St. Lawrence, across from Quebec.

Starting on September 16, 1775, Montgomery besieged Fort St. Jean, southeast of Montreal, for six weeks, his force of 1,000 augmented by 200 Canadiens. His militiamen were volunteers, mostly farmers, an undisciplined, reluctant group who were ravaged by disease. Hundreds were discharged as unfit for duty. Inside the fort were 662 defenders, most of

MAJOR-GENERAL BENEDICT ARNOLD ◆ March 1776. As an officer in the American Revolutionary army, Benedict Arnold was courageous, brash, and innovative and was twice wounded in battle. But he felt his military contributions had been overlooked by his commanders and his promotions insufficent and late in coming. A middle-aged man with a nineteen-year-old wife, Arnold also had financial difficulties. In July 1780, he offered to surrender West Point to the British for 20,000 pounds, a plan that ultimately failed. His treachery wiped out any memory of his successful military leadership and he entered the American lexicon as a synonym for traitor. The British appointed Arnold brigadier general and he ably served George III, looting Richmond, Virginia, and burning rebel ships and warehouses. But he was as unpopular in Britain as he had been in the United States and he died without a nationality. (*Anne S. K. Brown, Military Collection, Brown University*)

them British redcoats, the bulk of Carleton's force. Their supply lines had been cut and they were facing starvation.

On November 1, with the troops already demoralized, an eight-hour bombardment destroyed most of the buildings inside the fort. Jean André, a British major, described the scene: "The weather grew very cold and the situation of the sick and wounded was a very cruel one. They were neither out of reach of danger nor sheltered from the inclemency of the weather. As many as could find room in the cellars slept there. The rest, unable to get a place slept above in cold and danger. There was now nothing left but to frame the best articles we could for the garrison."

Major Charles Preston surrendered the fort the next day. In the articles of capitulation Montgomery praised the enemy's valour, adding that it was too bad it had not been for a worthier cause. Preston ordered the clause to be stricken or they would fight to the death. Montgomery agreed, conceding this small victory. Preston's larger victory, as it often was in Canada, came in delaying the enemy long enough to prevent them from invading Quebec before winter set in.

Montgomery moved on to now-defenceless Montreal, entering at the Récollet gate and offering the people "liberty and security." His army was welcomed by an address signed by some of the city's leading citizens. "Our chains are broken," it read, "blissful liberty restores us to ourselves. . . . We accept union as we accepted it in our hearts from the moment we learned of the address of 26th October, 1774." A committee of six English citizens and six French met with Montgomery to negotiate the capitulation of the city.

Carleton had ordered the city's evacuation hours earlier, though few had obeyed. He had already sent his wife and three children to London. Then, immediately before Montgomery arrived, Carleton escaped in a whale boat, disguised as a peasant.

Thérèse Baby stayed in Montreal, anticipating disaster. "We are in the worst possible situation," she wrote her brother François. "The governor has just told the Canadiens they are free to stay or to leave. I think we are doomed, we are waiting to be taken. I'm sure this will be the last letter I can send you. . . . I must admit I'm at my wit's end. It has not prevented me from pulling out an old sword to defend my family from the insults of what is certain to be an unruly army."

Carleton went to Quebec, though he did not have much hope for the fortress. "B. Arnold is on the Chaudière, with twelve or fifteen hundred Men, we have not one Soldier in the Town, & the lower sort are not much more loyal than here [Montreal]." Quebec was defended by its fabled, crumbling walls and its citizens of doubtful loyalty. "Could the people in the town be depended upon," he wrote to Lord Dartmouth, "I should flatter myself, we might hold out. . . . But, we have as many enemies within, and a foolish people, dupes to those traitors, with the natural fears of men unused to war, I think our fate extremely doubtful, to say nothing worse." His main hope lay in the deficiencies of the city's attackers and their impetuous commander.

Benedict Arnold was a short, round man with a placid, almost bovine face and a wild military appetite. He had left Maine in September with eight hundred volunteer militiamen and three hundred Pennsylvania and Virginia riflemen dressed in buckskins. His plan was to march them through nearly three hundred kilometres of wilderness and then surprise Quebec. But the map he had was outdated and inaccurate; the distance was more than twice what he'd anticipated. Worse, he was hit by a flash flood on a river that carried away some of his boats and destroyed food and supplies.

The army was hindered by uncharted swamps, early snow, and famine in the "direful, howling wilderness." They were reduced to eating their shoe leather, cartridge boxes, and a pet Newfoundland dog. They slept in the

A View of the Upper Town of Quebec, 1775. By now, more than 100 English merchants had come to Quebec and Montreal, demanding legal and political rights that would put the 65,000 French Canadians at a disadvantage. The British merchants were described as "a small group of schemers come either with the army or as clerks and agents from London, who in no way warrant preferential treatment – either from their behaviour or their lack of education, and are in themselves despicable . . . " (*Archives nationales du Québec*, C-040777)

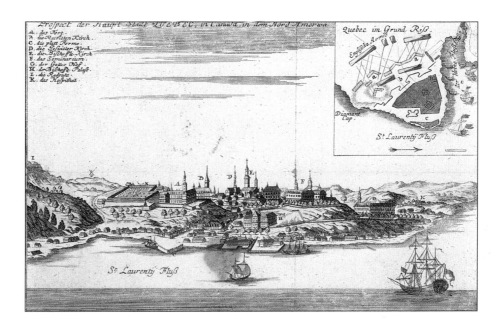

open under damp blankets and pneumonia preyed on them. By the time they got to the aptly named Dead River, many had either died or deserted. Some of those who remained were too hungry to walk. "We had all along aided our weaker brethren," Private George Morison recorded in his journal, "but the dreadful moment had now arrived when these friendly offices could no longer be performed. Many of the men began to fall behind, and those in any condition to march were scarcely able to support themselves, so that it was impossible to bring them along; if we tarried with them we must all have perished."

On November 8, more than a month behind schedule, Arnold arrived at Quebec with barely half of the twelve hundred men he had started with, and these were ragged and thin. But Arnold had lost none of his swagger. He wrote a letter to Hector Cramahé, Carleton's right-hand man, which read: "I am ordered by his excellency Gen. Washington to take possession of the town of Quebec. I do therefore, in the name of the United Colonies, demand immediate surrender of the town, fortifications & c. of Quebec to the forces of the United Colonies under my command . . ." Arnold, whom Carleton ridiculed as a "horse jockey" because of his short stature and the fact that he'd once made his living as a horse trader, was unable even to get his message delivered; his couriers were repeatedly turned away by musket fire. It took six days just to get the letter inside the walls.

Arnold's quixotic demand was met with prolonged silence. Still optimistic, he wrote to George Washington: "We arrived here and are making all possible preparations to attack the city, which has a wretched, motley garrison of disaffected seamen, marines and inhabitants, the walls in a ruinous situation, and cannot hold out long."

Inside the walls, Carleton had come to a similar conclusion. It was hard to gauge the loyalty of the townspeople. Would they fight the Americans or welcome them, as they had in Montreal? As the city prepared for the fourth siege in its eventful history, Carleton issued a proclamation: "In order to rid the Town of all useless, disloyal and treacherous persons . . . I do hereby strictly order all persons who have refused to enroll their names in the militia lists and to take up arms to quit the town in 4 days together with their wives and children under pain of being treated as rebels or spies."

On December 3, Montgomery arrived from Montreal with an army of three hundred and joined Arnold's force. Montgomery sent a letter to Carleton demanding surrender, but Carleton burned it unopened. A bombardment of the walls proved futile.

Like Wolfe before them, the attackers were pressed by winter to act quickly. They had another incentive; almost half of their armies' enlistments expired on December 31. Those men would be free to return home, and most would seize the opportunity. Smallpox and pneumonia plagued them, and the weather was numbing. In late December, an American deserter came to Quebec and told James Bain, captain of the militia, about the dispirited state of the attacking army. "He says all the people from the Old

The Death of General
Montgomery (Mort du
Général Montgomery
à l'attaque de Québec,
Décembre, 1775. *National
Archives of Canada,
c-046334*)

country wish to be at home," Bain recounted. "They are not fond of attacking the Town. . . . This man says we'll be attacked on the first snowy or
stormy night."

The last week of December started out clear and cold, a miserable, sus-
penseful Christmas. But on December 30, a blizzard arrived, and at 2:00 the
next morning, two rockets were fired, their muted light signalling the attack.

Montgomery approached the Lower Town from the southwest, his
men wearing hemlock twigs in their hats to distinguish them from the
British, who had the same uniforms. But the storm that Montgomery had
been waiting for was his undoing. He squinted ahead into the swirling snow,
seeing the shape of a house. Inside it were a few drunken British seamen, a
cannon, and thirty Canadien militia under the command of Captain Joseph
Chabot and Lieutenant Alexandre Picard. The Canadiens fired a single, fatal
volley of grapeshot and musketballs that ripped through the unsuspecting
American army. Montgomery was shot through the head and most of his
officers were killed. The rest fled the unseen enemy, leaving the wounded
and dead in the snow.

Arnold's seven hundred men came from the other side of Lower Town,
below the walls of the fortress, with the plan of meeting Montgomery and
then moving up to take the Citadel. Some had papers pinned to their hats
that read "Liberty or Death." Above them, Carleton's ad hoc force fired
down from the ramparts through the falling snow. "We could see nothing
but the blaze from the muzzles of their muskets," wrote American Private
John Henry.

Arnold fell, hit in the leg with a musketball, and was carried from
the field. His men staggered on to the rendezvous point and waited for
Montgomery's army, unaware of his fate.

151

While Arnold's men waited, Carleton brought a small force up behind the Americans and began firing down the street. "Confined in a narrow street," John Henry wrote, "hardly more than twenty feet wide . . . scarcely a ball, well aimed or otherwise, but must take effect upon us. . . . The enemy having the advantage of the ground in front, a vast superiority of numbers and dry and better arms, gave them an irresistible power in so narrow a space. . . . About nine o'clock, it was apparent to all of us that we must surrender; it was done."

Three hundred eighty-four men surrendered. Forty-two were wounded and thirty dead, with only eighteen Canadien casualties. Montgomery's frozen hand was found the next morning protruding from the snow. Another twenty corpses were discovered in the spring.

Even this dramatic defeat did not dampen Arnold's military spirit, however. "My wound has been exceedingly painful," he wrote to his wife, "[but] I have no thoughts of leaving this proud town until I first enter it in triumph." He and his much-reduced army were entrenched in farmhouses outside Quebec, recovering and hoping for reinforcements.

In Montreal, the genteel liberation had begun to sour. American General David Wooster had been left in charge of the occupying forces, and he had quickly alienated the Canadiens by banning Christmas mass and arresting a dozen leading citizens whom he suspected of being Loyalists. As the winter dragged on, the Americans ran out of gold to pay for their food. When Canadiens refused to accept their paper money, they took what they wanted by force.

"Ten of them went to see Monsieur de Tonnancour who gave them something to eat," wrote notary Jean-Baptiste Badeaux. "But they were not satisfied so they took his meat from the grill despite the cook's cries of protest. They left only after being threatened by their commander, shouting and stabbing their bayonets into the doors as they were leaving." The Americans plundered nearby farms, and their message of liberation was quickly buried beneath the demands of brute survival, bad manners, and cultural differences.

In April 1776, Congress sent three representatives to Montreal to rally support for the revolution. Led by the ailing, seventy-year-old Benjamin Franklin, they dragged a printing press along on the difficult month-long journey from Philadelphia, hoping to use words to sway Montrealers to their cause. But they found their own army mutinous and diseased and the Canadiens openly hostile. "We cannot find words strong enough to express our miserable situation," Franklin wrote. He was frail and bedridden most of the time and left, deeply discouraged, after only twelve days.

Even the indefatigable Benedict Arnold was finally driven away. On May 6, the ice broke up on the St. Lawrence River, and the HMS *Surprise* and two other Royal Navy ships arrived at Quebec, carrying 10,000 British troops. Arnold had command of 350 weary soldiers and 150 Canadians of failing loyalty; the sight of this fresh enemy was too much. He admitted

Benjamin Franklin. Franklin was essentially self-taught: a printer, politician, writer, scientist, and diplomat. He was an ideologue of American expansionism and an effective anti-Catholic propagandist. He also fathered several children with two different women. In his popular *Poor Richard's Almanac*, he wrote, "Where there's marriage without love, there will be love without marriage." He served on the committee that drafted the Declaration of Independence and also helped shape the American Constitution. In 1789 he wrote to a friend, "Our new constitution is now established, and has an appearance that promises permanency, but in this world nothing can be said to be certain, except death and taxes." (*Library of Congress*)

A statue of George III is pulled down in New York on July 4, 1776, after the Declaration of Independence. (*Pulling Down the Statue of King George III at Bowling Green, Lafayette College Art Collection*)

defeat and retreated up the Richelieu River to Lake Champlain. "As we pursued them," wrote the militia's Captain Ainslie, "we found the road strew'd with arms, cartridges, cloaths, bread, pork." The British offered a token pursuit, then stopped and ate the discarded food. On June 15, the Americans evacuated Montreal, unsuccessfully trying to burn it as they retreated.

After a bitter year, the American rebels gave up on their stubborn, unpredictable neighbours and focused their aggressions on their royalist countrymen.

Jacob Bowman was a farmer of German descent who was living on the Susquehannah River in New York when he was seized by American rebels. They accused him of remaining loyal to Britain. "He was surprised at night," his granddaughter Elizabeth later wrote, "while his wife was sick. . . . His house was pillaged of every article, except the bed on which his sick

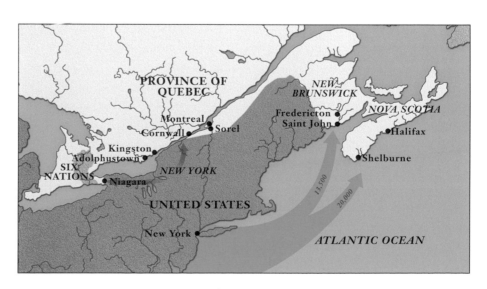

Loyalist Migration, 1783

LOYALIST ENCAMPMENT AT JOHNSTOWN, 1784 ◆ "It was sad and sorrowful for my Grandfather and especially for my Grandmother to have her neighbours' children coming to their house with their pale and wan faces and could not relieve them; there was one family especially in their neighbourhood who came for the parings from potatoes. My Grandfather shot some wild pigeons, just as they rose from the ground, and if I am not mistaken he killed twenty-five or thirty at one discharge of the gun. And at another time the cat dragged a rabbit into the house to be used for food. There was such a scarcity of food that one neighbour would share up as soon as he was fortunate enough to get anything to eat . . . . I had heard my father speak about a field of wheat that the people flocked to and carried away bags even before it was out of the milk and made broth of it, after shelling it first on a table so as not to lose one kernel of that precious field of wheat." From the unpublished *History of the Jones Family* by Andrew Jones. (*James Peachy, National Archives of Canada,* C-002001)

wife lay, and that they stripped of all but one blanket." His wife was pregnant and the shock of the attack induced premature labour. "Half an hour after my grandfather was marched off, his youngest child was born. This was in November."

Bowman and his sixteen-year-old son were taken to prison. "They were fastened together by a band of iron around their arms, and a chain with three links around their ankles," Elizabeth wrote. "In that condition they remained either three years and a half, or four years, until the flesh was worn away and the bones laid bare four inches."

Bowman's wife went to the Mohawk Valley, New York, and became part of a loyalist matriarchy of five women and thirty-one children, their husbands all in jail. They tried to grow corn and potatoes without much luck, and in the fall the British authorities from Fort Niagara took them to a refugee camp at Machiche, near Trois-Rivières, Quebec.

The Colonies were divided between those who supported the new Continental Congress and those who remained loyal to Britain, creating a checkerboard of conflicting alliances. In Virginia, Governor John Murray Dunmore declared martial law and called "upon every person capable of bearing arms to resort to his majesty's standard." In Philadelphia, the spirit

Joseph Brant. Born on the banks of the Ohio River in 1742, Brant quickly came to the attention of Sir William Johnson, the British superintendent of the northern American Indians, who sent him to Moor's Charity School for Indians at Lebanon, Connecticut (which later became Dartmouth College). Brant became a close friend of Johnson's and played an integral part in the fight against the Americans. He died in 1807, at age sixty-five, at Grand River, Upper Canada. (*George Romney, National Gallery of Canada, 8005*)

of independence was at fever pitch. New York held many Tories, as the Loyalists were called, but even there a statue of George III was melted down to make musket balls for the rebel army.

In the countryside, farm communities were torn apart. Tories were tarred and feathered, a ghastly process that sometimes left them scalded and badly injured. Beatings and lynchings were commonplace as the rule of law dissolved under revolutionary fever. Pathetic wagon trains of women and children moved north. In the largest mass migration in North America, more than 100,000 Loyalists fled the Thirteen Colonies, some returning to England, others seeking refuge in the West Indies or Canada.

The Loyalists fought back, forming guerrilla units that proved to be Britain's most effective weapon against the revolution. Butler's Rangers was a squad recruited by John Butler, a wealthy landowner from the Mohawk Valley who had dealt with natives since childhood and spoke several native languages. He recruited Loyalists and natives from the Six Nations to fight the Americans. The Rangers harassed and scalped Americans from the Hudson Valley to Kentucky. They disrupted supply lines, engaged in guerrilla skirmishes, and demoralized settlers.

Quebec refugee camps quickly filled with Loyalist families fleeing the fighting in the Colonies. Quebec Governor Frederick Haldimand did not want the camps; he thought the province was unsuitable for Loyalist settlement because of its predominantly French population. He also suspected some of the Loyalists of being opportunistic immigrants in search of free land. But Carleton, who was now responsible for evacuating Loyalist troops and refugees from New York, insisted that Haldimand take them, and he did so reluctantly, running the camps along harsh military lines. They were squalid, impromptu shelters that offered little relief. Families were separated and food shortages were endemic; children were put on quarter rations. The overcrowding and poor diet led to malaria, smallpox, and scurvy, which were crudely treated with vinegar, wine, and spruce beer.

In 1777, Jacob Bowman's next eldest son, Peter, turned thirteen, and he and his nine-year-old brother left Machiche to join Butler's Rangers, Peter as a soldier, his brother as a fifer. That summer they returned to the Mohawk Valley where the Bowman and Butler families had lived. They came to burn the valley, to destroy their own farms. Of the 850 homes in the valley at the beginning of the war, only 15 were left at the end of the revolution.

The Loyalists could never return. Butler said that his people "would rather go to Japan than go back among the Americans."

Joseph Brant, a Mohawk chief, allied himself with Butler's Rangers. Brant, who had been educated in English, was an articulate, dramatic-looking man who straddled two cultures without effort. His Mohawk name was Thayendanegea, "He Who Places Two Bets." Brant believed that the Mohawk could lose their land if America achieved independence. Governor Carleton had refused Brant's offer to fight the Americans and used the natives only as scouts. In 1775, Brant sailed for London to offer King George III his services.

"The Mohawks have been very badly treated in that country," he told Lord George Germain, secretary of state for the American colonies. "It is very hard when we have let the King's subjects have so much of our lands for so little value, they should want to cheat us . . . of the small spots we have left for our women and children to live on. We are tired out in making complaints and getting no redress."

In London, Brant was celebrated as an exotic. George Romney painted his portrait and Fleet Street journalists interviewed him about his impressions of London. He liked the horses and the women best, he said. After a performance of *Romeo and Juliet* he remarked on the couple's protracted courtship. "If my people were to make love in that way," he observed, "our race would be extinct in two generations."

He warned London of a more pressing threat of extinction: "We think the rebels will ruin us at last if we go on as we do, one year after another, doing nothing . . . we are in between two hells."

The king endorsed the native alliance. Brant was already a captain in the British army, and when he returned to Canada he quickly raised a native force among four of the Six Nations: the Mohawk, Onondaga, Cayuga, and Seneca. The Oneida and Tuscarora had remained neutral, though they leaned toward the Americans.

Together, Brant's force and Butler's Rangers began an effective campaign of disruption and terror. Brant commanded the natives at the battle of Oriskany in 1777, one of the bloodiest fights of the war; several hundred rebels were killed in an ambush and only a handful of natives and Loyalists died. Peter Bowman and his nine-year-old brother were there.

The Iroquois alliance with Britain prompted a brutal response from George Washington. "The immediate objects are the total destruction and devastation of their [native] settlements," he ordered, "and the capture of as many prisoners, of every age and sex, as possible. . . . Parties should be detached to lay waste all the settlements around, with instructions to do it in the most effectual manner, that the country not be merely overrun but destroyed."

Within two months, Washington's pogrom had almost destroyed the Six Nations. Homes and crops were burned, orchards destroyed, burial grounds defiled, and prisoners taken. The Oneida and Tuscarora were not rewarded for their neutrality; their farms were destroyed as well.

"The number of [Iroquois] towns destroyed by this army amounted to 40," wrote Major-General John Sullivan, "besides scattering houses. . . . Every creek and river has been traced, and the whole country explored in search of Indian settlements, and I am persuaded that . . . there is not a single town left in the country of the Six Nations."

In 1783, with the Treaty of Paris, Britain finally recognized the independence that the U.S. Congress had declared seven years earlier. But in the treaty, the Six Nations were not even mentioned. Brant felt that Britain had sold its allies to the Americans. "[Given] what friendship we had shown to the English," he wrote to Lord Stanley, "and being conscious of the active part . . . we have taken in their favour in every dispute they have had with their enemies, we were struck with astonishment at hearing we were forgot in the treaty. . . . We could not believe it possible such firm friends and allies could be so neglected by a nation remarkable for its honour and glory whom we had served with so much zeal and fidelity."

The Six Nations had effectively been destroyed as a political and military force, but nevertheless there was concern in Britain that they might rally to avenge their shabby treatment. As compensation, 275,000 hectares in the British-held country north of Lake Erie was granted to them. Brant and 1,800 followers settled along the Grand River in the fall of 1784. He had a vast home with several slaves and servants and favoured fine European clothes. American President George Washington sought his help in 1792, asking Brant to arrange a "peace with the Ohio Indians." Instead, Brant visited the natives and encouraged war.

He returned to London, again meeting with King George III, seeking compensation for Mohawk losses during the American revolutionary war. He also got money to build the first Anglican church in Upper Canada. But he refused to kneel to the king. "I bow to no man," Brant said, "for I am considered a prince among my own people. But I will gladly shake your hand."

For their services to Britain, Butler's Rangers received land on the west bank of the Niagara River. Butler settled there, and so did Peter Bowman, who had survived the brutal skirmishing. "My father settled on his land near the fort," Elizabeth Bowman wrote. "He drew an axe and a hoe from the Government. . . . My mother had a cow, a bed, six plates and three knives. . . . Men, women and children all went to work clearing the land. There were none to make improvements in [Upper] Canada then but the U.E. Loyalists and they . . . planted the germ of its future greatness."

John Butler died there in 1796, and at his native funeral ceremony, Joseph Brant said, "Our loss is the greater, as there are none remaining who understand our manners and customs as well as he did."

Brant died at his home in 1807. His last words were, "Have pity on the poor Indians; if you can get any influence with the great, endeavor to do them all the good you can."

Thirty-five thousand Loyalists settled in the Maritimes during and after the war; among them were several thousand blacks who had escaped slavery. David George was born of African slaves in Virginia. He saw his parents and siblings routinely whipped. His brother Dick once ran away but was caught and punished. "After he had received 500 lashes," George told two members of his church, "they washed his back with salt water, and whipped it in, as well as rubbed it in with a rag; and then directly sent him to work in pulling

HANNAH INGRAHAM ◆ Born in 1772 in Albany County, New York, Hannah Ingraham was four when the American Revolution disrupted her life. Her family were Loyalists, and her father joined the King's American Regiment at New York. She didn't see him again until she was eleven. In 1783 the family heard that there was land available for Loyalists in Nova Scotia and prepared to sail for Saint John. "Then on Tuesday, suddenly the house was surrounded by rebels and father was taken prisoner and carried away. Uncle went forward and asked those who had taken him that if he might come home he would answer for his being forthcoming the next morning. But no, and I cried and cried *enough to kill myself that night.* When morning came, they said he was free to go. We had five wagon loads carried down the Hudson in a sloop and then we went on board the transport that was to bring us to Saint John . . . .There were no deaths on board, but several babies were born. It was a sad sick time after we landed in Saint John. We had to live in tents. The government gave them to us and rations too. It was just at the first snow then and the melting snow and the rain would soak up into our beds as we lay. Mother got so chilled and developed rheumatism and was never well afterward.

"We lived in a tent at St. Annes until father got a house ready . . . .There was no floor laid, no windows, no chimney, no door, but we had a roof at least. A good fire was blazing and mother had a big loaf of bread and she boiled a kettle of water and put a good piece of butter in a pewter bowl. We toasted the bread and all sat around the bowl and at our breakfast that morning mother said: 'Thank God we are no longer in dread of having shots fired through our house.' This is the sweetest meal I ever tasted for many a day."

Ingraham was never married and died at the age of ninety-seven in 1869. (*Hannah Ingraham, 88 years old, Kings Landing, New Brunswick*)

off the suckers of tobacco." George escaped and became a Baptist preacher and a black Loyalist.

The escaped slaves were a natural target for recruitment by the British, whose slogan, "Freedom and a Farm," was seductive, though not entirely accurate. Of the tens of thousands of blacks who declared themselves Loyalists, few became farmers.

As the blacks retreated north with the British army, their numbers became a hindrance. They were sometimes so desperate that they clung to the sides of boats. "To prevent this dangerous practice the fingers of some of them were chopped off, and soldiers were posted with cutlasses and bayonets to oblige them to keep at proper distances. Many of them labouring under diseases, forsaken by their new masters, and destitute of the necessities of life, perished in the woods."

David George made it to Nova Scotia with 1,500 other black Loyalists, joining 15,000 white Loyalists who had just arrived (some of whom brought their own slaves). Nova Scotia Governor John Parr worried about the relentless tide of immigrants. "I have not yet been able to find any sort of place for them, and the cold [is] setting in severe," he said.

The white Loyalists were housed in tents, public buildings, and the holds of ships, and they picked up rations from hastily constructed street kitchens. "It was a sad, sick time after we landed in Saint John," wrote Hannah Ingraham, who was eleven when she and her family arrived in 1783.

They came from Albany County, New York. "We had a comfortable farm, plenty of cows and sheep," she wrote, "but when the war began and [Father] joined the regulars, they, the Rebels took it all away. . . . My father was in the army seven years. . . . Mother was four years without hearing from [him] whether he was alive or dead; anyone would be hanged right up if they were caught bringing letters. . . . Oh they were terrible times."

Like many other Loyalist families, the Ingrahams were allotted two hundred acres to homestead. The settlers fanned north from the mouth of the Saint John River to form Queenston, Gagetown, and St. Anne's (later Fredericton). During that first winter, hundreds died of famine or exposure. Graves were dug in the frozen earth with an axe. But in the spring the government distributed nails and tools and the Ingrahams built a house.

In Nova Scotia, the black Loyalists who had been promised farms thought they would have equal claim to free land, but found that was not the case. The land grant system had quickly become corrupt and overburdened, and some black Loyalists had to wait six years for land. David George received a quarter acre. "It was a spot where there was plenty of water," he wrote, "and which I had before secretly wished for, as I knew it would be convenient for baptizing at any time."

George sang and preached nightly, his thunderous, tearful sermons attracting both blacks and whites. But other whites resented his preaching and came to his church with threats. "I stayed and preached," George said, "and the next day they came and beat me with sticks, and drove me into a swamp."

They also destroyed his house in Shelburne. The blacks had built the town, but on July 26, 1784, they were driven out. "Great Riot today," deputy surveyor Benjamin Marston reported. "The disbanded soldiers have risen against the Free negroes to drive them out of Town, because they labour cheaper than they – the soldiers. [27 July] Riot continues. The soldiers force the Free negroes to quit the town – pulled down about 20 of their houses."

George became the most famous preacher in the province, moving through its black settlements, lending the people strength, appalled at the conditions in which they lived. To avoid destitution, some black Loyalists sold themselves to merchants for two or three years' service, effectively returning to the slavery they had escaped from. Famine was rampant, and crimes of desperation were punished harshly. In Shelburne, a black woman received two hundred lashes for stealing less than a shilling. George felt that he was no better off than he had been in Virginia.

While many blacks stayed and, against long odds, built a permanent community, George joined a second exodus. Almost 1,200 black Loyalists, a third of the population, returned to the continent their forebears had been taken from in chains. They established the colony of Freetown in Sierra Leone on the west coast of Africa, and they embraced it as home. Upon arrival, they offered up a hymn: "The Year of Jubilee has come, / Returned ye ransomed sinners home."

The Loyalists who remained wanted more than the land that had been promised them; they wanted their own colony. They had influence in London through their wealthy members, their sheer numbers, and the emphatic, moral weight they carried. In 1784, the British government agreed to divide Nova Scotia, creating the separate colony of New Brunswick, with its own elected assembly.

Loyalists in Quebec observed this development and argued that they had an even better case for their own colony. They had fought and suffered for England, and now they found themselves in a territory that retained many French laws and had no elected assembly. Petitions were taken up and presented to Governor Carleton, now Lord Dorchester. "The Petitioners do not ask for more than has already been granted to their fellow sufferers in Nova Scotia," a group of Loyalists argued. "We will be content only when Parliament has responded to our claims by giving us the same rights and privileges as the English and why not?" another Loyalist petition read. "We are English subjects just as they are." An uncomfortably familiar refrain was added: "Freedom, gentlemen, freedom at all cost."

The Canadiens, too, were agitating for their own elected assembly. A petition signed by influential merchants demanded "a house of representatives constituted indiscriminately of old and new Subjects, freely elected by the people of the province, the cities, towns and parishes." In this house, the Canadiens would inevitably form a majority.

The task of reconciling the claims of Loyalists and Canadiens fell to the British colonial secretary, twenty-nine-year-old William Grenville. He considered it an impossibility to accommodate the two groups politically. "If these two bodies and classes of men, differing in their prejudices and perhaps in their interest, were to be consolidated into one legislative body," he reasoned, "dissensions and animosities might probably prevail. . . . It should seem, therefore, that the natural remedy for this would be the separation of the province into two districts . . ." His solution was to create two distinct provinces, each with its own separate culture, system of law and land tenure, and its own elected assembly. In 1791, King George signed a bill dividing the colony of Quebec into Lower Canada and Upper Canada.

The new border was really a line drawn in the wilderness. Upper Canada was an area twice the size of France, thinly populated by ten thousand people. It looked, an observer noted, as though it had been "deserted in consequence of a plague." When John Graves Simcoe, its first lieutenant-governor, arrived in Newark (now Niagara-on-the-Lake) in 1792, it was the largest town in the province, a "wretched, straggling village with a few scattered cottages." Simcoe and his wife initially lived in a tent on the Niagara River, where Simcoe, an energetic monarchist, sang "God Save the King" before going to bed each night.

Simcoe wanted to recreate Britain here, to restore the colonial lustre that had been lost with America's independence. "The utmost attention should be paid that British Customs, Manners and Principles in the most

John Graves Simcoe. "I would rather die by more than Indian torture to restore my King and his Family to their just Inheritance. . . . Though a soldier, it is not by Arms that I hope for this Result . . . the Method I propose is by establishing a free, Honourable British Government, and a pure Administration of its Laws, which shall hold out to the solitary Emigrant, and to the several States, advantages that the present form of Government doth not and cannot permit them to enjoy." Upper Canada's first lieutenant-governor outlining his plan to populate the territory with Americans who were dissatisfied with their new democracy. (*Jean Laurent Mosnier, Metropolitan Toronto Library*)

YORK, UPPER CANADA, 1804 ◆ Simcoe wanted to develop York (Toronto) at the expense of existing towns like Kingston and Niagara. He transferred soldiers to the site and had them build roads (Yonge and Dundas streets among them), but his plan was mocked by Upper Canadian merchants and finally thwarted by his superiors in both Canada and London, who disapproved of stationing troops in the middle of nowhere. In 1804, York was still an isolated village with a good harbour. (*Elizabeth Frances Hale, National Archives of Canada, C-040137*)

trivial as well as serious matters should be promoted," he insisted. Simcoe believed that a sizable number of Americans were disillusioned with their newly minted democracy, and he wanted to attract them as settlers. "There are thousands of the inhabitants of the United States whose affections are centred in the British Government and the British name," he observed, "who are positively enemies of Congress and to the late division of the Empire . . . it will be true wisdom to invite . . . the emigration of this description of people."

The only enticement he had to offer was land. For an oath of loyalty to the king and a promise to cultivate the soil, white immigrants would receive two hundred acres. He advertised in English and West Indian newspapers and waited until the news trickled down to what he understood to be disgruntled Americans. "A great many settlers come daily from the United States," Simcoe's wife wrote in her diary, "some even from the Carolinas, about 2,000 miles. Five or six hundred miles is no more considered by an American than moving to the next parish is by an Englishman."

When Simcoe left in 1796, however, his dream had not yet materialized. Corrupt middlemen were selling the land to existing Upper Canada

THE EXECUTION OF KING LOUIS XVI OF FRANCE, 21 JANUARY 1793 ♦ His last words, largely eclipsed by drum rolls, were, "I die innocent of all the crimes laid to my charge; I pardon those who have occasioned my death; and I pray to God that the blood you are going to shed may never be visited on France." His severed head was shown to the large crowd, prompting cries of "*Vive la République.*" In Quebec, where the divine right of the monarchy was promoted by the Church, the execution turned the French-Canadian population against revolutionary and republican ideas. (*Bridgeman Art Library, Bibliothèque nationale, Paris*)

residents, and the exodus from the United States had been smaller than he had hoped. Simcoe had wanted York to replace Newark as the seat of government, but the town that would become Toronto still had only a dozen homes. He left, bitter and overwhelmed, but his vision would eventually be realized. By 1812, the Loyalists who had first settled the province would be outnumbered. Of the 75,000 people in Upper Canada, almost 60,000 would be recently arrived Americans.

The first elections in Upper and Lower Canada were wide-open affairs. Unlike in Britain, where the vote was restricted by religion and property, in Canada practically every male property owner could vote. The elections, which featured open voting, spirited public debate, and sometimes verbal and physical violence, lasted for weeks.

In Lower Canada, Pierre Bédard, the gifted son of a baker, was elected to the assembly in that first election in 1792. He was a lawyer who disliked

Napoleon Bonaparte. The War of 1812 in North America was essentially an outgrowth of the twenty-year struggle between revolutionary France and England for mastery in Europe. On September 7, 1812, a month after American General William Hull surrendered Detroit to Isaac Brock, Napoleon won the Battle of Borodino, which saw 80,000 casualties in a single day. Five days later he marched into Moscow with an army of 100,000. Less than a month later, he was forced to retreat from the Russian capital, his army in tatters. By November, they were fewer than 50,000, preyed upon by Russians and the winter. Napoleon wrote of the experience to the Abbé du Pradt, "From the sublime to the ridiculous is but a step." (*Mary Evans Picture Library*)

practising law and thought himself ugly and shy. Bédard turned to algebra as an escape from political turmoil, mental distress, and a dismal home life, seeking solace in the soothing rationality of numbers.

In 1807, the new governor, James Craig, arrived. He was a short, muscular man who had been a general in the Revolutionary War and was described by a friend as "hot, peremptory and pompous." Craig had an uncomplicated Tory view, a belief in harsh punishment, and a chronic illness. He was afflicted with dropsy (an abnormal swelling of joints and body cavities) and conducted his first colonial chores from his bed. He and Bédard faced one another like wounded lions, and their battles offered an early glimpse of the modern state.

Canadiens controlled the assembly, which was elected, but the English elite controlled the executive and legislative councils, which were appointed, and held the real power in the colony. The *Quebec Mercury*, voice of the anglophone merchants, dismissed the assembly as being too democratic. "What good do we have to expect from the assembly of Lower Canada, which emanates directly from the whole indiscriminate mass of population? An assembly not as in England and comprising the maximum of property, virtue, talents and valour of the state, but like a barroom of a country inn or a common stage coach filled with gentlemen, notaries, accountants and attorneys' clerks, country clowns, dram sellers and bankrupts." Whatever its faults, the assembly was a lively, disruptive place.

At a time when Napoleon was stalking Europe, wreaking havoc, Craig sensed that Quebec's sympathies lay with France. "They are in their hearts French yet," he wrote, "and whatever attachment they may affect to feel for [this] government . . . there would not be fifty dissentient voices to a proposition . . . for their re-annexation to France. . . . The general opinion among the English part of the inhabitants is that they [the Canadiens] would even join an American force, if that force were commanded by a French officer."

There were rumours that the French fleet would invade Canada and the English minority in Lower Canada was nervous. "This province is already too much of a French province for an English colony," read an editorial in the *Mercury*, "To *unfrenchify* it as much as possible, if I may be allowed the phrase, should be a primary object, particularly in these times, when our arch-enemy is straining every nerve to frenchify the Universe . . . after 47 years of possession of Quebec, it is time the province should be English."

Bédard had no wish to become English, but he embraced the English constitution and parliamentary democracy with an unmatched knowledge and zeal. "In what essential point are Canadien subjects different from English subjects?" he wrote in *Le Canadien*, the newspaper he co-founded. "Cannot a Canadien be, and is he not in reality, English, in his love of English liberty, in his attachment to the English government, and his aversion for French principles? Does loyalty consist in identity of language?"

Craig saw the province in pragmatic terms: Who could he count on? The French were a perennial threat. And now, the Americans were furious at Britain, whose warships were arbitrarily stopping their trading vessels on the high seas and seizing their cargoes to prevent them from reaching France. Worse, the Royal Navy seized American sailors and forced them into the British service. There was talk of invading Canada in revenge. Craig thought war was imminent. His province was an unknown quantity, and he wanted to assimilate the French and placate the Indians, to create a uniform, reliably British colony. The issue of loyalty, which had moved through the continent like a flu virus for more than fifty years, was again going to reach a fever pitch.

Although it was inevitable that the two men should have come into conflict, Bédard shared Craig's horror of war with the United States. "What would be the consequences if Canada were invaded by the United States?" he wrote, "We would quickly feel the greed and rapacious spirit of the Americans . . . on invading Canada, they would occupy most Canadien properties and reduce the Canadiens to the sad condition of slaves."

But there was no room in Craig's thinking for the idea of a loyal opposition; he saw Bédard, with his insistence on the assembly's rights, as his most immediate threat. "This son of a baker who possesses the best abilities of the lot," Craig wrote, "is by far the most dangerous of the set. Those who know him best . . . give it as their opinion that there are no lengths to which he is not capable of going." Twice Craig dissolved the assembly to thwart Bédard. In 1810 he seized the presses of *Le Canadien*, denouncing its "wicked, seditious, and traitorous writings." He imprisoned Bédard and his colleagues from the paper, releasing them one at a time, extracting bail and apologies from each. Bédard was alone in refusing to capitulate. He demanded a trial, which was refused, and he stayed in jail for a year.

Bédard helped drag into the open the essential tensions that existed in Lower Canada and helped sharpen the political conflict between Canadien democrats and their British rulers. He was a complex man who was the first colonist in British North America (and one of the first in the British empire) to espouse the idea of responsible government.

By 1811, Craig's dropsy had worn him out; he returned to London where he died the following year. After being released from jail, Bédard's political career was finished. He moved to Trois-Rivières, taking a judge's position and encouraging Canadiens to enlist in the forthcoming fight against the Americans.

Isaac Brock was brigadier general of the British forces in Upper Canada, a tall, unmarried career soldier with little actual battle experience. With Napoleon threatening all of Europe, Brock complained of being "buried in this inactive, remote corner." But by 1811, his remote corner was becoming dangerously active. "Every American newspaper teems with violent and hostile resolutions against England," he noted, "and associations are forming in every town for the ostensible purpose of attacking these provinces.

Sir James Henry Craig
(*Garrit Schipper, National Archives of Canada*, C-24888)

Major General Sir Isaac Brock
(*J.W.L. Forster, Government of Ontario Art Collection*)

Tecumseh. "I stood upon the ashes of my own home, where my own wigwam had sent up its fires to the Great Spirit, and where I summoned the spirits of the braves who had fallen in their vain attempts to protect their homes from the grasping invader, and as I snuffed up the smell of their blood from the ground I swore once more eternal hatred – the hatred of an avenger" – Tecumseh, after returning to Prophetstown, which had been destroyed by William Harrison's men. The Battle of Tippecanoe, as it was called, is sometimes cited as the first battle of the War of 1812. (*National Archives of Canada, C-000319*)

I consider the time arrived when every loyal subject should . . . come forward and show his zeal for His Majesty's service."

The mood in the United States Congress was hostile and acquisitive. "I shall never die contented," announced Kentucky Congressman Richard Johnson, "until I see [Britain's] territories incorporated with the United States. . . . The waters of the St. Lawrence and the Mississippi interlock in a number of places, and the great Disposer of Human Events intended those two rivers should belong to the same people."

On June 18, 1812, President James Madison signed a declaration of war against Canada. Brock heard the news while he was dining with American officers at Fort George, near Niagara Falls. They finished the dinner in peace, then withdrew to plan mutual destruction.

Former American president Thomas Jefferson thought that victory would simply be a formality. "The acquisition of Canada this year, as far as the neighbourhood of Quebec, will be a mere matter of marching," he felt. "Upon the whole I have known no war entered into under more favourable circumstances."

This certainly seemed true. Canada had 500,000 people (many of whom had recently been Americans) to America's 7 million. Brock had only 1,600 troops to defend a two-thousand-kilometre border. And he had the same worries that had plagued Guy Carleton in 1774: Would the citizens fight the enemy or embrace them? "My situation is most critical," Brock wrote to the adjutant-general in Montreal, "not from anything the enemy can do but from the disposition of the people – the population, believe me, is essentially bad – a full belief possesses them all that this province must inevitably succumb. . . . Most of the people have lost all confidence. I, however, speak loud and look big." It was difficult to look big given the state of affairs. To compound his problems, there was rampant desertion in the Canadian militia, with many men going over to the Americans.

Rather than spread his unreliable force in a thin, defensive pattern, Brock chose to assemble his soldiers and mount an audacious offensive. His target was Fort Detroit, defended by two thousand men and an eight-day march away. It was a risk; in concentrating his army there, he left the rest of the colony vulnerable to attack.

Brock had three hundred British regulars and four hundred Canadian militia. His army was augmented by six hundred natives under the leadership of Tecumseh, a stately, charismatic Shawnee chief who was a fan of *Hamlet*. Tecumseh's father had died when he was an infant and a brother had been killed by whites. His first battle had been fought at fifteen, against the Kentucky Volunteers. Tecumseh had been lobbying among the natives to halt American encroachment on native land throughout the Ohio Valley, visiting the Delaware, Wyandot, Kickapoo, Seneca, and Potawatomi to marshal support. He argued for a united native nation, a mirror of the Thirteen Colonies, and the military force he marshalled was formidable. "It was an extraordinary spectacle to see all these aborigines assembled together at one

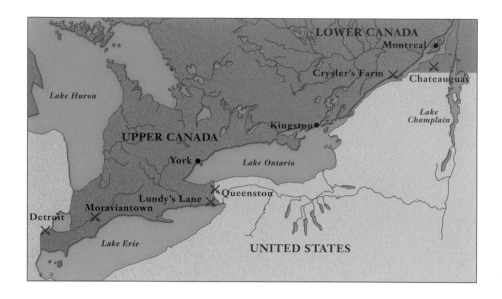

The War of 1812

time," wrote Thomas Verchères de Boucherville, a fur trader and volunteer in the militia, "some covered with vermillion, others with blue clay, and still others tattooed . . . from head to foot. . . . A European witnessing this strange spectacle for the first time would have thought . . . he was standing at the entrance to hell, with the gates thrown open to let the damned out for an hour's recreation on earth!"

Tecumseh paraded his warriors in front of Fort Detroit, presenting them three times to give the illusion of a larger force. Brock had dressed his Canadian militia in discarded British uniforms to create the look of a professional army. Their attack relied heavily on bluff, a tactic Brock had some experience with. As a young soldier, he had been provoked by a celebrated duellist, seeking to fight. Brock had insisted that instead of taking up the standard duelling distance he and his adversary should exchange shots over the width of a handkerchief. The duellist backed down and eventually left the regiment.

After assembling this theatrical force in view of Fort Detroit, Brock wrote a letter to the American commander, General William Hull: "Sir; It is far from my inclination to join a war of extermination, but you must be aware that the numerous body of Indians who have attached themselves to my troops will be beyond my control the moment the contest commences."

Montcalm had used the same scare tactic at Fort William Henry in 1757. Hull had civilians in the fort, among them his daughter and grandson. The spectre of an "Indian massacre" was entrenched in frontier mythology; it conjured scenes of torture and hell. While Hull was pondering this vivid image, Brock pounded the fort with cannon fire.

An officer emerged from the fort with a white flag, seeking an audience with Brock. "I was on the advance with the General Brock at the time," wrote Private Shadrach Byfield. "And from what we could hear, the officer wanted three days cessation; to which our General replied, that if they did not yield in three hours, he would blow up every one of them."

Battle of Queenston Heights
(*National Archives of Canada, c-276*)

Hull surrendered. Without sacrificing a life, Brock had acquired more than two thousand prisoners, an armoury of muskets and cannon, and money to pay his men. But the greatest benefit from his astounding victory was the change in attitude it inspired among the Canadians; their fragile patriotism was buoyed. "The militia have been inspired by the recent success with confidence," Brock wrote his brothers. "The disaffected are silenced."

The Americans were mortified by the capture of Detroit. "I declare to you," James Taylor of Virginia wrote to President James Madison on October 13, 1812, "I think the whole course of proceeding the most weak, cowardly and imbecile that ever came within my notice." William Hull was court-martialled for cowardice and sentenced to death. "I have done what my conscience directed," he said. "I have saved Detroit and the Territory from the horrors of an Indian massacre." He was pardoned but died in disgrace.

Their national honour shaken, the American military launched a response two months later. On October 13, before dawn, a low, insistent sound, like a strong, racing wind, reached Queenston Heights. Across the Niagara River, American artillery had begun to fire from their position at Fort Grey. Brock woke up and rode his horse, Alfred, toward the sound, anxious to determine if this was a real invasion or a diversionary tactic.

The American battery was directed by Major John Lovett, a lawyer, occasional poet, and pacifist who had never before fought in a battle. He viewed the war as a costly, inhumane waste. "If any man wants to see folly triumphant," he wrote to his friend John Alexander, "let him come here, let him view friends by friends stretched for hundreds of miles on these two shores, all loving and beloved; all desirous of harmony; all wounded by being coerced, by a hand unseen, to cut throats. . . . History, while recording our folly, will dress her pages in mourning, the showers of Posterity's tears will fall in vain; for the sponge of time can never wipe this blot from the American Name . . ."

The Americans were faced with the problem Brock had encountered months earlier: the desertion of soldiers, some of whom were going to the enemy. It was an unpopular war, despite the expansionist fire being preached by congressmen. It was clear that the war would not be a "mere matter of marching," as Jefferson had predicted, but a matter of killing and dying. Nevertheless, Lovett was committed to winning this misguided war, and he ordered the bombardment of Queenston. By sunrise, both sides were fully engaged.

"Day was just glimmering," wrote twenty-one-year-old John Beverley Robinson, a law student and future attorney general who had joined the Canadian militia. "The cannon from both sides roared incessantly; shells were bursting in the air, and the side of the mountain above Queenston was illuminated by the continual discharge of small arms."

The American attempt to cross the river was disastrous. They did not have boats large enough to transport their heavy guns, and the strong currents played havoc with the boats they did send across. Musket fire from the Canadians cut them down before they beached. Under the constitution of the United States, the militia was not required to fight on foreign soil. Some of the men exercised that right and refused to cross. Others crossed and returned. Still, almost twelve hundred made it to the Canadian side.

Under the command of the wounded Lieutenant-Colonel Solomon Van Rensselaer, the Americans were pinned below the cliffs that led up to Queenston Heights. They managed to find a fisherman's path up the cliff, and Van Rensselaer sent his men up under the command of a young captain, with the order to shoot anyone who tried to retreat. They captured Queenston Heights and took the upper ground. The battle was turning in their favour.

Brock tried to recapture the high ground. He felt that Queenston Heights was the key to Upper Canada; if it fell, the province would quickly follow. Brock's distinctive, scarlet uniform made him a natural target, and a sniper shot him in the centre of the chest, killing him instantly.

The last line of defence was the natives. In the woods surrounding the Heights, a band led by Joseph Brant's son John and his adopted nephew John Norton, who was half Scottish and half Cherokee, moved toward the Americans. Norton had begun the day with three hundred warriors. Moving through the forest they heard from retreating militiamen that six thousand Americans were at Queenston Heights. "Some Warriors answered – 'The more game the better hunting,'" Norton wrote in his journal. "These reports however had not the same effect upon all, – many were alarmed thereby. . . . We found ourselves much diminished in number by the imperceptible desertion of many; – there did not remain together more than Eighty Men, when coming to the Skirts of the Wood." The natives attacked repeatedly, retreating to the woods and regrouping. "Comrades and Brothers," Norton yelled, "remember the fame of ancient Warriors, whose Breasts were never daunted by odds of number. . . . We have found what we came for. . . . There they are – it only remains to fight."

Major John Norton. The adopted nephew of Joseph Brant, Norton was half Scottish and half Cherokee and he commanded a native force at the Battle of Queenston Heights. "The number of my Men was considerably reduced, – a great part had gone home, – the approach of Winter made them feel the Want of Warm Clothing, and in constant Marching they had worn out their Mocasins. The fall of the Leaf, the season for hunting the Buck, had arrived, & many had gone to the Woods, to supply their Wants by the Chase: – few would have remained, had not the Love of Glory animated their hearts, – & inspired Patience to Support them in their Sufferings, while they awaited the coming of the Enemy. There were then hardly Three Hundred Warriors remaining at Niagara." (*National Archives of Canada*, C-123832)

Prophet Tenskwatawa, Brother of Tecumseh. The Prophet, as he was known, was a one-eyed mystic who predicted that the Indians would be rescued from white oppression by divine intervention. The Americans, who "grew from the scum of the great Water when it was troubled by the Evil Spirit," would be vanquished by the Great Spirit. Miracles were attributed to the Prophet and his influence stretched across the continent. (*Charles Bird King, Gilcrease Museum*)

British reinforcements finally flanked them and they charged the Americans. "They had no place to retreat to," wrote John Beverley Robinson, "and were driven . . . to the brink of the mountain which overhangs the river. They fell in numbers. . . . Many leaped down the side of the mountain to avoid the horrors which pressed on them, and were dashed in pieces by the fall."

Back on the American side, Major Lovett encouraged his troops to cross the river to reinforce their compatriots but was unable to sway them. "The name of Indian," he wrote to his friend Joseph Alexander, "the sight of the wounded brought off, or the devil, or something else petrified them. Not a regiment, not a company, scarcely a man would go."

There would be no support or even rescue of those across the river. The Americans were pinned down below the cliffs, unsuccessfully trying to surrender. Twice, a soldier was sent out with a white flag; both were killed. Their capitulation was finally recognized in time to avert a wholesale slaughter. Nine hundred and twenty-five Americans surrendered, and there were two hundred and fifty casualties. On the Canadian side there were only fourteen dead and seventy-seven wounded. But one of the fourteen was Isaac Brock, a grievous loss. An ambitious soldier and brilliant tactician, he had personified the Canadian resistance, an elegant symbol of defiance.

Brock was buried at Fort George as the British gunners fired a twenty-one-gun salute. Across the river, the American guns at Fort Niagara matched the tribute. John Lovett watched the smoke of the guns disperse in the pale sky. He could not hear them; his day on the battery beside the guns had left him permanently deaf. "The 12th was all duty," he wrote to Joseph Alexander, "the 13th all death. My friend, the scenes of war are trying . . . to body and soul . . . and where, where in God's name are they to end?"

Tecumseh's younger half-brother Tenskwatawa, known simply as "the Prophet," was an angry, one-eyed mystic with a hot temper. He had gained early prominence, preaching a millennarian religion that urged a return to pure native values. Their present misery was a test, he said; soon they would be delivered from the predatory grasp of the white man. A few years earlier, Governor James Craig had heard about the Prophet and looked into buying his influence, hoping to use him as a weapon against the Americans. But the Prophet remained his own weapon.

Tecumseh, after four marriages, was resolutely single, devoted to a cause. He acted as the political arm of his brother's religious campaign, and together they lobbied natives from the Great Lakes to the Gulf of Mexico, trying to unite them into an effective continental confederacy. Tecumseh argued for communal land use among natives and an end to selling it to the whites. "The white men aren't friends to the Indians," he told them. "At first they only asked for land sufficient for a wigwam; now, nothing will satisfy them but the whole of our hunting grounds from the rising to the setting sun."

The man most responsible for the loss of native lands was Governor William Henry Harrison of Indiana Territory, who had bought up more than 40 million hectares. He procured half of present-day Indiana, as well as large parts of Wisconsin, Missouri, and Illinois, by bullying, deceit, fraud, cash, and whisky. Harrison intended to fill the spaces with settlers, to create a midwestern empire. The charismatic and tireless Tecumseh posed a threat to his plans. "The implicit obedience and respect which the followers of Tecumseh pay to him," Harrison noted, "bespeaks him one of those uncommon geniuses which spring up occasionally to produce revolutions. . . . If it were not for the vicinity of the U.S. he would perhaps be the founder of an Empire that would rival in glory that of Mexico."

Tecumseh and Harrison met at Vincennes, Indiana Territory, in 1810 to discuss their opposing viewpoints on land development. Tecumseh arrived with three hundred warriors. Harrison had hoped to use the meeting to defuse the growing native militancy, but Tecumseh seized the opportunity to make a political speech: "Sell a country! Why not sell the air, the clouds and the great sea, as well as the earth? Did not the Great Spirit make them all for the use of his children?" He talked for three hours and threatened to kill any chief who sold land to the white man. The outdoor meeting ended with brandished tomahawks, drawn swords, and a nervous departure.

The two would meet again. At the outbreak of war, Harrison was a major general in the American army, and in the autumn of 1813 he commanded an invasion force of three thousand men. A British force of three thousand led by General Henry Proctor was waiting at Fort Malden on the Detroit River, along with Tecumseh and his warriors. Tecumseh welcomed the chance to face his arch-enemy on the battlefield, but Proctor made the decision to retreat in the face of Harrison's army. Tecumseh had never entirely trusted the British – they were simply the less offensive whites – and now he accused Proctor of cowardice.: "We must compare our Father's conduct to a fat animal that carries its tail upon its back but when affrighted, it drops it between its legs and runs off. . . . We wish to remain here and fight our enemy. . . . You have got the arms and ammunition. . . . If you have an idea of going away, give them to us and you may go. . . . Our lives are in the hands of the Great Spirit. We are determined to defend our lands, and if it be his will, we wish to leave our bones upon them."

Proctor pulled his army up the Thames River, a slow retreat that was covered by Tecumseh's warriors. Harrison's men picked off the stragglers and took much of the British ammunition and supplies. By the time Proctor was ready to make a stand, at Moraviantown, near Chatham, some of his soldiers had not eaten in two days and were gravely disheartened. Many of Tecumseh's men had deserted, and he was left with roughly five hundred warriors.

Proctor had two days to prepare for Harrison's army, but he failed to take advantage of the terrain, or of his only military superiority, which was artillery. The British army was riddled with dissension and Proctor's

William H. Harrison. Harrison parlayed his military feats into a political career and eventually became the ninth president of the United States. In 1840, his running mate was John Tyler, leading to the campaign slogan "Tippecanoe and Tyler Too!" But Harrison's running mate, at times, seemed to be Tecumseh, who had been dead for twenty-seven years, but who still carried a mythic sense of menace, and Harrison invoked him to his political advantage. (*National Portrait Gallery, Smithsonian Institution/Art Resource, New York*)

leadership was being questioned. When Harrison's army approached, the British put up only a token fight.

Private Shadrach Byfield, veteran of Detroit and Queenston Heights, described the battle: "After exchanging a few shots, our men gave way . . . one of our sergeants exclaimed, 'For God's sake men, stand and fight.' I stood by him and fired one shot, but the line was broken and the men were retreating. I then made my escape farther into the wood."

Proctor tried to rally his men, riding among them, crying, "For shame 41st! What are you running away for? Why do you not form?" Then Proctor too made his escape into the wood. The actions of the 41st would be scrutinized in dismal detail at a court martial a year later. At the time, their retreat left five hundred natives fighting an American army of three thousand.

Tecumseh was in the woods, his men exposed on their left flank by the retreat of the British. The Americans advanced on horseback and were cut down. They dismounted and continued the fight, hand to hand. The battle lasted almost an hour before the British were overwhelmed. "I made my escape farther into the wood," wrote Shadrach Byfield, "where I met with some of the Indians, who said that they had beaten back the enemy on the right, but that their prophet [Tecumseh] was killed, and they then retreated." An American, Major Thomas Rowland, saw Tecumseh's corpse on the field: "He had such a countenance as I shall never forget. He did not appear to me so large a man as he was represented – I did not suppose his height exceeded 5 feet 10 inches, but exceedingly well proportioned. The British say he compelled them to fight."

The fate of his body remains a mystery. Some natives claim that he was carried off the battlefield and later buried, though there is no marked gravesite. Americans said his skin was torn off in strips by souvenir-hunters

The Death of Tecumseh at the Battle of the Thames (*Anne S.K. Brown, Military Collection, Brown University*)

and sold as razor strops, the mutilated corpse abandoned after yielding its morbid trinkets.

Dozens of men claimed to have killed Tecumseh. The dream of a unified native state died with him, and the symbolic value in having killed him carried significant political reward. His death was talismanic, influencing American politics for more than a generation. Richard Mentor Johnson, the expansionist Kentuckian, claimed the deed and rode it to the White House, where he served as vice-president. William Harrison's ongoing feud with Tecumseh fuelled his march to a brief presidency. Tecumseh's death became a popular political plank, no less effective for its frequent and varied use. The question echoed for fifty years, reduced to a children's rhyme, "Rumpsey, Dumpsey, Who killed Tecumseh?"

After its victory at Moraviantown, Harrison's army was poised to take Upper Canada, but it had reached the end of its supplies, and winter was at hand. Harrison retreated to Detroit, unable to conquer the weather or the land.

Maurice Nowlan was a lieutenant in the Prince Regent's County of Dublin regiment, which was made up almost entirely of Irish soldiers. In Montreal he wooed Agathe Perrault, a Catholic French Canadian, and they were married on February 10, 1812. A week after their wedding, they went to the Montreal circus, a comic respite that attracted most of the city. Mr. Menial performed acts of buffoonery on the tightrope and Mr. Manfredy "executed a grotesque dance with wooden shoes," the paper reported. After their brief honeymoon, Nowlan was called back to duty, and he wrote Agathe regularly.

In September, he wrote from Camp Blair Fundy, on Quebec's south shore, "... my Jewel, there is only one thing to trouble me; that is being away from you and the fear of your crying, don't be fretting, my love, the thoughts of that will be worse to me than all the Hardships of a Campaign ..."

By May of the next year, he was at Kingston. "General Proctor has General Harrison pinned up in a Small Fort with about 700 men which he intends to attack immediately. I am sure the next account will be that General Harrison will surrender to General Proctor without firing a shot. . . . I can't sleep for more than an hour at a time and then I start from my sleep with some frightful dream or other. Write to me my soul and give me some comfort as it is for you alone that I live."

By November, Harrison had routed Proctor's army. Nowlan was now at Stoney Creek in the Niagara Peninsula, and rumours arrived in waves, distorted and vigorous and threatening. He heard that the Americans were planning an attack on Montreal and he worried about his young wife. "My fears for you, my only Soul, are distressing beyond everything else. . . . Before this reaches you my Love, I hope the business that gives us so much uneasiness will be decided. It is shocking to hear the Indians, how they exclaim against Harrison's Army. The Prophet seeks Revenge for his Brother, he will cook their Hearts and feast his warriors with them, the Idea of such outrage is shocking my Love but they are so enraged it's all vain

Charles-Michel de Salaberry. At the age of fourteen, de Salaberry enlisted in the British Army's 44th Regiment of Foot, and he later joined the 60th Regiment, which was made up of professional soldiers from England, Prussia, Hanover, and Switzerland. There was one other French Canadian in the regiment, a man named des Rivières, who was killed in a duel with a Prussian. De Salaberry avenged his death, by duelling with the Prussian the next day and killing him. A colonel in the 60th reported to the Duke of Kent, "[de Salaberry] is a young man of distinguished bravery and he will make an excellent officer because he has a dedication to honour engraved in his soul." (*Musée du Chateau Ramezay*)

to try to prevent it. The Prophet says as they skinned his Brother to make razor straps he will eat of their flesh and quench his thirst with the soup. It will be shocking to witness such a doing but I hope for my Dear Wife's sake I may live to see all this. . . . My love tell me all the news my Sweet and muster all your courage for a few days and things will all be well . . ."

Maurice's last letter came before the battle of Fort Niagara. "I am just able to spare a few moments to say that I have received your very affectionate letter of the 28th last month, but I have to regret that I was obliged to commit it to the flames as soon as I read it, we have been making preparations since Sunday last to go and storm Niagara Fort. . . . I have great hopes to survive. . . . Now it is possible for me to bid my dear and loving wife adieu and perhaps the last time. . . . If the Almighty spares me till tomorrow my first care will be to write you. . . . My Dearest Jewel . . . it's but for you I live, the Almighty bless you my only Life."

The British attacked Fort Niagara at night, crossing the river about five kilometres upstream and moving quietly with scaling ladders and axes. It was planned as a surprise, and the men were to use bayonets and maintain strict silence. It was an almost bloodless victory. Only six men were killed, among them Maurice Nowlan. His brother wrote Agathe to tell her the news.

"My Dear Mrs Nowlan, With the most poignant grief and horror have I heard . . . my most affectionate and ever beloved brother is no more. . . . And now I may wander over the winter's snow or summer's heat of the distant region, no Season can ever bring him back to me. . . . But it's whispered in my ear that he has said – be kind and affectionate to my beloved Wife, yes this must have been his last desire, for never was one heart to another so linked as his to yours."

Agathe never remarried. She lived to the age of eighty-four, devoting her life to charity, and died in 1871.

Two weeks after the disaster of Moraviantown, the Americans invaded Lower Canada in a two-pronged attack. One army came down the Châteauguay River and a second down the St. Lawrence, with the plan of converging on Montreal.

Charles-Michel de Salaberry, whose grandfather had fought against the British and whose father had fought for them, commanded the resistance at Châteauguay. De Salaberry was from an old Canadien family, an imposing man and a career soldier who had once killed a Prussian in a sabre duel. French Canadians were already disposed to support Britain, and it was thought that the charismatic de Salaberry would effectively mobilize that support. He raised a company called Les Voltigeurs Canadiens with the promise of an immediate salary and fifty acres of land.

"The corps now forming under the command of Major de Salaberry is completing with a dispatch worthy of the ancient warlike spirit of the country," the *Quebec Gazette* reported. "They are to defend their king, known to them only by acts of kindness, and a native country long since

made sacred by the exploits of their forefathers." The *Gazette* might have been overstating the prevailing mood, but militia companies were raised and defended Lower Canada's borders at Lacolle River, Odelltown, and Four Corners.

De Salaberry chose to face the Americans on the banks of the Châteauguay, a strategically advantageous spot. His men destroyed bridges, felled trees, then waited three days for the enemy. His three hundred men on the front line faced an army of three thousand.

The Americans fired the first volley. "The fire from their right was so powerful as to force our skirmishers to shelter themselves," said Michael O'Sullivan, aide to de Salaberry. "The enemy mistook this for the beginning of a retreat and much mistaken they were. . . . Huzzas resounded from all parts of their army." But the Canadians returned fire from their entrenched positions, repeatedly rebuffing the Americans. Unable to penetrate the defences and vulnerable to fire, the Americans quit the field. "I write you just a word to let you know that the enemy commenced his retreat yesterday," de Salaberry wrote to his wife, Anne. "I believe that we have saved Montreal for this year. . . . I hope that they are going to let us rest and that I shall have the happiness to see you shortly. I am very tired. I kiss you a thousand times, also the little one."

Although the Americans were in retreat, de Salaberry thought they might simply be regrouping. For eight days, the Canadien and British forces

Battle of Châteauguay. On October 26, 1813, an American force of three thousand led by General Wade Hampton en route to Montreal was defeated by a much smaller force of Canadien volunteers commanded by Charles-Michel de Salaberry. (*Musée du Château Ramezay*)

Battle at Crysler's Farm
(*Crysler Farm Museum*)

stayed behind their barricades, waiting in the cold autumn rain. The weather became a more bitter enemy than the Americans. "We suffered so much from . . . foul weather that some of our men fell sick every day," wrote Lieutenant Charles Pinguet. "I now know that a man can endure without dying more pain and hell than a dog. There are many things that I can tell you easier than I could write them, but you will be convinced by this affair that Canadians know how to fight."

A few weeks after Châteauguay the second arm of the invasion met with the same fate, defeated resoundingly at Crysler's Farm by a much smaller force, and the Americans now abandoned their plan to take Lower Canada and turned their attention to the west.

Lower Canada had produced a surprisingly loyal and effective opposition, but in the Maritimes people were ambivalent about attacking the United States. "From the St. Lawrence to the Ocean an open disregard prevails for the laws prohibiting intercourse with the enemy," wrote Major-General George Izard.

British soldiers were living on beef imported from Vermont and Maine. The Americans were buying British textiles, pottery, and sugar. In the Maritimes, it was a time of unprecedented prosperity. "Happy state of Nova Scotia!" read an article in the *Acadian Recorder*. "Amongst all this tumult we have lived in peace and security; invaded only by a numerous host of American doubloons and dollars." Prostitution and venereal disease flourished on Halifax's Citadel Hill, where ten thousand British troops found ways to entertain themselves.

In Upper Canada, the British army provided merchants with a large, captive market, and they hiked their prices accordingly. Fortunes were made during the war. "I have lent money at the rate of 10% for 20 days which is upwards of 180% per annum," a merchant reported. "I do not think there was ever a place equal to this for making money."

Upper Canadians were less reliably loyal than their Lower Canadian counterparts. Simcoe's dream of American settlement in Upper Canada was not without its drawbacks: some of the settlers remained sympathetic to the United States. The leading critic of the British authorities was Joseph Willcocks, an Irishman who established the *Upper Canadian Guardian or Freeman's Journal* and was a member of the legislative assembly. The month that war broke out, he wrote, "I am flattered at being ranked among the enemies of the Kings Servants in this colony. I glory in the distinction. Is it truth and a constant adherence to the interests of the country that has excited so much alarm among the band of sycophantic office-hunters, pensioners and pimps!"

During the war, Willcocks turned from parliamentary opposition to outright treason when he started to spy for the Americans, passing on information about British troop movements. In 1813, he raised a company of Canadian Volunteers to fight for the Americans, and he led scouting and raiding parties and helped burn the Niagara Peninsula. In the spring of 1814, he and fourteen other Upper Canadians were charged with high treason. They were prosecuted by John Beverley Robinson, the veteran of Queenston Heights, who was now the twenty-three-year-old attorney general of Upper Canada. Eight of the men were convicted and sentenced to hang. On July 20, they were publicly executed at Burlington Heights. In a grotesque medieval display, the heads were then cut off and exhibited. But Willcocks was not among them. He had left Upper Canada to become a colonel in the American army. On the day of the executions, his army of traitors was part of America's last invasion force under the command of Brigadier General Winfield Scott.

By this time the Niagara Peninsula was a torched wasteland. Willcocks himself had burned the town of Niagara, which he had previously represented in the legislature. "In the village, at least 130 buildings were consumed," reported the *Ontario Repository*, "and the miserable tenants of them, to the number of nearly four hundred, consisting mostly of women and children, were exposed to all the severities of deep snow and a frosty sky, almost in a state of nakedness. How many perished by the inclemency of the weather, it is, at present, impossible to ascertain." One of the few buildings left untouched by the Americans was Willson's Tavern, a public house with a view of Niagara Falls. The proprietor, Deborah Willson, traded

The Battle of Lundy's Lane, July 25, 1814 (*Granger Collection, 4E758.12*)

information with both British and Americans, and both sides considered it neutral ground.

On July 25, 1814, American Brigadier General Winfield Scott stopped at the tavern seeking information on the enemy. Willson told him that British General Phineas Riall was at a nearby farm with 800 regulars and 300 Canadians. She was right about the location, but wrong about the numbers. About 1,500 men were waiting among the grave markers in a pioneer cemetery by Lundy's farm.

Scott took his army of 1,200 to confront them. "At the discovery of the formidable line," he wrote, "I dispatched a staff officer to the General-in-chief, with a promise to maintain my ground until the arrival of the reserve. By standing fast, the impression was made on the enemy that the whole American reserve was at hand and would soon assault his flanks. . . . [M]y brigade could not be withdrawn." Outnumbered, Scott's First Brigade was cut down; it lost 500 of its 750 men before sunset. "About 9 o'clock at night there was, as if by a common consent, a general cessation of firing," wrote Henry Ruttan, an orderly sergeant in the Canadian militia. "It was yet so dark as to prevent us from distinguishing our men from those of the enemy. We could plainly see a line forming in our front and hear every order given."

Reinforcements arrived, and 6,000 men now faced one another in the darkness. "The opposing lines were so near each other that at the flash of the enemy's guns," an American soldier wrote, "[we could] see the faces and even mark the countenances of their adversaries. . . . The darkness and smoke combined with the fitful light made the faces of those in the opposing ranks wear a blue sulphurous hue, and the men at each flash had the appearance of laughing . . ."

The two armies fired volleys, then engaged in hand-to-hand combat, stabbing and clubbing each other with blind desperation, killing their own men by accident in the darkness. Joseph Willcocks knew that if he was captured, he would be hanged for treason; he melted into the night. At midnight, the fighting ended without any order from either side. The Americans retreated, taking their wounded from the field.

"The morning light ushered to our view a shocking spectacle," observed British Sergeant James Commins, "Americans and English laid upon one another, occasioned by our advance and retreat. Nearly 2,000 was left on the field."

The battle of Lundy's Lane was among the bloodiest of the war. Both sides officially claimed victory. The Americans went home, burning villages and bridges as they went.

In August, almost four thousand British soldiers descended on Washington and burned most of it, including the White House and the Library of Congress. President James Madison fled, but his wife, Dolley, who had salvaged the original Declaration of Independence and a life-sized portrait of George Washington, watched the flames from a friend's house nearby in Virginia.

On the day before Christmas, 1814, the Treaty of Ghent was drawn up in Belgium. The war was officially over, although it took more than a month for the news to make it to North America. Britain recognized America's independence and agreed to return all seized territories.

For Canada and the United States, the war resulted in scorched settlements and two official victors. In Upper Canada, the war cemented the province's essentially British cultural and political nature. The tectonic plates that had been shifting in North America for more than a century – among French, British, and American forces – had finally settled into place; the continent would be American south of the Great Lakes and Canadian to the north.

JOURNEY TO THE SEA

At the beginning of the seventeenth century, the west was still a conceptual hole in the European imagination, a vast, uncharted space between Europe and China. It was the fur trade that transformed the territory, pushing its exploration, changing its culture as Europeans formed alliances with natives, and leading, inevitably, to settlement.

The Hudson's Bay Company was instrumental in this process, and it owed its name, and in some ways its existence, to the ill-fated Henry Hudson.

Hudson's early years are obscure. He enters history in 1607, already middle-aged, hired by the English Muscovy Company to find a way to China via the North Pole. His trip was a failure, but in 1610, the East India Company and the optimistically named Northwest Passage Company financed another attempt. Hudson was a gifted navigator; he had an outsized imagination and the courage necessary for exploration; but he was an erratic leader and a fatally flawed judge of men.

In his ship the *Discovery*, Hudson negotiated the treacherous tides and ice south of Resolute Island along what is now Hudson Strait, then entered what would be called Hudson Bay with a sense of destiny, assuming it was the Pacific Ocean. By October, after several weeks of exploring what we now call James Bay, a "labyrinth without end," it was clear that this was not the route to China. His crew blamed him for the failure, which brought for them

First Page of the Hudson's Bay Company Charter, May 2, 1670 (*Hudson's Bay Company Archives, Provincial Archives of Manitoba*)

The Last Voyage of Henry
Hudson (*John Collier, Tate Gallery*)

a number of unfortunate consequences: for one thing, they would not be
getting the promised bonus for finding the passage, and they would be spending the winter in the frozen north, poorly equipped and on short rations.

During that miserable, deprived winter, a mutinous schism formed
among Hudson's men. On June 12, the *Discovery* sailed for home, but eleven
days later the mutiny flowered. Hudson and seven men, including his son,
were set adrift in a small boat. The rebellious crew sailed north on the
Discovery, then anchored to investigate the remaining food supply, which
they thought Hudson had been hoarding.

While they were anchored, the shallop caught up to them. Some of the
mutineers argued to let Hudson and the others back on board, but the leader,
William Wilson, weighed anchor and sailed away, "as from an enemy."
Hudson and his men died in the wilderness, the facts of their fate unrecorded.

Hudson's fateful voyage set in motion an even greater enterprise: the
opening up of the Canadian west by English and French explorers and
traders. The mutineers took back with them knowledge of the route to the

west, and over the next two hundred years the territory would be transformed by an unlikely phenomenon, the popularity of the beaver hat, which propelled the fur trade. The Hudson's Bay Company was born out of a charter issued by Charles II in 1670. The natives who lived in the territories Hudson explored had long-established trading networks, which the company would tap with great success. But while Henry Hudson had supplied the essential geographical knowledge, the company itself was conceived by two Frenchmen, Pierre Esprit Radisson and Médard Chouart Des Groseilliers.

Pierre Radisson was from Provence, but he disdained national allegiances throughout his life, shifting his loyalties as it served his purposes. "For my own part, I will venture," he wrote in his informative, wonderfully baroque, though often inaccurate journal, "choosing to die like a man than live like a beggar. . . . It was my destiny to discover many wild nations, I would not strive against that destiny."

In 1651, not long after arriving in New France, the teenaged Radisson was captured by Iroquois during a raid. He was adopted by a prominent native family and quickly learned their language and customs, accompanying them on hunting expeditions and war parties. He eventually escaped but was recaptured before he could get back to Trois-Rivières. His punishment was a slow torture, and he was saved from death only by the intervention of his adoptive family, who gave him the name Oninga. When he visited Fort Orange (later Albany, New York), the governor offered to ransom Radisson, but he declined, surprisingly, and instead returned with the Iroquois. His perverse ambivalence led to another escape attempt, this one successful.

Radisson's brother-in-law, Médard Chouart Des Groseilliers, was a fur trader who had journeyed into the western country as far as Lake Huron, and in 1659 they teamed up to explore past the trading territories known to Europeans, to seek out new sources of fur. "We made our proposition to the Governor of Quebec that we were willing to venture our lives for the good of the country," Radisson wrote, "and go to the remotest countries with two Hurons."

The governor welcomed their offer but imposed his own terms: they would take along two government overseers and return half of their profits. "My brother was vexed at such an unreasonable demand," Radisson wrote. "To take Inexperted men to their ruine; . . . besides, that the governor should compare two of his servants to us. . . . We made the Governor a slight answer and told him for our part we knewed what we were; Discoverers before governors. . . . The Governor was much displeased at this, and commanded us not to go without his leave."

Disobeying the governor, they left in the middle of the night and paddled for two months, travelling up the Ottawa River, through Lake Nipissing, to the north shore of Lake Huron. They were Caesars, Radisson wrote, with no one to contradict them. But it was a dangerous trip: for several years the Iroquois had barred the route to the interior, determined

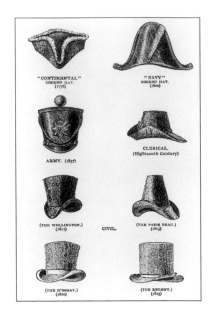

The underwool from beaver pelts was used to make the beaver hat, which remained fashionable for centuries. In 1634, Father Paul Le Jeune, the superior of the Jesuits at Quebec, observed that the natives thought the European desire for beaver belts was frivolous. "I heard my [Indian] host say one day, jokingly, *Missi picoutau amiscou*, 'The Beaver does everything perfectly well, it makes Kettles, hatchets, swords, knives, bread; in short, it makes everything.' He was making sport of us Europeans, who have such a fondness for the skin of this animal and who fight to see who will get it; they carry this to such an extent that my host said to me one day, showing me a very beautiful knife, 'The English have no sense; they give us twenty knives like this for one Beaver skin.'" (*National Archives of Canada, C-17338*)

to keep the lucrative role of fur-trade middleman to themselves. In the company of Ojibwa, Radisson and Des Groseilliers encountered some Iroquois, and a battle ensued. The victorious Ojibwa ate the flesh of their dead enemies and took the prisoners along "to burn them at our own leisure for the more satisfaction of our wives. We left that place of massacre with horrid cries," according to Radisson. "We plagued those unfortunates. We plucked out their nails one after another."

By winter they had paddled to Lake Superior, as far as any European trader had previously ventured. They buried their trade goods so they would not be stolen, then camped for the winter with a group of Ojibwa. When their food ran out they faced famine and resorted to eating their dogs. Then they boiled the bones repeatedly for a thin soup before finally grinding them into dust and eating that. They tried to dig roots out of the frozen ground, stripped bark from trees, and ate the hide from beaver pelts. Many of the Ojibwa died of starvation, and the survivors were sick and gaunt. "We mistook ourselves very often taking the living for the dead and the Dead for the living," Radisson wrote.

In the spring, the survivors had their reward. The Ojibwa took part in the Feast of the Dead: eighteen native nations came together for ten days of feasting near Lake Superior. For Radisson and Des Groseilliers it was an unprecedented trading opportunity; they feasted, observed the politics, and joined in the theatre. "We sang in our language as they in theirs, to which they gave great attention," Radisson wrote. "We gave them several gifts, and received many. They bestowed upon us above 300 robes of castors [beaver]." They also told the Frenchmen that thicker, more lustrous pelts could be found at a great northern bay.

The two traders returned to Montreal accompanied by three hundred natives in a flotilla of canoes laden with furs, expecting a heroes' welcome. Not only had they extended the fur trading territory substantially, they had convinced the inland natives to hazard the Iroquois blockade. Instead of being congratulated, however, they were fined by the governor, and Des Groseilliers was thrown in jail. "He made my brother prisoner for not having observed his orders and to be gone without his leave," Radisson wrote. "Was he not a tyrant to deal so with us after we had so hazarded our lives?"

Radisson and Des Groseilliers had planned to go farther north on their next trip, to find those marvellous furs. But after the reception in Montreal, and a subsequent rejection in Paris, they went to England with their proposal to find the northern bay, arriving in London in the plague year of 1665. English commerce was moving rapidly across the world at the time. The British East India Company had recently been chartered to gather the riches of India, and there was interest in the potential of North America. King Charles II granted them an audience and agreed to finance a voyage to Hudson Bay to search for the furs that the natives had described.

In 1668, Radisson set out for Hudson Bay on the *Eaglet* and Des Groseilliers sailed on the *Nonsuch*. Radisson had to turn back, his ship

HURON FEAST OF THE DEAD ◆ After spending a deprived winter near Lake Superior, Radisson and Des Groseilliers joined in the Feast of the Dead in the spring. Originating with the Huron, the ritual was initially held when the land was depleted for planting, usually after seven to ten years, and the village would move to a new site. All those who had died were disinterred and a feast was held to celebrate them. Among non-agrarian native societies, the ritual evolved into an opportunity to cement trading and political ties with other bands. For Radisson and Des Groseilliers it was not only a time of plenty after a winter of privation, it was a unique commercial opportunity.

"Severall kettles weare brought there full of meate. They rested and eat above five howres without speaking one to another. The Considerablest of our Companyes went and made Speeches to them. . . .The day following they arrived with an incredible pomp. This made me thinke of the Intrance that the Polanders did in Paris; saving that they had not so many Jewells, but instead of them they had so many feathers. The first weare yong people with their bows and arrows and Buckler on their shoulders, uppon which weare represented all manner of figures: according to their knowledge, as of the sun and moone, of terrestriall beasts, about its feathers very [artfully] painted. Most of the men their faces weare all over dabbed with severall collours. Their hair turned up, Like a Crowne: and weare Cutt very even, but rather so burned for the fire is their Cicers. . . . They present us with guifts of Castors skins, assuring us that the mountains weare elevated, the valleys risen, the ways very smooth, the bows of trees cutt downe to goe with more ease, and bridges erected over Rivers, for not to wett our feete. . . . The speech being finished, they intreated us to be att the feast. . . . After the feast was over, there comes two maidens bringing wherewithall to smoake the one the pipes, the other the fire. They offered first to one of the Elders, that Satt downe by us. When he had smoaked, he bids them give it us. This being done, we went back to our fort as we came." From the journal of Pierre Radisson (*National Archives of Canada*, C-113747)

---

damaged by a storm, but Des Groseilliers was gone for a year, and he returned with an impressive cargo of beaver pelts. With the stories of abundant beaver confirmed and an economical, direct route to the fur territory established, the Hudson's Bay Company (HBC) was born. Charles II issued a charter in 1670 that granted monopoly trading privileges and mineral rights to all the lands drained by the water flowing into Hudson Strait. Named Rupert's Land in honour of Prince Rupert, the king's cousin, it was an area fifteen times the size of Britain, almost 8 million square kilometres. Radisson and Des Groseilliers were not among the partners or investors of the new company; those positions were occupied exclusively by armchair adventurers in London who had the ear of the king.

For five years, Radisson and Des Groseilliers worked for the British administrators of the Hudson's Bay Company. Then, abruptly, they once again allied themselves with the French. Des Groseilliers returned to New France and died there before the turn of the century. Radisson joined the French navy and was involved in the effort to capture the Dutch colonies in Africa and the Caribbean. He later led a raid on the HBC post at Port Nelson, capturing the English governor, claiming the furs for France, and making it an outpost of the French empire. But by 1684, he was back in the employ of the Hudson's Bay Company. He then returned to Port Nelson and persuaded his nephew, Jean-Baptiste Des Groseilliers, who ran the post, to defect to the English.

Radisson flirted with different loyalties for much of his life. He was able to negotiate in the royal courts of two countries and live comfortably in the bush among the natives. But his only real allegiance was to himself. Radisson had a tenacity and singularity that suited him to exploration and commerce. He eventually retired to a London suburb and died in 1710, a roguish, decayed gentleman.

The company that he and Des Groseilliers helped create flourished. Trading posts were established on Hudson Bay, and a protocol developed with the Cree, who were courted as trading partners. The whole system depended on the natives bringing their furs to the posts, though they often had to cross hundreds of kilometres to get there.

The annual trading sessions began with the passing of a ceremonial pipe, which the Cree left at the fort to indicate that they would return the following year. There was a ritual exchange of gifts, and then they got down to the pragmatic issues of business. "You told me last year to bring many Indians," a Cree chief told the traders. "You see I have not lied. Here is a great many young men . . . give them good goods, I say! . . . Tell your servants to fill the measure and not to put their fingers within the brim. . . . We have come a long way to see you. The French send for us but we will not be there. We love the English. Give us good black tobacco; moist and hard twisted. . . . Do you understand me?"

The natives were tough negotiators. "The guns are bad," a Cree trading captain complained. "Let us trade light guns, small in the hand, and well shaped, with locks that will not freeze in the winter." The Europeans

White Trader with Indian Trappers (*Royal Ontario Museum, 966.136.2*)

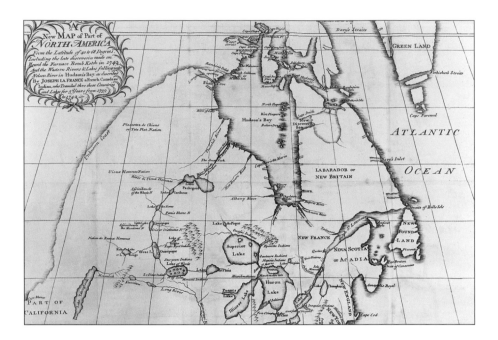

A New Map of North America,
1743 (Jacob Robinson, Hudson's
Bay Company Archives, Provincial
Archives of Manitoba)

accommodated them. The natives had long ago forged their own complex trading network; now a new commercial relationship had been established.

Pierre Gaultier de Varennes, Sieur de La Vérendrye, was the son of the governor of Trois-Rivières. He had been both a soldier and farmer before being put in charge of a French trading post near Lake Superior in 1715. La Vérendrye listened to the natives, who said they knew of a route to the Western Sea. The French maps of the west at the time were vague and fanciful, but some showed a large body of water that led to the Pacific. If the Western Sea could be found, trade with China would be direct and profitable. La Vérendrye felt he could find it.

"I acquainted myself with the route through different savages, who all made the same statement, that there are three routes or rivers which lead to the great river of the West," he wrote in his journal. "Consequently I had a map made of these three rivers, in order that I might be able to choose the shortest and easiest road."

To get the support of the governor and the French court, La Vérendrye offered a pragmatic argument. His proposed route from Lake Superior ran across the trapping grounds of the natives who traded with the Hudson's Bay Company. He would build inland trading posts and cut off the supply to the English. "The colony will receive a new benefit independently of the discovery of the Western Sea through the quantity of furs that will be produced which now . . . go to the English. I am only seeking to carry the name and arms of His Majesty into a vast stretch of countries hitherto unknown, to enlarge the colony and increase its commerce."

He left Montreal in June 1731 with a party of fifty that included his sons, a nephew, and an extensive supply of trade goods. Moving west, he encountered Cree and Assiniboins taking their furs on the long trip to a Hudson's Bay Company post and persuaded them to trade with him instead, which they were happy to do. "Provided there are Frenchmen on the road they travel, the savages will not go to the English," he wrote, "whom they do not like and even despise."

By 1743 he had established eight trading posts and staked out an enormous western territory for New France that eventually extended to the foothills of the Rocky Mountains. The various native nations were a checkerboard of allegiances, and La Vérendrye showed a politician's skills in picking his way through the warring tribes. But he was put to a crucial test by the Cree, who demanded that La Vérendrye's son Jean-Baptiste join them in a war party.

"I was agitated, I must confess, and cruelly tormented by conflicting thoughts, but put on a brave front. . . . How was I to entrust my eldest son to barbarians whom I did not know . . . to go and fight other barbarians of whose name and of whose strength I knew nothing? Who could tell whether my son would ever return?"

In the end, he let his son go with them. He did return, but two years later he was killed in a revenge attack. "They were all massacred by the Sioux in the most treacherous manner. . . . In that calamity I lost my son . . . to my lifelong regret."

When he returned to Montreal, La Vérendrye faced creditors and lawsuits. His ventures had cost him dearly, but he saw his accomplishments in a broader, patriotic light.

"People do not know me," La Vérendrye wrote. "Money has never been my object; I have sacrificed myself and sons for the service of His Majesty and the good of the colony; what advantages shall result from my toils the future may tell."

What he had done was lay down the foundations for a fur-trading empire that would rival that of the Hudson's Bay Company. He was planning another voyage to find the elusive Western Sea when he died in New France at the age of sixty-four.

The French sought out the natives, eliminating the considerable work involved for them in hauling pelts to a remote Hudson's Bay post. The HBC's response to La Vérendrye was Anthony Henday, a labourer who volunteered to travel inland and trade with the natives at their settlements. He left in June 1754, paddling down the Hayes River, then walking with a group of natives to the site of present-day Red Deer, Alberta. He was the first Englishman to meet with the Blackfoot and one of the first to witness the extraordinary spectacle of buffalo herds moving across the prairie like an earthquake. He wintered with the Blackfoot and admired their hunting skills.

"I went with the young men a Buffalo hunting," Henday wrote, "all armed with Bows & Arrows: Killed seven, fine sport. . . . So expert are the Natives, that they will take the arrows out of them when they are foaming and raging with pain, & tearing the ground up with their feet & horns until they fall down."

A BLACKFOOT ENCAMPMENT ◆ David Thompson spent the winter of 1787-88 in the tent of Saukamapee, a Peigan chief, who was almost eighty. Each night the chief told a story, which Thompson later recorded. Thompson heard of the battles with the Snake natives and the coming of horses to the Plains.

"We had more guns and iron headed arrows than before; but our enemies the Snake Indians and their allies had Misstutim [horses] on which they rode, swift as the Deer, on which they dashed at the Peeagans, and with their stone Pukamoggan knocked them on the head, and they had thus lost several of their best men. This news we did not well comprehend and it alarmed us, for we had no idea of Horses and could not make out what they were."

While the Snake had horses, the Peigan had guns, the two new technologies that would alter the Plains. "Those of us who had guns stood in the front line, and each of us [had] two balls in his mouth, and a load of powder in his left hand to reload. . . . We watched our opportunity when they drew their bows to shoot at us, their bodies were then exposed and each of us, as opportunity offered, fired with deadly aim, and either killed, or severely wounded, every one we aimed at."

A horse was shot as well. "Numbers of us went to see him, and we all admired him, he put us in mind of a Stag that had lost its horns; and we did not know what name to give him. But as he was slave to Man, like the dog, which carried our things; he was named the Big Dog." (*W. M. Armstrong, Royal Ontario Museum*)

Hudson's Bay Company Post
(*L. P. Hurd, Royal Ontario Museum*)

The Blackfoot embraced Henday as a guest, but not as a trading partner. "We have no hopes of getting them to the Fort," he wrote. "As what cloth & c. they had were French, and, by their behaviour I perceived they were strongly attached to the French interest." Henday tried to tempt one chief with the deals that could be made at Hudson Bay. "He made little answer: only said that it was far off, & they could not paddle." The Blackfoot were horsemen, a regal and powerful group who already had the French coming to them.

After a year, Henday began the trip home. The natives he met with had traded their best furs to the French, and then French traders stole most of Henday's furs. He returned to the post at York Factory with a few inferior furs and discouraging news.

With the loss of New France to the British in 1759, the French surrendered the northern half of the continent, along with control of the fur trade. This vacuum was filled by English merchants from Quebec who came west to trade, either individually or in small groups, using the trading network the French had developed. The natives had been allies of the French, and they did not embrace the English traders at first.

The British traders began to winter with the natives, and eventually a rapport was reached. The "pedlars," as the HBC dismissively called them, were mostly enterprising Scots and adventurers from the Thirteen Colonies. By the 1760s, the HBC had noticed a drastic decline in both the quality and number of furs. The pedlars were exploring rich new fur territories, while the HBC was trapping the already known territories near Hudson Bay.

These new traders cut into HBC profits, but they also undercut each another in desperate, sometimes violent competition. They realized finally that it would make more sense to ally than to continue this destructive competition. Benjamin Frobisher, who, along with his brother Joseph, had a small fur-trading enterprise, learned "that separate interests were the bane of the trade, we lost no time to form . . . a company."

In 1774, the North West Company (NWC) was born, made up of Montreal businessmen, including Simon McTavish, James McGill, Isaac Todd, and the Frobishers. Their motto was Perseverance. Following La Vérendrye's routes, they continued north as far as Lake Athabaska and west to the Peace River country. Within twenty-five years they would control 78 per cent of the Canadian fur trade.

As veterans of trading expeditions, the NWC partners understood the business at its most essential level. The HBC was run by London businessmen who were unfamiliar with the country and its customs and still ran their business with the blithe confidence of a monopoly. The key advantage for the "Nor'Westers" was that they took their business to the natives, fraternizing freely with them and cementing their commercial ties through strategic marriages. They were also prepared to use threats and intimidation when it served their purpose. The new company quickly brought in more than four times as many furs as its rival, making its partners very wealthy.

The Hudson's Bay Company realized that it would have to adopt the same tactics in order to survive. It had already made some concessions by sending employees inland to winter with the natives to try to persuade them to bring their furs to York Factory in the spring. But it was clear that the company would have to go further than that. "We are quite satisfied that the decrease of our trade is owing to the upland Indians being intercepted by the pedlars," the London Committee concluded, "who by means of a chain of rivers and lakes are got up to the back of many of our factories, but we are equally satisfied that this traffic might in a short time be got better of by sending some of our servants from each of our factories to those lakes or rivers and opening a trade with the natives in the same manner as they do." The HBC would no longer be "asleep by the frozen sea," as its critics had suggested.

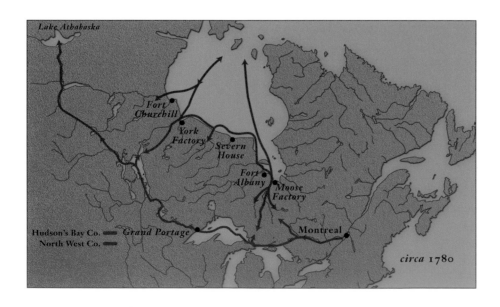

Trade routes of the Hudson's Bay Company and the North West Company

SAMUEL HEARNE ◆ "Whether it was from real motives of hospitality, or from the great advantages which they expected to reap by my discoveries, I know not; but I must confess that their civility far exceeded what I could expect from so uncivilized a tribe, and I was exceedingly sorry that I had nothing of value to offer them. However, such articles as I had, I distributed among them, and they were thankfully received by them. Though they have some European commodities among them, which they purchase from the Northern Indians, the same articles from the hands of an Englishman were more prized." Hearne's description of his encounter with the Copper natives, from *A Journey from Prince of Wales Fort in Hudson's Bay to the Northern Ocean* (*Hudson's Bay Company Archives, Provincial Archives of Manitoba*)

One of its first forays into the interior was not to find furs, though; it was to search for minerals. The HBC hoped to diversify its interests by venturing into whaling and mining, to compensate for diminishing fur profits. In 1762, Moses Norton, the factor at Churchill, had engaged a Dene native named Matonabbee to "go & trace to ye mouth of ye Largest Rivers to ye Northward" in the hope of finding minerals. Matonabbee returned in 1767 with a map to the Coppermine River drawn in charcoal on deerskin. Two years later, Samuel Hearne was given the task of retracing Matonabbee's route and returning with copper. The land was unknown and incredibly harsh; his journey was a monumental task of navigation and survival.

Hearne had fought in the Seven Years' War in the Royal Navy and joined the Hudson's Bay Company in 1763 as a ship's mate on the *Churchill*. He was chosen on the basis of his youth, his navigational skills, and his ability to snowshoe. Hearne made two abortive attempts before his definitive third journey. Matonabbee, who accompanied Hearne, ascribed the Englishman's early failures to bad guides and a lack of women. "For when all the men are heavy laden," Matonabbee argued, "they can neither hunt nor travel to any considerable distance. . . . Women were made for labour. One of them can carry, or haul, as much as two men can do. They also pitch our tents, make and mend our clothing, keep us warm at night; and in fact there is no such thing as travelling any considerable distance, or for any length of time, in this country, without their assistance." On his next trip, Matonabbee brought women, among them his numerous wives.

They left Churchill in December 1770. Hearne described Matonabbee as being nearly six feet tall, finely proportioned, courageous, and defiantly agnostic. "He was determined," Hearne noted, "as he came into the world, so he would go out of it, without professing any religion at all. Notwithstanding his aversion from religion, I have met with few Christians who possessed more good moral qualities, or fewer bad ones." They became close during the course of their travels, and Hearne saw European qualities in him: "to the vivacity of a Frenchman, and the sincerity of an Englishman, he added the gravity and nobleness of a Turk." Matonabbee was also a fierce warrior, an adept politician, and a practised guide, qualities Hearne needed to make the trip a success.

Hearne recalled a confrontation Matonabbee had with southern natives who were intent on robbing him. "'I am sure (said he) of killing two or three of you, and if you chuse to purchase my life at that price, now is the time; but if otherwise, let me depart without any further molestation.' They then told him he was at liberty to go, on condition of leaving his servant; but to this he would not consent. He then rushed into the tent and took his servant by force from two men; when finding there was no appearance of farther danger, he set out on his return to the frontiers of his own country."

To the natives known as the Copper Indians, who had never seen a European, Hearne was exotic, if not beautiful. "They flocked about me, and expressed as much desire to examine me from top to toe, as an European Naturalist would a non-descript animal. They, however, found and pronounced me to be a perfect human being, except in the colour of my hair and eyes; the former they said, was like the stained hair of a buffalo's tail, and the latter, being light, were like those of a gull. The whiteness of my skin also was, in their opinion, no ornament, as they said it resembled meat which had been sodden in water till all the blood was extracted."

Out on the tundra, Hearne, a reader of Voltaire, ruminated on the elusive nature of beauty. The native women aged quickly, he noted, worn with labour, but they were valued for the very qualities he abhorred. "Ask a Northern Indian, what is beauty? he will answer, a broad flat face, small eyes, high cheekbones, three or four broad, black lines a-cross each cheek, a low forehead, a large broad chin, a clumsy hook-nose, a tawny hide, and breasts hanging down to the belt."

Hearne noticed that when a woman was in labour, her people set up a small tent for her out of earshot of the main camp so they could not hear her shrieks. "These people never attempt to assist each other on those occasions," Hearne observed. "They entertain that nature is abundantly sufficient to perform every thing required. . . . When I informed them of the assistance which European women derive from the skill and attention of our midwives, they treated it with the utmost contempt; ironically observing, 'that the many hump-backs, bandy-legs, and other deformities, so frequent among the English, were undoubtedly owing to the great skill of the persons who assisted in bringing them into the world.'"

By the time Hearne's party reached the tundra, they had run out of food. "Indeed for many days before we had been in great want, and for the last three days had not tasted a morsel of any thing, except a pipe of tobacco and a drink of snow water; and as we walked daily from morning till night, and were all heavy laden, our strength began to fail." Hearne's pack had the sextant in it and weighed thirty kilograms.

Near their destination, Hearne's group was joined by a group of Dene, who were looking to battle with their traditional enemy, the Inuit.

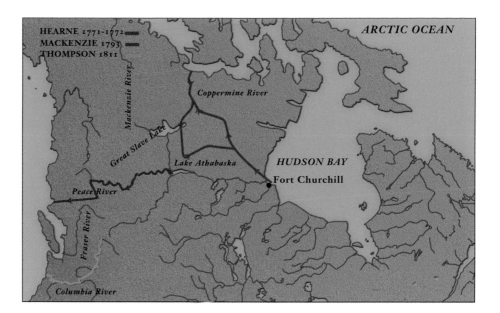

ARCTIC OCEAN

Mackenzie River

Coppermine River

Great Slave Lake

Lake Athabaska

HUDSON BAY

Fort Churchill

Peace River

Fraser River

Columbia River

The Voyages of Samuel Hearne, Alexander Mackenzie, and David Thompson, 1771-1811

Near the mouth of the Coppermine River they came upon a party of Inuit. Hearne tried to talk the Dene out of their fight but was mocked for lacking courage. In preparation for battle, the Dene painted their faces red and black, tied their hair back, and stripped to their breechcloths. At one in the morning, they attacked the sleeping enemy.

"Finding all the Esquimaux [Inuit] quiet in their tents, they rushed forth from their ambuscade, and fell on the poor unsuspecting creatures, unperceived till close at the very eves of their tents, when they soon began the bloody massacre while I stood neuter in the rear. In a few seconds the horrible scene commenced; it was shocking beyond description; the poor unhappy victims . . . ran out of their tents stark naked, and endeavoured to make their escape." Twenty-one Inuit were killed.

In the morning, as they were leaving, they noticed an old woman, probably deaf, catching salmon at the shore, oblivious to the slaughter. She was tortured and killed as well. "I cannot reflect on the transactions of that horrid day without shedding tears," Hearne wrote. He named the site Bloody Falls.

When he reached the river that was his destination, Hearne hoped to see a gleaming mountain of copper, but all he found was a single two-kilogram nugget. "This mine, if it deserve that appellation," he wrote, "is no more than an entire jumble of rocks and gravel. . . . I and almost all my companions expended near four hours in search of some of this metal. Among us all, only one piece of any size could be found." They turned around and walked home, completing a 4,000-kilometre journey.

His search had not yielded riches, but Hearne was the first European to reach the arctic overland, and this was the first step toward opening up the interior, a monumental leap forward. Hearne's journal, *A Journey from Prince of Wales Fort in Hudson Bay to the Northern Ocean*, became a lively entry in the genre of Canadian exploration writing, published in two English editions as well as in French, German, and Dutch translations.

After his extraordinary trip, Hearne established Cumberland House, the Bay's first inland trading post, and he eventually became the slightly eccentric factor at Fort Prince of Wales, where he kept a small menagerie of mink, muskrat, geese, foxes, hawks, and tame beaver. "They become so domesticated as to answer their name," he wrote, "and follow in the same manner as a dog would do; and they were as much pleased at being fondled, as any animal I ever saw. During the winter they lived on the same food as the women and were remarkably fond of rice and plum-pudding."

While at Fort Prince of Wales, Hearne worked on the manuscript for his *Journey*. In 1782, a French force of three ships under Jean-François de Galaup, Comte de Lapérouse, approached the fort. The French had 74 guns and 290 soldiers, while Hearne's fort held only 38 civilians. Hearne surrendered the fort – a logical but controversial decision. Lapérouse burned it down to its stone foundations. But he read Hearne's manuscript and praised it, urging him to publish. The French commander sent Hearne, his manuscript, and his men back to England on a Hudson's Bay Company ship.

When Matonabbee heard that Hearne had surrendered the fort, he hanged himself in shame. His six wives and four children starved to death that winter.

By the late eighteenth century, the west was slowly coming into focus for Europeans. Maps had been made, cobbled together from the limited observations of explorers and the natives' anecdotal evidence. James Cook's accounts of his Pacific voyage were published, offering a sense of the destination they sought. But still, no one had succeeded in finding an overland route to the sea. The Hudson's Bay Company was still looking for it, under pressure from critics in England, and in 1789 the North West Company began its own search.

The job fell to Alexander Mackenzie, a twenty-five-year-old fur trader who had been born in Scotland on the Isle of Lewis. He was given the task of finding a route to the Pacific coast, then sailing up to Alaska, across to Russia, and on to England in triumph.

In his first attempt, Mackenzie set a gruelling pace – at one point he covered 1,730 kilometres in fourteen days – but the trip was of no commercial use. His route took him from Fort Chipewyan on Lake Athabaska down what is now the Mackenzie River, which led him to the Arctic Ocean rather than the Pacific. Mackenzie was intensely pragmatic, and he decided to better prepare himself for his next trip. "In this voyage I was not only without the necessary books and instruments," he wrote, "but also felt myself deficient in the sciences of astronomy and navigation; I did not hesitate therefore, to undertake a winter's voyage to England, in order to procure one and acquire the other."

Mackenzie had little of the romance of explorers like Hearne, and he felt no inclination toward philosophical reflections on the alien landscape.

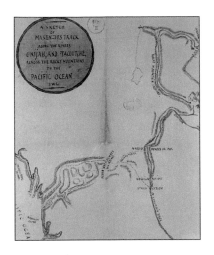

A sketch of Alexander Mackenzie's track along the rivers Unijah and Tacoutche, across the Rocky Mountains to the Pacific Ocean (*James Winter Lake, Hudson's Bay Company Archives, Provincial Archives of Manitoba*)

He saw the natives as tools to be used in reaching his destination and he was largely incurious about them. For Mackenzie, exploration was a commercial issue and a chance to win personal glory.

For the second voyage he had a compass, a sextant, a chronometer, a telescope, and a working knowledge of navigation. He wrote to a cousin, "I'm off to traffick with the Russians. . . . Should I be successful I shall retire to greater advantage. Should I be unsuccessful I cannot be worse off than I am at present."

Mackenzie set off with nine men, including two Chipewyan guides, and a dog on May 9, 1793, paddling up the Peace River, looking for the continental divide. Despite rough water, Mackenzie managed to cross the Rocky Mountains and reach the Fraser River on June 18. Shuswap natives warned him that the river was too dangerous to navigate and advised him to take the overland route they used to trade with the coastal tribes.

Mackenzie ran the idea past his men. "I stated the difficulties that threatened our continuing to navigate the river, the length of time it would require, and the scanty provisions we had for such a voyage; I then proceeded for the foregoing reasons to propose a shorter route, by trying the overland road to the sea. . . . I declared, in the most solemn manner, that I would not abandon my design of reaching the sea, if I made the attempt alone, and that I did not despair of returning in safety to my friends." Mackenzie was not a glamorous man, but he was a respected and determined leader, and his men followed him.

A party of Nuxalk natives guided them to a grease trail, named for the fish oil that coastal natives brought inland to trade. It took a month to reach Dean Channel, a saltwater arm of the ocean. There they encountered hostile Bella Bella natives, who had already had unfortunate dealings with whites arriving in ships, probably captained by the sternly imperial George Vancouver. One of the natives threatened Mackenzie, gesturing for him to leave. His terrified guide interpreted for him. "In relating our danger, his agitation was so violent that he foamed at the mouth. . . . My people were panic-struck, and some of them asked if it was my determination to remain there to be sacrificed."

Despite the imminent threat, Mackenzie took the time to fix his location, using his instruments to calculate the position of the sun. "I had now determined my situation," he wrote, "which is the most fortunate circumstance of my long, painful, and perilous journey, as a few cloudy days would have prevented me from ascertaining the final longitude of it."

He also left his mark on a large rock. "I now mixed up some vermillion in melted grease, and inscribed in large characters . . . this brief memorial: Alexander Mackenzie from Canada, by land. The 22nd of July, one thousand seven hundred and ninety-three."

Mackenzie had reached the salt water of the Pacific Ocean – he was within a few hours' paddling of the open sea, but he never actually saw it. He was the first European to cross the continent overland.

Of his voyages, Mackenzie wrote: "Their toils and their dangers, their solicitudes and sufferings, have not been exaggerated in my description. On the contrary, in many instances, language has failed me in the attempt to describe them. I received, however, the reward for my labours, for they were crowned with success."

He wanted to publish a version of his journal but was faced with writer's block. Undaunted by unmapped spaces, angry rivers, and hostile natives, Mackenzie was defeated by the blank page. He suffered a bout of depression and complained that his thoughts were scattered and unformed every time he tried to write. His book, *Voyages From Montreal*, was finally ghost-written by William Combe, an Englishman who had ghosted other heroic accounts, occasionally from debtors' prison.

Mackenzie's dry and detailed book was well received. Napoleon read it. So did Thomas Jefferson, who then commissioned Lewis and Clark to map the territory beyond the Mississippi. Mackenzie was knighted by King George III at St. James's Palace in London, and, through shrewd investments, he became a wealthy man, making him unique among the explorers of his time.

Mackenzie went on to become a listless, largely absentee parliamentarian, elected to the assembly in Lower Canada. After his career as an explorer, he found politics static and dull. He quickly abandoned his seat and retired to Scotland. At the age of forty-eight, he married a fourteen-year-old named Geddes Mackenzie with whom he had a daughter and two sons. By the time the second son was born, Mackenzie was afflicted with Bright's disease, a kidney ailment, and he died suddenly the next year, in 1820.

Mackenzie's contemporary David Thompson was called by his biographer, James Tyrell, "the greatest practical land geographer that the world had produced." Thompson worked for both the Hudson's Bay Company and the North West Company, and during his life he saw the fur trade rise to periods of giddy profits and sink into its eventual decline. He covered more territory than Mackenzie but never achieved the wealth or fame that Mackenzie did. Thompson more closely matched the description he gave of himself, "a solitary traveller unknown to the world."

The son of Welsh parents, Thompson was born in London in 1770 and from the age of seven attended the Grey Coat Hospital, a charity school for the poor and orphaned. He had an early obsession with numbers and liked to work out difficult mathematical problems on a slate. He thrilled to the adventures of Daniel Defoe's *Robinson Crusoe* and read Jonathan Swift's *Gulliver's Travels*. At the age of fourteen, he was recruited by the Hudson's Bay Company.

"In the month of May 1784 at the Port of London," Thompson wrote in his autobiography, "I embarked in the ship *Prince Rupert* belonging to the Hudson's Bay Company, as apprentice and clerk to the said company, bound for Churchill Factory." From the shores of Hudson Bay he watched the

Before Alexander Mackenzie left on his extraordinary trek to the Pacific, he wrote to his cousin Roderick that he wanted to leave the west. "I am fully bent on going down. I am more anxious now than ever. For I think it unpardonable in any man to remain in this country who can afford to leave it. What a pretty Situation I am in this winter. Starving and alone, without the power of doing myself or any body any Service." (*British Columbia Archives*)

Prince Rupert disappear. "I bid a long and sad farewell to my noble, my sacred country, an exile forever."

At Churchill he met Samuel Hearne, who had lost Fort Prince of Wales to the French two years earlier and whose reputation was in decline. "Mr. Samuel Hearne was a handsome man of six feet in height, of a ruddy complexion and remarkably well made, enjoying good health," Thompson noted. "As soon as the Hudson's Bay Company could do without his services they dismissed him for cowardice. Under him I served my first year."

Thompson's uncharitable view of Hearne might have had more to do with Hearne's religious beliefs than with any military shortcomings. "It was customary of a Sunday," Thompson wrote, "for a sermon to be read to the Men, which was done in [Hearne's] room, the only comfortable one in the Factory; one Sunday, after the service . . . he then took Voltaire's Dictionary, and said to us, here is my belief, and I will have no other." In his *Dictionnaire philosophique portatif, ou la raison par l'alphabet*, Voltaire argued against the idea that there was a hierarchy of created beings, from slug to ape to man to angel. But Thompson disagreed. He felt that God had given him "the power to examine his works on our globe; and perhaps to learn the order in which he has placed them." Where Hearne was a notorious freethinker, Thompson was a devout Christian.

Like a number of men who have lived in isolated circumstances, Thompson had found God in the vast, unkind landscape of the New World. Few conversions, though, are as dramatic as his.

"A strange incident happened to me and which some[times] happens to mankind which brings with it a strong influence on their conduct for the rest of their lives. I was sitting at a small table with the chequer board before me, when the devil sat down opposite to me, his features and colour were those of a Spaniard, he had two short black horns on his forehead which pointed forwards; his head and body down to his waist (I saw no more) was covered with glossy black curling hair, his countenance mild and grave; we began playing, played several games and he lost every game, kept his temper but looked more grave; at length he got up or rather disappeared. My eyes were open it was broad daylight, I looked around, all was silence and solitude, was it a dream or was it reality? I could not decide."

After this encounter, Thompson became a pious young man, and remained true to his faith until his death. His game of checkers with Satan was an unlikely foray into mysticism in a life that was otherwise governed by rigorous science.

At Churchill, Thompson expected to have the kind of adventure he had read about in London, but instead he found himself a shivering clerk enduring the rude surprise of a northern winter. "The cold is so intense that everything in a manner is shivered by it; continually the Rocks are split with a sound like the report of a gun," he wrote. "All our movements more or less were for self-preservation. All the wood that could be collected for fuel, gave us only one fire in the morning, and another in the evening.

The rest of the day, if bad weather, we had to walk in the guard room with our heavy coats of dressed Beaver." To keep warm, he paced the way he had in the Grey Coat schoolyard. Instead of adventure, he had the clerk's job of making lists of flannel, flint, gin, hardtack, and hatchets – a numbing alphabetical inventory.

The summer provided little relief. The mosquitoes tortured the men's flesh and their imaginations, but Thompson's natural scientific curiosity overcame his torment. He examined the mosquito under a microscope and wrote in meticulous detail about the ingenious system it employed to suck blood. This kind of inquisitiveness was applied to almost everything he encountered in the west.

After a cloistered year at Churchill Factory, Thompson finally got his first taste of adventure. His assignment was to travel to York Factory, 240 kilometres to the south, equipped with a blanket and a gun, delivering mail in the company of two Cree natives. "Every day we passed from 12 to 15 polar bears," he wrote. "Lying on the marsh, a short distance from the shore. . . . The Indian rule is to walk past them with a steady step without seeming to notice them."

The following year, Thompson went inland with a group of men on a company expedition to build a trading post on the western plains. For more than two months they paddled and walked, and Thompson got his first glimpse of the vast interior of the continent, where he would spend the next twenty-five years. "At length the Rocky Mountains came in sight, like shining white clouds on the horizon," he wrote. "As we proceeded, they rose in height, their immense masses of snow appeared above the clouds and formed an impassable barrier, even to the eagle."

In the foothills Thompson was struck by another remarkable sight – thousands of Peigan natives camped in a sprawling city of tents. The seventeen-year-old Thompson spent the winter in the tent of an elder named Saukamapee, learning the language, listening to his stories.

"Almost every evening for the time of four months, I sat and listened to the old man without being in the least tired . . . the habits, customs and manners, politics and religion, such as it was, anecdotes of Indian chiefs, and their means of gaining influence in war and peace, that I always found something to interest me."

Night after night, in the smoky darkness of the teepee, huddled under a blanket, Thompson listened to the hypnotic cadences of Saukamapee, relishing the kinds of stories he had cherished and longed for in London. One of the stories Saukamapee told described the first tragic effects of contact with Europeans.

The Peigan had approached the camp of an enemy band with stealth, slitting open the tents with their knives to attack the sleeping men. "But our war whoop instantly stopt," Saukamapee said. "Our eyes were appalled with terror, there was no one to fight but the dead and the dying, each a mass of corruption."

Half Breed Encampment
(*Paul Kane, Royal Ontario Museum, 912.1.25*)

They were dying of smallpox, a disease the natives had never seen before and to which they had no immunity. The Peigan took the infected possessions of their enemy and returned home.

"The second day after, this dreadful disease broke out in our camp," Saukamapee said, "and spread from one tent to another, as if the bad spirit carried it. We had no belief that one man could give it to another, any more than a wounded man could give his wound to another. . . . We believed that the Good Spirit had forsaken us, and allowed the Bad Spirit to become our master. . . . Our hearts were low and dejected, and we shall never be again the same people."

In 1788, Thompson broke his leg and convalesced at Cumberland House, where he met Philip Turnor, the Bay's chief surveyor, and at last found his calling. "Mr. Turnor was well versed in mathematics. . . . Under him I regained my mathematical education, and during the winter became his only assistant, and thus learned practical astronomy under an excellent master of the science." Thompson studied obsessively. "By too much attention to calculations in the night, with no other light than a small candle my right eye became so much inflamed that I lost its sight . . ."

At the end of this protracted apprenticeship, Thompson was half blind but eager. He wrote the HBC in London that, instead of the suit of clothes that they regularly gave employees who had finished their apprenticeship, he would prefer a set of surveying instruments. The HBC, who recognized Thompson's talent, sent him both.

For the next twenty years he measured the latitude and longitude of every place he visited; the natives called him "The Man Who Looks at

Canot de Maître of 1882
(J. Halkett, Hudson's Bay
Company Archives, Provincial
Archives of Manitoba)

Stars." "Both Canadians and Indians often inquired of me why I observed the sun, and sometimes the moon, in the daytime, and passed whole nights with my instruments looking at the moon and stars. [When] I told them it was to determine the distance and direction from the place I observed to other places, neither the Canadians nor the Indians believed me, for both argued that if what I said was truth, I ought to look to the ground, and over it, and not to the stars."

Thompson's reputation as a surveyor soon spread throughout the territory, and he was wooed by the rival North West Company. In 1797, he accepted their offer and left the Hudson's Bay's Reindeer Lake post in the middle of the night, walking 130 kilometres south to his new employer. "May 23rd, Tuesday. At 3 -1/2 a.m. set off . . . this day left the service of the Hudson's Bay Co. and entered that of the company of merchants from Canada. May God almighty prosper me."

It was a time of heightened competition: the Bay had opened 242 trading posts scattered throughout the west and the North West Company 342. Sometimes the rivals set up shop within a few hundred metres of one another. There were not enough beaver to support both companies, and so they relentlessly pushed their territories to the north and to the west, looking to exploit the land west of the Rockies, looking for a route to the Pacific that would be more practical than Alexander Mackenzie's torturous path.

In 1799, Thompson married a Métis woman named Charlotte Small; he was twenty-nine, she was thirteen. He often took her and their children along with him on his extended trips. Thompson became the chief surveyor of the North West Company, wandering the unmapped plains with his family, making notes and consulting the stars. He was a poor judge of distances without his instruments. But his accomplishments were enormous. He surveyed the territory west of Lake Superior, as well as the 49th parallel. In his seventy-seven journals, he described the customs and beliefs of different natives and analyzed their languages. He noted the habits and diet of moose, deer, fox, and field mice, and examined the nature of rivers, their flows and idiosyncrasies. He mapped not just the geography of the space but what filled it as well, parsing the Great Plains into something Europeans could understand.

The North West Company set him the perennial challenge of finding a convenient route to the Pacific Ocean, to open up trade with the coastal natives and to establish trade with China. It was a problematic journey for Thompson, who had been hoping to return to civilization for the first time in twenty-five years. "For the last 20 months I have spent only bare two months under the shelter of a hut, all the rest has been in my tent, and there is little likelihood the next 12 months will be much otherwise."

When he ventured into the Rocky Mountain foothills, the territory of his old friends the Peigan, Thompson encountered hostility. The North West Company had supplied the Flathead, a traditional enemy of the Peigan, with guns. In response, the Peigan pursued Thompson through the forests along the foothills and then blocked his way into the mountains. If Thompson was going to proceed, he would have to make a lengthy detour. "We must now change our route to the defiles of the Athabasca River, which would place us in safety, but would be attended with great inconvenience, fatigue, suffering and privation; but there was no alternative."

It was a two-month detour through an avalanche zone. The snow was two metres deep in places, and the horses they had brought were useless and had to be abandoned. Each evening, Thompson spent an hour fixing their coordinates, mapping his place in the blank wilderness with a sense of rapture. His men were less enraptured; all but three deserted. "My men were not at their ease, yet when night came they admired the brilliancy of the stars, and as one of them said, he thought he could almost touch them with his hand. As usual when the fire was made, I set off to examine the country before us. . . . Many reflections came to my mind; a new world was in a manner before me."

Once across the mountains, Thompson made camp and waited for winter to end.

In the spring, the resourceful Thompson made a cedar canoe and explored the upper Columbia River, the first European to do so. He made contact with the Simpoil, Nespelim, Methow, and Wenatchee natives, extolling the trading opportunities they would enjoy with the North West Company. "Very large cargoes with goods of all kinds would arrive, by which they would be supplied with clothing and all they wanted if they were industrious hunters."

He made it to the coast in 1811, only to find that American traders of the Pacific Fur Company had arrived by ship before him.

Through his efforts, the interior of what is now British Columbia was claimed for the North West Company. He had also found a usable route to the sea. "Thus I have fully completed the survey of this part of North America from sea to sea," he wrote, "and by almost innumerable astronomical Observations have determined the positions of the Mountains, Lakes and Rivers and other remarkable places of the northern part of this Continent; the Maps of all have been drawn, and laid down in geographical position, being now the work of twenty-seven years." It was Thompson's last heroic trip; he had mapped almost all the unknown areas of the west. "The age of guessing is passed away," he wrote.

In 1812 Thompson retired to Montreal to educate his children. He had a little money, but it was quickly exhausted in a series of failed business ventures: potash production, two general stores. Personal tragedy accompanied his business losses. His five-year-old son, John, died, and his seven-year-old daughter followed soon after. His eldest son, who had worked for him, rebelled, then left, and Thompson never spoke to him again. He had walked or paddled more than 8,000 kilometres, and all that was left for him now were odd jobs surveying for land development.

He kept refining his maps, working on them over the years. His magnum opus was five maps that charted the west, each giant map measuring one metre by three metres. For the first time, there was a reliable map of that vast territory. "Nothing less than an unremitting perseverance bordering on enthusiasm could have enabled [me] to have brought these maps to their present state," he wrote. "In early life [I] conceived the idea of this work, and Providence has given [me] to complete, amidst various dangers, all that one man could hope to perform."

Thompson had been driven by a sense of divine mission: to describe and catalogue all of God's work, His flora, fauna, weather, geography, and every variation of man. But sadly, his life's work failed to find a market. Arrowsmith, a London map company, valued the maps at a paltry 150 pounds, then did not publish them. Instead they used his information to correct their existing maps and did not credit Thompson. The trail that he had blazed across the plains would soon be carved up by land speculators; he was a man out of time.

Thompson was now almost destitute and took on the humiliating job of surveying Alexander Mackenzie's former estate in Montreal. Poverty continued to plague him; he was forced to pawn his warmest coat and, finally, his surveying tools.

He moved in with his daughter and son-in-law and wrote about his exploration of North America, trying to turn his journals into something publishable and popular. But his earlier problems with his eyes worsened and his vision was failing. The American writer Washington Irving (author of "Rip Van Winkle") offered to buy Thompson's manuscript, with the aim of turning it into an entertainment, but Thompson refused. His manuscript remained unfinished and unpublished. He died in obscurity in 1857 and was buried in Montreal. His reputation would not be made until the following century, when the Canadian geologist James Tyrell would examine, edit, and publish his work, declaring his genius.

Trade and exploration forged ahead, thanks to the singular efforts of men like Thompson and Mackenzie. In their wake, a society slowly formed on the prairie. As posts were established, more traders wintered with the natives. The men took native wives, and a rough culture formed around them. A new people – the Métis – arose.

THE FRANKLIN EXPEDITION ◆ The mysterious, ill-fated 1845 Franklin expedition to the Arctic haunted the nineteenth-century imagination. Thirty expeditions were sent to look for Franklin after his ships were frozen in the pack ice off King William Island. There was no journal to explain what had happened, but Franklin had kept a journal on an earlier, 1819 expedition, when nine men died.

"After our usual supper of singed skin and bone soup, Dr. Richardson acquainted me with the afflicting circumstances attending the death of Mr. Hood and Michel, and detailed the occurrences subsequent to my departure from them. . . . Hepburn went hunting, but was as usual unsuccessful. . . . In the afternoon Peltier was so much exhausted, that he sat up with difficulty, and looked piteously; at length he slided from his stool upon his bed, as we supposed to sleep, and in this composed state he remained upwards of two hours, without our apprehending any danger. We were then alarmed by hearing a rattling in his throat, and on the Doctor's examining him, he was found to be speechless. He died in the course of the night. . . . Semandre sat up the greater part of the day, and even assisted in pounding some bones; but on witnessing the melancholy state of Peltier, he became very low, and began to complain of cold and stiffness of the joints. Being unable to keep up a sufficient fire to warm him, we laid him down and covered him with several blankets. He did not, however, appear to get better and I deeply lament to add he also died before daylight. . . .

"We generally avoided speaking directly of our present sufferings, or even of the prospect of relief. I observed, that in proportion as our strength decayed, our minds exhibited symptoms of weakness, evinced by a kind of unreasonable pettiness with each other. Each of us thought the other weaker in intellect than himself, and more in need of advice and assistance. So trifling a circumstance as a change of place, recommended by one as being warmer and more comfortable and refused by the other from a dread of motion, frequently called forth fretful expressions which were no sooner uttered than atoned for, to be repeated perhaps in the course of a few minutes. . . . On one of these occasions Hepburn was so convinced of this waywardness that he exclaimed, 'Dear me, if we are spared to return to England, I wonder if we shall recover our understandings.'" (*The Franklin Expedition Crossing Lake Prosperous, Northwest Territories, attended by a Tribe of Copper Mine Indians, National Archives of Canada, c-0403*)

THOMPSON MAP ◆ Of the western explorers, David Thompson had the greatest natural curiosity, an interest in everything made by God and most things made by man. When he arrived at Fort Churchill as a teenager, the mosquitoes were an unrelenting summer plague. While others cursed them to the point of madness and covered themselves in sturgeon oil to ward them off, Thompson analyzed the enemy with his usual scientific rigour. "Summer, such as it is, comes at once, and with it myriads of tormenting Musketoes; the air is thick with them, there is no cessation day nor night of suffering from them. Smoke is no relief, they can stand more smoke than we can, and smoke cannot be carried about with us. . . . The Musketoe Bill, when viewed through a good microscope, is of a curious formation, composed of two distinct pieces; the upper is three sided, of a black colour, and sharp-pointed, under which is a round white tube, like clear glass . . . drawn back, and the clear tube applied to the wound, and the blood sucked through it into the body, till it is full; thus their bites are two distinct operations, but so quickly done as to feel as only one; different Persons feel them in a different manner; some are swelled, even bloated, with intolerable itching; others feel only the smart of the minute wounds; Oil is the only remedy and that frequently applied; the Natives rub themselves with Sturgeon Oil, which is found to be far more effective than any other oil. All animals suffer from them, almost to madness, even the well feathered Birds suffer about the eyes and neck . . . . A sailor finding swearing of no use, tried what Tar could do, and covered his face with it, but the musketoes stuck to it in such numbers as to blind him, and the tickling of their wings were worse than their bites." From *David Thompson's Narrative 1784–1812* (*Ontario Archives*)

One of the traders was Daniel Harmon, who came to Montreal from Vermont in 1799 at the age of twenty-one and signed on with the North West Company as a clerk. Harmon kept a journal for nineteen years, a record of the daily struggles of the fur trade. It did not have the sweep of the explorers' journals, but it captured the world they helped create.

Harmon's initial trip west with the voyageurs was arduous, and the cultivated young Yankee did not like their company. "They are great talkers but in the utmost sense of the word thoughtless," he wrote. "All of their chat is about horses, dogs, canoes and women, and strong men who can fight a good battle. The voyageurs make very indifferent companions, and with whom I cannot associate."

Harmon found no comfort among the native women, either. At Fort Alexandria, a Cree chief offered his daughter in matrimony, but Harmon refused, after briefly considering both the physical comforts and trading advantages such a union would bring. "Thanks be to God alone," he wrote in 1802, "if I have not been brought into a snare laid no doubt by the Devil himself." Without a wife or companions, he spent his time reading books, his "dead friends" as he called them.

Still, Harmon was unbearably lonely, and he accepted the next offer of a wife, which came from the father of fourteen-year-old Lizette Duval, a Métis girl. He rationalized that it was common practice at the trading posts

Daniel Harmon was from a prosperous Vermont family, an odd background for a fur trader. He had trouble adapting to both the geography and personalities of his new business. "Rainy evening and I for the first time am to pass the night in a Tent. . . . [The voyageurs] I am told have many of the Sailors customs, and the following is one of them: – from all who have not passed certain places they expect a *treat* or some thing to drink, and should you not comply with their whims, you might be sure of getting a Ducking which they call *baptizing*, but to avoid that ceremony I gave the People of my Canoe a few Bottles of Spirits and Porter, and in drinking which they got rather merry and forgot their Relations, whom they had but a few Days before left with heavy hearts and eyes drowned in tears." (*Hudson's Bay Company Archives, Provincial Archives of Manitoba*)

to have a "country wife," a stay against loneliness and celibacy. But he told himself that the arrangement would only be temporary. "My intentions now are to keep her as long as I remain in this uncivilized part of the world, but when I return to my native land, I shall endeavour to place her into the hands of some good honest man, with whom she can pass the remainder of her days in this country."

With Lizette he had two sons and nine daughters, and the household spoke a mixture of Cree, French, and English. "I now pass a short time every day, very pleasantly," he wrote, "teaching my little daughter Polly to read and spell words in the English language, in which she makes good progress, though she knows not the meaning of them. In conversing with my children, I use entirely the Cree, Indian language; with her mother I frequently employ the French."

Harmon travelled the prairies, trading with the natives, recording these meetings in his journal. "When we got within a mile of the natives camp, 10 or a dozen of the chiefs and most respected men, came on horseback to meet and conduct us to their dwellings. . . . One of the chiefs sent his son to invite me and my interpreter to go to his lodge and as soon as we were seated, the old men caused meat and berries (in short the best of everything they had) to be set before us. . . . During several days that we remained with those people we met with more real politeness than is often shown to strangers in the civilized part of the world, and much more than I had expected to meet with from savages, as the Indians are generally called, but I think wrongfully."

Harmon met David Thompson and kept up a correspondence with him. Like Thompson, he found God on the plains. His conversion came when he was left alone in the fort after everyone had gone berry-picking. In that grand solitude he reflected on his life, "and in so doing I am struck with astonishment and grieved to find it has been so different from that of a true Christian! . . . Until this day, I have always doubted whether such a saviour as the scriptures describe, ever really existed, and appeared on earth!" He resolved to be a better man, living under God's eye on the naked plain.

Harmon spent nineteen winters in trading posts across the west before moving east to educate his children in a "civilized and christian manner." Harmon toyed with the idea of leaving his "country wife," as he had originally planned to. Most of the North West traders did. But Harmon felt he could not. "We have wept together over the early departure of several children, and especially, over the death of a beloved son. We have children still living, who are equally dear to us both. How could I spend my days in the civilized world, and leave my beloved children in the wilderness? The thought has in it the bitterness of death. How could I tear them from a mother's love, and leave her to mourn over their absence, to the day of her death."

Harmon and his family went to Montreal, then Vermont, where he married Lizette in a church and had their children baptized. But he eventually returned to the fur trade, managing a trading post near Fort Frances, on Rainy Lake. He worked in modest capacities throughout his trading career,

Shooting the Rapids, Quebec, 1879 *(Frances Anne Hopkins, National Archives of Canada, C-2774)*

but in middle age he tried to leave his mark by founding a settlement named for himself. Harmonsville did not prosper, though, and Harmon died in 1843, poor and unrecognized.

The tensions that had always existed between the Hudson's Bay Company and the North West Company found a tragic focal point in Red River, the colony founded by Thomas Douglas, the fifth earl of Selkirk. Douglas was the seventh child of a Scottish aristocrat, a well-educated, fragile boy who came to his title after the unexpected deaths of his five older brothers. He was intelligent, quietly ambitious, and had his father's progressive nature.

In 1792, Selkirk toured the Scottish Highlands, where tenant farmers were being crowded out to make room for sheep, which were more profitable. It was an impoverished and dispirited place, and Selkirk became involved in the Highlanders' plight, even learning Gaelic to better understand them. He wrote a book, *Observations on the present state of the Highlands of Scotland, with a View of the Causes and probable consequences of Emigration* (1805). In it, he argued that emigration was inevitable: why not direct it in a way that benefited everyone?

He travelled around North America, looking for a suitable site for a Scots colony. "I thought that a portion of the ancient spirit might be preserved among the Highlanders of the New World," he wrote. But it was Alexander Mackenzie's *Voyages* that first inspired him to establish his colony on the stark plains of the Red River, even though Mackenzie had suggested that the area was in fact unsuitable for settlement.

The idea of founding a colony perfectly reflected Selkirk's character and ambition. It satisfied his humanitarian instincts to offer the Highlanders a fresh start. A successful colony would also give him some political prominence; he could redefine himself in much the same way as his settlers. And there was the hope of a significant profit, always a strong incentive. He

LORD SELKIRK ◆ During his travels through Upper and Lower Canada, Thomas Douglas, the Fifth Earl of Selkirk, closely observed the politics. "The English at Quebec & Montreal cry out in the true John Bull style against [the French Canadians'] obstinate aversion to institutions which they have never taken any pains to make them understand – & are surprised at the natural & universally experienced dislike of a conquered people to their conquerors & to every thing which puts them in mind of their subjection. . . . The only chance of reconciling the people would have been either to use every effort to change them entirely in language & Institutions & make them forget that they were not English – or keeping them as French to give a Government adapted to them as such, & keep every thing English out of sight - neither of these plans has been followed, & the policy of Govt. has been a kind of vibration between them." (*Raeburn, 2365*)

was interested in new agricultural techniques and believed they could be successfully implemented in the New World.

The land that Selkirk had his eye on was controlled by the Hudson's Bay Company. In 1808, Selkirk began to buy stock in the company and persuaded members of his family to do the same. The Napoleonic wars had disrupted the market for furs, and HBC stock had plummeted from 250 pounds a share to 60 pounds, making it affordable. Selkirk and his circle came to control almost a third of the company's shares, giving him considerable influence, which he used to push his settlement plan. To gain government support, Selkirk astutely suggested that British settlement in the west would provide a bulwark against American encroachment.

The most vocal opponent was Sir Alexander Mackenzie, who had retired from business but still defended the interests of the North West Company. He was aware that settlers were the natural enemy of the fur trade. Watching Selkirk's plan unfold, Mackenzie wrote to an NWC partner, prophetically, "He will put the North-West Company to a greater expense than you seem to apprehend, and, had the Company sacrificed 20,000 pounds, which might have secured a preponderance in the stock of the Hudson's Bay Company, it would have been money well spent."

Mackenzie attacked the idea of settlement as preposterous. As someone who knew the area, he said, he could attest that it was never intended for man, but for raw nature. Even Selkirk's friends were skeptical. "By God, sir, if you are bent on doing something futile," one asked, "why do you not . . . plough the desert of the Sahara, which is so much nearer?"

There was opposition within the HBC as well as from the NWC; Selkirk's colony would not necessarily be in the interests of either party. A settlement on the Red River could prove to be the beginning of the slow, inexorable civilizing of the west, crowding out the fur trade. Despite strident opposition, however, Selkirk persuaded the company to sell him 300,000 square kilometres – five times the area of Scotland – for ten shillings.

SAULTEAUX NATIVES ◆ The Saulteaux occupied the Red River Valley at the time Selkirk's settlers arrived.
When the Métis started to burn the settlers' homes, the Saulteaux attempted to negotiate on the settlers' behalf.
They were unsuccessful, but helped move the settlers to the safety of Jack River, where they spent the winter. After
the settlement was re-established, Selkirk paid the Saulteaux 100 pounds of tobacco per tribe annually to give up any
claim to the land, defined as the area that extended two miles on either side of the Red River. (*H. Jones, Hudson's Bay
Company Archives, Provincial Archives of Manitoba*)

He had the land; now he needed settlers. Selkirk wrote an "Advertisement and Prospectus" that described the Red River area in the flattering
terms available only to someone who had not yet visited, and had the advertisement distributed throughout Scotland.

Bishop John Strachan of York had never been to the area either, but he
labelled the advertisement "one of the most gross impositions that ever was
attempted on the British public, and must be attended with the most baneful
consequences to all those unfortunate men, who, deluded by the false promises held out to them, shall leave their homes for such a dreary wilderness."

Both men were partially right about the territory. The Red River country was hostile, flood-prone, and barren for most of the year. It was also a
huge blank canvas on which oppressed Highlanders could create a new life
for themselves, and it offered wonderfully fertile soil, if a desperately short
growing season.

Despite the extraordinary hardships in the Highlands, it was not easy
to recruit settlers. The North West Company placed stories in Scottish

Hudson's Bay Company job posting (*National Archives of Canada, C-125856*)

newspapers warning of savage attacks from the local natives. Miles Macdonell, who was hired to be the governor of Assiniboia, as the colony was called, tried to counter the scare tactics. He travelled around the north, telling Highlanders that Red River was the Promised Land and offering incentives. In this way, he managed to recruit a boatload of settlers, who quickly came to dislike and distrust him. Macdonell was an arrogant, hot-tempered military officer who saw the job of governor as a career move.

The first group came over in 1812, and a second wave arrived the following year. The Saulteaux natives, who were the HBC's allies in Red River, welcomed them. But settlement was difficult and tentative. Crops failed, and famine was a continual threat. Fever and scurvy left the settlers weak and brittle.

There were also confrontations with the local Métis, who had a substantial settlement nearby. The Métis supplied the North West Company with buffalo meat, and they resented the settlers' presence. It was a delicate political situation, and the indelicate Macdonell soon made it worse. In January 1814, he issued a proclamation ordering that "no persons trading Furs or Provisions within the Territory . . . shall take out any provisions, either of flesh or game or vegetables." It effectively banned the export of food from Red River, threatening the North West Company's ability to supply its trading posts. It became known as the "pemmican proclamation."

John Duncan Cameron of the North West Company predicted violence: "Macdonell is now determined not only to seize our pemmican but to drive us out of the Assiniboia district and consequently out of the north west. Hostilities will no doubt begin early this spring."

Cameron rallied the Métis behind him. "You must assist me in driving away the colony," he told them. "If they are not drove away, the consequence will be that they will prevent you from hunting. They will starve your families, and they will put their feet in the neck of those that attempt to resist them. You can easily see how they mean to finish by what they have begun already."

Cameron, a gifted provocateur, urged the Métis on with praise for their people and their accomplishments, emphasizing that this was their nation to defend. He told them that they could keep anything they looted from the settlers and suggested they put on war paint and pose as Saulteaux. The Métis followed Cameron's lead.

"They immediately began to burn our houses in the day time, and fire upon us during the night, saying the country was theirs," wrote John Pritchard, one of the settlers. "If we did not immediately quit the settlement, they would plunder us of our property, and burn the houses over our heads."

With the help of the Saulteaux, the settlers retreated to Jack River, an HBC trading post at the north end of Lake Winnipeg. They were disillusioned with the New World and angry with Selkirk, their sponsor. Macdonell was depressed and suffered a nervous breakdown.

Later that year, the settlers returned to Red River to rebuild, but the worst was yet to come.

A BUFFALO HUNT ◆ In the mid-nineteenth century, the west was being transformed at a rapid pace. As settlers arrived in the wake of the explorers, the natives, Métis, and fur traders were being crowded out. The west as an idea was in flux as well: was it an Edenic paradise or a decaying romantic notion? Artist Paul Kane's vision of the west was resolutely romantic, as seen in both his paintings and his writing.

"Towards evening, as we were approaching the place where we were to cross the river, I saw some buffaloes idly grazing in a valley, and as I wished to give a general idea of the beauty of the scenery which lies all along the banks of the Saskatchewan from this point to Edmonton, I sat down to make a sketch, the rest of the party promising to wait for me at the crossing place. It was the commencement of Indian summer; the evening was very fine, and threw that peculiar soft, warm haziness over the landscape, which is supposed to proceed from the burning of the immense prairies. The sleepy buffaloes grazing upon the undulating hills, here and there relieved by clumps of small trees, the unbroken stillness, and the approaching evening, rendered it altogether a scene of most enchanting repose." (From *Wanderings of an Artist among the Indians of North America*)

At the same time that Kane was idealizing the Plains in his art, Henry Youle Hind saw a dying culture. Hind was a Toronto chemistry professor who was part of the Canadian government's 1857 Red River expedition, and his journal presents the antithesis of Kane's rosy descriptions: "We now began to find the fresh bones of buffalo very numerous on the ground, and here and there startled a pack of wolves feeding on a carcass which had been deprived of its tongue and hump only by the careless, thriftless Crees. . . . Within a circular fence 120 feet broad . . . lay tossed in every conceivable position over two hundred dead buffalo. From old bulls to calves of three months old, animals of every age were huddled together in all the forced attitudes of violent death. . . . The flesh of many of the cows had been taken from them, and was drying in the sun on stages near the tents. It is needless to say that the odour was overpowering, and millions of large blue flesh flies, humming and buzzing over the putrifying bodies was not the least disgusting part of the spectacle." (Half Breeds Running Buffalo, *Paul Kane, Royal Ontario Museum*)

The Selkirk Settlement
(*Anon., National Archives of Canada, C-8714*)

On June 19, 1816, the skirmishes, arson, and terrorism finally culminated in a massacre. At Seven Oaks, near the HBC's Red River trading post, twenty-five Bay employees and settlers, including Governor Robert Semple, rode out from Fort Douglas to meet sixty-one Métis wearing war paint who were riding by. Semple approached a French Canadian named Boucher and words were exchanged, then shots. It was never clear who fired first. "In a few minutes, almost all our people were either killed or wounded," reported John Pritchard, one of the few surviving settlers. "Captain Rogers, having fallen, rose up again and came towards me. . . . I called out to him, 'for God's sake give yourself up.' He ran toward the enemy for that purpose, myself following him. He raised up his hands . . . and called out for mercy. A half-breed shot him through the head and another cut open his belly with a knife." About twenty of Semple's party were killed and only one Métis.

The remaining settlers were spared but their houses were pillaged. They surrendered the next day and again retreated to Jack River. Each party claimed self-defence, and a Canadian commission determined that it was a private war between two rival companies and condemned both sides. It was the bloodiest battle between the two companies, and one of the last. In 1821, exhausted by the competition and violence, the North West Company and the Hudson's Bay Company did the unthinkable: they agreed to join forces.

Selkirk's unlikely colony prospered, though he did not live to see it. By 1818, his health was failing and he was plagued by lawsuits from the North West Company, which suggested that he had no legal right to the land. Selkirk moved to the French Pyrenees as a curative measure and died there in 1820 at the age of forty-eight.

An 1822 census of the Red River colony counted 234 men, 161 women, 886 children, 126 houses, and 160 gardens. Selkirk's settlers had endured scurvy, frostbite, and murder. Winters were a frightening wasteland, and in the summer the Red River flooded its banks, birds ate the seed out of

Voyageurs at Dawn, 1871
(*Frances Anne Hopkins, National Gallery of Canada, C-2773*)

the fields, and locusts ate whatever grew. In the beginning they had lived on wild parsnips and nettles and suffered the winter in English shoes. But eventually they thrived. Alexander Ross, a settler, had initially described Red River as being "as gloomy as the Ultima Thule." Thirty years later, he proclaimed, "No farmers in the world, no settlement or colony of agriculturalists can be pronounced so happy, independent, and comfortable as those in Red River."

The eventual success of Red River signalled the eclipse of the fur trade, as many had feared, and had a dramatic effect on the plains natives. They had supplied the fur trade and guided the explorers in a partnership that had become increasingly unequal. The Saulteaux had helped the early Red River colonists, saving them from starvation. But as the settlement matured, they were viewed as an impediment to its future growth.

A wary amalgamation of the Hudson's Bay Company and the North West Company brought an end to the hostilities and lawsuits. But the new company, using the Hudson's Bay name, was now burdened with duplication and inefficiency. The job of making the company lean and efficient fell to George Simpson, a veteran of the sugar trade. Simpson was born in the Scottish Highlands, an illegitimate child who was raised by his aunt and ultimately sent to London to find employment. He was a compact, autocratic man who had enormous physical stamina and a natural passion for efficiency in all things: travel, business, and romance.

One of his first acts as governor was to bring together seventy-three employees from the former North West Company and the Hudson's Bay Company for a banquet at York Factory in an effort to get rid of the lingering ill will. Two of his guests had recently fought a duel with one another. "They had hacked and slashed at each other with naked swords only a few months before," John Tod, a guest, noted. "One of them still bore the marks of a cut on his face, the other, it was said, on some less conspicuous part of the body." The dinner went off without incident, an encouraging start.

Simpson left York Factory in August 1824 with twelve voyageurs, an ornate snuff box, and a terrier named Boxer. "I intend devoting this ensuing winter to a . . . tour of the Columbia where the broom and pruning knife are I believe much required." He had a penchant for speed, and he made the trip from Hudson Bay to Fort George (in Oregon) in just eighty-four days, breaking the existing record by twenty days.

Along the way, Simpson made detailed notes; he was searching for economies. "The table appointments throughout the county have hitherto been upon much too large a scale," he wrote, "far exceeding the consumption of most respectable families in the civilized world and I think you may safely reduce the usual supplies by 50 per cent. Tin plates . . . no tableclothes . . . no earthenware dishes: a few tumblers which answer for wine glasses. Knives and forks ought to last at least half a dozen years."

The trading posts in the territory north of the Columbia River were managerial disasters. "The Columbia department from the day of its origin to the present hour has been neglected, shamefully mismanaged and a scene of the most wasteful extravagance and the most unfortunate dissension," he wrote. The expanded HBC had new competitors; the Americans and the Russians were both trading along the Pacific coast. The company needed to prepare itself for this fresh threat.

For eight years, Simpson was paddled around the country, visiting every trading post, analyzing everything he saw, especially the people. In what he called his "Character Book" he made notes on 157 Hudson's Bay employees – witty, ruthless portraits of their corporate worth. Colin Robertson was "a frothy trifling conceited man who would starve in any other Country and is perfectly useless here." John Clarke was a "boasting, ignorant low fellow who rarely speaks the truth and is strongly suspected of dishonesty . . ." John Stuart was "exceedingly vain, a great Egotist, Swallows the grossest flattery . . ." Like a horseman assessing breeding stock, Simpson went through the company personnel, describing some as active, useful, and honourable, others as weak-minded, violent, and stupid. He had a gift for determining a man's moral qualities and his use to the company, two things that did not always overlap. Donald McIntosh was "a very poor creature in every sense of the Word, illiterate, weak-minded and laughed at by his colleagues. . . . Speaks Saulteaux, is qualified to cheat an Indian, and can make & set a Net . . ." Samuel Black was honest, tyrannical, and intensely paranoid, with "Dirks, Knives and Loaded Pistols concealed about his Person and in all directions about his Establishment even under his Table cloth at meals and in his Bed. He would be admirably adapted for the Service of the North West coast . . ." The Character Book was a psychological accounting of the men of the fur trade, an entertaining and insightful record.

Simpson visited every post in the northern territory, closed down seventy-three, fired half of the employees, and stopped the practice of ritual gift exchanges with the natives, a tradition that had existed for almost two hundred years. "During the heat of opposition in some districts it was necessary to give Indians expensive presents in clothing, guns, etc. . . . This ruinous practice has been discontinued and nothing beyond tobacco and ammunition in some parts and a few trifles such as fire steels, needles, vermillion etc. in others have last year been given, and occasionally a dress to a chief or Indian of considerable influence."

Simpson's efficiency extended to his own life. He impressed his superiors with his reforms and was amply rewarded, becoming a wealthy man. When he started to move among Montreal society, he jettisoned his native wives and children with the same cold eye he had turned on the company. His native country wife, Margaret Taylor, was pregnant with their third child when Simpson left the family. He wrote to a friend: "Pray keep an Eye on the commodity if she bring forth anything in proper time & of the right colour let them be taken care of but if anything be amiss let the whole be bundled about their business."

At the age of forty-three, he travelled to London to find an English wife suitable to his needs. He married his eighteen-year-old cousin, Frances Ramsay, perhaps as much for her proximity as for her social stature. She entered into life with George less than enthusiastically. "On the 4rth of March," she wrote in her journal, "I arise from my Bed, at 5 AM (for the first time in my life) with an aching heart, and a mind agitated by the various emotions of Grief, Fear, & Hope."

As the daughter of a prominent London merchant, she had been accustomed to a life of refinement and pampering. Now she was in a canoe filled with voyageurs, paddling to Red River. "The morning was cold & disagreeable after the incessant rain of yesterday," she wrote, "but neither that nor the fatigue of the forced march we were making, served to depress the Spirits of our voyageurs; who paddled, sung, laughed & joked, as if on an excursion of pleasure, until one of them who seemed to feel the force of a joke, which his neighbour indulged in, at his expense, returned it upon him in a still more forcible manner by a blow, which gave rise to a battle in the Canoe. Mr. Simpson was asleep at the time, but the noise awoke him, and put him into nearly as great a passion as the combatants, upon whom, he bestowed a shower of blows with a paddle which lay at hand, and brought about an immediate cessation of hostilities . . ."

If the company was rough, the scenery offered some compensation. She described the Mattawa River as the "most wild & romantic place I ever beheld: it reminded me of the description I have read (in some of Sir Walter Scott's beautiful tales) of Scottish scenery. . . . [O]n either side are stupendous rocks of the most fantastic forms: some bear the appearance of Gothic

Sir George Simpson
(*Hudson's Bay Company Archives, Provincial Archives of Manitoba*)

FRANCES SIMPSON ◆ The wife of the indomitable George Simpson was the well-bred daughter of a London merchant. She kept a cheery journal of her canoe trip to the west. "Our Canoe, a most beautiful craft, airy and elegant beyond description, was 35 feet in length. . . . The sun intensely hot today and the water of the Grand, or Uttowas river as smooth as glass: the Country on either side a thick Forest; the trees near the edge of the Water low, & branching, chiefly Aspen: while those behind were Pine, straight as Arrows, and growing to an enormous height: every thing was calm & quiet, not a sound to be heard excepting the stroke of the paddle, and the clear mellow voice of our principal vocalist Tomma Felix, singing 'La Belle Rosier' and other sweet Voyageur airs. . . .

"The Establishment at which we encamped last night, may be considered the boundary between the Civilized and Savage Worlds, as beyond this point, the country is uninhabited by Whites, except where a Trading Post of the Honourable Hudson's Bay Company occasionally presents itself."

Life in the bush proved to be too much for Frances. She left Red River, never to return, and died at the age of forty-one. (*Hudson's Bay Company Archives, Provincial Archives of Manitoba*)

Castles, others exhibit rows of the most regular, and beautifully carved Corinthian Pillars: deep Caverns are formed in some, while others present a smooth level surface, crowned with tufts of Pines, and Cedars."

They settled in Red River, where Frances was friendless and delicate, suffering from a litany of ills. Her first pregnancy in 1831 was difficult, and her constitution was not suited to western life. "My poor wife you'll be sorry to learn is very ill indeed," Simpson wrote to a friend. "Almost entirely confined to her room and altho not in an immediately dangerous state much worse than women generally are while in such situations." Her suffering and London ills were largely ignored by the locals, who resented her. Simpson had left no provision for his native wives, a cultural and social faux pas in the fledgling prairie society, and Frances paid for his ruthlessness.

In 1833 she went back to England and stayed for five years on her own. George was spending more time in Montreal now, a wealthy gentleman with investments to oversee. He bought part of Alexander Mackenzie's estate, recently surveyed by the luckless David Thompson, who lived nearby.

Simpson led the life of an English gentleman, with a mansion and servants. But his desire for travel never left him. Periodically, he made long, arduous trips throughout the extended HBC empire. "It is strange that all my ailments vanish as soon as I seat myself in a canoe," he said. In 1842, at the age of fifty-six, Simpson made his way around the world, first crossing North America, then sailing to the Sandwich Islands (Hawaii), trekking across Siberia to Europe, and finally travelling overland to England. His circumnavigation was accomplished in nineteen months and nineteen days – a blistering pace, especially given the fact that he stopped to conduct business periodically and occasionally backtracked.

By 1860, the fur trade was in decline. The beaver hat had been supplanted by the silk hat, which had been introduced in 1824; its glossy look had taken almost twenty years to catch on. Simpson had prolonged the natural lifespan of the fur trade by streamlining it, but he could not keep civilization at bay. He tried, testifying at an investigation of the HBC that the Red River area was spectacularly unsuitable for European settlement. But the west had been mapped by Thompson and Hearne and Mackenzie. Captain John Palliser was currently out on the prairies, measuring the land for settlement. A railway line would soon connect Red River with St. Paul, Minnesota. The links were falling into place, making it easier and faster to get there.

In 1860, the Prince of Wales (later Edward VII) came to Canada on a royal visit. Simpson entertained him at his estate on Dorval Island, recreating an old Nor'Wester-style dinner complete with canoes and an honour guard of brightly dressed natives. The elaborate, sanitized re-enactment of the fur trade was a theatrical coda for the industry. Nine days later, Simpson suffered an attack of apoplexy and died. He was the last fur trader to travel with the zeal and purpose of an explorer, but he was also the harbinger of the modern efficiency experts, that cold army of men who would whittle the next century into something profitable.

REBELLION AND REFORM

At the beginning of the nineteenth century, the ideals of both the French and American Revolutions still echoed around the globe. Uprisings broke out, triggering brutal repression in the Austro-Hungarian, Russian, and Turkish empires. Occasionally, the protesters won: Simón Bolívar drove Spain from much of South America; in 1830, the Belgians freed Brussels from the Dutch army; and in 1836, Texas won independence from Mexico (in 1845 it would be annexed by the United States).

The ideals of justice and liberty inspired passions in British North America, too. The six colonies now boasted almost a million inhabitants, and many of them resented the fact that even the most insignificant local decisions required the assent of London. The colonial houses of assembly adopted laws but had no real power. A governor appointed by London, and the councillors named by him, controlled the decision-making process. As a result, there were constant conflicts between the representatives of the people and an unelected government.

Militant newspapers began to appear, criticizing the colonial regime. In York (now Toronto), the capital of Upper Canada, William Lyon Mackenzie, a Scottish immigrant, published the *Colonial Advocate*. In it, he complained, "I had long seen the country in the hands of a few shrewd, crafty, covetous men, under whose management one of the most lovely and

"Nothing can be more imposing than the situation of Quebec," Catharine Parr Traill wrote on August 14, 1832, "built on the sides and summit of a magnificent rock, on the highest point of which stands the fortress overlooking the river, and commanding a most superb view of the surrounding scenes."(*J. R. C. Smyth*, Quebec from the Château, *National Archives of Canada*, C-001038)

desirable sections of America remained a comparative desert. The most obvious improvements were stayed; dissention was created among classes; large estates were wrested from their owners in utter contempt of even the forms of the courts." Mackenzie denounced the privileged few who influenced the governor, coining for them the expression "Family Compact," which quickly entered the political lexicon. This network, he wrote, governed Upper Canada through a handful of narrow-minded, sectarian individuals.

The attorney general of Upper Canada, John Beverley Robinson, denounced Mackenzie as a "reptile . . . a conceited red-headed fellow with an apron." But Mackenzie continued his attacks. In one typical broadside, he denounced the governing clique for their total control of the colonies finances: they were the self-appointed "treasurers, receivers, auditors, King, Lords and Commons."

Mackenzie's virulent criticism did not go unanswered. In 1826, a gang of young men from York's finest families destroyed the printing presses of the *Colonial Advocate*. Mackenzie took the vandals to court and won his case, and he was awarded enough money to replace the presses. Encouraged by this support, the fiery journalist entered the political arena.

In Halifax, Joseph Howe's newspaper, the *Novascotian*, was also critical of the government. "Whatever goes to extend or to secure the advantages which of right ought to flow to the People," Howe vowed, "we shall steadily and fearlessly uphold." This self-taught Reformer, the son of a Loyalist American, was a strong and blunt speaker, but for all his zeal, he had no desire to sever ties with Great Britain. "We are desirous of a change," he said, "not such as shall divide us from our brethren across the water, but which will ensure to us what they enjoy. . . . Gentlemen, all we ask is what exists at home in England – a system of responsibility to the people."

The *Novascotian* described the colony as "a young and poor country, where the sons of rich and favoured families alone receive education at the public expence – where the many must toil to support the extortions and exactions of a few. . . . It requires no ordinary nerve in men of moderate circumstances and humble pretensions, to stand forward and boldly protest against measures which are fast working the ruin of the Province." Nova Scotia's political leaders took Howe to court, accusing him of publishing seditious articles. Howe defended himself, denouncing his accusers "as the most negligent and imbecile, if not the most reprehensible body, that ever mismanaged a people's affairs. . . . They may expect much from the result of this trial; but before I have done with them, I hope to convince them that they, and not I, are the real criminals here." Howe was acquitted by the jury. The trial bolstered his popularity, and, like Mackenzie, he entered politics.

In Quebec, the capital of Lower Canada, two Montreal journalists, Ludger Duvernay and Daniel Tracey, dared to attack the legislative council appointed by the governor, which had the power to reject the resolutions of the elected assembly, and frequently did so. "The current Legislative Council being possibly the greatest nuisance we have, we must take steps

WILLIAM LYON MACKENZIE ◆ William Lyon Mackenzie was born in 1795 in Dundee, Scotland. His father, a weaver, died soon after he was born. Mackenzie obtained a scholarship and studied in a parochial school, and for the next fifteen years worked as a journalist. With his mother, he opened a general store that went bankrupt during the economic crisis that followed the Napoleonic Wars. After that, Mackenzie led a bohemian life, travelling in France and in England before emigrating to Canada in 1820. (*Heritage Toronto*)

JOSEPH HOWE ◆ In 1827, Joseph Howe took over the *Novascotian*, which, under his direction, became the most influential newspaper in Nova Scotia. During his first years as a journalist, Howe travelled throughout the province, which he described in a series of articles published from 1828 onwards. He also wrote more than 150 parliamentary reports, denouncing the way a small group of men had taken control of all public affairs in Nova Scotia. (*Public Archives of Nova Scotia*)

CATHARINE PARR TRAILL ◆ Catharine Parr Traill was born in 1802 into a middle-class family in Kent, England. When she was sixteen years old, her father, Thomas Strickland, died suddenly, and Catharine undertook a literary career to support the family. Before departing for Canada, Catharine had already published a dozen books. Her husband, Thomas Traill, was the scion of a distinguished Scottish family from the Orkney Islands, but neither his British Army officer's pension nor the meagre income he derived from his property enabled them to live well in Scotland. Like many people in the British Isles, Thomas and Catharine felt they could improve their lot by emigrating to Canada. (*Thomas Cheeseman, from* Letters of a Lifetime)

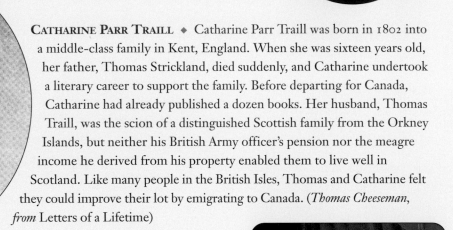

LOUIS-JOSEPH PAPINEAU ◆ Louis-Joseph Papineau was a well-educated man, as the books in this painting show: speeches by the classical Greek orator Demosthenes, a copy of *The Spirit of Laws* by the French philosopher Montesquieu, speeches by the great British parliamentarian Charles James Fox and by the American president Thomas Jefferson. (*Antoine Plamondon, National Gallery of Canada, 17919*)

to rid ourselves of it and demand its abolition," they wrote. They were thrown into jail for forty days for publishing their attacks in *La Minerve* and the *Vindicator*, organs of the Parti Patriote, the colonial government's leading adversary.

Louis-Joseph Papineau was the undisputed leader of the Patriotes. A seigneur and lawyer, he was also speaker of the House of Assembly. He was a tall, vigorous man who could galvanize a crowd with his rousing speeches. Like Howe and Mackenzie, Papineau struggled to establish a government responsible to its electors. In a March 8, 1831, letter to his wife, Julie, he wrote that "the votes and actions daily adopted by the legislative councillors can be explained by their passionate hatred of Canadiens, their unbridled love of money and the most disgraceful egoism."

Initially, Papineau had admired the British constitution and parliamentary institutions, thinking they would help him obtain justice for French Canadians. But after fifteen years of political struggle, he had come to favour American-style democracy. In a letter to his wife, Papineau wrote that he did not believe it was possible to be "happy and well-treated under the colonial regime." In the February 18, 1834, edition of *La Minerve*, he predicted that all of North America would eventually become republican.

The political struggles in the colonies coincided with an unprecedented wave of immigration. Most of the newcomers landed in Quebec, the port of entry for the Canadas. In the early 1830s, almost 30,000 immigrants a year came through a city with a settled population of only 28,000. Many immigrants were fleeing the economic crisis that had followed the Napoleonic Wars in Europe.

Among the newcomers, in May 1832, was Catharine Parr Traill, published author of a dozen children's books. Her husband, Thomas Traill, a retired military officer who was heavily in debt, had been convinced to emigrate to Upper Canada by a land agent, who described it as an agricultural paradise. Her sister Susanna came as well, with her husband, John Dunbar Moodie, and their child. Together, the two women would help lay the foundations of the country's literature. "Canada is *the* land of hope," Catharine wrote. "Here, everything is new; everything going forward; it is scarcely possible for arts, sciences, agriculture, manufactures, to retrograde; they must keep advancing."

She was impressed by the country's newness, but surprised by its wilderness. "Much as I had seen and heard of the badness of the roads in Canada, I was not prepared for such a one as we travelled along this day," she wrote. "Indeed, it hardly deserved the name of a road. . . . Sometimes I laughed because I would not cry."

The pioneers appealed to the government for better roads and schools, but their pleas were ignored. Some of them, like Robert Davis, a farmer of Irish descent, became disenchanted. He had built his own roads and bridges, cleared the land, and educated his children himself, and in the process he had

Bush Farm near Chatham, Ontario, 1838. This pioneer's cabin was made of logs, with a roof of earth or bark. After a hard day of cutting trees, the settler warmed himself in front of a cast-iron stove or a hearth made of wood and earth. (*Philip John Bainbrigge, National Archives of Canada, C-011811*)

been crushed by a falling tree, had his feet lacerated by an axe, "and suffered almost everything except death."

While Upper Canada was the fastest-growing colony in the British empire, Lower Canada still had more people, almost 400,000 inhabitants. The English and French lived in separate districts, divided by language, religion, and economic status. Despite tensions and mutual suspicion, they coexisted peacefully, for the most part. Louise Aylmer, wife of the governor, socialized with the Papineaus and with Monseigneur Jean-Jacques Lartigue, the bishop of Montreal. She felt more comfortable in the company of French Canadians, she said, than among her own compatriots, whom she found too reserved.

In the Lower Canadian countryside, tenant farmers lived under the seigneurial regime. Each year they had to give part of their harvest as payment to the landowner. In the mid-1830s, most of the fertile lands of the old seigneuries were occupied, and the seigneurs, whether French or English, were demanding ever higher rents. The hapless tenants protested. A petition in the county of Deux-Montagnes, dated November 23, 1832, asserted that "a good many seigneurs have exercised absolute power over their lands, selling them at exorbitant prices, and illegally, without His Majesty's Canadien subjects receiving any protection from these abuses." These exactions and the shortage of land forced the young habitants to clear fields in ever more remote regions, or abandon agriculture altogether and find work in the city.

In the spring of 1832, Montreal had 27,000 inhabitants, who were divided between the Upper and the Lower towns, between grand greystone mansions and modest wooden homes. The citadel that had blocked Nôtre Dame Street to the northeast had just been razed to the ground and a new cathedral on Place d'Armes was under construction. The city had a brilliant economic future, but English and French did not share equally in this bounty. Montreal was divided by an invisible barrier: language. During his stay in Montreal in 1832, the great French writer Alexis de Tocqueville

PLACE D'ARMES, 1828 ◆ The construction of the Nôtre-Dame Basilica, shown in the background of this water-colour by Robert Auchmaty Sproule, began in 1824. The church in the foreground was the old cathedral that was subsequently destroyed. During the first half of the nineteenth century, there was a considerable decrease in religious observance in Lower Canada. One-third of Montreal parishioners did not take communion at Easter, and the authority of the Church was called into question. The legislative assembly had to intervene to prevent people from drinking alcohol and talking during mass. (*R. A. Sproule, National Archives of Canada, c-002639*)

wrote: "The French newspapers I read kept up a constant and vigorous opposition to the English."

The English Party, representing Quebec's English-speaking elite, was mainly supported by Canadians of Scottish, English, and American origins. The militants of the Parti Patriote were mostly French Canadians and immigrants from Ireland, who shared a profound distrust of British power. During elections, the two parties often used thugs to intimidate voters of the other camp and to control access to polling stations, which sometimes had to be closed. On May 21, 1832, after a polling station was shut down, supporters of the English Party taunted a group of Patriotes and a fight broke out. The 15th Regiment was called in to establish order, and they opened fire on the crowd. Three Canadiens were struck down: Casimir Chauvin, Pierre Billet, and François Languedoc. The day after the shooting, it was announced that the Parti Patriote had won the by-election by a margin of four votes.

Cholera Epidemic. In an attempt to prevent a cholera epidemic in 1832, authorities in Lower Canada set up a quarantine station at Grosse-Ile, downstream from Quebec. But an Irish immigrant in a rooming house was infected, and the epidemic subsequently spread throughout the province. (*Joseph Légaré, National Gallery of Canada 7157*)

Louis-Joseph Papineau was greatly upset by the death of his compatriots and wrote to the governor general, Lord Aylmer: "My heart is racked with pain, and my letter will find you in the same situation, since you will have learned by now of the disastrous events which yesterday bloodied our streets. The troops sent to protect His Majesty's subjects shot them. No such tragedy has ever before afflicted Canada." The political climate quickly deteriorated.

At the beginning of June, a new tragedy struck the colony. The *Carrick*, a ship that had come over from Ireland, reached Quebec with a few feverish immigrants on board. Three days later, cholera took its first victim, and the illness spread like wildfire to Montreal and into Upper Canada, an epidemic that moved through the shanty neighbourhoods of the urban poor. The lack of sewers and garbage collection contributed to water contamination, and hundreds died each day. *La Minerve* tried to prevent panic from spreading, advising that "as soon as the illness breaks out, people should immediately consult a doctor and follow his directions. All pharmacists have the necessary remedies and their prices are within reach of everyone." This was not true: doctors were overwhelmed and powerless. They thought that cholera was transmitted by fumes carried through the atmosphere. To purify the air, English officers tried firing cannons, and the Sanitary Office burned tar.

By the end of 1832, the epidemic had claimed nine thousand lives, more than half of them in Lower Canada. Some Canadians held Britain responsible for this misfortune, claiming that its emigration policy was negligent, if not malevolent. This climate of death, fear, and mistrust helped inflame the political situation.

In Quebec, the deputies of the Parti Patriote had enjoyed a majority in the House of Assembly for the last fifteen years, but their demands had been blocked consistently by the governor and the advisers he had appointed to the executive and legislative councils. In 1834, the Patriotes took their cause directly to London, drawing up a list of grievances and claims known as the Ninety-Two Resolutions. They demanded that the legislative council be elected rather than appointed, and that the colony's budget be controlled by the House of Assembly. They wanted the same powers, privileges, and immunities enjoyed by the British parliament: "This House is no wise disposed to admit the excellence of the present Constitution of Canada, although His Majesty's Secretary of State for the Colonies has unseasonably and erroneously asserted that it has conferred on the two Canadas the Institutions of Great Britain." The resolutions contained veiled threats that Lower Canada would break free and pursue annexation to the United States. "We will do nothing to hasten our separation from the Mother Country," Papineau said, "apart from preparing and moving forward our people for an era which will be neither monarchist nor aristocratic."

The radical tone of the Ninety-Two Resolutions, followed by the dramatic victory of the Patriotes in the 1834 elections, shook up the English Party and its supporters. During a public meeting in December, John Molson, a powerful Montreal businessman, issued a warning to the Patriotes: "Recent events have roused us to a sense of impending danger. . . . The French party may yet be taught, that the majority upon which they count for success, will, in the hour of trial, prove a weak defence against the awakened energies of an insulted and oppressed people." Molson violently criticized the seigneurial regime, which was, he said, an outdated institution that should be relegated to the garbage heap of history: "Every person who clears, or otherwise improves a farm, erects a building, either in town or country, or invests capital in landed estate, bestows one-twelfth of his outlay on the Seignior, whenever the property is brought to sale. . . . The profits which accrue to the Seignior from this state of things are obvious; and the interest of the French Lawyer and Notary, in maintaining a system of law that fosters litigation and produces corresponding expense is equally intelligible."

Julie Papineau wrote to her husband in Quebec on December 26, describing the growing tensions in Montreal: "I am not the type to indulge in vain fears, but I know how to assess the true extent of rage and hatred which this party [the Tories] bears towards us. The state in which we find ourselves is deplorable; they want to dominate us or crush us and if we do not have the energy to free ourselves from their power, they will find ways to hurt us."

In 1834, the town of York was renamed Toronto, and it now had more than nine thousand inhabitants. William Lyon Mackenzie had never been so popular. In addition to being the publisher of an influential newspaper, he was now mayor of a new municipality and a member of the Upper Canada Legislative Assembly. Like Papineau, Mackenzie helped draft a list of demands, which he sent to London. The *Seventh Report on Grievances*, a five-hundred-page

document, slammed the government of Upper Canada: "One great excellence of the English constitution consists in the limits it imposes on the will of a king, by requiring responsible men to give effect to it. In Upper Canada no such responsibility can exist. The lieutenant-governor and the British ministry hold in their hands the whole patronage of the province; they hold the sole domination of the country, and leave the representative branch of the legislature powerless and dependent."

Joseph Howe was now a member of Nova Scotia's House of Assembly, and he adopted much the same tone in his writings for the *Novascotian*. "I am approaching now the root of all our evils . . . that gross and palpable defect in our local Government. . . . Compared with the British Parliament, this House has absolutely no power," he wrote on February 23, 1837. Howe also drafted a list of resolutions that argued for political change, but he remained a moderate reformer, and his Loyalist origins prevented him from going as far as Papineau or Mackenzie. "I know that I shall hear the cries of republicanism and danger to the constitution," he wrote. "But the idea of republicanism, of independence, of severance from the Mother Country, never crosses my mind. . . . I wish to live and die a British subject – but not a Briton only in name."

The year 1837 started off badly. In Lower Canada, poverty and despair were endemic, particularly among the French. "It is easy to see that the French are a defeated people," Alexis de Tocqueville had written a few

Toronto, 1835. In 1834, York was renamed Toronto. City streets now had sidewalks and gas lighting began to make an appearance. This view of Toronto shows the original courthouse and jail on the north side of King Street. (*Thomas Young, Royal Ontario Museum*)

Halifax, 1835. The steam-powered ferry *Ogle* in the background of this watercolour by William Eager is a sign of Halifax's prosperity. (*Royal Ontario Museum*)

years earlier. "The rich classes are almost all made up of the English race. Although French is the most commonly-spoken language, most newspapers, notices and even the commercial signs of French merchants are in English."

For several years the harvests had been poor. Near Quebec, the situation was so desperate, *Le Canadien* reported, "that some habitants have taken to eating their own horses. Harvests have fallen short for four years now and many habitants don't have even a potato. The ones who are better off, barely have enough for themselves and their families to get by. What will all these poor souls do from now until May? It is certain that most of them will die of hunger, if relief is not provided to them."

This widespread poverty was accompanied by a political crisis. After three years of reflection, London had rejected the Ninety-Two Resolutions. The British government thought that acceding to the demands of the Patriotes would mean the end of any political hold over its North American colonies. In Lower Canada, civil and military authorities took note and strengthened the garrison as a precaution.

In the villages of the Richelieu Valley, a warning of imminent revolt came when a traditional custom began to be used to send a political message. A *charivari* was an event in which people would surround the house of new-lyweds, or anyone judged to be odd or unwelcome, and make a tremendous, frightening racket with noisemakers of all kinds. During the summer of 1837, the *charivari* was used to stigmatize people who refused to join the

Patriotes, including justices of the peace and other representatives of the Crown. It had become a form of violent demonstration.

Other popular customs also took on political import. Militiamen had the habit of driving a post into the ground in front of their captain's residence to show that they accepted his authority. During the turbulent early months of 1837, Patriote militias cut down the posts of captains who refused to give up their officer's commissions. Starting in October 1837, the Patriotes organized public meetings in which they elected their own militia officers and justices of the peace, replacing their predecessors, who, they felt, had lost the confidence of the people. This movement started in the region of Deux-Montagnes and spread throughout the countryside.

On October 23, 1837, at the Assembly of the Six Counties, five thousand people met in St. Charles in the Richelieu Valley under the green, white, and red flag of the Parti Patriote. They had come to hear the most powerful speaker of the colony: Louis-Joseph Papineau. He alone could find the words to express their disillusionment and discontent.

First, the speaker of the assembly, Dr. Wolfred Nelson, rose and addressed the crowd. This forty-five-year-old was an English Protestant from Sorel who spoke falteringly in his adopted language. He had married a Canadien woman and raised his children as Catholics. Now he had taken up the cause of the Patriotes, a surprising stance for someone who was distantly related to Admiral Horatio Nelson, the hero of Trafalgar.

Next Papineau stood and walked up to the rostrum. When the crowd saw the great man, they cheered, and the militia fired a volley in his honour. "Fellow citizens! Brothers who share our suffering!" he bellowed. "All of you, whatever your origin, your language or your religion, to whom equal laws and the rights of man are precious, we call on you to take that position which alone will bring respect for yourselves and success for your demands, organizing systematically in your respective parishes and townships."

Papineau knew that here, in this little village in the Richelieu Valley, he was getting ready to defy the most powerful empire in the world. His public position was bold, but his private writings showed that he harboured no illusions: without help from outside, from the American republic and progressives in London, the Patriotes would be heading toward catastrophe. But he was buoyed by the revolutionary winds, and he supported the ideas inspired by the American and French revolutions. He called on all Patriotes to elect their own judges and militia officers. It was a rebellious act, he knew: the first step on the way to forming a provisional government. "Assemble together," he thundered, "and elect your justices of the peace, the way your reformist brothers have done in Deux-Montagnes, in order to protect your people from the vengeance of their enemies."

Papineau had never gone so far before. But it was still not enough for the more radical Patriotes. Dr. Nelson then spoke: "I say that the time has come to melt down our dishes and tin spoons to make bullets." The crowd exploded with enthusiasm.

QUEEN VICTORIA'S FIRST MEETING WITH HER CABINET ◆ Queen Victoria acceded to the the throne of Britain and Ireland just as the protest movement reached a crescendo in Lower Canada. The young, seventeen-year-old sovereign was subjected to the gibes of Patriotes, who called her a prostitute, among other slurs. (*Sir David Wilkie, Royal Collection Enterprises, Windsor Castle*)

That same day, in Montreal, four thousand demonstrators gathered in Place d'Armes to listen to Peter McGill, the president of the Bank of Montreal and one of Montreal's anglophone business elite. "We must admit their constitutional right to meet and discuss . . . and to petition and remonstrate . . . if they feel or fancy themselves aggrieved," he said, at first adopting a conciliatory tone, "but any and all of them who overstep the bounds prescribed by the laws in doing so, who outrage the feelings of loyal and well disposed peaceable citizens by overt acts verging on rebellion, ought to be made to understand, that such conduct can be no longer tolerated with impunity."

A tragic, unavoidable conflict was brewing, and everyone had to decide which camp to join. The Church had been supporting the established authorities, but which side would it take now? In a pastoral letter of October 24, 1837, Monseigneur Jean-Jacques Lartigue, bishop of Montreal, issued a warning to the Patriotes: "Have you seriously thought about the horrors a civil war would bring? Have you imagined the rivers of blood flowing through the roads and countryside, and innocent people overwhelmed along with the guilty in the same series of disasters? Have you considered that every popular revolution, almost without exception, is a blood-letting?" Lartigue was a conservative man who feared that a rebellion would bring on the excesses of the French Revolution.

In Upper Canada, William Lyon Mackenzie supported the Patriotes. "People of Upper Canada," he wrote in the *Colonial Advocate*, "Canadians . . . Fellow colonists . . . Behold the oppressors!! in order to enslave a free People encamp soldiers all over their country [Lower Canada]!! . . . If the British Kingdom can tax the People of Lower Canada against their will, they will do so with you when you dare to be free."

For several weeks, Mackenzie travelled through the country north of Toronto, trying to get the support of dissatisfied people, who for years had been asking in vain for schools, roads, and bridges. "Oh, men of Upper Canada, would you murder a free people?" he would ask. "[Lieutenant Governor] Head has sent down his troops, next he will try and send you down to put down your countrymen. Before you do so pause, and consider the world has its eyes on you – history will mark your conduct – beware lest they condemn. Oh who would not have it said of him that, as an Upper Canadian, he died in the cause of freedom! To die fighting for freedom is truly glorious. Who would live and die a slave? Never . . . Never . . . Never . . ."

The crowds would respond, "Never! Never!"

Mackenzie organized fifteen public meetings to keep up the pressure for reform. He was a tireless campaigner and a persuasive speaker, though not everyone liked his fiery speeches. He received death threats and was physically attacked on occasion. But his protest movement was gathering steam.

Starting in October, Mackenzie's supporters began to conduct military drills. A young Reformer, Thomas Sheppard, described them: "We would take our muskets and join the other Reformers who were drilled by an old soldier who worked I think in Mackenzie's printing office. . . . Mackenzie used to ride from the city . . . to watch the old soldier put the farmers through their facings."

These military drills did not go unnoticed. The surveyor general of Upper Canada, John Macaulay, wrote to his mother: "In the rear of the Town the disaffected meet in squads with arms and are drilling and I have no doubt they are in correspondence with the Lower Canadian Malcontents – The time may not be far distant when our muskets may again [bear] requisition – not in foreign, but civil war – The Papineau and Mackenzie faction seem almost infuriated and I do not see how matters can end but in a resort to arms."

Popular unrest in Toronto was not the government's greatest concern. But the lieutenant governor, Sir Francis Bond Head, wanted to prove he had the situation well under control, and made a fateful decision. The British troops stationed in Upper Canada were all sent to Lower Canada, where the situation seemed more serious. By early November 1837, not a single soldier of the regular forces remained in Toronto. And that month the countryside of Lower Canada exploded in violence. In the county of

General John Colborne was the only son of an Anglican minister. A deeply religious and rigorously disciplined man, he walked to church every Sunday and insisted that his servants do the same. Every morning, he rose at four o'clock to study foreign languages before beginning his work day. (*Metropolitan Toronto Reference Library*)

Deux-Montagnes, and in the Richelieu Valley, south of Montreal, the Patriotes threatened the justices of the peace and militia officers who refused to join them.

They faced a formidable adversary in General John Colborne, commander of the British troops. He had participated in the terrible expedition under Wellington to drive the French from Spain, and at Waterloo, with the 52nd Regiment, he had taken on the troops of Napoleon's Vieille Garde and thrown them into disarray. Many in Britain considered Colborne to be a strategist second only to Wellington himself. He had recently resigned his position as lieutenant governor of Upper Canada and was getting ready to sail back to England when a dispatch arrived, ordering him to take command of the military in the two Canadas. This was unfortunate for the Patriotes; they were now facing a seasoned strategist, rather than a mediocre colonial officer.

"[The] revolutionists are running over a large section of the country armed and menacing every individual who hesitates to join them," Colborne wrote to Governor General Archibald Acheson, Earl of Gosford, on November 12, 1837. "If we neglect to profit by the offers from the Upper Province and those of the inhabitants of Montreal to assist by raising corps, while we permit the declared revolutionists to arm quietly, we shall lose the Province."

In fact, the Patriotes were planning to organize a convention and declare the independence of Lower Canada. In mid-November, arrest warrants were about to be issued for the leaders, with prices on their heads. They sought refuge in the strongholds of the Richelieu Valley and the county of Deux-Montagnes.

Governor General Gosford now reluctantly faced an insurrection. Gosford was a man of compromise. In Ireland, this sixty-year-old Protestant had taken a stand against the anti-Catholic Orangemen, and he enjoyed good relations with the Irish Catholic reformer Daniel O'Connell, a friend of the Canadiens. Gosford had been ordered to conduct a commission of inquiry into the crisis in Lower Canada, but he had procrastinated endlessly. Finally, under direct pressure from the pro-British circle in Montreal, he agreed to send in the army against the Patriotes.

"The civil authorities . . . have called for the military to assist them in apprehending these persons," Colborne wrote. "It is of the greatest importance to drag the leaders of the revolt from their meeting places." The general ordered his troops to undertake a pre-emptive strike against the Patriote leaders sheltering in the Richelieu Valley. He wanted to act first and disperse the rebels. Five companies left Chambly, headed for St. Charles. Five other companies left Sorel, bound for St. Denis. Their orders were to take over the villages and proceed to the armed Patriote camp in St. Charles.

After marching all night in the mud and freezing rain, a party of troops got to within a few kilometres of St. Denis. Daniel Lysons was a lieutenant in the First Infantry Regiment, the "Royal Scot": "It soon became evident

CANADA: A PEOPLE'S HISTORY

that the rebels were on the alert; the church bells were heard in the distance ringing the alarm, and parties of skirmishers appeared on our left flank." A group of Patriotes ran out of a stone house and opened fire from behind a barricade. The soldiers approached the St. Germain house on the highway to Sorel and sought shelter behind a stone wall. And so began the Battle of St. Denis.

Dr. Wolfred Nelson was in charge of defending the village. Papineau and the other Patriote leaders counted on his leadership to throw the British troops back. He was at the head of eight hundred men. One hundred of them had taken up position inside and around the St. Germain house. Among them were ordinary citizens, including the merchant Louis Pagé, a surveyor named David Bourdages, and farmer Antoine Lusignan. Nelson rallied his men. Their lives were at stake, he said, and they would have to show exemplary courage. They had to be steadfast, aim carefully, save powder, and avoid unwarranted risks.

The commander of the British troops, Colonel Charles Gore, divided his three hundred soldiers into three columns and positioned his cannon a few hundred metres away from the fortified house. But the cannon did little damage.

Few men fell during six hours of combat. In the middle of the afternoon, the defenders of St. Denis received reinforcements from neighbouring villages. The English soldiers were tired after their long and difficult march. They had not expected to meet such resistance and they were running out of ammunition. Colonel Gore finally ordered a retreat. Twelve British soldiers and thirteen Patriotes were dead.

The Patriotes celebrated their victory, but Louis-Joseph Papineau was not in St. Denis to celebrate with them. Later on, some people would claim that Nelson himself had asked Papineau to leave the scene of battle, so that the leader's life would not be put unnecessarily at risk. Others accused him of having fled from the fighting.

While his men celebrated, Nelson thought about the consequences of the battle. "We have now passed the Rubicon – our very lives are at stake," he wrote. "There is no alternative; even a mean, cringing submission will scarcely protect us from every kind of ignominy, insult and injury, worse to bear than death itself, if, indeed, this event do not befall us at once. We see, now, but the painful necessity of taking up arms in good earnest, and manfully awaiting the occurrences which our attitude may provoke." Nelson knew that they had won only a skirmish with the world's most powerful army. The war was just beginning.

In the fall of 1837, after the surprise victory of the Patriotes in St. Denis, General John Colborne wrote to the lieutenant governor of Upper Canada, Sir Francis Bond Head: "The Civil War has now commenced in this Province. I entreat you, therefore, to call out the Militia of Upper Canada and endeavour to send to Montreal as many corps as may be inclined to volunteer their services at this critical period."

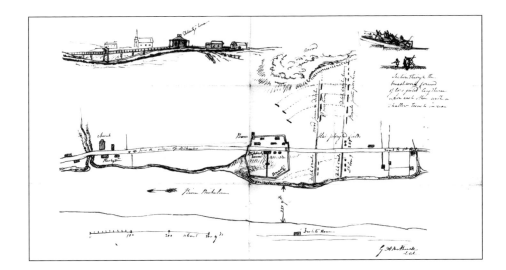

This map of the Battle of St. Charles was drawn by Lieutenant-Colonel George Augustus Wetherall on the day of the British victory. (*National Archives of Canada*, NMC-43316)

On November 25, Lieutenant-Colonel George Wetherall launched an attack on St. Charles with 425 men who had come down from Fort Chambly – a move intended to smash the resistance of the Patriotes in the Richelieu Valley.

The fate of the rebellion was at stake in St. Charles. Two hundred and fifty Patriotes took up a position behind a barricade they had thrown up around the seigneurial manor house. One of them, thirty-seven-year-old journalist and teacher Jean-Philippe Boucher-Belleville, wrote in his memoirs, *Diary of a Patriote*: "We were totally on the defensive, and the question for us came down to this: should we hand over our properties, our women and children, without fighting, to these barbarians who were coming, not out of respect for law, but to conquer by fire and sword and to haul away their booty? Much as in St. Denis, most of our brave blue-hatted Patriotes showed a zeal and courage that could only bring us victory. Even the women cast bullets and made cartridges; the elderly and children wanted to share in the dangers of combat."

British Lieutenant Charles Beauclerk, a twenty-four-year-old amateur painter, also took part in the battle. "Colonel Wetherall hoped that a display of his force would induce some defection among the infatuated people," he wrote, "but, unfortunately for the sake of humanity, it was far otherwise. . . . From behind the breastworks, a continual fire was directed against the centre of the line, ordered in consequence to lie down; notwithstanding which, from the exposed position, it materially suffered. This gave rise to an order for the three centre companies, headed by Colonel Wetherall in person, to fix bayonets and charge the works."

The Royals, one of the toughest regiments in the British army, was covered by fire from the other soldiers and advanced relentlessly on the barricade in close formation, despite devastating gunfire from the Patriotes. It was an unequal struggle: on the one hand were poorly equipped and inexperienced civilians holding makeshift weapons; on the other, crack professional troops.

THE BATTLE OF ST. CHARLES ◆ On November 25, 1837, the British Army faced the Patriotes at St. Charles in the Richelieu Valley. This painting is by Lieutenant Charles Beauclerk, one of the English officers participating in the battle. After returning to England, Beauclerk published a set of lithographs as well as his memoirs of the 1837 rebellion. (*National Archives of Canada, C-000393*)

The Royals advanced, pushing the insurgents into the frigid waters of the Richelieu River. Lieutenant Beauclerk's eyewitness account is the only one to have survived. As he described it, a group of Patriotes awaited the soldiers on their knees, with their rifles upside down, as if they wanted to surrender, but then at the last moment they opened fire. The soldiers yelled their war cry and charged the Patriotes. It was a slaughter. "This act of treachery caused, until restrained by the officers, a general massacre; which, whilst it lasted, was indeed dreadful."

By the end of the day, 150 Patriotes and 3 British soldiers lay dead on the battlefield. Louis-Joseph Papineau, Wolfred Nelson, Jean-Philippe Boucher-Belleville, and hundreds of other Patriotes fled the Richelieu Valley to seek refuge in the United States. Some were captured and ended up in Montreal's prison, the Pied-du-Courant, in appalling, nearly medieval conditions.

News of the clashes in the Richelieu Valley quickly reached Upper Canada. A week after the Battle of St. Charles, William Lyon Mackenzie was convinced that the time had come to attack Toronto. His speeches, and those of his lieutenants, like Samuel Lount, fired the blood of the people, and each day brought him fresh supporters. Charles Doan, a farmer from the village of Hope, east of Toronto, told how he had been recruited by the rebels: "Lount said there was a war in Lower Canada and there was reason to believe that Martial Law would be declared in this province. In order to prevent which, it would be necessary to proceed to the City. He said he thought the City would be taken without firing a gun. He didn't know the exact day the attack was to be made. Lount recommended to take such guns as we had with us."

Mackenzie recruited discontented farmers in particular, telling them to report to Montgomery's Tavern north of Toronto, which had been transformed into his headquarters. With no British troops in Toronto, Mackenzie decided to seize power and form a provisional government. "Up then Brave Canadians!" he wrote in a December 1 pamphlet. "Get your rifles, and make short work of it; a connection to England would involve us in all her wars, undertaken for her own advantage, never for ours, with governors from England, we will have bribery at elections, corruption, villainy and perpetual discord in every township, but Independence would give us the means of enjoying many blessings."

On December 4, at nightfall, 150 men from the villages of Holland Landing, Sharon, and Lloydtown met at Montgomery's Tavern. They were tired, hungry, and completely disorganized. Mackenzie, Lount, and the other leaders could not agree on the best time to descend on Toronto. More rebels arrived during the night. The next day, Mackenzie and Lount marched down Yonge Street, leading hundreds of ragtag insurgents. Twenty militia faithful to the British Crown were waiting for them. The militia fired, then retreated, while the rebels shot back.

"Colonel Lount and those in the front fired – and instead of stepping to one side to make room for those behind to fire, fell flat on their faces," Mackenzie wrote. "The next rank did the same thing. Many of the country people, when they saw the riflemen in front falling down and heard the firing, they imagined that those who fell were killed by the enemy's fire, and took to their heels. This was almost too much for the human patience. The city would have been ours in an hour, probably without firing a shot. But 800 ran, and unfortunately the wrong way."

Two days later, one thousand militia and volunteers loyal to the government were given weapons and ammunition, with orders to drive the rebels out of Montgomery's Tavern. Mackenzie's men were waiting for them along Yonge Street. There were only four hundred insurgents left, and only half of them had guns; the rest were armed with picks.

When their adversaries came in sight, Lount ordered his men to shoot. But the militia returned their fire with a barrage from their field artillery. Surprised by the thunderous cannon, the rebels threw down their weapons and fled. The battle lasted only a few minutes. The militia burned Montgomery's Tavern to the ground, and Upper Canada's rebellion was over. Mackenzie's dream had collapsed, and a reward was offered for his capture.

In Lower Canada, martial law was declared in the district of Montreal. Only one rebel stronghold remained: the county of Deux-Montagnes. On December 14, General John Colborne led a military expedition to the village of St. Eustache. A twenty-one-year-old woman, Emélie Berthelot, described the arrival of the British troops in her diary: "Around ten in the morning, on Thursday, with the weather clear and very cold, about 1,500 English troops took the Chemin du Roy [the King's Way]: infantry, artillery, cavalry, the general staff in brilliant uniforms, commanded by Sir John Colborne; then the war machines, mortars and red eight-seater carriages for transporting the wounded. All of that passed by slowly, as if in a spirit of defiance."

Most Patriotes realized that there was no hope of victory, and they fled. Only 250 defenders remained. One of them, Dr. Jean-Olivier Chénier, holed up in the church with a handful of men. He was small, well-built, and physically imposing, with a frank and open face. When it was suggested that he flee, Chénier replied: "Do what you want, but as for me, I am here to fight, and if I am killed, I am going to take a few of them before dying." Some of his men worried that they did not have enough weapons. "Rest assured," he told them, "some men will be killed, and you can take their guns."

General Colborne ordered his artillery to bombard the church. The priest, Father Jacques Paquin, was against the rebellion and was present during the cannonade. "All the cannons together started striking the church

Canonnade against the church of St. Eustache. On December 14, 1837, for more than two hours, the church of St. Eustache was battered by four six-pound cannons and two twelve-pound howitzers. Dr. Jean-Olivier Chénier and a handful of die-hard Patriotes resisted the assault until the church was finally engulfed in flames. (*Charles Beauclerk, National Archives of Canada, C-000392*)

St. Eustache. This painting shows the final moments of the Battle of St. Eustache. The Patriotes are in flight, surrounded by the St. Eustache Loyal Volunteers under Captain Maximilien Globensky, the Royal Montreal Rifles under Captain Pierre-Edouard Leclère, and the rearguard of the 83rd Infantry Regiment of the British Army. (*Charles Beauclerk, National Archives of Canada, C-396*)

with surprising speed," he wrote in his diary. "The masonry-work was extremely solid and stood up to a huge number of cannon balls that were fired without ceasing." For two hours, the church held up to the artillery fire.

At nightfall, General Colborne gave the order to drive the Patriotes out of their hiding place. A detachment of the Royals entered the church and had to stop near the altar under the fire of the Patriotes. "We got round to the back of the church," Lieutenant Daniel Lysons wrote in his memoirs, "and found a small door leading into the sacristy which we battered in. We then turned to our left and went into the main body of the church. Here the rebels began firing down our heads. We could not get up to them for the staircases were broken down." Before leaving the church, they set fire to the altar cloth. The defenders feared being roasted alive and had to flee.

Father Paquin witnessed the last moments of the battle: "Dr. Chénier, seeing all hope had been lost and he could not dream of defending himself within the church, which was now ablaze, brought some of his men together and jumped with them through the windows on the convent side. He wanted to escape but he could not get out of the cemetery, and soon was caught by a bullet, dropped to the ground and died almost immediately." Seventy Patriotes and three soldiers were dead.

In the days that followed, the soldiers and volunteers spread terror throughout the county of Deux-Montagnes. St. Eustache and St. Benoit

Reward for the arrest of Louis-Joseph Papineau. On December 1, 1837, Governor General Gosford offered a reward of either 1,000 pounds or 4,000 dollars to whomever succeeded in capturing Louis-Joseph Papineau, who was accused of high treason. (*Archives nationales du Québec à Québec*)

were looted and burned. In St. Joachim, Ste. Scholastique, and Ste. Therese, the army burned the houses of the rebel leaders. Hundreds of Patriotes from the region were taken prisoner before they could get across the American border, Dr. Wolfred Nelson and the journalist Jean-Philippe Boucher-Belleville among them.

Louis-Joseph Papineau wrote from exile in the United States to his wife, Julie, who had sought refuge in St. Hyacinthe with her children: "My dear, very dear friend – During my perilous escape, I narrowly escaped so many dangers, I experienced such heart-wrenching anguish to see the suffering of my country, of my family, of my friends. . . . I believe, however, despite the immense disasters we have suffered, that Providence will one day shine brightly on us, setting us to the task of liberating our unfortunate country, and reuniting us all as a family."

Julie replied to her husband: "When your letter arrived, informing us that our future was as uncertain as our current situation . . . I felt extremely discouraged. With the renewal of Martial Law, the arrival of troops who will spread out through the countryside, I fear that we will suffer many more humiliations this winter."

In Upper Canada, a few months later, many of the rebels were pursued as they tried to reach the American border. Mackenzie got as far as Buffalo, in New York State, but hundreds of others were not so lucky. Most of them were given amnesty after serving a few months in prison, but an example was made of Samuel Lount and another rebel, Peter Matthews. In the spring, they were hanged in front of Toronto's prison.

The British government was now determined to end the crisis in the two Canadas. In May 1838, the new governor general arrived in Quebec City to conduct a far-reaching inquiry into the rebellions. John George Lambton, first Earl of Durham, was a forty-five-year-old aristocrat and a skilful diplomat. In England, his adversaries had nicknamed him "Radical Jack." He was as comfortable with royalty as he was with the workers in his father's coal mines. Durham was granted extraordinary, almost dictatorial powers and an enormous budget to maintain a suite of secretaries, aide-de-camps, musicians, and friends.

"I beg you to consider me as a friend and arbitrator," he wrote on May 29 in a proclamation to the people of the colonies, "ready at all times to listen to your wishes, complaints, and grievances, and fully determined to act with the strictest impartiality." His first step was to grant an amnesty to the Patriotes, who were rotting in prison, in the hopes of restoring calm. On the day of Queen Victoria's coronation, 150 prisoners were freed, while eight leaders remained in jail, after pleading guilty in exchange for the release of their comrades.

Dr. Wolfred Nelson and seven others were exiled to Bermuda. "We belong to our country and we will gladly sacrifice ourselves on the altar of her liberties," Nelson wrote to Durham on June 18, 1838. "We rose in revolt neither against the person of Her Majesty nor of her government, but against a vicious colonial administration." Papineau and the other Patriote leaders who had found refuge in the United States faced the death penalty if they returned to Lower Canada.

"Not one drop of blood has been shed," Durham wrote to Queen Victoria on June 28. "the guilty have received justice, the misguided mercy; but at the same time, security is afforded to the loyal and peaceable subjects of this hitherto distracted province."

While Durham was undertaking his inquiry, a group of Patriotes were preparing a new insurrection. They had formed a secret society, the Société des frères chasseurs (Hunters' Lodges), which recruited members in Lower Canada and among exiled Patriotes in the United States. They had an initiation ritual something like that of the Freemasons: the novice had to get down on his knees wearing a blindfold, surrounding by his comrades. A bible was placed in his hands and he took an oath: "I solemnly swear, freely and before almighty God, to observe the secret and mysterious signs of the Society of Hunters, to obey all the rules and regulations the Society may establish. I commit to this unreservedly, failing which I consent to my property being destroyed and my own neck severed to the bone." Then the blindfold was pulled off.

The Frères chasseurs were led by radical Patriotes, among them Robert Nelson, the brother of Wolfred, a respected Montreal surgeon. This forty-three-year-old revolutionary had been imprisoned in 1837. Now he was alongside Chevalier de Lorimier, an idealistic thirty-five-year-old notary who had played a part in the uprising and yearned to take up the good fight once again. "I am always ready to shed my blood on the soil that witnessed my birth," de Lorimier wrote to a friend on July 6, 1838, "in order to overthrow the despicable British government – from the top of its branches to its roots – everything. But I must confess that my heart bleeds at the thought of leaving my family with no means to subsist. This thought has often brought tears to my eyes." De Lorimier was a tireless organizer and possessed a daunting physical courage.

Papineau, however, dissociated himself from the group. Once the governors of Vermont and New York had proclaimed their neutrality, he firmly believed that the government of the United States would refuse to back another uprising, and he concluded that a new rebellion would end in failure.

In Lower Canada, the Frères chasseurs hoped for broad support. "Having spent the summer in the country," one Patriote said during interrogation after being arrested, "I must say that most people are ripe for revolution, and that the indecision and lack of resolve and courage they showed in some cases can only be attributed to a feeling of inferiority in terms of discipline, military organization and weaponry. The destruction of lives and property, far from snuffing out the flame of the rebellion, has only kindled it."

In the fall of 1838, Lord Durham resigned under pressure. In condemning the Patriote leaders to exile in Bermuda, which was not a penal colony, Durham had exceeded his legal authority. On November 1, he left North America, bound for England. "I little expected the reward I have received from home, – disavowal and condemnation," he wrote to Lord Glenelg on September 29, 1838. "In these circumstances I have no business here – My authority is gone – all that rests is military power, that can be better wielded by a soldier, and Sir John Colborne will, no doubt, do it efficiently." Lower Canada was about to suffer violence once again.

In the fall of 1838, the Frères chasseurs launched an invasion from the United States, timed to coincide with an uprising in Lower Canada. They attacked the seigneurial manor of Beauharnois, which belonged to Edward Ellice, one of the richest landowners in Lower Canada and an influential member of the Whig Party in Great Britain. Inside the imposing house were the seigneur's son and daughter-in-law, Jane Ellice. "We had not been in bed five minutes before a long, loud, horrid yell close to the house made us start up," Jane Ellice wrote in her diary. "The house was surrounded on all sides. Guns going off in all directions, striking the house, breaking the windows on every side."

In less than an hour, three hundred Frères chasseurs overran the manor. Sixty villagers loyal to the British Crown were taken prisoner, including the seigneur's son, also Edward Ellice, who was Durham's personal secretary. The prisoners were escorted to the parish of Châteauguay, five kilometres away.

The family was treated well. "I wanted to make this measure as tolerable as possible for the people to whom it was applied," the Patriote

Jane Ellice was the wife of the younger Edward Ellice, private secretary to Lord Durham. On July 10, 1838, the Ellices moved into the seigneurial manor of Beauharnois, where they planned to stay until their departure for England. They were taken prisoner when the second rebellion erupted. (*William Charles Ross, National Archives of Canada, C-131638*)

Patriotes in rebellion in November 1838. This watercolour is by Jane Ellice, who was held captive by these men for six days in 1838. (*National Archives of Canada*, C-13392)

François-Xavier Prieur wrote in *Notes of an 1838 political convict*, "and so I went to Madame Ellice, who was with another lady said to be her sister, to reassure them that their husband and fellow prisoners risked no danger, and to offer them all the consolations we could. When these ladies expressed the wish to seek refuge in the Beauharnois presbytery, six of the most respectable farmers were ordered to accompany them, while we placed a regular guard at the manor to protect the properties from any attacks. A courier was placed at the disposal of Madame Ellice so she could communicate with her husband, and every day our prisoners and the ladies shared news." Nevertheless, Jane Ellice described her captors as terrifying French revolutionaries: "My sister and I were left seated en chemise de nuit and robe de chambre, in the

Julie Papineau and her daughter Ezilda in 1836. Julie and Louis-Joseph Papineau had six boys and three girls. Four of them died at an early age, typical for the infant mortality rate in Canada in the nineteenth century. (*Antoine Plamondon, National Gallery of Canada, 17920*)

midst of five or six of the most ruffian looking men I ever saw except in my dreams of Robespierre and without a single being to give us either advice or assistance." After six days in captivity, Jane Ellice and her family were freed.

The rebellion suffered a serious setback when weapons and ammunition being sent north by American supporters were seized at the border. The Frères chasseurs went from one defeat to another, and history repeated itself. The rebels hurried to the border to seek asylum in the United States. The uprising had only lasted a week, but the consequences would be devastating.

Julie Papineau now joined her husband in Albany. She wrote to her son Amédée: "You say that you don't understand why the whole people didn't rise up in revolt? They were told arms and money would be coming, along with a big army from the United States: they were told a lot of tall tales."

In the days that followed, one thousand Glengarry Highlanders and militia from elsewhere in Upper Canada looted and burned the whole Beauharnois region. Jane Ellice witnessed the devastation: "The Glengarries' boast is 'No fear of our being forgotten, for we've left a trail six miles broad all thro' the country.' They seem to be a wild set of men. One of them told

PATRIOTES EXECUTED IN 1838 ◆ This drawing by Henri Julien shows the hanging of Chevalier de Lorimier, Charles Hindelang, Pierre-Rémi Narbonne, Amable Daunais, and François Nicolas. One of their friends who escaped the scaffold, François-Xavier Prieur, described their tragic end: "Lorimier went up on the scaffold with a firm step and gave no sign of weakness until the very last moment. . . . Lorimier smiled several times and approvingly nodded his head at the enthusiastic words of his comrade in adversity. Hindelang had hardly finished speaking when the signal was given, and the trapdoor underneath him fell open." (*From La Presse, June 24, 1893, National Archives of Canada, C-013493*)

me that the houses they had spared in coming down the country, they would surely burn in going back." The Glengarries were not alone in laying waste to the land. With the full support of civil and military authorities, the army and the volunteers sowed terror in the countryside to the south of Montreal. A journalist from the *Montreal Herald* described the scene: "All the country back of Laprairie presented the frightful spectacle of a vast expanse of livid flame. . . . It is sad to reflect on the terrible consequences of the revolt, of the irreparable ruin of so great a number of human beings, whether innocent or guilty. Nevertheless the supremacy of the laws must be maintained inviolate, the integrity of the Empire respected, and peace and prosperity assured to the English, even at the expense of the whole Canadian people."

One of the victims of this devastation was the Patriote shopkeeper François-Xavier Prieur, who had just opened a general store. "It was about eleven in the evening," he wrote, "when I found myself in front of the still smoking ruins of my new store, and that was only after passing other ruins along the road, where soldiers had set fire to several inhabited houses and barns full of grain. I met nobody on the road, the darkened houses seemed to want to hide from view the terrors of the women, children and the suspects inside them." Because of the pointless and barbarous torching of hundreds of houses, Sir John Colborne was nicknamed "the old firebrand."

Like Papineau, William Lyon Mackenzie, still in exile in the United States, had abandoned the idea of armed resistance. But in Upper Canada, American adventurers kept the struggle alive. Throughout 1838, these "Patriote hunters" launched border raids, without the approval of the United States government. The cause of the Canadian people touched the hearts of Americans who dreamed of freeing Upper Canada from British domination. But their determination was shattered once and for all in December 1838, when almost all of them were captured by the Canadian militia after a crushing defeat at Windsor.

In 1838 and 1839, hundreds of imprisoned rebels were convicted of high treason. In Upper Canada, seventeen men were executed, and in

Lower Canada, twelve men were hanged. "I only have a few hours to live," Chevalier de Lorimier wrote, "but I wanted to devote these last precious hours to my religious duties and my comrades. For them, I die the infamous death of a murderer on the gallows, for them I tear myself away from my young children, my wife . . . and for them I die calling out 'Long live Liberty, long live Independence.'"

In the fall of 1839, more than 130 prisoners from Upper and Lower Canada were exiled to the penal colony of Australia. The rebels had been utterly defeated. Two hundred had died on the battlefield or been hanged, while many more had been sent into exile. Twenty years of work for parliamentary reform had come to nothing. The Tories were triumphant. In Lower Canada, the constitution was suspended and the assembly dissolved. A special council, appointed by the governor general, ruled the colony with an iron hand.

In London, Lord Durham tabled a *Report on the Affairs of British North America*, the legacy of his brief tenure as governor general. "It is not by weakening, but strengthening the influence of the people on its Government," he wrote, "that I believe that harmony is to be restored, where dissension has so long prevailed; and a regularity and vigour hitherto unknown, introduced into the administration of these Provinces."

In this respect, Durham seemed to agree with Papineau, Mackenzie, and Howe. He proposed that the governor choose his councillors from among men who enjoyed the confidence of the assembly. This would end the quarrel between the representatives of the people, who sought to increase their power, and a non-elected government, which invoked imperial authority in order to defend its privileges.

Durham stated that there was another, more serious problem in the case of Lower Canada: "I expected to find a contest between a government and a people: I found two nations warring in the bosom of a single state: I found a struggle, not of principles, but of races; and I perceived that it would be idle to attempt any amelioration of laws or institutions until we could first succeed in terminating the deadly animosity that now separates the inhabitants of Lower Canada into the hostile divisions of French and English."

Durham proposed to unite the two Canadas. He thought that Canadiens, whom he described as a people without history and without literature, would ultimately benefit. Once they had become a minority, they would gradually abandon their nationality. "The language, the laws, the character of the North American Continent are English," Durham stated, "and every race but English appears there in a condition of inferiority. It is to elevate them from that inferiority that I desire to give the Canadians our English character."

But in London, the government refused to make the colonial parliamentary system more democratic. The English ministers worried that colonial autonomy would lead to the disintegration of the empire. Nevertheless, they approved of Durham's idea of uniting the two Canadas.

Robert Baldwin. On January 11, 1836, Robert Baldwin's wife, Elizabeth, died after a long illness, and Baldwin never completely recovered from the loss. "I will have to continue my pilgrimage alone," he wrote shortly after his wife's death, "and in the emptiness that spreads before me, I can only hope to find joy in the knowledge that the happiness of our dear children will recall our former happiness, and I shall wait humbly for that blessed hour, if God wills it, when I shall be again, and forever, at the side of my Eliza." (*Théophile Hamel, Château Ramezay Museum*)

Eighteen months after publishing his report, Lord Durham died of tuberculosis at the age of forty-eight.

In Halifax, Joseph Howe, who had been a member of the House of Assembly for four years now, urged the colonial secretary in London to support the recommendations contained in the Durham Report: "The principle of responsibility to the popular branch must be introduced into all the colonies without delay. It is the only simple and safe remedy for an inveterate and very common disease."

Once again, the Halifax elite tried to keep Howe quiet. He had made an unfavourable comparison in the *Novascotian* between the children of rich families and the apprentices he employed in his print shop, which was considered an intolerable insult. This time, however, the challenge came not in the courts, but in the form of a duel, which Howe accepted. "During the political struggles in which I have been engaged," he said, "several attempts have been made to make me pay the penalty of life for the steady maintenance of my opinions. Hitherto providence has spared my life . . . this may not be the case always. . . . I feel that I am bound to hazard my life rather than blight all prospects of being useful. If I fall, cherish the principles I have taught – forgive my errors – protect my children."

His opponent shot first but missed, leaving Howe a clear shot. Instead, he raised his pistol and fired into the air. "All is well that ends well," he said. "I never intended to fire at him and would not for Ten Thousand Pounds – all that was necessary was for me to let them see that the Reformers could teach them a lesson of coolness and moderation."

Far to the west, two other men were trying to follow the path of political tolerance and democracy. In Toronto, a thirty-six-year-old lawyer named Robert Baldwin had become the leader of the Reformers. Heir to one of the colony's largest fortunes, Baldwin was a big man with stooped shoulders and a phlegmatic manner. He was a former student of Dr. John Strachan, the powerful and conservative Anglican bishop of Toronto.

During the 1837 rebellion, Baldwin had tried, unsuccessfully, to mediate between William Lyon Mackenzie and the lieutenant governor, Sir Francis Bond Head. Now he wanted to bring the Reformers from Lower and Upper Canada together. He knew that without the support of French Canadians, the Reformers would not be able to win a majority in the new assembly of United Canada. "There is, and must be no question of races," he wrote to Louis-Hippolyte La Fontaine, who had become one of the most influential politicians in Lower Canada, since most of the Patriote leaders had gone into exile. "It were madness on one side, and guilt, deep guilt on both to make such a question. The Reformers of Upper Canada are ready to make every allowance for the unfortunate state of things and are resolved, as I believe them to be, to unite with their Lower Canadian Brethren cordially as friends, and to afford every assistance in obtaining justice." La Fontaine replied: "It is in the interest of reformers of both provinces to meet on

LOUIS-HIPPOLYTE LA FONTAINE ◆ In the early years of his political career, Louis-Hippolyte La Fontaine was one of Louis-Joseph Papineau's most ardent admirers. But shortly before the rebellion, he broke ranks with the Parti Patriote. La Fontaine feared the consequences of resorting to violence, and, at the last minute, he appealed to the governor general, Lord Gosford. "In my humble opinion," he wrote on November 19, 1837, "the only effective way to restore peace to the country will be to call Parliament into session. Because it is a hundred times better to reign through the confidence and love of the people than through force." La Fontaine failed to move Gosford, and went to London to seek a compromise. But he was too late; the first shots of the rebellion had already been fired. (*Théophile Hamel, Château Ramezay Museum*)

legislative ground, in a spirit of peace, union, friendship and brotherhood. United action is needed now more than ever."

Now thirty-two years of age, La Fontaine bore a striking resemblance to Napoleon, which he cultivated through his hairstyle. He was born of a modest family, on the Boucherville seigneury, east of Montreal, had studied law, and had quickly become a respected politician. In 1837, he tried to reconcile the Patriotes and the colonial authorities, without success. La Fontaine saw the union of Upper and Lower Canada as an act of injustice and despotism, but Baldwin's letter gave him fresh hope.

"I have no doubt that, the reformers of Upper Canada feel the desire to join forces, the way we do," he declared in an open letter to the electors in his riding of Terrebonne, "and that during the first legislative session, they will give us unambiguous proof, which I hope will be the sign of a lasting and mutual bond of trust."

In February 1841, the new constitution came into effect. Kingston was chosen as capital of the United Province of Canada. In the house of assembly, the two former provinces had the same number of representatives, a system designed to reduce the political clout of French Canadians. Even if La Fontaine's Reformers were to win all the majority French-speaking ridings in Lower Canada, they could not control the House of Assembly without Baldwin's help. Baldwin's Reformers, meanwhile, faced stiff opposition from Conservatives, who had held a powerful position since the failure of the rebellion. They could not form a majority without La Fontaine's support. Each group needed the other.

The alliance of Reformers from both Canadas received its baptism by fire during the first election after the rebellions. In Lower Canada, Governor General Charles Edward Poulett Thomson, Lord Sydenham, used every means at his disposal to help the Conservatives win: he redrew electoral boundaries and placed polling stations as far as possible from villages with French-Canadian majorities. During the election, violence broke out and

The House of Assembly, Montreal. In 1844, Montreal became the capital of United Canada. Saint Anne's Market was transformed into the seat of Parliament, inaugurated on November 28, 1844. (*J. Duncan, Musée des Beaux Arts du Canada*)

there were even some deaths. The army intervened only to protect candidates of the English Party.

In Terrebonne, where La Fontaine was seeking re-election, the governor general placed the only polling station at New Glasgow, a village with an English majority. When La Fontaine and his supporters went to vote, they were threatened with violence, and La Fontaine decided to withdraw from the race to avoid bloodshed. The election was a disaster for his Reformers, who saw only twenty-four of their forty-four candidates elected.

Without La Fontaine in the House of Assembly, the Reformers' alliance was in peril. In August 1841, Baldwin wrote to his father, William, a candidate in a Toronto riding: "I think it would be very desirable that you should, even tho' you may have already accepted the nomination for North York, suggest to them the expediency of accepting your retirement and of returning Mr. La Fontaine, if he will accept the nomination instead of you. I am satisfied that nothing could be done at this conjuncture [that] would have a better effect upon the state of parties in the House than his return just now for North York." La Fontaine accepted the offer, and, much to everyone's surprise, he won the election in the riding of North York. Later, he would return the favour to Baldwin, who would be elected in the riding of Rimouski, after losing an election in the riding of York, on January 30, 1843. These gestures of goodwill sealed both a political alliance and a friendship between the two men.

QUEEN AND NAPOLEON'S WHARVES, QUEBEC ◆ In the early nineteenth century, the port of Quebec depended on the trade in squared timber. Between 1812 and 1834, the number of ships anchoring there each year went from 362 to 1,213. (*Mary Millicent Chaplin, National Archives of Canada, C-000860*)

In the years that followed, Robert Baldwin and Louis-Hippolyte La Fontaine struggled side by side to create a democratic government, but they were disappointed by London's refusal to grant autonomy to its North American colonies.

The political malaise was mirrored by a devastating plague. In the spring of 1847, the *Syria* brought 241 miserable immigrants fleeing the Great Famine in Ireland. They were anchored off Grosse-Ile, an island below Quebec where immigrants with typhus, cholera, and smallpox were quarantined. The Irish immigrants brought an epidemic that would rage throughout Canada.

One immigrant's account, published under the name of Robert Whyte, described the scene at Grosse-Ile. "We lay at some distance from the island," he wrote in his 1847 diary, "the distant view of which was exceedingly beautiful. However, this scene of natural beauty was sadly deformed by the dismal display of human suffering that it presented – helpless creatures being carried by sailors over the rocks on their way to the hospital, boats arriving with patients some of whom died in their transmission from their ships. Another, and still more awful sight, was a continuous line of boats, each carrying its freight of dead to the burial ground and forming an endless funeral procession."

During the stiflingly hot summer of 1847, fifty people died each day at Grosse-Ile. Six men worked full time digging graves. At the end of the year, the toll was tragic: twenty thousand Irish immigrants had lost their lives.

"The year 1847 shall be remembered in our history," said *La Minerve* on January 3, 1848, "as the year of emigration. Close to 100,000 unhappy souls left Ireland to seek their daily bread on the banks of the St. Lawrence. To compound their misery, fever decimated them at sea, in quarantine stations, in the villages, towns and countryside of the colonies of British North America."

The Great Famine in Ireland put pressure on London to abandon the preferential tariffs that gave colonial products privileged access to the British market. The victims of famine needed food, and at low prices, but preferential tariffs kept food prices high. Britain, which had been moving in the direction of free trade for some time now, finally abandoned colonial preferences, much to the satisfaction of the English industrialists who had been lobbying for this since the beginning of the century.

Now that the colonies no longer enjoyed a privileged trading position, there was no compelling reason for Britain to control their domestic politics. London finally granted the Reformers of British North America what they had been after for decades: the power to govern themselves. The new rules were laid out in a letter dated November 3, 1847, that would have a decisive effect on the future of the colonies. "It is neither possible nor desirable," declared the colonial secretary, Lord Grey, to John Harvey, lieutenant-governor of Nova Scotia, "to carry on the government of any of the British provinces in North America in opposition to the opinion of its inhabitants."

The moment Joseph Howe had long been waiting for had finally arrived. In early 1848, his party took power in Nova Scotia after winning a general election, forming the first colonial government within the British empire to be freely elected. "It will be our pride to make Nova Scotia a Normal School for the rest of the Colonies," Howe wrote in February of that year, "showing them how representative Institutions may be worked, so as to insure internal tranquility, and advancement, in subordination to the paramount interest and authority of the Empire."

In United Canada, the Reformers, led by Robert Baldwin and Louis-Hippolyte La Fontaine, won a similar victory. "The union of the two provinces was originally devised in order to annihilate the French Canadians," La Fontaine declared. "But things have changed since then. The author of this measure made a mistake. He wanted to lay low a whole category of citizens, because of their origin. But the facts today show that people of all origins are on an equal footing."

In December 1847, Robert Baldwin had anticipated this sentiment in a speech to the voters of York riding: "The Province has passed through a long and arduous struggle for the establishment of a system of government founded on the broad basis of British Constitutional principles. Your favour, and the confidence of a large portion of the people of my country, placed me in a position in which I was called upon to perform no unimportant part in the great battle of the constitution. The battle has been fought. The victory has been achieved."

Louis-Joseph Papineau had been granted amnesty in 1845 and returned to Canada. In 1848 he was elected to represent St. Maurice, and he immediately called for a repeal of the union. But times had changed. The former Patriote leader did not find many supporters for his views, apart from the young radicals of the newspaper *L'Avenir*. His former allies had moved over to support La Fontaine. Wolfred Nelson, the hero of St. Denis, accused his former leader of cowardly flight from the battlefield in 1837. Newspapers circulated rumours to discredit the great man. A year after his return to public affairs, Papineau was a broken politician. He abandoned public life and withdrew to his manor at Montebello. By this time, almost all the former Patriotes and rebels had been granted amnesty. In 1849, Mackenzie was the last to be allowed back.

British North America now had more than two million inhabitants. But on King Street in Toronto, on St. Paul Street in Montreal, and on Water Street in Halifax, businessmen were bracing for an uncertain future. Jobs were scarce, and merchants blamed the situation on Great Britain's free trade policy. English industrialists were now buying their raw materials wherever they were cheapest, which meant that the colonies were losing out to foreign competition.

On top of these economic woes, a fresh political crisis had emerged. In the Parliament of United Canada, now based in Montreal, the Baldwin-La Fontaine government proposed to compensate the Lower Canadians who had lost property during the rebellions. They would receive compensation on condition that they had not been convicted of sedition and they could offer proof of their losses. However, it was well known that numerous Patriotes who had taken part in the rebellion had never been convicted. In the Assembly, Conservatives protested vigorously against what they considered a reward for treason.

There was also opposition to the measure outside Parliament. Influential men got together in order to thwart the Baldwin-La Fontaine government's plan. "Fellow Countrymen," read a manifesto outlining the grievances of Tory merchants, "it has been deemed by those who now address you that the present is a fitting time to ascertain public opinion upon many important subjects, intimately connected with the social, commercial, and political welfare of the inhabitants of this Province. . . . It is evident, from the known character of our race, that patient submission to any ascendency founded on feelings of nationality alone . . . never has been, and never will be for any length of time, endured by Britons."

Extra edition of the *Montreal Gazette*. An edition of the *Montreal Gazette* invited the English citizens of Montreal to protest against the adoption of the indemnity law for losses undergone during the insurrections of 1837 and 1838. (*Public Record Office of the United Kingdom*)

BONSECOURS MARKET, MONTREAL ◆ Between 1815 and 1851, the population of Montreal more than tripled, from 15,000 to 57,000. The Bonsecours Market was one of the largest in the city. Habitants sold their surplus crops there: wheat, peas, hemp, linen, corn, carrots, cabbages, onions, squash, strawberries, apples, and pears. (*William Raphael,* Behind Bonsecours Market, *National Gallery of Canada, 6673*)

In the spring, the new governor general, Lord Elgin, was faced with a difficult decision. He was a skilful diplomat, from a great Scottish family, and it was now up to him to implement the recommendations of his father-in-law, Lord Durham. If he did not accept the Rebellion Losses Bill, then he would be undermining the foundation of responsible government. If he did accept it, then he would antagonize most of the English population of Montreal.

In the spirit of responsible government, he chose to sanction it. The English felt betrayed, and when Elgin left the assembly building, an angry crowd bombarded his carriage with rotten eggs. On April 25, 1849, the *Gazette* issued a call to arms: "The Disgrace of Great Britain Accomplished! Canada Sold and Given Away! Rebellion Losses Bill Passed. The Governor Pelted with Rotten Eggs! . . . The End has begun. Anglo-Saxons you must live for the future. Your blood and your race will now be supreme, if true to yourselves. You will be English 'at the expense of not being British.' . . . A Mass Meeting will be held on the Place d'Armes this evening at 8 o'clock. Anglo-Saxons to the struggle, now is your time."

That evening, the crowd was whipped up by the fire chief, Alfred Perry, and its rage was turned toward Parliament. "Last night about 8 o'clock while

BURNING OF THE PARLIAMENT BUILDING, MONTREAL ◆ The newspaper *La Minerve* was outraged by the burning of Parliament that followed the adoption of the Rebellian Losses Bill: "Under the pretext of refusing to pay an indemnity of 90,000 pounds sterling, they have caused the country an irreparable and incomparably greater loss. Some renegade firemen took great pleasure in this dreadful conflagration. They let the fire, usually their greatest enemy, wreak its destruction." (*Attributed to Joseph Légaré, Musée McCord Museum*)

Parliament was still sitting," wrote William Rufus Seaver, a Congregationalist pastor who witnessed the riot, "a mob (it can be called nothing else tho' composed of some of our most worthy citizens) assembled around the House, and commenced the distruction of the building, by breaking windows etc. Soon the doors were broken open and a stout fellow sprang into the speakers chair with the exclamation 'I dissolve Parliament'. This was the Signal – and immediately in the face of the members, and an immense multitude of spectators, the Gas Pipes were fired in a dozen places, and the building wraped in flames – the 'Golden Mace', sacred emblem of Royalty, was seized by the infuriated mob and borne into the street amid shouts of derision & scorn. The Members barely escaped with their lives, and that splendid Building with its rare paintings, all the records of the Provinces from the first settlement, all the acts of Parliament, that Library, worth alone, £100,000, all, all, are distroyed. That splendid portrait of the Queen, which you may remember was dropped into the street, and torn into a thousand pieces. All was lost, nothing saved, and the structure now is but a heap of smoking ruins. . . . The quarrel is a war of Races – English speakeing people will not be ruled by a Canadian Government, and none can see what the end of these things will yet be – Shall it be the extermination of the Canadian Race? God only knows – But we are in trouble enough now, and blood will be shed worse yet than in the Rebellion of '37."

In this volatile atmosphere, a group of English merchants, who were already angry about free trade, demanded annexation to the United States. They signed petitions and formed a peculiar alliance with the radicals of the newspaper *L'Avenir*. These young intellectuals, who called themselves *les Rouges*, believed that French Canadians would be better treated if they joined the United States; they believed that Lower Canada, which had forcibly been united with Upper Canada in 1840, could become a new state in the American union. But the campaign in favour of annexation did not get very far. The Tories of Montreal did not succeed in getting the support of other English citizens of United Canada, and the *Rouges* were not strong enough to take on La Fontaine's powerful machine, which had built a united party and enjoyed the support of the Church.

"The opposition leaders who are very low in the World at the moment," wrote the governor general on March 1, 1849, "have taken advantage of the circumstance to work upon the feelings of the old loyalists as opposed to Rebels, of British as opposed to French, and of Upper Canada as opposed to Lower, and thus to provoke from various parts of the Province the expression of not very temperate or measured discontent."

Joseph Howe was shocked to learn what had happened in Montreal. In an open letter, he condemned the mob for attacking the governor general and torching Parliament. "We hear a great deal about anglifying the French-Canadians; and a union of the Provinces is sometimes advocated with a view to swamping and controlling that portion of the population which, being of French origin, still preserve their ancient religion, manners and language. . . . If the process of anglifying is to include any species of injustice to that large body of British subjects, who already form at least one-half of the population of United Canada, to such a design, no matter in what form pressed or by whom entertained, we will be no parties."

In 1851, Robert Baldwin retired from public life. He was only forty-seven years old, but the parliamentary struggles he had waged for a decade had exhausted him. He spent time gardening on his property north of Toronto, and died eight years later.

Louis-Hippolyte La Fontaine left politics just a few months after his friend Baldwin. He, too, was tired. At forty-three, La Fontaine took up the practice of law and travelled to Europe. He died in Montreal in 1864.

After returning from exile, William Lyon Mackenzie was elected to the Parliament of United Canada. He took up his pen again to denounce political corruption. But people no longer paid attention. He became bitter, retired from politics in 1859, and died two years later in Toronto, at the age of sixty-six.

Louis-Joseph Papineau lived with his wife, Julie, on the Petite-Nation seigneury, in the Ottawa Valley. "You will believe me, I hope, when I tell you: I love my country," he told a meeting of the Institut Canadien in 1867. "Did I love her wisely? Did I love her foolishly? Opinions may vary on the subject. Nevertheless, when I conscientiously look into my heart and my mind, I believe I can say that I have loved her the way she ought to be loved." He died in 1871, a few days before his eighty-fifth birthday.

Joseph Howe was the only one to continue in politics. After Nova Scotia became the first colony of the British Empire to obtain responsible government, Howe took up a new cause. He became the champion of the railway, symbol of the Industrial Revolution and potential builder of a new country.

"I am neither a prophet nor a son of a prophet," he said in 1851, "yet I will venture to predict that in five or six years we shall make the journey hence to Quebec and Montreal, and home through Portland and St. John, by rail; and I believe that many . . . will live to hear the whistle of the steam engine in the passes of the Rocky Mountains and to make the journey from Halifax to the Pacific in five or six days."

CONFEDERATION

In the 1860s, the British settlements in North America were facing pressure from two sides. Britain was growing tired of the high cost of defending its apparently ungrateful colonies. And to the south, the outbreak of civil war had created a new military power and a renewed threat; its might could easily be turned north, with the aim of annexation.

The British colonies were not easily defended, or even easily defined. They were lightly populated and geographically diverse. Much of the vast northwestern territory was still loosely held by the Hudson's Bay Company. The plains were a vast area already coveted by the United States and sparsely inhabited by natives, Métis, and fur traders. British Columbia, cut off by the Rocky Mountains, was in the throes of a gold rush, which was bringing Americans up by the thousands. In the east, Newfoundland sat in splendid isolation, and the separate colonies of Prince Edward Island, New Brunswick, and Nova Scotia had little to do with one another. In the centre loomed the bickering, hulking United Province of Canada. None of these elements boded well for nationhood.

Within a decade, however, the northern half of the continent would assume a new shape. The scattered colonies would ally to create a transcontinental nation distinct from the United States, largely free of direct colonial control from London, and possessed of the greatest reservoir of undeveloped land and resources in the world.

The Fathers of Confederation at Charlottetown, P.E.I., September 11, 1864 (*National Archives of Canada*, C-733)

The men who engineered Canada's Confederation formed an unlikely alliance. Like the colonies they represented, they were divided by religious, political, and regional animosities. John A. Macdonald was a Scot who distrusted the English; George-Etienne Cartier was a conservative Quebecker who had fought the British in the 1837 rebellion; George Brown was a liberal Scots Presbyterian who wanted to eliminate aristocratic privilege; and Thomas D'Arcy McGee was an Irishman who once proudly signed a letter "Thomas D'Arcy McGee, A Traitor to the British Government." Together, they argued a constitution into existence.

Some citizens were not impressed by their leaders, though. "John A. Macdonald and some others at the Ministry are in town," Amelia Harris wrote in 1860, when the political circus came to London, in Canada West. Harris was a Loyalist who had settled there in 1834 and whose diary provides an interesting record of social and political events. "They are making a tour of the province before the meeting of parliament. The public dinner given to them is to come off tomorrow." Two days later she wrote: "The dinner is called a success, a great many people were there. The Ministry stayed until very late and were very tipsy, there were John A. Macdonald, Mr. van Koughnet, Mr. Morrison and Mr. Sidney Smith. They knocked each other's hats off, tore each other's coats and did several equally clever things. They were not by themselves, there were a number of their entertainers joined in their drunken sport."

Macdonald stayed for another three days. "The Premier, J. A. Macdonald, did not leave town until today," Harris reported. "Mr. Jackson saw him at the station. When he left Mr. Jackson looked as if he knew a good deal, so I suppose J.A. has been on a spree. They give him a public dinner tonight in Hamilton. What a pity to see such men at the head of affairs in Canada."

But Viscount Charles Monck, the new governor general, was oddly impressed by the colony's politicians: "On the whole I find here more knowledge, more ability, and I think quite as much, if not more, tenderness of conscience as amongst the same class in England."

John Alexander Macdonald was the most prominent Upper Canadian politician, a flawed and witty man with a gift for organizing and an enviable stamina. He had an impressive grasp of constitutional law and a public taste for alcohol. Born in 1815 in Glasgow, of Highland parents, Macdonald came to Kingston at the age of five but maintained a Celtic distrust of "overwashed Englishmen, utterly ignorant of this country and full of crotchets as all Englishmen are." Two of Macdonald's siblings had died young, and his own childhood had ended early; by the age of fifteen he was supporting himself, articling with a Kingston lawyer. He became a prominent lawyer himself and won a seat on the town council before moving to provincial politics. He was tall and loose-limbed, with dark, unruly hair, and a bulbous nose beloved by political cartoonists. Still, he was courtly and flirtatious and had many women admirers.

JOHN A. MACDONALD ◆ "The question of Colonial Union is one of such magnitude that it dwarfs every other question on this portion of the continent. It absorbs every other idea as far as I am concerned. For twenty long years I have been dragging myself through the dreary waste of colonial politics. I thought there was no end – nothing worthy of ambition, but now I see something that is well worthy to be weighed against all I have suffered in the cause of my little country. There may be obstructions, local differences may arise, disputes may occur, local jealousies may intervene, but it matters not – the wheel is now revolving, and we are only the fly on the wheel, we cannot delay it. The union of the colonies of British America under one sovereign is a fixed fact." From a speech given by Macdonald after the Charlottetown Conference, while he was in Halifax, en route to the Quebec Conference, 1864 (*National Archives of Canada, C-004154*)

JOHN A. MACDONALD'S FIRST WIFE, ISABELLA ◆ "Isabella has been ill – very ill – with one of her severest attacks. She is now just recovering and I hope has thrown off for the time her terrible disease. . . . She is weaker than she has ever yet been, and there are symptoms, such as an apparent numbness of one limb, and an irregularity in the action of the heart, which made me send for Dr. Samson." John A. Macdonald described his wife's illness in this 1845 letter to his sister. Isabella was sick for thirteen of their fourteen years of marriage. Although the official cause of her death was given as pneumonia, the exact nature of her illness was never clear. Her symptoms included fainting spells, fatigue, hysteria, tics, various pains, and what Macdonald referred to as "uterine neuralgia." In the course of her lengthy treatment, she became addicted to opium. (*National Archives of Canada, C-98673*)

GEORGE-ETIENNE CARTIER ◆ After Confederation was achieved, the Queen knighted John A. Macdonald but awarded others, including Cartier, the lesser title of Companion of the Bath. Cartier refused the title, writing to Governor General Monck, "I beg that you will be kind enough to allow me to express to Your Excellency my most sincere feelings of gratitude for the honour so graciously conferred on me by Her Majesty, in the selection of myself as one of the Companions of the Bath, in connection with the Federal Union of the British North American Provinces, now forming the Dominion of Canada, and the expression of my grateful thanks. . . . I have had more than any public man to contend with in allaying the sensibilities of a large class of her Majesty's subjects in Lower Canada. In reference to the question of Confederation, in fact, I jeopardized . . . my political position, and in Canada as well as in England, I did not spare labour and trouble to bring the scheme of Confederation to successful issue. As political leader and co-worker my position is inferior to that of no other. . . . I am under the necessity of praying that Her Majesty will be pleased to allow me to decline the honour conferred on me." (*Musée McCord Museum, Notman Photographic Archives*)

Macdonald married his first cousin, Isabella Clark, who was five years his senior. Isabella became an invalid not long after, bedridden with an undiagnosed illness. To deal with the pain, she took opium mixed with wine, and came to depend on it. Despite her agonies, she gave birth to their first son, John, in 1847. "My very soul is bound up in him," she said. But at the age of thirteen months, the baby died, the cause of death unclear. Macdonald never got over John's death, and he kept a box of the child's toys until his own death almost fifty years later. Another son, Hugh, survived, but on December 28, 1857, Isabella died. Her death was not unexpected, but Macdonald was devastated.

Macdonald was able to dominate Upper Canadian politics through a combination of charisma, will, and shrewd negotiation. "Good or bad, able or unable, weak or strong, he wraps them around his finger as you would a thread," noted Joseph Rymal, a Liberal rival.

In Lower Canada, George-Etienne Cartier's was the principal political voice, the "chief of the French-Canadian nationality." He grew up on a large estate on the Richelieu River and attended the strict Collège de Montréal from the age of ten. Cartier began his career as a lawyer, but in his twenties he took an interest in politics and was caught up in the rebellion of 1837. Joining the Patriotes in their fight against arbitrary rule by the colonial administration, he fought in the battle of St. Denis. When the Patriotes were defeated and accused of treason, Cartier fled to the United States for six months, returning to Montreal only after the charges were annulled.

Cartier ran for office in 1848 at the age of thirty-four and was elected as a member of the Legislative Assembly of United Canada. His oratorical gifts were such that he once spoke for thirteen hours in Parliament, delivering a passionate critique of the government.

His wife, Hortense, was a dour woman, and their marriage was more of a business merger than a love match. Cartier soon began a lifelong affair with his wife's cousin Luce Cuvillier, who was eleven years older than Hortense. Luce loved politics and often advised Cartier. She wore pants, smoked cheroots, and read Byron and the novels of George Sand.

Cartier wore a miniature of Napoleon around his neck; he had a taste for champagne and a stubborn habit of singing in public. "Mr. Cartier dined in full uniform! No one knows why," reported Frances Monck, a snobbish, indelicate gossip. "Mr. Cartier sang, or croaked, after dinner and made every one he could find stand up, hold hands and sing a chorus."

Though Cartier and Macdonald seemed to have little in common, they shared a private grief: each had lost a child at the age of thirteen months – Cartier a daughter, Macdonald a son. And they shared a similar, conservative vision that included a vigorous commitment to economic growth and the accommodation of the religious animosities that plagued the United Province of Canada.

In 1841, the former colonies of Lower and Upper Canada had been forced into an unhappy political marriage. Although Lower Canada had a much larger population, the two provinces had been given the same number of elected representatives, and French Canadians resented this inequality. By 1850, immigration had changed the balance, giving Upper Canada (or Canada West, as it became known, although the names Upper and Lower Canada persisted) a larger population.

The political animosities were difficult to separate from religious differences. The Roman Catholic majority in Canada East believed that they were members of the one true, universal Church, that schools should be operated by the Church, and that religious orders should be granted a place of privilege in society. Most Protestants, on the other hand, believed that no one Christian denomination should be given precedence over the others. The debate often degenerated into charges of papist plots and godlessness. Political deadlock was a regular problem, and to overcome political stalemates, Macdonald and Cartier came to depend upon one another to deliver votes from their respective sides of the House. Eventually, the two formed a political alliance.

Their alliance was vilified by George Brown, the founder of *The Globe*, Canada West's most influential newspaper. Brown was six-foot-four and barrel-chested, a mountainous man who used *The Globe* to give voice to his liberal philosophy and criticize his political enemies. He was enraged that Canada West, with its larger population, had the same number of representatives as its largely French counterpart. He argued for representation by population, an issue he had scrupulously avoided when Canada East was larger.

The embodiment of Upper Canadian Protestant virtue, Brown denounced Macdonald's ministers as "Corruptionists" and described Cartier as "that damnable little French Canadian." Brown believed that the Conservatives were particularly debauched, and that Macdonald was a gifted Conservative. He never passed up an opportunity to ridicule him. On an occasion when Macdonald wore the ceremonial British civil uniform to meet with visiting royalty, Brown wrote, "A great deal of time has been wasted by John A. Macdonald in learning to walk, for the sword suspended to his waist has an awkward knack of getting between his legs, especially after dinner." Macdonald responded that the voters "would rather have a drunken John A. Macdonald than a sober George Brown." The voters eventually got both when Brown won office in 1851, running in the southwestern county of Kent as a Reform candidate, representing a movement with a rural, defiantly Protestant base.

Thomas D'Arcy McGee was an Irish Catholic editor, journalist, and ex-revolutionary. He first came to America in 1842, when he was seventeen; two years later he was the editor of the Boston *Pilot*. In 1845 he returned to Ireland, where he continued to work as a journalist and became involved with Young Ireland, a group of nationalists who advocated rebellion against England. In a police notice offering 1,500 pounds for his capture, McGee was described as "Five foot three inches in height – Black hair, dark face – Delicate, thin man – Dresses generally black shooting coat, plaid trousers,

GEORGE BROWN ◆ Anne Nelson Brown sent her husband letters offering shrewd, practical advice on political matters. Brown responded with love letters. "Say not a word, my own dear Anne, about having left me alone! How glad I would have been had you been with me this past fortnight – what a comfort it would have been to consult you from hour to hour & be guided by your sound common sense & unerring woman's instinct as to what was right & honourable to do. . . . Oh dear Anne! I wish you knew how I live upon your love – I really believe I should die if a doubt that you loved me fondly were to take possession of my mind. Even to do what you were to think wrong – to know that you thought I had done that which was mean or dishonourable, were to be insupportable. If ever man thoroughly respected his wife, fondly admired her, devotedly loved her – I do my Anne. When my friends speak of you I have often the greatest difficulty in refraining from breaking out & telling how good you are, how much I owe you."

On March 25, 1880, a former *Globe* employee named George Bennett, who had been fired for intemperance, came into George Brown's office. The two men argued and Bennett produced a gun and shot Brown in the leg. The wound was minor but quickly became infected. In May, Brown became feverish and fell into a coma, dying on May 9 at the age of sixty-one, the third member of the Confederation ministry to fall. (*John Colin Forbes, Government of Ontario Art Collection*)

THOMAS D'ARCY MCGEE ◆ Born in Ireland, McGee came to North America in 1842, one of an estimated 93,000 Irish who emigrated that year. His vast energy was channelled into poetry, literature, and politics. In 1867 he ran for a seat in both the provincial legislature and federal Parliament. He published poems under the pseudonym "Amergin"; more than 300 were published in a collection after his death. He also wrote a novel and more than a dozen popular histories, the most successful of which was *A popular history of Ireland* (1863). The most eloquent of the fathers of Confederation, perpetually indebted, and a sporadically heavy drinker, McGee described himself as having "with impudence, volubility and combativeness, the life and soul and fortune of ten thousand lawyers." But he was more poet than lawyer.

"I dreamed a dream when the woods were green,
And my April heart made an April scene,
In the far, far distant land,
That even I might something do
That would keep my memory for the true,
And my name from the spoiler's hand."

(*Ellison and Co., National Archives of Canada, c-021541*)

light vest." McGee himself listed his good qualities as "a bold face, a fluent tongue and a love for argument." He was praised by the first archbishop of New York, Archbishop Hughes, as having "the biggest mind" and being "unquestionably the cleverest man and the greatest orator that Ireland has sent forth in our time."

He married Mary Theresa Caffrey in 1847 and they moved to Boston after the Irish rebellion of 1848. Their first child, Dorcas, died at the age of three, and another baby, Rose, died of scarlet fever. Of six children, only two survived their father.

After ten years in the United States, McGee still felt like an exile, and he was burdened with poverty and the weight of his children's deaths. He decided to move to Canada, a country whose "character is in the crucible." McGee had been to Canada before, speaking about ways to relieve the horrors of the Irish famine, including massive immigration to Canada, an idea that was criticized by journalist George Brown in *The Globe* as "[a] deep scheme of Romish Priestcraft to colonize Upper Canada with papists . . . a movement to swamp the Protestantism of Canada by bringing into the Province 800,000 unenlightened and bigoted Romanists."

McGee moved to Montreal in 1857 and launched a nationalist newspaper, *New Era*. He was elected to the legislative assembly that same year. "The one thing needed for Canada is to rub down all the sharp angles, and to remove these asperities which divide our people on questions of origin and religion," he wrote. "The man who says this cannot be done is a blockhead."

Amelia Harris began to keep her diary in 1857, after she was widowed at the age of fifty-two. She lived in Eldon House, a gracious, two-storey home on a four-hectare lot overlooking the Thames River. As well as recording her lively criticisms of various politicians, she noted the quotidian rhythms of life in Canada West. That spring she and her family viewed the local entertainments: "In the evening all of the Eldon party went to see Merchant of Venice murdered. The performance was even worse than they expected." And her account is not without its tragedies. When her daughter Amelia Andrina gave birth to a stillborn child, she wrote, "Mr. Griffin brought the baby to me on a pillow, it looked so pretty and so sweet and its little cold face but there was nothing there to make a mother's heart glad. It had come and gone." She recorded how the son of a local member of Parliament was shot in the head in a brothel ("Poor miserable boy – how wretched his father must feel"); how a neighbour lost her breast to cancer ("About this time next year she will die, poor woman"); how a girl killed herself for love and her body was taken by body-snatchers. She discussed the false promise of a nearby oil discovery, the corrupting influence of politics ("I think politics does away with all the finer feelings"), and the economic hardship surrounding her ("Distress in the country is very great," she wrote in 1859. "The first soup kitchen that has been in London has been established here within the past week and it gives relief to 70 poor families").

Her own situation was comfortable, as evidenced by her long struggle to find a decent cook. "May 3: Our new cook has come and proved to be another failure. . . . May 10: Our new cook came. I sent her away after four hours. She did not even know how to boil asparagus. . . . May 14: Our new cook is not a success. I do not think we can keep her. . . . July 28: The cook is so bad tempered . . . that no servant will live with her so that she will have to go." She felt that incompetent cooks were part of a larger, unwelcome

THE AMERICAN CIVIL WAR ◆ The American Civil War resulted in an estimated 618,000 deaths (Confederate dead were 258,000; Union dead 360,000), more than the number of Americans who died in both world wars and Vietnam combined. More men died of disease than bullets. Britain's position on the war was summed up in a ditty published in *Punch* magazine.

"Though with the North we sympathize
It must not be forgotten
That with the South we've stronger ties
which are composed of cotton . . ."

(*Dead near Dunker Church, Library of Congress*)

social change. Describing a recent ball, Harris wrote, "There is a new set who pushed themselves forward, who a few years ago were tailors & soap boilers but now they wish to take the lead."

Her daughter Amelia was married to Gilbert Griffin, the London postal inspector, and the young Amelia met John A. Macdonald at a dinner in 1862. "J. A. Macdonald took Amelia in to supper and paid her a good deal of attention," her mother wrote. "Amelia had only seen him once before in her life and that only for a few minutes. He is a clever man whose moral character I despise." Harris felt that politics made one crude, but she possessed an unwelcome streak of political pragmatism herself: "At the same time, from the position he has held and will probably hold again in the country, it would not do for Amelia, whose husband holds a public office, to be rude to him . . ." Macdonald talked to the younger Harris about matrimony and the *louche* charm of Quebec society. "This is the conversation of J. A. Macdonald *sober*," Harris wrote, appalled. "He condemns and despises what in drunkenness and debauchery he gives himself up to. How melancholy that men of sense and talent, who know the right, will yet choose the wrong."

In 1861, when the American states were in the first year of their fratricidal slaughter, Harris followed the action closely. In November, two Confederate agents named Mason and Slidell headed to Britain on the *Trent*, a Royal Mail carrier, seeking European support for the Confederate cause. The commander of a nearby American vessel, the *San Jacinto*, detained the mail carrier and seized the two agents. The seizure of a British vessel at gunpoint was virtually a declaration of war. "The British Government demands an apology from the American Government," she wrote, "and that Mason and Slidell shall be given up to the British flag again. Troops are to be sent to Canada, and the militia are advised to organize & drill."

The Duke of Newcastle, the colonial secretary, wrote to Governor General Monck: "You must have heard of the affair of the *Trent* and the serious implications which it must produce. I am bound to warn you that war is too likely to be the result. . . . Every preparation should be made to defend Canada from invasion."

Some Americans welcomed the prospect of a fight. "In the event of England, in her folly, declaring war against the United States," read an article in the *New York Herald*, "the annexation of the British North American possessions . . . will unavoidably follow. We could pour 150,000 troops into Canada in a week, and overrun the Province in three weeks more. In this invasion, we should be aided by a large portion of the inhabitants, two-thirds of whom are in favour of annexation with the United States."

The real American invasion, however, came in the form of immigrants and refugees rather than soldiers. "The all exciting subject is the American conscription," Amelia Harris wrote. "To avoid it, the Americans are coming into the country by hundreds." Of the 776,000 men drafted into the Union army, 161,000 "failed to report," many of them fleeing to Canada. They joined the approximately 30,000 escaped slaves who had come via the Underground Railroad to Canada, which they saw as Canaan, the Promised Land. Southern slave-owners tried to discourage flight to Canada, telling them that the Detroit River was three thousand miles wide, that the abolitionists were cannibals: "they get you darkies up there, fatten you up and then boil you."

Among those who came to Canada was Mary Ann Shadd, a striking, freeborn black woman from Delaware. She eventually settled at Chatham, a town of 3,585 in Canada West, where half the citizens were black. Most of Shadd's family followed her to Canada, and her father, Abraham, was elected to the Raleigh township council, the first black to win office in Canada.

Shadd countered the plantation owners' propaganda with a forty-four-page booklet titled *A Plea for Emigration, or; Notes of Canada West in its Moral, Social and Political Aspect*, written for American blacks: "In Canada as in recently settled countries, there is much to do, and comparatively few for the work. . . . If a coloured man understands his business, he receives the public patronage the same as a white man . . ."

Following the escaped slaves were American slave-hunters who came to take them back. First they searched the churches, where the liberated slaves could be counted on to congregate. The First Baptist Church in Chatham had a trap door by the pulpit where the pursued could escape to the basement, then out a window to the woods.

When they could not find who they were looking for, the slave-hunters often took someone else. In September 1858, a ten-year-old boy named Venus was being returned to slavery on board a train that was scheduled to pass through Chatham. Mary Shadd's brother Isaac marshalled a crowd, who stormed the train. Venus was freeborn, it turned out, and his captor, a patent-medicine salesman, was planning to sell him into slavery.

The raid on the train angered some Canadians. Amelia Harris, although an abolitionist, took the southern side. "A great outrage has been committed on the Great Western at Chatham," she wrote. "A southern gentleman was passing through with a slave boy of ten years old. Some negro made the discovery here and telegraphed to the coloured people in Chatham who

Mary Ann Shadd fought for an integrated school system; Canada West had separate schools for Protestants and Catholics, and for blacks and whites. In an abandoned army building in Windsor, she opened a school for any child who wished to come. At night she taught adults, and on Sundays, bible class. She became the first black woman in North America to found and edit a newspaper, the *Provincial Freeman*, whose motto was "Self Reliance is the True Road to Independence." In 1883, she received a law degree from Howard University. (*National Archives of Canada*, C-29977)

assembled a mob of three hundred and when the train stopped at the station they took the boy forcibly from his master although the child cried and did not wish to go. . . . It will turn the American travel from Canada." For Harris, it was a class issue; the South, with its elaborate manners and Old World aristocracy, was more genteel than the industrial North. She sided with the "southern gentleman" and worried about the blow to tourism.

Isaac Shadd and six others were found guilty of rioting. Unable to pay the heavy fines they had been assessed, several of them went to jail. Isaac's aunt, E. J. Williams, wrote from her home in Delaware, "I am much afraid that Canada is not going to prove what it was cracked up to be . . . American gold will bye it in time and Canada will . . . become the hunting ground for the American bloodhound."

For more than a decade, British public opinion had been in favour of reducing, if not eliminating, government spending on the North American colonies, especially for defence. Now, the *Trent* scare raised the possibility of an expensive full-scale war in North America. Britain was determined that the colonies be equipped to defend themselves and to absorb the considerable costs. A militia bill was introduced in the Canadian legislature in 1862, prodded by Governor General Monck and supported by the Macdonald-Cartier alliance. The bill called for the creation of a Canadian militia of one hundred thousand men, an expensive and unpopular undertaking in a colony that had, until now, been defended by British troops. Macdonald knew there would be little support for it, and the bill was repeatedly delayed. He finally introduced the bill with a disjointed speech and was absent the next day, causing the bill's second reading to be postponed.

"Mr. J. A. Macdonald," observed a frustrated Monck, "was prevented from attending in his place in the House during the whole of last week, nominally by illness, but really as everyone knows, by drunkenness."

The militia bill was attacked in the House from all sides, as well as by George Brown in the pages of the *Globe*. When it was defeated, the Macdonald-Cartier administration was forced to resign. The militia bill faded from the political agenda, drawing outrage from London. "It is, perhaps, our duty to defend the Empire at all hasards," read an editorial in the London *Spectator*, "it is no part of it to defend men who will not defend themselves."

British troops arrived in Canada in the wake of the *Trent* crisis, and the garrison towns themselves became battlegrounds for bored soldiers and resentful locals. Drunkenness and prostitution were widespread, and in Halifax a gang fight between soldiers and civilians erupted after an argument over who had won a "greasy pole" contest.

In Canada West, the wealthy were sending their money to England for safekeeping in the event of invasion. "The militia are advised to organize & drill," Amelia Harris noted. "Mr. Scott is trying to get up some volunteer companies. . . . There appears to be a good deal of jealousy among the volunteers. The men all want to be officers. . . . It is said that 2,000 troops are to be stationed in London, all the public buildings have been taken for Barracks and the rents have doubled."

In 1864, the crisis waned, and some of the British troops were sent home. "The troops got their marching orders today," Harris wrote. "We are all so sorry to see them go. London will be very dull without the red coats. . . . It is very doubtful whether there will be any more British soldiers stationed in London as the home government say they will not defend the colonies."

As the American Civil War reached its grim denouement, there was a renewed fear in Canada that the victorious North would turn its army on the poorly defended British territories. To protect itself, British North America first had to be consolidated. Alone, each colony was ripe for invasion, or at least seduction into the American republic.

"I do not believe it is our destiny to be engulfed into a Republican Union," D'Arcy McGee wrote. "We can hardly join the Americans on our own terms and we never ought to join them on theirs. A Canadian nationality, not French-Canadian, nor British-Columbian, nor Irish-Canadian – patriotism rejects the prefix – is, in my opinion, what we should look forward to – and that is what we ought to labour for, that is what we ought to be prepared to defend to the death."

In 1862, George Brown travelled to Britain, a cheerless, upright, forty-three-year-old bachelor who had lost his seat in Parliament after ten years as a member. Brown was the pre-eminent political voice of Canada West, especially in the growing city of Toronto and the farm communities that stretched west to Lake Huron. His single-minded pursuit of the policy of representation by population, his angry distrust of what he saw as Catholic scheming, and his interest in annexing the Hudson's Bay Company's lands were all presented in the *Globe* on a regular basis. He had emerged as the leader of the Reformers. But now he was facing severe financial problems, and his health had deteriorated. For two months he had been bedridden with depression, and he was going to Britain to recuperate.

In Scotland, Brown met Anne Nelson, the daughter of a prominent publisher, and was smitten by her sophistication. He proposed to her within weeks. "How well I remember every event of that day," he later wrote to her, "the walk to the station to meet you . . . the hope & the fear, the despair & the joy, changing every hour until all was settled in that delightful walk along the shore. I was very much in love."

They were married in November 1862, and Brown brought his bride to Toronto just after Christmas. Five thousand people were there to meet them at the train station, and they were serenaded by a band and escorted on a torchlight procession through the city. At his door, he declared that he had returned "with a better knowledge of public affairs and with a more ardent desire to serve."

Softened by love, Brown was prepared to consider the unthinkable – joining forces with his natural enemies, the "Corruptionists," and working toward the union of British North America. Despite his antipathy toward "French Canadianism" and his distaste for debauched Conservatives, he allied with Cartier and Macdonald in a new coalition government whose singular cause was to promote the union of the colonies. Brown saw it as the only way to achieve representation by population and the annexing of the west. "I trust that . . . whenever the great interests of Canada are at stake," he wrote, "we will forget our merely political partisanship and rally round the cause of our country."

McGee applauded Brown's gesture. "Brown has the given the greatest exhibition of moral courage I ever knew," he wrote. "Next to him the man who has taken the greatest risk to his political career is Cartier."

Cartier was attacked in Lower Canada for allying himself with Brown, whose anti-French views were well documented. But Cartier felt that the union of colonies would have several advantages for Canada East. A federation would put an end to the political impasse that paralyzed the union of Upper and Lower Canada. While the new federal government would have power over defence, currency, and foreign trade, the provinces would control their own schools and social institutions, which would bring an end to the bitter religious conflicts. Upper Canadian Protestants and Lower Canadian Catholics would no longer involve themselves in each other's school systems. Cartier also realized that representation by population was inevitable, and it would be preferable to have its application limited to the senior level of government.

Cartier was closely connected to both railway and banking enterprises, and he saw that a larger federation offered the chance for economic growth. For the last two decades, French Canadians had been leaving to work in the mills of New England, which were desperate for cheap labour. Tens of thousands had already gone, and as long as they continued to go, the prospect of new markets in the west and new jobs in Montreal's railway shops were big incentives to endorse Confederation.

Governor General Monck saw an opportunity to promote Confederation among the Maritime provinces, which had been talking idly of a union with one another for several years. As Britain's representative, Lieutenant-Governor Arthur Gordon of New Brunswick pursued Maritime union at every opportunity. A conference was planned to discuss the issue further, and Monck asked that the Canadians be invited to their talks, "to ascertain whether the proposed Union might not be made to embrace the whole of the British North American Provinces." A date was set for September 1, 1864, in Charlottetown, Prince Edward Island.

Brown, Macdonald, McGee, and Alexander Galt, a businessman, finance minister, and railwayman, travelled to the conference on the *Queen Victoria*, a 191-tonne steamer. "We had great fun coming down the St. Lawrence," Brown wrote, "having fine weather, a broad awning to recline under, excellent stores of all kinds, an unexceptionable cook, lots of books, chessboards, backgammon and so forth." They occupied themselves by mapping the proposed union, anticipating resistance, and refining their arguments. On board was $13,000 worth of champagne.

They arrived at Charlottetown at the same time as Slaymaker's and Nichol's Olympic Circus, the first circus to visit the island in twenty years. The harbour was deserted, with most of the town under the tent watching contortionists and clowns. The delegates to the conference formed a different, political circus – a marathon of speeches, protests, lobster lunches, resolutions, picnics, alliances, flirtations, and champagne balls.

On the first official day, Macdonald spoke at length on the benefits of a union of all of British North America. The next day, Galt presented a well-researched description of the financial workings of such a union. On the third day, George Brown discussed the legal infrastructure. And on the fourth day, McGee praised the nationalist identity, one that he saw bolstered by a vivid Canadian literature. The larger union overwhelmed the separate issue of a Maritime union, reducing it to a subtext. By the end of their talks, the delegates were unanimous in their pledge to create a new federation, "if the terms of union could be made satisfactory."

"Cartier and I made eloquent speeches – of course," Brown wrote to his wife, "and whether as a result of our eloquence or the goodness of our champagne, the ice became completely broken, the tongues of the delegates wagged merrily, and the bonds of matrimony between all the provinces of British North America having been formally proclaimed and all manner of persons duly warned then and there to speak or forever after to hold their tongues – no man appeared to forbid the banns and the union was thereupon completed and proclaimed."

The celebration party continued in Halifax and Saint John and Fredericton. But the need still remained to make the terms satisfactory, a daunting political task. The delegates agreed to meet again in Quebec the following month.

The thirty-three delegates to Quebec arrived in October 1864 and were met by oppressive storms that began with snow and tapered to rain. Most of them stayed at the St. Louis Hotel, which was filled with railwaymen who took a keen interest in the negotiations. Among them was C. J. Brydges, general manager of the magnificent and financially disastrous Grand Trunk, which had ambitious plans to expand west to the Pacific.

The railways had a lively political momentum, despite the fact that they had already driven Canada, New Brunswick, and Nova Scotia deep into debt. There was also an entrenched culture of bribery and corruption between railway promoters and politicians. The locomotive was the emblem of a powerful, steam-driven future – the tense every politician was happiest in. Macdonald hoped a refinanced and consolidated railway system would help both trade and unity. For his part, Cartier benefited materially and

GREAT WESTERN RAILWAY ENGINE, HAMILTON, JUNE 1864 ◆ The railway was one of the most potent symbols of nineteenth-century progress. It signalled a victory over the harsh climate and intimidating geography; winter ice and mud roads could no longer bring commerce to a halt. It was a boon for both businessmen and politicians, but it was enormously expensive. The sparse population and vast distances made it impossible for a privately owned company to make a profit, and governments quickly became involved. In Nova Scotia and New Brunswick, the government owned the railway. In the United Province of Canada (Ontario and Quebec), they were heavily (and endlessly) subsidized. Seduced by the railroad's promise of limitless progress and economic growth, the colonial governments built hundreds of kilometres of track. The largest operation was the Grand Trunk Railway of Canada, which stretched from the shores of Lake Huron to the Atlantic Ocean. But costs were staggering and revenues disappointing, and the governments accumulated massive debts.

For many railway boosters, Confederation offered a way out. If it went through, the British government promised to provide a large, low-cost loan, allowing the new nation to link up the separate lines in Nova Scotia, New Brunswick, and Canada. This new, government-owned Intercolonial Railway would, for the first time, connect the St. Lawrence colonies with Halifax. And there were hopes of an even greater project, a transcontinental railway that would reach all the way to the Pacific Ocean. It was no surprise that railway contractors, investors, and bankers were prominent bystanders as Confederation was hammered out at the Quebec Conference in 1864. (*Canadian National Railways, National Archives of Canada, C-028860*)

politically from the fact that the trains were manufactured in Montreal, supplying jobs. He was also the Grand Trunk's solicitor, a lucrative practice. This intimate professional connection was typical of an era that had no laws prohibiting conflicts of interest.

The meetings in Quebec were conducted in Masonic secrecy; no press was allowed, but notes were taken by delegates. On October 10, it was moved that "the best interests and present and future prosperity of British North America will be promoted by a Federal Union under the Crown of Great Britain, provided such union can be effected on principles just to the several Provinces." The key concept of federalism – the idea that the central government would be granted certain powers while the provinces retained others – was by turns caressed and hammered into shape. But Macdonald led the way with his vision of a powerful central government.

On Wednesday night there was a dinner at Government House. Mercy Coles, daughter of one of the P.E.I. delegates, described the evening: "D'Arcy McGee took me to dinner and sat between Lady McDonnell and I. Before dinner was half over he got so drunk he was obliged to leave the table. . . . The sun has not shone for two hours since we have been here. I was never in such a place."

Lord Monck and family, Rideau Hall, 1866. Frances Elizabeth Owen "Feo" Monck was Governor General Monck's sister-in-law. In her snide, entertaining diary, she described the social world of the elite, including a military production of *Macbeth* performed in drag by the garrison players. "Captain E. was very good, and looked so hideous in a yellow coat covered with red hearts. Mr. Stoney made a most lovely woman. Everyone was in uniform and the room looked gay.

"In one scene they all had a ballet in night-gowns. The band was lovely. In the witch scene, where they made apparitions, was Mr. Collis, in a nightgown, followed by his enormous Maltese dog, also in a night dress and night cap; it ran in on its hind legs. Such a sight I never saw; the house almost came down with applause. Lady Macbeth, in a pink sunbonnet and watering pot, was delicious." (*Samuel McLaughlin, National Archives of Canada*, C-021006)

On October 14, the idea of a senate was debated. It had already been established that representation by population would prevail in the House of Commons. The senate was a way of balancing power between Canada and the smaller Maritime provinces. It was proposed that the senate have three equal blocks of seats: one for Lower Canada, one for Upper Canada, and one for the four Atlantic provinces combined as a single entity.

That night there was a Delegates' Ball for 1,400 people held at Parliament House where they danced to the 25th Regiment's string band and dined on partridge, lobster salad, and tongue. Frances Elizabeth Owen Monck ("Feo" to her family) was a plump, vivacious, and condescending woman who was married to the brother of the governor general, and who kept a diary offering a snide account of social events. She thought of herself as a medium, wore an eyeglass, and had a morbid fear of thunder. For Feo, the Delegates' Ball meant polite conversation and an endless string of obligatory dances with elderly politicians. According to her account, the evening began as a tableau of "grace, loveliness and politeness." By four in the morning, however, the elegant waltzes and quadrilles had descended into mayhem. "F.B.'s account of the ball was most amusing," she wrote, "such drunkenness, pushing, kicking, and tearing, he says, he never saw; his own coat tails were nearly torn off; the supper room floor was covered with meat, drink, and broken bottles."

The next day, the composition of the senate was proposed: thirty seats for Upper Canada, thirty for Lower Canada, ten each for Nova Scotia and New Brunswick, and five each for Newfoundland and Prince Edward Island. The eastern delegates argued that each Atlantic province should have an equal number of senators. Brown countered that Upper Canada should then have more senators. Hector Langevin protested any inequality between Lower and Upper Canada.

On the evening of October 19, there was a ball at Madame Tessier's, wife of the speaker of the House. "At French parties there are no fast dances," Feo Monck complained, "all quadrilles and lancers; it seems so odd." The bishop of Quebec had forbidden intimate dancing, fearing that it would lead to something worse. Feo danced with George Coles, part of the Prince Edward Island delegation, a former premier and successful brewer: "Old Coles is, I believe, a retired butcher, and oh! so vulgar, I could not describe him. He is gray haired and red faced, and looks as if his legs were fastened on after the rest of his body, to support his fat." They danced and drank until late, and Feo Monck gleefully reported on Macdonald's erratic behaviour: "He is always drunk now, I am sorry to say, and when some one went to his room the other night, they found him in his night shirt, with a railway rug thrown over him, practising Hamlet before a looking glass. At the drawing room he said to Mrs. G. he should like to blow up Sir R.M. [Sir Richard Graves Macdonnell, lieutenant-governor of Nova Scotia] with gunpowder."

Despite his vigorous and eclectic social calendar during the conference, Macdonald did much of the actual work on the constitution, drafting fifty of the seventy-two resolutions, and his desire for a strong federal government was reflected in the document. Macdonald was convinced that the American tradition of "states' rights" was a dangerous doctrine that had led to attempted secession and civil war. He was determined that Canada would have a pre-eminent central government.

Macdonald was the only one present with a background in constitutional law. "As it is, I have no help," he told his friend Sir James Gowan. "Not one man of the conference (except Galt in finance) has the slightest idea of Constitution making. Whatever is good or ill in the Constitution is mine."

Brown already had the representation-by-population clause he cherished – a necessary weapon in the fight against what he felt to be French dominance. Cartier was satisfied that Lower Canada would flourish economically, and French control of the provincial government would allow it to retain its unique character. The Maritime provinces were less enthusiastic. "I object to the proposed system," said Edward Chandler, of the New Brunswick delegation. "You are now proceeding to destroy the Constitutions of the Local Governments." He argued that under a system of representation by population, the smaller provinces would be overwhelmed by the rest of the country. They would lose control of their financial affairs and trade policy and be stuck with a share of the responsibility for the sizable Canadian debt.

The weeks of negotiating, bullying, and parties took their toll on most of the delegates. "The festivities interfere somewhat with the progress of business," the *Montreal Gazette* reported. P.E.I. delegate Edward Whelan concurred: "May the good prayers of all our friends at home be copiously offered to us, to the end that we may be removed from this dear, charming, abominable, killing, pleasure ridden City."

In the fractious atmosphere of the meetings, the delegates found that one of the safest ways to define the new country was to attack the American model. "The great evil in the United States is that the President is a despot for four years," Macdonald said. "Under the British constitution, with the people having always in their hands the power and with the responsibility of a Ministry to Parliament, we are free from such despotism."

There was the issue of defence as well. "Separated as we are," said Cartier, "we cannot defend ourselves. . . . When we bring the country all together all our means would be united to repel an enemy."

Brown warned that the Americans were encroaching. The best route to peace with them was to be powerful, Macdonald argued. "Our present isolated and defenceless position is, no doubt, a source of embarrassment to England," he noted. "For the sake of securing peace . . . we must make ourselves powerful."

While at Quebec, a telegram arrived that brought into sharp relief the need for defence against the Americans. On October 19, a group of Confederate soldiers who had been hiding out in Canada had posed as Canadians on a fishing holiday and looted several banks in the town of St. Albans, Vermont. They had then fled back to Canada with $200,000, followed by a posse of angry Americans.

Governor General Monck ordered out the militia, who captured fourteen of the raiders. They were later tried in a Montreal court but released on a technicality. Their stolen money was returned to them, causing outrage in the United States. Tensions quickly escalated on both sides. Cartier and Macdonald met at Monck's house. "John A.'s appearance was grotesque," Feo Monck happily reported, "with his hair flying in all directions like a Spanish caricature." Monck marshalled two thousand troops to police the American border.

American General John Dix ordered that "all military commanders are instructed to cross the boundary into Canada and pursue the rebels wherever they take refuge." President Lincoln recognized the incendiary potential of Dix's command and revoked it, but he announced that Canadians would now have to produce passports to gain entry to the United States. As expected, the Reciprocity Treaty of 1854, which abolished the duties on many goods moving across the Canada-U.S. border, was revoked.

In Canada, the incident left a climate of hostility and a fresh resolve to unite. The terms agreed on by the delegates, known as the Quebec Resolutions, were adopted. The document steered clear of the revolutionary phrases that France and America had employed a century earlier. It adopted the language of a careful contract, promising peace, order, and good government.

Brown wrote to his wife, "Conference through at six o'clock this evening – constitution adopted – a most creditable document. . . . A complete reform of all the abuses and injustice we have complained of!! Is it not wonderful? The old French domination is entirely extinguished. . . . Some will say our constitution is dreadfully Tory – and so it is – *but we have the power in our hands (if it passes), to change it as we like. Hurrah!*"

There remained the task of selling Confederation to the citizens. In Nova Scotia, Charles Tupper faced the fierce resistance of Joseph Howe, a defeated but revered politician. "Did anybody ever propose to unite Scotland with Poland or Hungary?" Howe wrote in the *Halifax Chronicle*. "Inland countries 800 miles off in the very heart of Europe." At the time, Nova Scotia, with its population of 330,857, was a prosperous colony, and Howe believed it could stand alone. It had been the first colony to introduce responsible government. If Nova Scotia were to join any political body, Howe declared, it would be the Imperial Parliament in Westminster, not the unfinished chamber still being erected in Ottawa, a backward, inland lumber town.

In New Brunswick, Premier Samuel Leonard Tilley was a supporter of union and the railway that would result, and he was confident of backing from his electorate. But when he held an ill-advised snap election, he was soundly beaten and his government replaced by an anti-Confederation administration. Both Prince Edward Island and Newfoundland rejected the Quebec Resolutions.

In the Canadas the idea was not secure either. Macdonald and Cartier announced that they would not hold an election on the Quebec Resolutions, which created resentment. Antoine-Aimé Dorion, the leader of the opposition *Rouges*, said, "If Confederation should be adopted without the people of this province's sanction, the entire country will sorely learn to regret it." Where Cartier emphasized the powers that would be held by the new province of Quebec, Dorion stressed that French Canadians would be reduced to a small minority of the seats in the federal Parliament, down from their current 50 per cent. And there would be debts and new taxes for building railways, and for acquiring the Hudson's Bay territories, which would be populated largely by intolerant Ontario Protestants.

The Catholic Church helped sway the people. Parishioners were encouraged from the pulpit, and occasionally from the confessional, to support Cartier and Confederation.

The Quebec Resolutions were voted on in Parliament, finally, with ninety-one members in favour and thirty-three opposed. Among the Canada East constituencies with a French-speaking majority, the division was roughly fifty-fifty.

The Maritime vote was influenced by events in Canada but also by what was happening in the United States, where the Civil War had ended in April 1865. The Fenians were an Irish Catholic group that hoped to free Ireland by attacking the British colonies in North America. Mostly Irish Americans who had fought for the North in the war, they were now forming small units intent on raiding Canada. Rumour reached New Brunswick that the Fenians intended to occupy Campobello Island, in the mouth of Passamaquoddy Bay. The invasion collapsed, but it instilled in Maritimers the fear of possible war. Another election was called, corrupt even by the standards of the day, and Tilley and the Confederationists were returned

CHARLES TUPPER ◆ "I have always supposed that the great object, in every country, was to draw as many capitalists into it as possible," Charles Tupper wrote. Tupper was a doctor, the first president of the Canadian Medical Association, a father of Confederation and a member of Macdonald's first Confederation cabinet. The son of a Baptist pastor, Tupper gained the nickname the "ram of Cumberland" because of his reputation as a womanizer. In 1891, an American typist named Josephine Bailey filed a lawsuit against Tupper, claiming she had become pregnant by him and had been advised to have an abortion. The suit was dropped or settled out of court. Tupper was ambitious, ruthless, humourless, and made enemies easily. Among his many accomplishments was the passing of the first Free School Act, which established a system of subsidized schools. He was the last father of Confederation to die, living to see the surprising slaughter of the First World War. (*National Archives of Canada*, PA-26317)

JOSEPH HOWE ◆ "I am not one of those who thank God that I am a Nova Scotian merely, for I am a Canadian as well. . . . I have looked across the broad continent at the great territory, which the Almighty has given us for an inheritance. . . . What a country to live in! And why should union not be brought about? Is it because we wish to live and die in our insignificance, that we would sooner make money, than that our country should grow? God forbid!"

Howe delivered this speech at a dinner in Halifax in 1864. Soon afterward he reversed his position and became one of the leading opponents of Confederation. In the *Morning Chronicle* he published a series, called the "Botheration Letters," that helped sway public opinion in Nova Scotia against union. (*National Archives of Canada*, C-007158)

SAMUEL LEONARD TILLEY ◆ A drug store owner, low-church Anglican, and premier of New Brunswick, Tilley became a temperance advocate after a drunken man murdered his own wife with a butcher knife. Their eleven-year-old daughter ran for help and encountered Tilley. "There lay the mother weltering in her blood," Tilley wrote, "her little children crying around her, and the husband and father under arrest for murder, and rum the cause of it all." Tilley was on the committee of the Portland Total Abstinence Society and in 1854 he was elected to the highest position in the Sons of Temperance.

At the London conference in 1867, the question arose of what to call the new country. It was neither a kingdom nor a republic. Tilley, who read the Bible daily, cited psalm 72:8, "His dominion shall be also from sea to sea." It was decided to call the new country the Dominion of Canada. (*National Archives of Canada*, C-10115)

ANTOINE-AIMÉ DORION ◆ Antoine-Aimé Dorion was a lawyer, newspaperman, and leader of the Parti Rouge. In 1849, he helped found the Club National Democratique, saying its members were "democrats in conscience and French Canadian in origin. . . . We [demand] the powerful right of sovereignty . . . education of the masses, trade, and universal suffrage." He died in May 1891, a few days before his political enemy, John A. Macdonald. (*Ellison and Co.*, *National Archives of Canada*, PA 74105)

Battle of Ridgeway, Ontario, June 2, 1866 (*National Archives of Canada, C-18737*)

to office, partly on the threat of a Fenian invasion and partly through bribes to the electorate.

The Fenians presented a more palpable threat in Upper Canada. "The Fenians this morning invaded Canada," Amelia Harris wrote on June 1, 1866. "They crossed the river from Buffalo below Black Rock. It is telegraphed that there are about 1,500 of them. 1,000 Volunteers & some companies of the 16th have gone to repel them. It is to be hoped that we shall have a good account of them by tomorrow. . . . The garrison had arranged for a picnic . . . but on account of the Fenians no one was allowed to leave the Barracks, so the picnic was turned into a dance in the mess room. Edward, Sophia & George went . . ."

Two days later, the news that thousands of Fenians had crossed into Upper Canada reached Harris in church, and the militia in the congregation left during the Litany. The volunteers clashed with the Fenians at Ridgeway and were routed. Ten Canadians were killed and thirty-eight wounded. "It was very exciting," Harris wrote. But by June 5, the fear in London, at least, had waned. "The Fenian excitement continues but not so absorbing as it was," she reported. "There is a great feeling against [militia commanders] General Napier & Colonel Peacock. . . . It is said that Gen Napier was drunk and that Col Peacock delayed so that the volunteers at [the Battle of] Ridgeway were sacrificed."

On June 18, the volunteers all returned to their homes, and by fall, Harris had moved on to other events. "Mr. Portman did not return until 4 o'clock in the morning. Bessy Dewar is a very bad girl. She wanted him to take her as a mistress but he declined. How wickedly he has spent his summer."

In the spring the Fenians threatened again. Macdonald suspended the protection of habeas corpus for anyone suspected of being involved with them. McGee condemned them publicly and with a special vehemence. But the Fenians remained a largely ineffective group. Their main gift was instilling fear, and their unfocused military personality was celebrated in song:

Many a battle has been fought
Along with the boys in blue
So we will go and conquer Canada
For we've nothing else to do.

Although the Fenians failed to mount a decisive military action, they made a vivid bogeyman – one more reason to unite.

Both Newfoundland and Prince Edward Island had declined the offer to join Confederation, but Macdonald and his colleagues still had an effective blueprint for the country. All that was left was to get the British North America bill passed in London. The Confederation team – including Macdonald, Cartier, Galt, and Brown – travelled to London and stayed at the Westminster Palace Hotel. Also in London was Joseph Howe, who was trying to get Nova Scotia out of the deal. He had dragged along an anti-Confederation petition containing thirty thousand signatures.

While in London, Macdonald, Cartier, and the others fine-tuned their bill, and by Christmas a preliminary draft was ready to send to Sir Frederic Rogers, the permanent undersecretary of the Colonial Office, who witnessed the drama surrounding the document. "Macdonald was the ruling genius and spokesman," Rogers observed. "I was very greatly struck by his power of management and adroitness. The French delegates were keenly on the watch for anything which weakened their securities; on the contrary, the Nova Scotia and New Brunswick delegates were very jealous of concessions to the arrière province. . . . Macdonald had to argue the question with the Home Gov on a point on which the slightest divergence from the narrow line already agreed on in Canada was watched for – here by the French, and there by the English – as eager dogs watch a rat hole; a snap on one side might have provoked a snap on the other; and put an end to the concord. He stated and argued the case with cool, ready fluency, while at the same time you saw that every word was measured . . ."

When not working on the plan for Confederation, the delegates took in the sights. Macdonald ran into Susan Agnes Bernard, a woman he had unsuccessfully wooed in Canada after his wife's death. While in London, he pursued her once more.

Construction of the Parliament Buildings, Ottawa, Ontario, 1863. In 1857, the Macdonald-Cartier ministry asked Queen Victoria to choose the site for a capital. Quebec, Montreal, Toronto, Kingston, and Ottawa were candidates; the queen chose Ottawa. The Legislative Assembly voted on the issue and decided that "in the opinion of this House the City of Ottawa ought not to be the permanent seat of government of this province." The Macdonald-Cartier ministry resigned, replaced by the ministry of George Brown and Antoine-Aimé Dorion, who lasted two days in power. Macdonald and Cartier returned to office, with John A. referring to Brown's tenure as "His Excellency's most ephemeral administration." The Parliament Buildings stayed in Ottawa. *(Samuel McLaughlin, National Archives of Canada, C-000773)*

Macdonald also narrowly avoided catastrophe. He woke up one night to find that he and his bed were on fire. He went next door to Cartier's room to get help. "We made no alarm," Macdonald wrote to his sister, "and only Cartier, Galt and myself knew of the accident. . . . Had I not worn a very thick flannel shirt under my nightshirt I would have been burnt to death. As it was my escape was miraculous." His hair and hands were singed and his shoulder was burned badly enough to require medical attention.

The British North America bill had to crawl through the tedious, halting machinery of the Commons and the House of Lords. It was delayed several times, causing consternation among the Canadian delegates. Between the first and second reading of the bill, Macdonald married Agnes Bernard in St. Georges Church in Hanover Square, the service performed by the bishop of Montreal.

The bill was finally signed by Queen Victoria on March 29, 1867, and Macdonald and his colleagues left for home. On July 1, at noon, New Brunswick, Nova Scotia, and the Province of Canada were proclaimed the Dominion of Canada, with John A. Macdonald its first prime minister.

A cannon was fired on the Plains of Abraham to mark the day. In Toronto, children were given Union Jacks to wave and an ox was roasted in front of St. Lawrence Hall, with the meat then distributed to the poor. In Ottawa, a military review on Parliament Hill fired a salute, neglecting to take the ramrods out of their rifles, which arched over Sparks Street.

In Halifax, the *British Colonist* trumpeted: "The days of isolation and dwarf-hood are past; henceforth we are a united people, and the greatness of each goes to swell the greatness of the whole." The *Morning Chronicle* offered a different view: "Died! Last night at 12 o'clock, the free and enlightened Province of Nova Scotia." At the waterfront, an effigy of Charles Tupper was burned alongside a live rat.

Governor General Monck dispensed honours for the gruelling work and political genius that had gone into the creation of Canada. Cartier, Galt, Tupper, Tilley, and a few others were made Companions of the Bath. Macdonald, whom Monck saw as the principal architect of Confederation, was knighted – a distinction that wounded both Cartier and Galt. They respectfully declined their honours and wrote to Monck about the royal slight.

George Brown wrote to commiserate with his old rival, Cartier: "You ran the risk of political death by the bold course you took, Mr. Macdonald ran no risk whatever." But Brown, who was omitted entirely from the honours, claimed paternity of Confederation for himself: "Of course, I believe that my fifteen years' contest for constitutional reform, and my bold action in 1864 won the battle – that you and Macdonald were made to 'move on' in spite of yourselves. . . . I live very much in the consciousness of having done the work – but I don't care one straw for a ribbon or a title, as a Canadian – which I always expect and wish to be."

Brown said he was happy to be out of politics and asked that Cartier come and visit him sometime: "Now that all our electoral, educational and ecclesiastical bickering are at an end, would not such a visit be a pleasant thing. No one would be happier to see it than my good wife."

Cartier eventually was awarded a baronetcy, an equivalent title, and Galt got the knighthood he had been seeking.

Thomas D'Arcy McGee celebrated with his new countrymen, but he had already offered this dark, Celtic caveat: "So long as we respect in Canada the rights of minorities, told either by tongue or creed, we are safe. For so long it will be possible for us to be united. But when we cease to respect these rights, we will be in the full tide towards that madness which the ancients considered the gods sent to those whom they wished to destroy."

McGee was forty-two years old, in poor health, and chronically broke. "There are only two things on earth I fear," he wrote to a friend in New York. "Death and debt." During the winter of 1867-68, he campaigned to raise money for destitute Nova Scotia fishermen. He had a law degree from McGill and had written twenty books, including several volumes of poetry. McGee had been instrumental in convincing the Irish population to support Confederation, which they initially viewed as similar to the despised British rule of Ireland. But McGee had always been an eloquent and harsh critic of the Fenians, which made him unpopular with some Irish Catholics. In Ireland he had experienced the savagery of secret societies. "Secret Societies are like what the farmers in Ireland used to say of scotch grass," he wrote in the *Montreal Gazette*. "The only way to destroy it is to cut it out by the roots and burn it into powder."

McGee was considered to be the country's greatest orator. His last speech in the House began at midnight on April 6, 1868; it was an eloquent defence of Charles Tupper, who had been criticized by Dr. Parker, a Nova Scotia MP.

"Dr. Tupper's character has been assailed," McGee told the House. "And it would show but a base spirit to sacrifice the man in his absence who had sacrificed himself for Confederation. . . . What we need above everything else is the healing influence of time. It is not only the lime and the sand and the hair in the mortar, but the time which has been taken to temper it. And if time be so necessary in so rudimentary a process as the mixing of mortar, of how much greater importance is it in the work of consolidating the Confederation of these Provinces." What began as a defence of Tupper became a compelling argument for Confederation. "And I, Sir, who have been and still am its warm and earnest advocate, speak here not as the representative of any race or of any Province but as thoroughly and emphatically a Canadian."

Watching his performance from the visitor's gallery was an Irishman named Patrick James Whelan.

Shortly after 1:00 a.m., McGee left the House, lit a cigar, and walked to Mrs. Trotter's boarding house on Sparks Street, where he stayed while in Ottawa. It would be his birthday in six days, and he was looking forward to returning to Montreal to celebrate it with his wife and family. As he was turning his key in the lock, he was shot in the head and died immediately.

It was generally believed that the murder was the work of Fenian terrorists. Patrick James Whelan was arrested within twenty-four hours. He was tried and found guilty, though he maintained his innocence, and it was never proven that he was a Fenian. He was hanged in front of a crowd of five thousand people – the last public hanging in Canada. McGee's funeral, held on what would have been his forty-third birthday, was the largest that Montreal had seen.

In 1868, Montreal was a city of more than 100,000 people, offering a bleak contrast between Canada's most wealthy and its most destitute citizens. The Square Mile, an enclave on the south slope of Mount Royal, housed the anglophone commercial elite. They controlled two-thirds of the country's wealth, fortunes that came from beer (John Molson), furs (James McGill), sugar (John Redpath), and flour (the Ogilvies). The richest among them was Hugh Allan, a piratical shipping magnate who shunned tobacco and alcohol, preferring hard work and curling. His thirty-four-room mansion, Ravenscrag, overlooked the city from the lower slope of Mount Royal. From his bell tower, he could look through a brass telescope to the harbour to watch his ships being unloaded. William Cornelius Van Horne, a railway-man who also lived in the Square Mile, personified the commercial spirit. "I eat all I can," he said, "drink all I can, I smoke all I can, and I don't care a damn for anything."

Many of those in the Square Mile were unyielding Scots Presbyterians who had come to Canada with little money or education. They had built fortunes and then a corresponding kingdom. The homes of the merchant princes incorporated the random details of castles in a child's imagination.

THE BUILDING OF VICTORIA BRIDGE, MONTREAL, 1859 ◆
The Victoria Bridge in Montreal was more than two kilometres long and took seven years to build, the largest bridge in the world at the time of its completion. The project was overseen by James Hodges, an Englishman who had worked on suspension bridges and railway track before coming to Montreal. The 3,000 men who worked on the bridge routinely went on strike. Twenty-six of them died, mostly from drowning. Others went blind from the glare of the sun off the ice. Cholera also affected the workmen, who lived on the banks of the St. Lawrence in a shantytown with a school, chapel, and library. On August 25, 1860, the Prince of Wales inaugurated the structure named for his mother as 500 people waved Union Jacks. (*William Notman, Musée McCord Museum, Notman Photographic Archives*)

A dozen architectural styles vied for attention – Italianate, Neo-Gothic, Victorian – sometimes within a single oversized house. These men were the country's aristocracy, and they were eager to associate with British royalty.

In 1860, a royal visit from the Prince of Wales dominated the social calendar. A ball for three thousand was held in the prince's honour in a ballroom that was one hundred metres long. The dinner menu was printed on pink silk and listed sixty dishes, including lobster mayonnaise, oysters in aspic, pâté de foie gras, beef, mutton, salmon, and duck. Fountains burbled with champagne; another sprayed eau de cologne. "The Prince of Romance," as he was dubbed before he became the stout, roué King Edward VII, stayed until 4:30 a.m., dancing twenty of twenty-one dances.

Among the prince's royal duties was the official inauguration of the railway bridge named for his mother. The Victoria Bridge spanned the St. Lawrence River and linked Montreal with the United States via the Grand Trunk Railway. It was the most audacious structure of its era, an engineering marvel that had taken three thousand men seven years to construct. As the prince delicately and inexpertly spread mortar over the last of the six-tonne blocks of stone to be set in place, five hundred people waved Union Jacks. The bridge was essentially a tube, and after he set the final rivet, he was almost asphyxiated by the smoke from the locomotive rushing through. Afterward, invited guests went to the Grand Trunk workshops in Pointe St. Charles for lunch with the men who had built the bridge – a rare juxtaposition of the classes. Located in the heart of the working-class district, the Grand Trunk workshop employed three thousand men, most of whom lived nearby in overcrowded houses, 95 per cent of them without indoor toilets. There was a single, half-hectare park, Richmond Square, to service the neighbourhood. Most of the area was without running water.

The prince addressed the workers, telling them to take pride in the fact that the bridge's engineer had come from the working class: "Let me further

Ignace Bourget, second Roman Catholic bishop of Montreal (1799-1885). Bishop Bourget's diocese spanned the territory from the American border to James Bay. He believed that the Church should be the dominating influence on politics and French-Catholic society. Under Bourget, the clergy played an increasingly important role in schools, colleges, hospitals, and charities in Montreal. His liberal opponents in the democratic Parti Rouge and the Institut Canadien wanted the clergy out of politics entirely. Bourget won that battle, though he lost his war on sex. In 1871 a handbook on sexuality and reproduction was distributed in Montreal, and Bourget condemned it as "harmful to the sacredness of virginity and celibacy." Five years later it was in its 90th edition. (*National Archives of Canada*, PA 138830)

remind you, that England opens to all her sons the same prospect of success to genius combined with honest industry. All cannot claim the prize but all may strive for it."

Between 1845 and 1848, 100,000 Irish immigrants had come to Canada to escape famine, and many had settled in Montreal. At the same time, French Canadians were beginning the long exodus from rural areas to the city, looking for work in the new industries. Despite the Irish immigration, the 1860s was the decade when Montreal went from a city with an anglophone majority (52 per cent in 1861) to a francophone majority (53 per cent in 1871).

Montreal had one of the highest levels of infant mortality in North America; one in three children died before reaching the age of five. Children were abandoned in heartbreaking numbers, left to the mercy of the Grey Nuns. In 1867, the nuns took in 662 infants. Within a month, 369 had died; at the end of the year, only 39 had survived. As the century moved forward, provincial allocations for the care of the foundlings were reduced: from $33 annually per child in 1845 to less than $5 in 1868.

Sister Jane Slocombe was one of the nuns who ministered to the infants. An orphan herself, she had been born Protestant but converted to Catholicism in her teens. She was tall, blond, and melancholy, and while caring for the poor during the cholera epidemic of 1847 she had contracted the disease herself. She recovered and quickly moved up through the ranks of the Grey Nuns, promoted to the top job by the age of forty-three. She was aided by her ambition, her bilingualism, and the appalling death rate of those who dealt with the sick; there were few elderly nuns, and regular opportunities for promotion.

The convent of the Grey Nuns was a clearing house for illegitimate children. The babies were found by the river, left in baskets at the orphanage's doors, or discovered wrapped in newspapers. The few survivors were farmed out to rural families. A report compiled by the Montreal Sanitary Association was discouraging. "The sad condition of neglect in which these 'unwelcome children' were received from their unnatural parents . . . Naked – 31, wounded by instruments – 32, tainted with syphillis – 120, sick 210, unwashed 104, hemorage of lungs 33. 147 with feet frozen. One asleep for three days from the effects of opium."

The following year, the number of foundlings increased. "Can you believe we took in 729 of them last year [1865]?" Slocombe wrote. "Incredible isn't it? Everything is increasing except our revenues."

A few years later, Prince Arthur, the Queen's youngest son, was posted to Montreal as a subaltern in the Rifle Brigade, and he became the focal point of a brilliant social season, offering a pale encore of the magic that his brother had injected into local society a decade earlier.

During the sweltering summer, Arthur was a guest at Hugh Allan's summer home, Belmere, on Lake Memphremagog, and cruised on his yacht, the *Ormond*. That winter, a fancy-dress skating carnival was arranged for

Arthur at the Victoria Rink. Bishop Oxenden described it as "one of the most beautiful sights I ever beheld. The place was hung with the gayest flags, most tastefully arranged. It was indeed a fairy scene to look upon, the skating was wonderful, and the dresses gorgeous." In his fur hat, the prince stared mournfully at the skaters shyly circling him: Montreal society dressed as Indians and Highlanders and cavaliers.

There was a flood in the spring of 1871 that covered much of the workers' neighbourhood and caused renewed outbreaks of typhoid and cholera. Sister Jane Slocombe began to experience symptoms of typhoid. She became increasingly feeble and her stays in hospital lengthened. In 1871, she wrote of the death of another sister, though she could have been describing herself: "She suffered for a long time, or perhaps it just seemed to be a long time, but now that it's gone, it was but a little wrinkle in time. How time is short and eternity endless." She died in 1872, just before the completion of a magnificent new convent for her order.

At the Collège de Montréal, one of Sister Slocombe's charges was Louis Riel. In St. Boniface, in Rupert's Land, Bishop Alexandre-Antonin Taché had been looking for Métis candidates for the priesthood, and Riel was one of four he had selected. He was a good student, though introverted and moody. "He knew about pemmican and the tomahawk," classmate Eustache Prud'Homme said, recalling Riel's stories of the exotic west. "There were scenes of terrible prairie fires in the west, of children crushed or kidnapped by the wild horses of fearless hunters who could jump over a large river in a single bound."

In 1864, while in Montreal, Riel received the news that his father, Jean-Louis, had died. Jean-Louis had been the de facto spokesman of the almost six thousand French Métis who lived on the prairie. After his father's

A composite photograph of a skating party, taken by William Notman, a Scot who came to Montreal and became the city's pre-eminent photographer. The ambrotype, wet-plate technique that he used required the subject to remain motionless for forty seconds, making action shots impossible. Notman achieved the illusion by posing subjects separately in his studio then placing the result against a painted backdrop. *(William Notman, Musée McCord Museum)*

Alexandre-Antonin Taché. As the Catholic bishop at St. Boniface, Taché spotted Louis Riel's talents and sent him to Montreal to study for the priesthood. Taché was instrumental in establishing the Catholic religion and French-Canadian culture in the west. (*National Archives of Canada, PA 74103*)

death, Riel's interest in the priesthood waned and he became more introspective. His mood was made blacker by a failed romance; the girl's parents would not allow her to marry a Métis.

"Louis is still in Montreal," wrote Sister Slocombe. "No one knows when he will leave. He has announced his departure for the fifth of this month, but he has been seen around here recently. This young man is incomprehensible and behaves most suspiciously. I fear this poor child does not have a good head on his shoulders. He needs someone to guide him, someone to follow him, but here he is on his own and none of his former friends have confidence in him. I fear it will all end badly."

Riel's sister Sara was attending college in Manitoba, on her way to becoming a nun. Riel withdrew from the Collège de Montréal in March, before graduating. He was the oldest in a family of eleven children and his father had left no money. Riel stayed in Montreal working as a clerk in a law firm, sending money home. He left in 1866 but lingered in Chicago and St. Paul for almost two years before returning to Red River in July 1868. There he was met by a plague of grasshoppers of biblical proportions. "They penetrated into the parlours, and kitchens, bed chambers and bedding, pots, pans, kettles, ovens, boots and coat pockets," the *Globe* reported. "One scarcely dared to open one's mouth. On the river they floated like scum or were piled two feet on the banks where they rotted and stunk like carrion." They ate the crops with noisy efficiency, destroying the harvest and threatening the settlement with famine.

The territory was also on the cusp of a profound transformation. The Hudson's Bay Company was reluctantly selling Rupert's Land, almost 8 million square kilometres that included parts of northern Quebec, northern Ontario, most of the prairies, as well as parts of what is now Nunavut. American Secretary of State William Seward had just paid Russia $7.2 million for Alaska in 1867, and he was looking for other properties to annex. "I know," he announced, "that nature designs that this whole continent, not merely these thirty-six states, shall be sooner or later, within the magic circle of the American union."

The Canadians were equally proprietorial. George Brown saw the west as "[t]he vast and fertile territory which is our birthright – and which no power on earth can prevent us occupying." Brown was also aware of the fact that they were running out of good land in Canada West. Thomas D'Arcy McGee had viewed the west with the sense of romance he brought to most ideas: "Towards the sunset lies the new Canada West, the field for another great province."

Prime Minister John A. Macdonald did not share McGee's romantic vision. As always, he was a pragmatist. "I would be quite willing to leave that whole country a wilderness for the next half century," Macdonald said, "but I fear that if Englishmen do not go there, Yankees will."

The Hudson's Bay Company was prepared to sell to the Americans, who would pay top dollar, but the British government would not allow it. So the west sat suspended, waiting for a real estate deal.

Louis Riel and his Council,
1869-70 (*National Archives
of Canada*, C-6692)

The headquarters for American annexationists was the Davis Hotel in
Winnipeg. Oscar Malmros was the American consul there, on hand to guard
against threats to American interests, one of which came from Riel, who saw
the territory as the Métis homeland. Malmros reported that Riel was "ambitious, quick of perception, though not profound, of indomitable energy,
daring, exessively suspicious of others and of a pleasing and rather dignified
address." Down the street from the Davis Hotel, John Christian Schultz's
drugstore was the focal point for those who wanted union with Canada. The
Métis were in the middle, largely without a voice, simply part of the deal.

On March 20, 1869, the Hudson's Bay Company reluctantly, and
under pressure from Great Britain, sold Rupert's Land to the Government
of Canada for $1.5 million. The sale involved roughly a quarter of the con-
tinent, a staggering amount of land, but it failed to take into account the
existing residents.

"No explanation it appears has been made of the arrangement by
which the country is to be handed over," Macdonald told Cartier. "All these
poor people know is that Canada has bought the country from the Hudson's
Bay Company and that they are handed over like a flock of sheep to us."

In 1869, Macdonald sent a party of surveyors to Red River to outline a
grid of townships, the new owners' first step toward imposing their vision.
The land was currently divided in the Quebec fashion, in long, thin strips
that rose up from the river.

On October 11, a survey party led by Captain Adam Clark Webb
began to survey the property of André Nault, a Métis farmer. Nault protested the intrusion, then called his cousin, Louis Riel, who arrived and
stood on the surveying chain, demanding that they stop.

"Further progress with the survey had been stopped by a band of some
18 French half-breeds, headed by a man named Louis Riel," one of Webb's

party reported. "Mr. Webb was ordered by the leader of the party at once to desist from further running the line." The surveyors withdrew.

This was the first act of what would be known as the Red River Rebellion. Riel quickly gained status among the Métis as the man who had stared down the Canadian government, and he consolidated his leadership by visiting the local parishes. The six thousand French-speaking Métis rallied around him, but the four thousand English-speaking "county-born" were more cautious. Some endorsed his views but felt he was too militant; they refused to join him. "Go," he told them. "Return peacefully to your farms. Stay in the arms of your wives. Give this example to your children. But watch us act. We are going ahead to work and obtain the guarantee of our rights and yours. You will come to share them in the end."

Riel presented an early test of Macdonald's leadership. "These impulsive half-breeds have got spoiled by this *émeute* [riot]," Macdonald said, "and must be kept down by a strong hand, until they are swamped by an influx of settlers." He sent out William McDougall as the first Canadian lieutenant-governor of the North-West Territories. "McDougall goes with a large party," Macdonald told George Brown. "I anticipate that he will have a good deal of trouble, and it will require considerable management to keep those wild people quiet."

Macdonald knew that Canada's claim to ownership of the area was tenuous. Riel was also aware of this, and on November 2, 1869, in the name of the recently formed National Committee of the Métis, he had a group of his men turn McDougall away at the border. McDougall camped in a tent in North Dakota, infuriated by his political impotence. During the night of November 30, he crossed the border alone and screamed the proclamation he had written into the winter wind.

While Riel's men were turning McDougall back, Riel rode to Fort Garry, the administrative centre of the area, with a group of 120 men. They seized the fort from the ailing, elderly William Mactavish, governor of Rupert's Land, and Riel asserted authority. "Most of us are half-breeds," Riel said. "We all have rights. We claim no half rights . . . but all the rights we are entitled to. Those rights will be set forth by our representatives and what is more, we will get them." Riel compiled a List of Rights that had fourteen points. Essentially, the Métis would accept annexation to Canada as long as they were not stripped of their property or denied Catholic religious rights or French language rights.

The Grey Nuns, who had a mission in Red River, were sympathetic to Riel: "War, nothing more, nothing less, is upon us. The Métis, desiring to defend their rights and to save their religion, have taken up arms. All the paths have been barricaded. They have decided that they would rather shed blood than let those men enter the country. It is so very admirable to know the reasons inspiring our dear Métis."

Back in Montreal, Sister Jane Slocombe was worried that her nuns were becoming too involved: "I know that I do not need to tell you to be

A Tragedy at Fort Garry, March 4, 1870. Thomas Scott, a Protestant Irishman and member of the Orange Lodge, was executed on orders from Louis Riel. Though Scott was an unsympathetic figure, in Ontario he quickly gained the status of martyr, becoming the subject of a romantic novel and an epic poem. (*Front cover of the Illustrated Canadian News, April 23, 1870, Glenbow Collection*)

very watchful, so that no indiscretions are committed, spoken or written. Our sisters must remain silent on all political matters. It is the only way to avoid indiscretion."

There were rumours that John Christian Schultz had put a price on Riel's head and was organizing an armed resistance. On December 7, 1869, Riel seized forty-five of Schultz's followers and held them in the Hudson's Bay Company stockade. The next day, Riel set up a provisional government for Red River.

Macdonald tried to placate Riel, sending Donald Alexander Smith (who would later drive the last spike in the Canadian Pacific Railway line) as emissary. Smith offered amnesty, money, and employment to Métis leaders, and assured them that land titles would be respected by the Canadian government. Riel agreed to send a delegation to Ottawa to negotiate terms for the entry of Red River into Confederation, and he released the men he held at Fort Garry.

Some of Schultz's men gathered in Portage la Prairie, enlisting support in the Scottish parishes for the overthrow of Riel's provisional government. Again they were captured by Riel's supporters and held at Fort Garry. Among them was Thomas Scott, a big, aggressive Ontario Orangeman who insulted his guards and threatened to shoot Riel if he ever got free. Riel's actions to date had been temperate, but with Scott he overreacted and appointed a military tribunal to try the prisoner for treason. The Orangeman was convicted, sentenced to death, and executed by a firing squad in the courtyard of Fort Garry. It was Riel's largest miscalculation and an act that cost him the moral high ground. Scott's death triggered an angry response in Protestant Ontario and made him an unlikely martyr.

While Macdonald was negotiating with the Manitoba delegation in Ottawa, 1,200 British troops, headed by Colonel Garnet Wolseley, were sent out to Red River. Wolseley had been a young officer enjoying the social whirl in Montreal, and the trip west offered a dramatic contrast. The ninety-six days of gruelling travel involved forty-seven portages, dragging boats across muskeg while being feasted on by mosquitoes. Wolseley and his men entered Fort Garry to find it empty, with Riel's unfinished breakfast still on the table. It was a rude anticlimax to their heroic journey. Riel was watching the scene from horseback, three hundred metres away.

"Personally I was glad that Riel did not come out and surrender, as he at one time said he would," Wolseley said, "for I could not then have hanged him as I might have done had I taken him prisoner when in arms against the sovereign."

Wolseley's troops took out their frustrations on the locals. Winnipeg was chaos, according to an observer, "littered with bodies of drunken soldiers, Indians, and one pet bear on the loose." The British troops hunted down Elzéar Goulet, one of the jurors in Scott's trial, and he died trying to get away. No arrests were made.

Alexandre-Antonin Taché, the bishop of St. Boniface who had originally recommended Riel for the Collège de Montréal years earlier, wrote his old friend George-Etienne Cartier, appalled at Goulet's murder: "You know for a certainty that two soldiers had a hand in poor Goulet's drowning! These men are in the ranks, they are known, and yet nothing [has been done about] this crime. . . . If I wanted to enumerate every reprehensible act that has been committed with impunity since the transfer, the list would be a long one. . . . Why, therefore, are there two standards, two measures?"

Cartier was caught between Macdonald's hard-nosed politics and the issue of French rights in the west, now personified by Riel. In Parliament, Cartier was indignant: "I do not approve of what the people of the North-West have done, any more than I like hearing them constantly described as rebels and insurgents. What! rebels? When did they ever wish to submit to the Queen's sovereignty? I do not doubt that their resistance was premeditated, but Canada had no authority there yet. . . . I will not dwell on the troubles that have taken place in the Territory."

French Canadians believed that the west would be open to them as much as to English Protestants; the issues of language and religion in Manitoba were important because they would fulfill or falsify that promise.

Behind the scenes, Ottawa had quietly acceded to most of the conditions Riel had set. On May 12, 1870, the Manitoba Act was passed, and the territory entered Confederation as the fifth province. But Riel's demand for amnesty was not granted, and he became a fugitive. After getting food from a sympathizer, Riel gave him a message: "Tell the people that he who ruled Fort Garry only yesterday is now a homeless wanderer with nothing to eat but two dried fish."

Riel went south to the United States and lived there briefly as an exile. In 1873 he returned and won a seat in a by-election in the Manitoba riding of Provencher. He went to Ottawa, but he was still wanted for Scott's murder, and he was expelled from the House. He was re-elected in the general election of 1874 but was again expelled and returned to exile. His sister Sara wrote to him, seeking news: "Write to me about the lands for Métis children . . . may heaven send us assistance; our number is insufficient, the missions suffer, we have five school children, sixteen orphans. . . . I would like to reveal to you the secrets and consolations that I find in isolation and sacrifice."

While Manitoba was now part of Canada, British Columbia was still isolated on the coast. In March 1867, the United States had bought Alaska, leaving British Columbia hemmed in by the Americans to the north and south, with the Rocky Mountains to the east. The American secretary of state had actually proposed that B.C. be given to the United States as settlement of claims against Britain arising from the Civil War (an idea that got some support from B.C. merchants) but Britain had refused. British Columbia felt vulnerable and detached, a colony of less than forty thousand; (thirty thousand of these were natives, their population reduced dramatically by a smallpox epidemic in 1862 that killed ten thousand).

The merits of joining Confederation were argued by, among others, the exquisitely named Amor de Cosmos, a Nova Scotian who had come to Victoria in 1858 by way of California. De Cosmos, whose original name was William Smith, founded a newspaper, the *British Colonist*. In 1863, he was elected to the Vancouver Island assembly (the island and mainland B.C. were separate colonies until 1866) and became the obstreperous, often drunken leader of the opposition, occasionally getting into fights in which he would use his walking stick as a weapon.

De Cosmos lobbied James Douglas, Vancouver Island's governor, to join Canada. He also met, uneventfully, with John A. Macdonald. Macdonald opted instead to work with a council member named Dr. R. W. Carrall. There was support for B.C.'s inclusion, both in the colonies and

For the easterner, Winnipeg represented the edge of civilization. Henri Julien, a French-Canadian artist, visited in the 1870s and wrote, "This narrow strip of planking [the station platform] was the dividing line between civilization and the wilderness. Behind us lay the works of man, with their noises: before us stretched out the handiwork of God, with its eternal solitudes." (Civilization and Barbarism, *Anon.*, *Provincial Archives of Manitoba*)

Amor de Cosmos
(*British Columbia Archives*)

in Ottawa, and by 1869 the British government was taking an active role in prodding British Columbia toward union. The mainland colony's new governor, Sir Anthony Musgrave, was appointed with instructions to make Confederation happen.

In 1870, a delegation from British Columbia went to Ottawa to negotiate terms and made the modest yet wildly impractical demand that a wagon road be built from Lake Superior to the Pacific. The road would be impassable in the winter and a slow chore during summer. The Ottawa negotiator was Cartier (Macdonald was indisposed, due to one of his periodic bouts of alcoholic fatigue), who surprised the B.C. group by offering them a railway instead. Construction would begin within two years and be completed in ten years. Cartier also agreed to take over the colony's considerable debt of almost $1.5 million and provide an annual subsidy of $216,000.

In 1871, British Columbia entered Confederation, and in the following year Amor de Cosmos became premier, the first in what would become a tradition of singular provincial leaders.

In 1869, Agnes Macdonald had given birth to a hydrocephalic girl, Mary Margaret. John A. initially held out hopes for his daughter's recovery, but finally resigned himself to her disability. He was also in desperate financial straits. His salary as a politician had never kept pace with his expenses, and his law practice had incurred debts.

By 1872, Macdonald's personal life was a burden and his political life was perilous. The election was looming, and the transcontinental railway he was proposing was an expensive and unpopular issue with Ontarians. They pointed out that it would merely link Canada with a handful of white settlers on the Pacific coast – not much of a bargain. But the Manitoba crisis had demonstrated that communication and transportation were vital in securing Canada's interests in the west. The central government could not control a territory if it took ninety-six days to get an army there. Macdonald needed money to entice the electorate and provide the standard incentives to vote Conservative: rides to the polling stations in hired carriages, whiskey to smooth the way.

Most of the money came from Hugh Allan, president of the Canada Pacific Railway Company. He wanted the government charter to build the railroad and was prepared to pay whatever costs came along with it.

Cartier sent a letter to Allan: "Dear Sir Hugh, The friends of the government will expect to be assisted with funds in the pending elections, and any amount which you or your company shall advance for that purpose shall be re-couped to you. A memorandum of immediate requirements is below. Sir John A. Macdonald $25,000; Hon. Mr. Langevin $15,000. Sir G.E.C [Cartier] $20,000 . . ." The total came to more than $350,000.

Macdonald was re-elected prime minister in 1872 and Allan got the charter to build the railway. Macdonald and Cartier assumed that Allan's board of directors, which had a number of Americans on it, would now

Victoria, British Columbia, 1850s *(National Archives of Canada, C-11347)*

be made wholly Canadian. "Never will a damned American company have control of the Pacific," Cartier proclaimed. What neither Macdonald nor Cartier knew was that the money they had received from Allan had actually come from Americans.

On New Year's Eve 1872, George McMullen, owner of the Chicago *Post*, visited Macdonald's office in the East Block. He was one of the American investors who had given money to Hugh Allan in return for the promise of shares in the syndicate to build the Canadian Pacific Railway. Now Allan was reneging on the deal, and the Americans were furious. McMullen produced documents showing money paid to the Conservative Party by Allan and threatened to make the documents public.

Macdonald was furious with Allan and confided to a friend: "Entre nous, Allan seems to have lost his head altogether, and has made a series of stupendous blunders with respect to the whole matter. . . . He is the worst negotiator I ever saw in my life."

The issue became public after the Liberals bribed a clerk in the office of Hugh Allan's lawyer and stole incriminating documents. In April, Liberal Seth Huntington rose in the House and charged that American money was financing the CPR and that senior members of the Conservative government had taken money from Allan.

Cartier was in London and missed the political firestorm. He had been ailing for some time, constantly fatigued, his ankles swollen and his movements afflicted by a subtle palsy. He had hypertensive nephritis, also known

Cariboo Camels. During the B.C. Gold Rush, prospectors found the terrain difficult to negotiate, and their demand for pack animals led to the wonderfully ill-conceived idea of importing camels from the Middle East. When these desert animals proved to be unsuitable for mountain treks, they were set loose, which led, briefly, to a wild camel population in the interior. (*Frank Laumeister, British Columbia Archives*)

as Bright's disease, a degenerative kidney condition, and in September 1872 he had sailed to London to consult a specialist. Before his departure, his confessor had urged him to break with his mistress, Luce. Instead, Luce had followed him to Europe. Cartier's wife Hortense was already there; she and their daughters had been living in Europe, on and off, for a year. Over the years his lover and his wife had come to resemble one another, both stern-looking women in dark dresses.

Cartier met his family at the Westminster Palace Hotel, the same hotel he and Macdonald had stayed in while working on the Confederation bill. His condition worsened, and on May 20, he died, uttering the prosaic words, "I am dying." He had been a conservative leader, a logical man, and a talented capitalist. His death had political repercussions, both in Canada and in Manitoba, where he was known as a champion of French-Catholic rights.

News of Cartier's death reached Canada by transatlantic cable the same day. When Macdonald read the telegram in the House, he was overcome by tears and sat down, unable to speak. Cartier's body arrived in Canada eleven days later aboard the *Druid*, lying in a candlelit chapel, bells tolling, with a band playing the "Dead March." Along the shore, church bells tolled as the ship passed. "Cartier was bold as a lion," Macdonald said. "But for him Confederation would not have carried."

Cartier's funeral was the most elaborate in the country's history and it brought out all of Montreal – with the notable exception of his wife, Hortense. Macdonald mourned and drank with equal resolve. In his will,

Cartier beseeched Luce to have masses said for his soul and asked that she give his daughters the sound advice she had once given him. Hortense and her daughters moved to France and never returned to Canada.

On July 18, 1873, the *Globe* printed a telegram from Macdonald to Hugh Allan: "Immediate. Private. I must have another ten thousand. Will be the last time of asking. Do not fail me. Answer today." During that summer, the Pacific Scandal, as it was labelled, rarely left the papers, but the government hung on until the fall. For several days, no one could find Macdonald. A story was fabricated by the opposition that he had killed himself, leaping from the pier at Rivière du Loup, and the *Globe* related the rumour with a sense of optimism.

He was at the nadir of his political career and in a dark, alcoholic mood, but he found time to write his daughter Mary: "The garden looks lovely just now. It is full of beautiful flowers and I hope you see them before they are withered. . . . You remember that Mamma cut my hair and made me look like a cropped donkey. It has grown quite long again. When you come home you must not pull it too hard. . . . [A]nd so goodbye my pet and come home soon to your loving papa."

Macdonald appeared back in Parliament on November 3, looking haggard and lost. He listened to a lengthy debate on the Pacific Scandal and finally rose to speak. Fuelled by gin, looking older than fifty-eight, he addressed the packed gallery. "We have faithfully done our duty," he said. "We have had party strife setting province against province. . . . I have been the victim of that conduct to a great extent; but I have fought the battle of Confederation, the battle of Union, the battle of the Dominion of Canada. I throw myself upon this House; I throw myself upon this country; I throw myself upon posterity; and I believe, and I know, that, notwithstanding the many failings of my life, I shall have the voice of this country, and this House, rallying around me. And, sir, if I am mistaken in that, I can confidently appeal to a higher court – the court of my own conscience, and to the court of posterity. . . . There does not exist in this country a man who has given more of his time, more of his heart, more of his wealth, or more of his intellect and power, such as they may be, for the good of this Dominion of Canada."

Two days later, Macdonald failed to show up at a cabinet meeting, and the minister of agriculture was sent to find him. He found the prime minister in bed, reading a novel. He came to the meeting two hours late and said, "I suppose I shall have to go to Rideau Hall and hand in your resignations." He and his government resigned on November 5, 1873.

BIBLIOGRAPHY

GENERAL:

Canadian History: A Reader's Guide
(Toronto: University of Toronto
Press, 1994).
—— Vol. 1, *Beginnings to
Confederation*. M. Brook Taylor (ed.)
—— Vol. 2, *Confederation the the
Present*. Doug Owram (ed.)
*Guide d'histoire du Québec du régime
français à nous jours: Bibliographie
commentée*, sous la direction
de Jacques Rouillard (Laval,
Québec: Éditions du Méridien,
2nd edition, 1993).
Cook, Ramsay (general ed.) and Jean
Hamelin (directeur général adjoint).
Dictionary of Canadian Biography,
14 vols (Toronto, Buffalo and
London: University of Toronto
Press, 1966-98).
The Canadian Encyclopedia (Toronto:
McClelland & Stewart, 1999).
Historical Atlas of Canada (Toronto:
University of Toronto Press,
1987-1993).
—— Vol. 1, *From the Beginning to
1800*. Geoffrey Matthews (cartogra-
pher), R. Cole Harris. (ed.)
—— Vol. 2, *The Land Transformed,
1800-1891*, Geoffrey Matthews
(cartographer), R. L. Gentilcore (ed.)
—— Vol. 3, *Addressing the Twentieth

Century, Geoffrey Matthews
(cartographer), Donald Kerr and
Deryck W. Holdsworth (eds.)
R. Craig Brown (ed.) *Illustrated
History of Canada* (Toronto: Key
Porter Books, 2000; rev. ed.)
Buckner, Phillip A. and John G. Reid
(eds.) *The Atlantic Region to
Confederation: A History* (Toronto,
Buffalo, London and Fredericton:
University of Toronto Press/
Acadiensis Press, 1994).
Forbes, E. R. and D. A. Muise (eds.)
*The Atlantic Provinces in Confedera-
tion* (Toronto, Buffalo, London and
Fredericton: University of Toronto
Press/Acadiensis Press, 1993).
Mathieu, Jacques. *La Nouvelle-France:
Les Français en Amérique du Nord,
XVI-XVIIIe siècle* (Ste-Foy, Quebec:
Les presses de l'Université Laval,
1991).
Friesen, Gerald. *The Canadian
Prairies: A History* (Toronto:
University of Toronto Press, 1984).
Barman, Jean. *The West Beyond the
West: A History of British Columbia*
(Toronto: University of Toronto
Press, 1991).
Dickason, Olive Patricia. *Canada's
First Nations: A History of Founding
Peoples From Earliest Times* (Toronto:

Oxford University Press, 1997,
2nd ed.)
Morton, Desmond. *A Military History
of Canada* (Edmonton: Hurtig, 1990;
new, rev. and updated ed.)
Bliss, Michael. *Northern Enterprise:
Five Centuries of Canadian
Business* (Toronto: McClelland
& Stewart, 1987).
Prentice, Alison, et. al. *Canadian
Women: A History* (Toronto:
Harcourt Brace Jovanovich, 1988).
Palmer, Bryan D. *Working-Class
Experience: Rethinking the History of
Canadian Labour, 1800-1991* (Toronto:
McClelland & Stewart, 1992).
Magocsi, Paul R. (ed.) *Encyclopedia of
Canada's Peoples* (Toronto: Published
for the Multicultural History
Society of Ontario by the University
of Toronto Press, 1999).

CHAPTER 1

Arima, E.Y. (ed.) *The Whaling Indians:
West Coast Legends and Stories*
(Ottawa: National Historic Parks
and Sites, Deptartment of Canadian
Heritage, 1997).
Clark, Ella E. *Indian Legends of
Canada* (Toronto: McClelland &
Stewart, 1981).

Cook, Ramsay. *The Voyages of Jacques Cartier* (Toronto: University of Toronto Press, 1993).

Howley, James. *The Beothucks or Red Indians: The Aboriginal Inhabitants of Newfoundland* (Toronto: Coles Publishing Company, 1974).

McGhee, Robert. *The Burial at L'Anse-Amour* (Ottawa: Archeological Survey of Canada; National Museum of Man, 1976).

Jewitt, John R. *The Adventures and Sufferings of John R. Jewitt: Captive of Maquinna*, annotated and illustrated by Hilary Stewart (Vancouver, Seattle: Douglas & McIntyre, 1987).

Whitehead, Ruth Holmes. *Stories from the Six Worlds: Micmac Legends* (Halifax: Nimbus Publishing Ltd., 1988).

CHAPTER 2

Best, George. *The Three Voyages of Martin Frobisher* (London: Hakluyt Society, 1867).

Champlain, Samuel de. *The Works of Samuel de Champlain* (Toronto: University of Toronto Press, 1971).

Hakluyt, Richard. *The principall navigations, voyages, and discoveries of the English nation* (Cambridge: Hakluyt Society and Peabody Museum of Salem at the University Press, 1965).

Quinn, David B. (ed.) *New American world: A Documentary History of North America to 1612*, 5 vols. (New York: Arno Press, 1979).

Sagard, Gabriel. *The Long Journey to the Country of the Hurons* (Toronto: Champlain Society, 1939).

Schlesinger, Roger (ed.) *Andre Thevet's North America: A Sixteenth-Century View* (Kingston, Ont.: McGill-Queen's University Press, 1986).

Trigger, Bruce. *Children of Aataentsic: A History of the Huron People to 1660* (Kingston, Ont.: McGill-Queen's University Press, 1987).

—— *Natives and Newcomers: Canada's Heroic Age Reconsidered* (Montreal: McGill-Queen's University Press, 1985).

CHAPTER 3

Bégon, Élisabeth. *Lettres au cher fils: correspondance d'Élisabeth Bégon avec son gendre* (Montreal: Boréal, 1994).

Boucher, Pierre. *Pierre Boucher, textes choisis et présentés par Raymond Douville* (Montreal: Fides, 1970).

Charlevoix, Pierre-François-Xavier de. *History and General Description of New France*, translated, with notes, by John Gilmary Shea (Chicago: Loyola University Press, 1962).

Cox, Isaac Joslin. *The journeys of Réné Robert Cavelier de la Salle: as related by his faithful lieutenant, Henri de Tonty* (New York: Barnes, 1905).

Dechêne, Louise. *Habitants and Merchants in Seventeenth-Century Montreal* (Montreal: McGill-Queen's University Press, 1992).

Griffiths, Naomi. *The Acadian Deportation* (Toronto: Copp Clark, 1969).

—— *The Contexts of Acadian History, 1686-1784* (Montreal: McGill-Queen's University Press, 1992).

Lescarbot, Marc. *The History of New France*, edited by W.L. Grant and H.P. Biggar (Toronto: Champlain Society, 1907-1914).

Marshall, Joyce (ed.) *Word from New France: the Selected letters of Marie de l'Incarnation* (Toronto: Oxford University Press, 1967).

Thwaites, Reuben (ed.) *The Jesuit Relations and Allied Documents* (Cleveland: Burrows Bros., 1896-1901).

CHAPTER 4

Bougainville, Louis Antoine de. *Adventure in the Wilderness: the American Journals of Louis Antoine de Bougainville, 1756-1760*, Hamilton, Edward (ed. and trans.) (Oklahoma: University of Oklahoma Press, 1990).

Doughty, Sir Arthur G. And George William Parmalee. *The Siege of Quebec and the Battle of the Plains of Abraham*, 6 vols. (Quebec: Dussault & Proulx, 1901).

Frégault, Guy. *Canada: the War of the Conquest* (Toronto: Oxford University Press, 1969).

Knox, John. *An Historical journal of the campaigns in North America for the years 1757, 1758, 1759 and 1760*, Doughty, Arthur G. (ed.) (Toronto: Champlain Society, 1914-16).

Stevens, Sylvester K., Donald H. Kent, and Emma E. Woods (eds.) *JCB: Travels in New France* (Harrisburg: The Pennsylvania Historical Commission, 1941).

Stacey, C.P. *Quebec 1759: The Siege and the Battle* (Toronto: Macmillan Co., 1984).

Willson, Beckles. *The Life and Letters of James Wolfe* (London: W. Heinemann, 1909).

CHAPTER 5

Archibald, Mary (ed.) "Boston King" in *United Empire Loyalists: Loyalists of the American Revolution*. Toronto: Dundurn Press, 1977.

Berton, Pierre. *The Invasion of Canada: 1812-13*. (Toronto: McClelland & Stewart, 1980).

—— *Flames across the border: 1813-1814* (Toronto: McClelland & Stewart, 1981).

Byfield, Shadrach. *A Narrative of a light company's service in the 41st regiment of Foot, during the late*

American war (Toronto: Baxter Publishing Co., 1964).

Cruikshank, Ernest A. *The Documentary History of the Campaign upon the Niagara Frontier, 1812-1814* (Welland: Lundy's Lane Historical Society, 1896-1908).

Lanctôt, Gustave. *Canada & the American Revolution* (Toronto: Clarke, Irwin, 1967).

Roberts, Kenneth (ed.) *March to Quebec: Journals of the Members of Arnold's Expedition* (New York: Doubleday, Duran & Co. Inc., 1938).

Stanley, George F. G. *The War of 1812: Land Operations* (Toronto: Macmillan, 1983).

—— *Canada Invaded: 1775-1776* (Toronto: Samuel Stevens Hakkert, 1977).

Sugden, John. *Tecumseh: A Life* (New York: Henry Holt & Co., 1998).

Talman, James J. (ed.) *Loyalist Narratives from Upper Canada* (Toronto: Champlain Society, 1946).

Tippet, William H. "The Hannah Ingraham Story" in *Annual Transactions of the United Empire Loyalists Association of Canada*, No. 6 (1904-1913).

Walker, James W. St. G. *The Black Loyalists: The Search for a Promised Land in Nova Scotia and Sierra Leone* (Toronto: University of Toronto Press, 1992).

CHAPTER 6

Adams, Arthur T. (ed.) *The Explorations of Pierre Esprit Radisson* (Minneapolis, Minn.: Ross & Haines, Inc., 1961).

Gough, Barry. *First Across the Continent: Sir Alexander Mackenzie* (Toronto: McClelland & Stewart, 1997).

Hearne, Samuel. *Journey from Fort Prince Wales, in Hudson's Bay, to the Northern Ocean* (Philadelphia: Joseph & James Crukshank, 1802).

Innis, Harold. *The Fur Trade in Canada*, with a new introductory essay by Arthur J. Ray. (Toronto: University of Toronto Press, 1999).

Isham, James. *Observations on Hudson's Bay* (Toronto: Champlain Society, 1949).

Lamb, W. Kaye (ed.) *Sixteen Years in the Indian Country: The Journals of Daniel Williams Harmon* (Toronto: Macmillan Co. of Canada Ltd., 1957).

Nisbet, Jack. *Sources of the River* (Seattle: Sasquatch Books, 1994).

Ray, Arthur. *Indians in the Fur Trade* (Toronto: University of Toronto Press, 1974).

Selkirk, Thomas Douglas, Earl of. *The Collected Writings of Lord Selkirk, 1799-1809*, Vols. I and II (Winnipeg: Manitoba Record Society, 1984).

Simpson, Sir George. *Fur Trade and Empire: George Simpson's Journal* (Cambridge: Harvard University Press, 1931).

Thompson, David. *David Thompson's Narrative, 1784-1812* (Toronto: Champlain Society, 1962).

Warkentin, Germaine (ed.) *Canadian Exploration Literature* (Oxford: Oxford University Press, 1993).

CHAPTER 7

Beauclerk, Charles, Lord. *Lithographic views of military operations in Canada during the late insurrection* (London: A. Flint, 1840).

Beck, Murray (ed.) *Joseph Howe: Voice of Nova Scotia* (Toronto: McClelland & Stewart, 1964).

Bernard, Jean-Paul. *The Rebellions of 1837 and 1838 in Lower Canada*

(Ottawa: Canadian Historical Association, 1996).

Buckner, Phillip. *The Transition to Responsible Government in British North America, 1815-1850* (Westport, Conn.: Greenwood Press, 1985).

Craig, Gerald. *Lord Durham's Report: An Abridgemnet of the Report on the Affairs of British North America* (Ottawa: Carleton University Press, 1982).

Greer, Allan. *The Patriots and the People: The Rebellion of 1837 in Rural Lower Canada* (Toronto: University of Toronto Press, 1993).

Keegan, Gerald. *Famine Diary: Journey to a New World*, edited and presented by James J. Mangan (Dublin: Wolfhound, 1991).

Mackenzie, William Lyon. *The Selected Writings, 1824-1837* (Toronto: Oxford University Press, 1960).

Nelson, Wolfred. *Écrits d'un patriote, 1812-1842* (Montreal: Comeau & Nadeau, 1998).

Ouellet, Fernand. *Lower Canada, 1791-1840: Social Change and Nationalism* (Toronto: McClelland & Stewart, 1980).

Papineau, Julie. *Une femme patriote: correspondance, 1823-1862* (Sillery, Quebec: Septentrion, 1997).

Papineau, Louis Joseph. *Papineau: Textes*, choisis et présentée par Fernand Ouellet (Quebec: Les presses universitaires Laval, 1967).

Read, Colin and Ronald Stagg. *The Rebellion of 1837 in Upper Canada: A Collection of Documents* (Toronto: Champlain Society, 1985).

Senior, Elinor Kyte. *Redcoats and Patriotes: The Rebellions in Lower Canada, 1837-38* (Stittsville, Ont.: National Museums of Canada, 1985).

Stewart, Yolande (ed.) *My Dear Friend: Letters of Louis Hippolyte Lafontaine & Robert Baldwin* (Whitby, Ont.: Plum Hollow Books, 1978).

Traill, Catharine Parr. *The Backwoods of Canada* (Ottawa: Carleton University Press, 1997).

CHAPTER 8

Careless, J.M.S. *Brown of the Globe: Voice of Upper Canada, 1818-1859* (Toronto: Dundurn Press, 1989).

—— *Brown of the Globe: Statesman of Confederation, 1860-1880* (Toronto: Dundurn Press, 1989).

Creighton, Donald. *John A. Macdonald: The Young Politician, the Old Chieftain* (Toronto: University of Toronto Press, 1998).

Doughty, Sir Arthur G., Duncan A. McArthur, Adam Shortt and Nora Story (eds.) *Documents Relating to the Constitutional History of Canada* (Ottawa: S. E. Dawson, 1907-1935).

Harris, Robin S. and Terry G. Harris (eds.) *Eldon House Diaries: Five Women's Views of the Nineteenth Century* (Toronto: Champlain Society in co-operation with the government of Ontario, 1994).

Hill, Daniel G. *The Freedom Seekers: Blacks in Early Canada* (Agincourt, Ont.: Book Society of Canada, 1981).

Macdonald, John A. *The Letters of Sir John A. Macdonald*, edited by J.K. Johnson and Carole B. Stelmack (Ottawa: Public Archives of Canada, 1969).

Mackay, Donald. *The Square Mile: Merchant Princes of Montreal* (Vancouver: Douglas & McIntyre, 1987).

Mitchell, Estelle. *Mère Jane Slocombe, neuvième supérieure générale des Soeurs Grises de Montreal, 1819-1872* (Montreal: Fides, 1964).

Morton, William L. *The Critical Years: The Union of British North America, 1857-1873* (Toronto: McClelland & Stewart, 1964).

Shadd, Mary Ann. *A Plea for Emigration, or Notes of Canada West* (Almonte, Richard, ed. Toronto: Mercury Press, 1998).

Siggins, Maggie. *Riel: A Life of Revolution* (Toronto: HarperCollins, 1994).

Swainson, Donald. *Sir John A. Macdonald: The Man and the Politician* (Kingston, Ont.: Quarry Press, 1989).

Waite, Peter B. *The Life and Times of Confederation: 1864-1867* (Toronto: University of Toronto Press, 1962).

Young, Brian. *George Etienne Cartier: Montreal Bourgeois* (Kingston, Ont.: McGill-Queen's University Press, 1981).

INDEX

Italics indicate references in captions to illustrations.

Aataentsic, 8; *see also* Ataensiq
Abenaki, 138
Abercromby, James, 112, 117
Acadia, *28*, *60*, *61*, *64*, 97, 98, 103-106; and Expulsion, 104-106, 110
Acton, Robert, 127
Agouhanna, 24
A-i-tiz-zart, 37
Alaska, 288
Albany, 66, 86, 90, 92, 182; Albany County, *158*, 159
Albert Edward, Prince of Wales, 216, *280*, 280-81
Aleut, 4, 5, *36*
Aleutian Islands, *36*
Alexander, John, 167
Alexander, Joseph, 169
Alexandria, Fort, 204
Algonkin, 9, 63-64, 72, 112, 127
Allan, Hugh, 279, 281, 289-90, 292
Alsop, Richard, 41
Amherst, Jeffery, *114*, 115, *115*, 116, 118, 125, 133, 138
Anadabidjou, 63, 64
André, Jean, 148
Andros, Edmond, 91, 92
Annapolis Royal, *see* Port-Royal
Anne (of Austria), *81*

Anse à la Famine, 91
Anse au Foulon, 126
Anse de la Coromandière, 116, 126
Anticosti Island, 19
Arbor Croche, 139
Armstrong, Lawrence, 104
Arnold, Benedict, 147, *148*, 149-50, 151-53
Arthur, Duke of Connaught, 281-82
Assiniboia, *see* Red River settlement
Assiniboine, 9
Ataensiq, 68; *see also* Aataentsic
Athabaska, Lake, 190, 194
Athapaskan Beaver, 8, 9
Australia, *146*, 244
L'Avenir, 250, 253
Aylmer, Louise, 222
Aylmer, Matthew, fifth Baron, 224
Aztec, 20, *44*

Baby, François, 146, 149
Baby, Thérèse, 146, 149
Bacqueville de la Potherie, Le Roy, 94
Badeaux, Jean-Baptiste, 152
Baffin Island, *49*
Bailey, Josephine, 274
Bain, James, 150-51
Baldwin, Elizabeth, *245*
Baldwin, Robert, 245, 245-48, 249-50, 253
Baldwin, William, 247

Barbary, Françoise, 91
Barbary, Marguerite, 91
Barker, James Nelson, 42
Beaubassin, 103, *105*
Beauclerk, Charles, 233-34, *234*
Beauharnois, François de, 95
Beauharnois estate, *240*, 240-43
Beaumont, 118
Beauport, *93*, *113*, 118, 124, 125, 126, 127, 129, 130
Bécancour, 97
Bédard, Pierre, 162-63, 164
Bégon, Marie-Elisabeth, 100-101, *101*, 102-103
Bégon, Michel, 97, 100, *101*
Belgium, 218
Bella Bella, 195
Belle Isle, Strait of, 19
Belle-Humeur, Alexandre Bourg, 104
Belmont, François Vachon de, 91; *History of Canada*, 91
Bennett, George, *261*
Beothuk, 9, 10, 13-17, 19, 29, 56-57; Beothuk Institution, 15
Bermuda, 239, 240
Bernier, Benoit-François, 131
Berthelot, Emélie, 236
Best, George, 47, 48
Biard, Pierre, *28*
Bigot, François, 121, 134
Billet, Pierre, 223
Black, Samuel, 213

Blackbird, Andrew, 139
Blackfoot, *4*, 4-5, 9, 187-89
Bligh, William, *32*
Blood, 4, 9
Bloody Falls, 193
Bolívar, Simón, 218
Bonaparte, Napoleon, *see* Napoleon I
Borodino, Battle of, *163*
Boston, 92, 97, 99, 104, 139, *141*,
　142, 261
Boucher, Pierre, 77, 78, 80, 82, 83,
　84, 85, 97
Boucher-Belleville, Jean-Philippe,
　233, 234, 238; *Diary of a Patriote*, 233
Boucherville, Thomas de, 166
Boucherville, 97
Bougainville, Louis Antoine de,
　112-14, *113*, 118, 119, 121-22,
　126, 130, 134
Bouquet, Henry, 138
Bourdages, David, 232
Bourget, Ignace, *281*
Bowman, Elizabeth, 153-54, 157
Bowman, Jacob, 153-54, 155
Bowman, Peter, 155, 156, 157
Brant, John, 168
Brant, Joseph, *155*, 155-57, 168, *168*
Brébeuf, Jean de, 70, 73, 74
Brendan, Saint (the Navigator), 10, *11*
Briand, Jean-Olivier, *134*, 147
Britain: colonial policy of, 79, 91-92,
　224, 227, 239, 244, 248, 249, 250;
　and establishment of territories in
　the New World, 12-14, 27-29, 31,
　32, 44-45, 47-53, 54, 55-57, 79, 80,
　82, 86, 89-92, 95, 96-97, 98, 103,
　104, 105, *105*; *see also* Seven Years'
　War; War of 1812
British Columbia, 256, 288-89, 291
Brock, Isaac, *163*, *164*, 164-67,
　168, 169
Brown, Anne Nelson, *261*, 266, 272
Brown, George, 257, 260, 261, 262,
　265, 266-68, 270, 271, 272, 276,
　277, *277*, 278, 283, 285
Brûlé, Etienne, 67, 70
Brydges, C. J., 268
Buchan, David, 16, *17*

Buffalo, 238, 275
Burlington Heights, 176
Butler, John, 155, 157; Butler's
　Rangers, 155, 156, 157
Buts, William, 29
Buttes-à-Neveu, 126, 127, 132
Byfield, Shadrach, 166, 171

Cabot, John, 10, 12-13, *14*, 19, 27,
　45, 51
Caboto, Giovanni, *see* Cabot, John
Callicum, *33*
Callières, Hector de, 93
Cameron, John Duncan, 209
Campobello Island, 273
Canada East, 260, 267, 273; *see also*
　Lower Canada
Canada Pacific Railway Company,
　289-90
Canada, United Province of, 246, 247,
　249, 250, 256, 259-60, 268, 269, 277
Canada West, 257, 260, 262, 264, *264*,
　266, 283; *see also* Upper Canada
Canadien, Le, 163, 164
Canso, 115
Cantino, Alberto, 14, *15*
Cap Rouge, *113*
Cap Tourmente, 62
Cap-Diamant, *62*
Cape Breton, 49, 60, 97, *108*
Cap-Rouge, Rivière du, 30
Caragnial, Pierre de Rigaud de
　Vaudreuil de, *see* Vaudreuil, Pierre
　de Rigaud de
Caribbean, 44, 49, *97*
Carleton, Guy, *140*, 141, 146-47,
　148-49, 150, 151, 155-56, 160, 165
Carrall, R. W., 288
Cartier, George-Etienne, 257, *258*,
　259, 260, 265, 267, 268-69, 271,
　272, 273, 277, *277*, 278, 284, 287,
　289-92
Cartier, Hortense, 259, 291-92
Cartier, Jacques, *6*, *18*, 19-27, *22*, 23,
　24, 27, 28, *28*, 29-30, *31*, 51, 53, 57,
　58, 62, 64
Cataracoui, Fort, 86, *86*

Cathay Company, 48, 49
Caulfield, Thomas, 103
Cavendish, William, fifth Duke, *141*
Cayuga, 9, 66, 67, 156
Chabot, Joseph, 151
Chambly, 231, 233
Champlain, Hélène (Boullé) de, 68-69
Champlain, Samuel de, *58*, 60, 60-70,
　62, 65, 68, 74; *On Savages*, 60
Champlain, Lake, 66, 67, 79, 80, 112,
　147, 153
Champlain Sea, 7
Chandler, Edward, 271
Charles I (of England), 70
Charles II (of England), 182, 183, 184
Charles V (of Spain), 58
Charlesbourg-Royal, 58
Charlevoix, Pierre-François-Xavier
　de, *80*, 91, 102, *102*; *History and
　General Description of New France*,
　91, *102*
Charlotte Sophia (of England), *146*
Charlottetown, *256*; Charlottetown
　Conference, *258*, 267-68
Chaste, Aymar de, 60
Châteauguay, 240; Battle of, *174*,
　174, 175
Châteauguay River, *173*
Chatham, 170, 222, 264-65
Chaudière River, 147, 149
Chauvin, Casimir, 223
Chebucto Bay, 104
Chénier, Jean-Olivier, *236*, *236*, 237
Cherokee, 168, *168*
Chilcotin, 9
China, 45, 47, 48, 54, 88, 180, 186, 201
Chinook, 9
Chipewyan, 9, 195
Chipewyan, Fort, 194
Chipps, Gillette, *32*
Choiseul, Etienne-François de, 135
Churchill Factory, 196-98
Churchill, Fort, 191, *204*
Clallum, *3*
Clarke, John, 213
Clinton, Michael, 127
Colbert, Jean-Baptiste, 82, *82*, 84,
　85, 86

Colborne, John, 231, *231*, 232, 236-37, 240, 243
Coles, George, 271
Coles, Mercy, 269
Colonial Advocate, The, 218, 230
Columbia River, 201, 213
Columbus, Christopher, 13
Combe, William, 196
Commins, James, 178
Company of Merchants, 68
Company of One Hundred Associates, 69, 78
Constantinople, *13*
Contrecoeur, Antoine Pécaudy de, 82
Cook, James, *32*, *36*, 194
Copper, 9, *191*, 192
Coppermine River, 191, 193
Cormack, William, 15-16, 19
Cortés, Hernando, *44*
Coteeakun, 2
Coudres, Ile aux, 62
Coureurs des bois, 85-86, 87
Craig, James, 163-64, *164*, 169
Cramahé, Hector, 150
Cree, 7-8, 9, 185, 186, 187, 198, 204
Crysler's Farm, Battle of, 175, *175*
Cudouagny, 23-24
Culloden, 125, 127
Cumberland House, 194, 199
Cuper's Cove, 56
Cuvillier, Luce, 259, 291, 292

Daniel, Antoine, 74
Darby, John, 127
Dartmouth, William Legge, second Earl, 146, 149
Daunais, Amable, *243*
d'Auteuil, Ruette, 100
da Verrazzano, Giovanni, 51, 58
Davis, Robert, 221-22
Dead River, 147, *150*
Dean Channel, 195
de Cosmos, Amor, 288, 289, *289*
de Courcelle, Daniel de Rémy, 79-80
Defoe, Daniel, 196; *Robinson Crusoe*, 196

Dekanahwidah, 8-9
de la Visitation, Marie, 122-23, 124, 130, 131-32
Delaware, 165
de l'Incarnation, Marie, 72, 77, 79, 80-81, 82-83, 85
de Maisonneuve, Paul de Chomedey, 72, 77
de Manthet, Nicolas D'Ailleboust, 92
Demasduit, 16-18, *17*, 19
De Meulles, Jacques, *91*
de Monteil, François Tapie, 79, 80, 82
de Monts, Pierre du Gua, 60-62, 68
Demosthenes, *220*
Dene, 9, 191, 192-93
Denonville, Jacques-René de Brisay, Marquis de, 90-91
de Salaberry, Anne, 174
de Salaberry, Charles-Michel, *173*, 173-74, *174*
Des Grosseilliers, Jean-Baptiste, 185
Des Grosseilliers, Médard Chouart, 182-85, *184*
des Ormeaux, *see* Dollard des Ormeaux
Detroit, 172; Battle of, *163*, 171
Detroit, Fort, 109, 137-38, 165, 166-67
Detroit River, 170, 264
Deux-Montagnes, County of, 222, 228, 231, 236-38
d'Iberville, *see* Le Moyne d'Iberville, Pierre
Dinwiddie, Robert, 106
Dionne, Germain, 146
Disney, John, 140
Dix, John, 272
Doan, Charles, 235
Dollard des Ormeaux, Adam, 77
Domagaya, 21-24, 25, 26
Dongan, Thomas, 89
Donnacona, 21, 22, 23, 25, 26-27, 53
Dorchester, Guy, first Baron, *see* Carleton, Guy
Dorion, Antoine-Aimé, 273, *274*, 277
Dorset, 10
Douglas, James, 288
Douglas, Fort, 211

Drake, Francis, 47, 49, *50*, 55
Drucour, Augustin de, 115
Drucour, Marie-Anne, 115
Duchesneau, Jacques, 87, 90
Duckworth, John Thomas, 16
Duhaut, Pierre, 88
Dunmore, John Murray, 154
Dupont-Gravé, François, 62
du Pradt, Abbé, *163*
Duquesne, Fort, 110, *111*
Durham Report, *see* Durham: *Report on the Affairs of British North America*
Durham, John George Lambton, first Earl, 239, 240, *240*, 244-45, 251; *Report on the Affairs of British North America* (Durham Report), 244
Duval, Lizette, 204-205
Duvernay (Jesuit), 67
Duvernay, Ludger, 219-21

Eager, William, *227*
East India Company, British, 180, 183
Elgin, James Bruce, eighth Earl, 251, 253
Elizabeth I (of England), 45, *46*, 47, 48, 49, 50, 51, 54, *54*, 55
Ellice, Edward, Jr., 240, *240*
Ellice, Edward, Sr., 240
Ellice, Jane, *240*, 240-43, *241*
English Party, 223, 225
Erie, Lake, 108, *144*, 157
Etchemin, 64
Eu-stoch-ee-exqua, 37, 38-39, 41
Exploits Bay, 14-15
Exploits, River, 15

Felix, Tomma, *215*
Fénélon, Abbé, 87
Fenians, 273, 275-76, 278
Filles du roi, 82-84, *83*
Five Nations Confederacy, 8-9, 66, 76, 81; *see also* Six Nations
Flathead, 9, 201
Florida, 50, 54, *61*, 65
Four Corners, 174
Fox, Charles James, *220*

France, *58, 69, 81,* 81, 91-92, 102-103, 104, 231; and establishment of territories in the New World, 19-27, 29-30, 53, 54, 58-60, 69, 76, 78-79, 81-85, 86-92, 95, 96-97, 103; and French Revolution, 218, 228, 230; and Wars of Religion, 58, *58,* 61; *see also* Acadia; New France; Seven Years' War

Frances, Fort, 205

François I (of France), *19,* 26-27, 29, 58

Franklin, Benjamin, 9, 142, 152, *152;* *Poor Richard's Almanac, 152*

Franklin, John, *203*

Franquet, Louis, *92, 99*

Fraser, Alexander, 127

Fraser, Malcolm, 125, 128-29, 131, 132

Fraser, Simon, 127

Fraser River, 195

Fredericton, 159, 268

Freetown (Sierra Leone), 159

Frigon, François, 83, 84

Frigon, Marie-Claude (Chamois), 83, 84

Frobisher, Benjamin, 189-90

Frobisher, Joseph, 189-90

Frobisher, Martin, *45, 46,* 47-49, *48, 49,* 51, 53, 55

Frobisher Strait, 47

Frontenac, Fort, *see* Cataracoui, Fort

Frontenac, Louis Buade, Comte de, *86,* 86-87, 88-89, 90, 91-92

Fundy, Bay of, 55, 61

Gagetown, 159

Gallina, Gallo, *36*

Galt, Alexander, 267-68, 271, 276, 277, 278

Garry, Fort, 285, 286, *286,* 287

Gaspé, Baie de, 21

Genghis Khan, *12*

George II (of England), 104, *115,* 117, 133, *140*

George III (of England), *129,* 141, 146, *146,* 147, *148,* 153, 155, 156, 157, 160, 196

George, David, 157-58, 159

George, Dick, 157

George, Fort, 165, 169

George, Fort (Oregon), 213

Georgian Bay, 7, 64

Germain, George, first Viscount Sackville, 156

Gilbert, Humphrey, 49-53, *50,* 54

Girave, Barthélemy, 127

Glenelg, Charles Grant, first Baron, 240

Globe, The, 260, 261, 262

Globensky, Maximilien, 237

Gordon, Arthur, 267

Gore, Charles, 232

Gosford, Archibald Acheson, second Earl, *231, 238,* 246

Gosselin, Clément, 146

Gouffre, Rivière du, 62

Goulet, Elzéar, 287

Gowan, James, 271

Grand-Pré, Charles de Goudalie de, 104

Grand River, *155,* 157

Grand Trunk Railway of Canada, 268-69, *269,* 280

Grand-Pré, 103, 105, *105*

Grasshopper, Pat, 8

Gray, Thomas, 119; "Elegy Written in a Country Churchyard," 119

Greenland, 47

Grenville, William, 160

Grey, Fort, 167

Grey, Henry, third Earl, 249

Griffin, Amelia Andrina, 262

Griffin, Gilbert, 262, 263

Grosse-Ile, *224,* 248-49

Guadeloupe, 135

Guy, John, 55-57, *56*

Guyart, Marie, *see* de l'Incarnation, Marie

Haida, 8, 9, 41

Haies, Edward, 52, 53

Hakluyt, Richard, 45-47, *46,* 49, 50-51, 52-55, 57-58; *Divers Voyages touching the discoverie of America,* 47, 50-51; *Principall Navigations, Voyages and Discoveries of the English Nation,* 57

Haldimand, Frederick, 155

Halifax, 104, 109, 176, 219, 227, 245, 250, 258, 265, 268, 269, 274, 277

Hall, Charles Francis, *49*

Hamilton, Alexander, 142

Hamilton, Charles, 16, *17*

Hampton, Wade, *174*

Han, 9

Harmon, Daniel, 204-206, *205*

Harmonsville, 206

Harris, Amelia, 257, 262-64, 265-66, 275-76

Harrison, William Henry, *165, 170,* 170-71, 172

Harvey, John, 249

Hatanville, Marie, 84

Hayes River, 187

Hayman, Robert, 56; "A Skeltonicall Continued Ryme, In Praise of My Newfoundland," 56

Head, Francis Bond, 230, 232, 245

Head-Smashed-In, 5

Hearne, Samuel, 190-94, *191, 193,* 197, 216; *A Journey from Prince of Wales Fort in Hudson's Bay to the Northern Ocean, 191,* 193, 194

Henday, Anthony, 187-89

Henri IV (of France), *58,* 58-60, 68, 69

Henry VII (of England), 12, *14*

Henry VIII (of England), 29

Henry, John, 151, 152

Hill, Samuel, 39, 40, 41

Hind, Henry Youle, *210*

Hindelang, Charles, *243*

Hochelaga, 23, *24,* 24-25, 29, 64

Hocquart, Gilles, *99,* 101

Hodges, James, *280*

Holland Landing, 235

Hope, 235

Hore, Richard, 27-29

Howe, Joseph, 219, *220,* 221, 226, 244, 245, 249, 253, 254, 273, *274,* 276

Hudson, Henry, 180-81, *181,* 182

Hudson Bay, 86, *95,* 97, 180, 183, 185, 189, 196, 213

Hudson River, 66; Hudson Valley, 76, 155

Hudson Strait, 97, 180, 184

Hudson's Bay Company (HBC), 42, 180, *180*, 182, 184-86, 187, 189, *189*, 190, 190-91, 194, 196-200, 206, 207, 209, *209*, 211, 212-14, 215, *215*, 216, 256, 266, 273, 283-84, 286

Hughes, John Joseph, 261

Hull, William, *163*, 166-67

Hunters' Lodges, *see* Société des frères chasseurs

Huntington, Seth, 290

Huron, 7, *7*, 8, 9, 10, 63, 64-68, *66*, 70-74, *73*, 76, *81*, 90, 91, 94, 137, 182, *184*

Huron, Lake, 67, 182, 266, *269*

Huronia, 7, 67, 68, 70-74, *73*, 81

Hwui Shan, *36*

Ile d'Orléans, *see* Orléans, Ile de

Iles-aux-Oiseaux, 20

Illinois (natives), 90

India, *146*, 183

Indiana Territory, 170

Indocott, John, 105

Ingraham, Hannah, *158*, 158-59

Ingram, David, 49, 51

Inuit, 4, 5-7, 9, *45*, 47-48, *48*, *49*, 192-93

Ireland, 223, 248, 249

Iroquois, 7, 8, 9, 63, 64-67, *66*, 70, *71*, 72-74, 76-81, 82, 89-93, 95, 112, 127, 156, 182-83; Iroquois Confederacy, 66, 67, 81, *90*; St. Lawrence Iroquoians, 21-27

Irving, Washington, 202

Izard, George, 175

Jack River, *208*, 209, 211

Jacques Cartier River, *113*

James Bay, 180, *281*

James I (of England), *54*, 55, *55*

Jefferson, Thomas, 165, 168, 196, 220

Jesuits, 70-74, 76, *81*, 95, 97, 102; *The Jesuit Relations*, 59, 71, *71*, *73*, 76, 77, 79

Jewitt, John R., 31, 34-42; *The Armourer's Escape*, 40, 42; *a Journal Kept at Nootka Sound*, 41; *A Narrative of the Adventures and Suffering of John R. Jewitt*, 41-42

Jogues, Isaac, 71, 74

John III (of Portugal), 26

Johnson, Richard Mentor, 165, 172

Johnson, William, *155*

Johnstown, *154*

Jolliet, Louis, 87, 88

Jones, Andrew, *154*

Jones, Hester, 41

Jonson, Ben, *46*

Joutel, Henri, *88*

Juchereau, Jeanne-Françoise, 94

Julien, Henri, *243*, *288*

Kane, Paul, *210*

Kaska, 9

Kennebec River, 147

Kingston, 86, *86*, *161*, 172, 257, 277

Kickapoo, 165

Kirke, Louis, 69-70; Kirke brothers, 69-70

Kji-Kinap, 8

Kluskap, 10

Knox, John, 117, 118, 127, 128, 131, 133, 134

Kondiaronk, 91, 94

Kublai Khan, 12

Kwakiutl, 9-10

La Barre, Joseph-Antoine Le Febvre de, 90

Labordore, Jean, 106

Labrador, 10, 13, 19

Lachine, 91; Lachine Rapids, 60

Lacolle River, 174

La Fontaine, Louis-Hippolyte, 245-48, 249, 250, 253

La Jonquière, Jacques-Pierre, Marquis de, 104

Lalemant, Charles, 70, 73, 74

Langevin, Hector, 270, 289

Languedoc, François, 223

Lapérouse, Jean-François de Galaup, Comte de, 194

Lartigue, Jean-Jacques, 222, 229-30

La Salle, René-Robert Cavelier de, 86, *87*, 88, *88*

Laval, François de, 86

La Vérendrye, Jean-Baptiste, 187

La Vérendrye, Pierre Gaultier de Varennes, Sieur de, 186-87, 190

Lawrence, Charles, 105

Leclère, Pierre-Edouard, *237*

Le Jeune, Paul, 59, 70-71, *71*, 72, 74, *182*

Le Mercier, François-Joseph, 9, 79, 81, 82, 84, 85

Le Moyne, Charles, 95

Le Moyne de Sainte-Hélène, Jacques, 92

Le Moyne de Bienville, Jean-Baptiste, 96

Le Moyne d'Iberville, Pierre, *80*, 92, 95-96

Le Royer de la Dauversière, Jérôme, 72

Lescabot, Marc, 61; *A History of New France*, 61; *The Theatre of Neptune in New France*, 61

Lévis, François-Gaston, Chevalier de, *113*, 125, 131, 132, 133

Lincoln, Abraham, 272

Lloydtown, 235

Lok, Michael, *46*

London (Canada), 257, 266

London (England), 44; London Conference, 274, 276-77, 291

Lorette, *113*

Lorimier, Chevalier de, 239-40, *243*, 244

Louis XIII (of France), 70

Louis XIV (of France), *78*, 78-79, *79*, *81*, 81-82, 84, 86, *86*, 87, 88, 89, 90, 92, 96, 97

Louis XV (of France), 98-99, 103, *120*, 121, 133, 135

Louis XVI (of France), *162*

Louisbourg, 99, 103, 104, 109, *114*, 114-16, *115*, 139

Louisiana, *87*, 88, 106, 109, 110, *111*

Lount, Samuel, 234-35, 238

Lovett, John, 167-68, 169

Lower Canada, 162-64, 173-75, 176, 196, 219-21, 222-25, *223*, *224*, 226-34, 246-47, 253, *258*, 259-60, 267, 270, 271; creation of, 160; 1837 rebellion in, 231-34, 235, 236-38, 250; 1838 rebellion in, 239-44, *241*, 250; union of with Upper Canada, 244, 245-46

Lowther, Katherine, 119

Loyalists, *153*, 153-55, *154*, 156, *158*, 158-60, 162, 219, 226, 257

Lundy's Lane, Battle of, *177*, 177-78

Lusignan, Antoine, 232

Lysons, Daniel, 231-32, 237

Macaulay, John, 230

Macdonald, Hugh, 259

Macdonald, Isabella (Clark), *258*, 259

Macdonald, John (infant), 259

Macdonald, John A., 257-59, *258*, 260, 263, 265, 267-69, 271-72, 273, 274, 276-77, *277*, 278, 283, 284, 285, 286, 287, 288, 289-90, 291, 292; and Pacific Scandal, 289-92

Macdonald, Mary Margaret, 289, 292

Macdonald, Susan Agnes (Bernard), 276, 277, 289

Macdonell, Miles, 209

Macdonnell, Richard Graves, 271

Machiche, 154, 155

Mackenzie, Alexander, *193*, 194-96, *195*, *196*, 200, 202, 206, 207, 215, 216; *Voyages from Montreal*, 196, 206

Mackenzie, Geddes, 196

Mackenzie, William Lyon, 218-19, 220, 221, 225-26, 230, 234-35, 238, 243, 244, 245, 250, 254

Mackenzie River, 194

Mactavish, William, 285

Madison, Dolley, 178

Madison, James, 165, 167, 178

Magellan, Ferdinand, *50*

Maine, 54, 175

Malartic, Maurès de, 128

Malden, Fort, 170

Malmros, Oscar, 284

Mance, Jeanne, 72

Mandrou, Robert, 20

Manitoba, 283, 286, 288, 289, 291; Manitoba Act, 287

Maquinna, 31-41, *33*, 42

March, Mary, *see* Demasduit

Marguerie, François, 67

Maritime provinces, 157, 175-76; union of, 267-68; *see also* Acadia

Marquette, Jacques, 88

Marsolet, Nicolas, 67

Marston, Benjamin, 159

Martin, Claude, 85

Matonabbee, 191-92, 194

Mattawa River, 214

Matthews, Peter, 238

Mazarin, Jules, 78

McDougall, William, 285

McGee, Dorcas, 261

McGee, Mary Theresa (Caffrey), 261

McGee, Rose, 262

McGee, Thomas D'Arcy, 257, 260-62, *261*, 266, 267-68, 269, 276, 278-79, 283; *A popular history of Ireland*, 261

McGill, James, 190, 279

McGill, Peter, 229

McIntosh, Donald, 213

McMullen, George, 290

McTavish, Simon, 190

Medici, Marie de, 59

Megapolensis, Johannes, 66

Membertu, Henri, 20, 28

Methow, 201

Métis, 200, 202, 204, *208*, 209, *210*, 211, 256, 282-83; and Red River rebellion, 285-88

Mexico, 44, 58, 218

Mexico, Gulf of, 49, 86, 88, *95*

Miami, 90

Michilimackinac, 91, 94

Michilimackinac, Fort, 135

Mi'kmaq, 7, 8, 9, 10, 20, *20*, 28, *60*, 96, 103, 104

Minerve, La, 221, 224, 249, 252

Minorca, 135

Minweweh, 135-36

Mississippi River, 109, 165, 196, 86, 88, 96; Mississippi Valley, *20*

Moctezuma II, *44*

Mohawk, 8, 9, 66, *67*, 77, *129*, 155, 156, 157

Mohawk Valley, 112, 154, 155

Mohican, 76

Molson, John, 225, 279

Monck, Frances (Feo), 259, *270*, 270-71, 272

Monck, Viscount Charles, 257, *258*, 263, 265, 267, *270*, 270, 272, 278

Monckton, Robert, 124

Montagnais, 9, 62, 63-64;

Montcalm, Louis-Joseph, Marquis de, *110*, 110-12, *111*, 113, *113*, 118-21, 123-24, 125, 126, 127-28, 130, *130*, 131, 132, 166

Montesquieu, Charles Louis, Baron, *220*; *The Spirit of Laws*, 220

Montgomery, Richard, 125, 147-48, 150, 151, *151*, 152

Montmagny, Charles Huault de, 72

Montreal, 23, *67*, 71, 76, 77, 86, 90, 93, 94, 95, 100, 109, 133, *137*, 139, 140, 146, 147, 148-49, *149*, 150, 152-53, 172, 173, 174, *174*, 183, 214, 215, 222-23, *223*, 224, 225, 229, 231, 232, 236, 247, 250-53, *251*, 252, 259, 262, 267, 269, 277, 279-82, *280*, 283

Moodie, John Dunbar, 221

Moodie, Susanna, 221

Moraviantown, 170, 172, 173

Morison, George, 150

Moscow, *163*

Mouet, François, 127

Mouret, Antoine, 127

Murray, James, 124, 131, 132, *134*, 139-41, 147, *147*

Muscovy Company, 180

Musgrave, Anthony, 289

Napoleon I (of France), 114, 163, *163*, 164, 196, 231, 246, 259; Napoleonic wars, 163, 164, 207, 220, 221

Narbonne, Pierre-Rémi, *243*

Natel, Antoine, 63, 64

Nault, André, 284

Navarre, Robert, 138

Nelson, Horatio, 228

Nelson, Robert, 239

Nelson, Wolfred, 228, 232, 234, 238, 239, 250

Nespelim, 201

Netherlands, *58*, 60, 218; and settlements in New World, 66, 79, 80

New Albion, *see* San Francisco Bay

New Brunswick, 160, 256, 267, 268, *269*, 270, 271, 273, *274*, 276, 277

New England, 97, 267

New France, 58-74, *65*, *72*, 76-103, 109; *see also* Quebec

New Glasgow, 247

New Holland, 66

New Orleans, 96, 110

New York, 89, 91, 97, *153*, 155, *158*, 238, 240

Newark, 160, 162

Newcastle, Henry Pelham-Clinton, fifth Duke, 263

Newcastle, Thomas Pelham-Holles, Duke, *115*

Newfoundland, 10, 13, *16*, *17*, 19, 45, 50, 51-52, *52*, 53, 55-57, *56*, *95*, 95 96, 97, 98, 256, 270, 273, 276; Grand Banks, 45, 52, 98

Newfoundland Company, *56*

Niagara, *161*, 176

Niagara Falls, 108, 165, 176

Niagara, Fort, 154, *168*, 169; Battle of, 173

Niagara River, 157, 160, 167

Niagara-on-the-Lake, 160

Nicolas, François, *243*

Nicollet, Jean, 67

Ninoch-Kiaiu, *4*

Nipissing, 112

Nipissing, Lake, 182

Nisga'a, 9

Nootka, *see* Nuu'chah'nulth

Nootka Sound, *32*, 33, *34*, 34-41, *38*

North West Company (NWC), 190, *190*, 194, 196, 200-201, 204, 205, 206, 207, 208-209, 211, 212-13, 216

Northwest Passage, 47-48, *48*, 49, 51, 54

Northwest Passage Company, 180

North-West Territories, 285

Norton, John, 168, *168*

Norton, Moses, 191

Norumbega, 49, 51

Notman, William, *282*

Nova Scotia, 103, 104, *105*, *108*, 134, 158, 160, 175-76, 220, 226, 249, 254, 256, 268, *269*, 270, 271, 273, *274*, 276, 277, 278

Novascotian, 219, 220, 226, 245

Nowlan, Maurice, 172-73

Nunavut, 283

Nuu'chah'nulth, 3-4, 9, 10, *32*, 33, 36, 42; Moachat band, 31-41

Nuxalk, 195

O'Connell, Daniel, 231

Odelltown, 174

Ogilvy family (Montreal), 279

Ohio (natives), 157

Ohio River, 88, *155*; Ohio Valley, 110, 134, 142, 165

Ojibwa, 9, 135, 183

Oneida, 9, 66, 67, *90*, 156

Onondaga, 9, 66, 67, 156

Ontario, *286*, 289; *see also* Canada West; Upper Canada

Ontario, Lake, 91, 112

Orange, Fort, 66, 182

Order of Good Cheer, 61

Oriskany, Battle of, 156

Orleans, 22

Orléans, Ile d', 62, 74, 118

O'Sullivan, Michael, 174

Oswego, Fort, 112

Ottawa (natives), 90, 110, 136, 137, 138, 139;

Ottawa (Ontario), 273, 277, *277*, 287

Ottawa River, 77, 182

Oxenden, Bishop, 282

Pacific Fur Company, 201

Pagé, Louis, 232

Palliser, John, 216

Papineau, Amédeus, 242

Papineau, Ezilda, *242*

Papineau, Julie, 221, 222, 225, 238, 242, *242*, 254

Papineau, Louis-Joseph, 220, 221, 222, 224, 225, 226, 228, 230, 232, 234, 238, *238*, 239, 240, 242, *242*, 243, 244, *246*, 250, 254

Paquin, Jacques, 236-37

Paris, Treaty of, *see* Seven Years' War

Parmenius, Steven, 51, 52-53

Parr, John, 158

Passamaquoddy Bay, 273

Patriote, Parti, 221, 223, 224-25, 227, 228-34, *229*, 234, 236, 236-38, *237*, 239-44, *241*, *243*, 245, *246*, *246*, 250; Ninety-Two Resolutions, 225, 227

Paul II (Pope), 29-30

Pawnee, 97

Peace River, 190, 195

Péan, Angélique-Geneviève, 121, 134

Péan, Michel-Jean-Hugues, 121, 134

Peigan, 4, *4*, 9, *188*, 198-99, 201

Peoria (natives), 139

Perrault, Agathe, 172-73

Perrot, Nicholas, 88, *90*, 93, 97; *Brief on the Morals, Customs, and Religion of the Savages of North America*, 90

Perry, Alfred, 251

Perry, Oliver Hazard, *144*

Peru, 58, 59

Peteojack, *105*

Peyton, John, Jr., 15, *17*, 19

Philadelphia, 60, 154-55

Philip II (of Spain), *54*, 54-55

Philip V (of Spain), 97

Philipps, Richard, 103, 104

Phips, William, 92, *93*

Picard, Alexandre, 151

Pinguet, Charles, 175

Pitt, William, 114, *114*, 116-17, 118, *129*, 133, 135, *135*, *140*

Pitt, Fort, 137, 138

Plains of Abraham, 277; Battle of the, *111*, 126-30, 131, 132, 139, *140*, 141

Point Pelée, 137
Pointe St.-Charles, 280
Polo, Marco, *12*
Pompadour, Jeanne Antoinette, Marquise de, *120, 121*
Pontchartrain, Jérôme Phélypeaux, Comte de, 85, 97
Pontiac, 136-39, *138*
Port Nelson, 184
Portage la Prairie, 286
Port-Royal, *28*, 55, 61, *61*, 92, *93*, *94*, 103
Portugal, 45, *54*, 96
Potawatomi, 137, 165
Poutrincourt, Jean de Biencourt de, 61-62
Preston, Charles, 148
Prieur, François-Xavier, 241, 243, *243; Notes of an 1838 political convict*, 241
Prince Edward Island (P.E.I.), 256, 269, 270, 271, 273, 276
Prince of Wales, Fort, 194, 197
Pritchard, John, 209, 211
Proctor, Henry, 170-71, *172*
Prophet, The, *see* Tenskwatawa
Prophetstown, *165*
Provincial Freeman, The, 264
Prud'Homme, Eustache, 282
Puants, Baie des, 88

Quebec: American siege of, 147, 149, 150-52; British siege of, *119*, 121-33, *140*, 146; city of, 77, 79, 80, 82, 83, 85, *89*, 92, *93*, 95, *98*, 100, 102, 109, 110-11, *111*, *113*, 115, 116, 118-19, *140*, *149*, 160, *162*, *182*, *218*, 219, 221, 224, *224*, 227, 248, *248*, 263, 277; settlement of, 63-64, 67, 69-70, 74; *see also* Canada East; Lower Canada; New France
Quebec Act, 141-42
Quebec Conference, *258*, 268-72, *269*; Quebec Resolutions, 272, 273
Quebec Mercury, The, 163
Queenston, 159

Queenston Heights, Battle of, *167*, 167-69, *168*, 171, 176

Rabelais, François, 26; *Pantagruel*, 26
Radisson, Pierre Esprit, 77, 182-85, *184*
Ragueneau, Paul, *73*
Raimbault, Pierre, 100
Raleigh, Walter, 54, *54*, 55
Ramezay, Jean-Baptiste-Nicholas Roch de, *111*
Rebellion Losses Bill, *250*, 250-53, *252*
Red River, 283, 284-85; expedition, *210*; Rebellion, 285-88, 289
Red River settlement, 206-12, *211*, *214*, 215, 216
Redpath, John, 279
Reformers, 219, 230, 245-47, 249
Resolute Island, 180
Resolution Cove, *see* Ship Cove
Resolution Island, 47
Revere, Paul, 142
Riall, Phineas, 177
Richelieu, Armand-Jean Du Plessis, Cardinal and Duke, 69, *69*, 70
Richelieu River, 66, 79, 82, 99, 147, 153, 234, 259; Richelieu Valley, 227-28, 231-32, 233-34, *234*
Ridgeway, Battle of, 275, *275*
Riel, Jean-Louis, 282-83
Riel, Louis, 282-83, *284*, 284-88
Riel, Sara, 283, 288
Rivière au Boeuf, Fort de la, 137
Robertson, Colin, 213
Roberval, Jean-François de la Rocque de, 29, 58
Roberval, Marguerite de, 58
Robinson, John Beverley, 168, 169, 176, 219
Rogers, Frederic, 276
Romney, George, 156
Ross, Alexander, 212
Rouge, Parti, 253, 274, *281*
Rousseau, Jean-Jacques, 53
Rowland, Thomas, 171
Roy, Catherine (Ducharme), 84

Roy, Pierre, 84
Royale, Ile, 97, 98-99, 114, 116
Rupert's Land, 184, 282, 283-85
Rutherford, James, 127
Ruttan, Henry, 177
Rymal, John, 259

Sagana, *see* Saguenay
Sagard, Gabriel, 68
Saguenay, 26, 29
St. Anne's, *158, 159*
Saint Augustine (Florida), *61*
St. Benoit, 237-38
St. Boniface, 282, *283*, 287
St. Charles, 228, 231; Battle of, *233*, 233-34, *234*
St. Charles River, 92, 128
St. Denis, Battle of, 231-32, 233, 250, 259
St. Eustache, Battle of, *236*, 236-38, *237*
Saint-Germain-en-Laye, Treaty of, *61*
St. Jean, Fort, 147-48
Saint John, 158, 268
St. John's, 15, 16, *16*, 17, 19, 96; St. John's harbour, 30, 52
St. Lawrence River, 7, 22, 23, 24, 27, 30, 60, 62-63, 76, 92, 99, 109, *111*, 114, 115, 116, 117, 119, 124, 133, 146, 147, 152, 165, 173, 280
St. Louis, Fort, 80
St. Louis, Lake, 91
St. Pierre and Miquelon, 135
Ste. Croix, 61
Sainte-Foy, Battle of, 132-33, 139
Salaberry, *see* de Salaberry
Salem (Massachusetts), 106
Salières, Henri de Chastelard, Marquis de, 79-80, 82; *Memoirs*, 79
Salter, John, 34, 39
San Francisco Bay, *50*
Sandwich Islands (Hawaii), *32*, 215
Sarcee, 4, 8
Saukamapee, *188*, 198-99
Saulteaux, *208*, 209, 212
Sault-Saint-Louis, 92
Saunders, Charles, 117

Savage, Thomas, 92

Schenectady, 80

Schultz, John Christian, 284, 286

Schuyler, Pieter, 92

Scott, Thomas, 286, *286*, 287, 288

Scott, Winfield, 176, 177

Seaver, William Rufus, 252-53

Sekani, 9

Selkirk, Thomas Douglas, fifth Earl, 206-208, *207*, 209, 211; *Observations on the present state of the Highlands of Scotland, with a View of the Causes and probable consequences of Emigration*, 206

Selkirk settlement, *see* Red River settlement

Semple, Robert, 211

Seneca, 9, 66, *67*, 156, 165

Seven Oaks, 211

Seven Years' War, *109*, 110-135, *135*, *120*, 141, 191; Treaty of Paris, 135, *136*, 156, 189

Seward, William, 284

Shadd, Abraham, 264

Shadd, Mary Ann, 264, *264*; *A Plea for Emigration, or; Notes of Canada West in its Moral, Social and Political Aspect*, 264

Shadd, Isaac, 264-65

Shakespeare, William, 44, *46*; *The Merchant of Venice, 46*; *Twelfth Night, 46*

Sharon, 235

Shawnadithit, 14-16, 19

Shawnee, 165

Shelburne, 159

Sheppard, Thomas, 230

Ship Cove, 31

Shirley, William, 104

Shuswap, 195

Simcoe, Elizabeth, 161

Simcoe, John Graves, *160*, 160-62, 176

Simcoe, Lake, 7, 64

Simpoil, 201

Simpson, Frances Ramsay, 214-15, *215*

Simpson, George, 212-16, *214*

Sioux, 9, 187

Six Nations, 8-9, 155, 156-57

Skittle, Abel, 127

Slocombe, Jane, 281, 282-83, 285-86

Small, Charlotte, 200

Smith, Donald Alexander, 286

Smith, Sidney, 257

Smith, William, *see* de Cosmos, Amor

Snake, *188*

Société des frères chasseurs, 239, 240-42

Society of Jesus, *see* Jesuits

Sorel, Pierre de, 82

Sorel, 228, 231

Spain, *46*, 54, *54*, 78, 96, 218, 231; and the Armada, 44, *46*, 49, 55; and establishment of territories in the New World, 44-45, 48, 50, 54-55, 58, 59, 60, 79, 88, *96*

Sproule, Robert Auchmaty, 223

Squamish, 7, 10-11

Stadacona, 22, 25-26, 30, 64

Stone, Edward, 127

Stoney Creek, 172

Strachan, John, 208, 245

Strickland, Thomas, 220

Stuart, Charles Edward, 127

Stuart, John, 213

Sullivan, John, 156

Sully, Maximilien de Béthune, Duc de, 59

Superior, Lake, 183, *184*, 186, 289

Susquehannah River, 153

Swift, Jonathan, 108, 196; *Gulliver's Travels*, 108, 196

Sydenham, Charles Edward Poulett Thompson, first Baron, 246

Taché, Alexandre-Antonin, 282, *283*, 287

Tacoutche River, *195*

Tadoussac, 60, 62, 63, 69

Tagish, 9

Tahiti, 134

Taignaogny, 21-24, 26

Talon, Jean, 79, *82*, 84-85, 86

Taylor, James, 167

Taylor, Margaret, 214

Tecumseh, *165*, 165-66, *169*, *171*, 169-73

Tenskwatawa, 169, *169*, 172-73

Texas, *88*, 218

Thames River (Upper Canada), 170, 262; Battle of, 170-71, *171*

Thevet, André, 27, *27*, 53-54

Thomas, John, 105

Thompson, David, *188*, *193*, 196-202, *204*, 205, 215, 216

Thompson, James, 127

Thompson, John, 35, 36-37, 39, 40, 41

Ticonderoga Point, 65

Tilley, Samuel Leonard, 273-75, *274*, 278

Tippecanoe, Battle of, *165*, 170

Tod, John, 213

Todd, Isaac, 190

Tootoosch, 37

Tocqueville, Alexis de, 222-23, 226-27

Toronto (York), *161*, 162, 218, 225, *226*, 230, 234-35, 245, 247, 250, 266, 277, *277*

Townshend, George, 124, *124*

Tracey, Daniel, 219-21

Tracy, Alexandre de Prouville, Marquis de, 79, 80

Trafalgar, Battle of, 228

Trahan, Joseph, 128, 129-30

Traill, Catharine Parr, *218*, 220, 221

Traill, Thomas, 220, 221

Trinity Bay, 56, 57

Trois-Rivières, 76, 77, 100, *101*, 154, 182, 186

Tsimshian, 9

Tsonnontouan, 90

Tupper, Charles, 273, *274*, 277, 278-79

Turenne, Henri de La Tour, Vicomte de, *113*

Turnor, Philip, 199

Tuscarora, 9, 156

Tutchone, 9

Tyler, John, *170*

Tyrell, James, 196, 202

Ulatilla, 39

Underground Railroad, 264-65

Unijah River, *195*

United States, *152*, 218: and American Revolution, 144-53, 218, 228; and annexation of Lower Canada, 225, 253; and Civil War, 256, *263*, 263-66, 273, 288; and support for rebellions, 240, 242, 243; and War of 1812, 163, 165-78

Upper Canada, 164-69, 176-78, 218-19, 221-22, 224, 225-26, 230, 231, 232, 242, 253, 259-60, 267, 270, 275; creation of, 160; 1837 rebellion in, 234-35, 238; 1838 rebellion in, 243-44; union of with Lower Canada, 244, 245-46; *see also* Canada West; Ontario

Upquesta, 37

Utrecht, Treaty of, *61*, 97

Van Horne, William Cornelius, 279

Van Rensselaer, Solomon, 168

Vancouver, George, *32*, 195

Vancouver Island, 3, 31, 42, 288

Varennes, René Gaultier de, 82

Vaudreuil, Jeanne-Charlotte de Fleury (Deschambault) de, *111*

Vaudreuil, Philippe de Rigaud, Marquis de, 97

Vaudreuil, Pierre de Rigaud, Marquis de, 110-12, *111*, 113, *113*, 121, 124, 133, 134

Venango, 137

Verchères, François de, 82

Vermont, 175, 204, 240

Verrier, Etienne, 99

Victoria (of England), 229, 239, *258*, 277, *277*, 280, *280*

Victoria (British Columbia), *290*

Villebois, Honoré-Michel de la Rouvillière de, 101, *101*

Ville-Marie, 76; *see also* Montreal

Vindicator, 221

Virginia, 54, 106, 110, 154, 157, 159

Voltaire, 114, 192, 197; *Candide*, 114; *Dictionnaire philosophique portatif, ou la raison par l'alphabet*, 197

Walker, Thomas, 139-41, 145-46

Walpole, Horace, *129*

Walsingham, Francis, 51

War of 1812, *163*, 165-78, *166*; Treaty of Ghent, 178

Warwick, Mount, 48

Washington, George, *111*, 142, 147, 150, 156, 157, 178

Waterloo, Battle of, 231

Webb, Adam Clark, 284-85

Wellington, Arthur Wellesley, first Duke, 231

Wenatchee, 201

West, Benjamin, *129*; *The Death of General Wolfe*, *129*, 135

West Indies, 134, 155, 161

Wetherall, George Augustus, 233, *233*

Whelan, Edward, 271

Whelan, Patrick James, 279

Whitbourne, Richard, *52*

Whyte, Robert, 248

Willcocks, Joseph, 176, 178

William Henry, Fort, 112, 113, 166

Williams, E. J., 265

Willson, Deborah, 176-77

Wilson, William, 181

Windsor, 243, *264*

Winnipeg, 284, *288*

Winnipeg, Lake, 209

Winslow, John, 105, *105*

Wolfe, James, *111*, 116-21, 123-30, *125*, *129*, *130*, 131, *132*, 134-35, *140*, 150

Wolfe, Walter, 116

Wolseley, Garnet, 287

Wooster, David, 152

Wyandot, 165

Yakima, 2

Yarmouth, Sophia, Countess, *115*

York, *161*, 162, 208, 218, 219, 225, 226; *see also* Toronto

York Factory, 189, 190, *190*, 198, 213

Yoscaha, 68

Yroquet, 63, 64